BETWEEN STATE CAPITALISM
AND
ECONOMIC STATECRAFT

CHINA INC.

BETWEEN STATE CAPITALISM AND ECONOMIC STATECRAFT

CHINA INC.

Aravind Yelery

PENTAGON PRESS LLP

CHINA INC.: Between State Capitalism and Economic Statecraft
By Aravind Yelery

First Published in 2021

ISBN 978-93-90095-35-3

Disclaimer: The views and opinions expressed in the book are the individual assertion of the Author in his personal capacity and do not have any offices endorsement. Moreover the Publisher does not take any responsibility for the same in any manner whatsoever. Attributability of the contents lies purely with Author.

Published by
PENTAGON PRESS LLP
206, Peacock Lane, Shahpur Jat
New Delhi-110049
Phones: 011-64706243, 26491568
Telefax: 011-26490600
email: rajan@pentagonpress.in
website: www.pentagonpress.in

Printed at Aegean Offset Printers, Greater Noida, U.P.

For Vivaan and Aadi

Especially Vivu, who had to share my tenderness with my obsession for China Studies. On innumerable travels, he, with a simple smile and a lot of courage, would let me go away silently.

Contents

Acknowledgements

Writing this book would not have been possible without the support of my Chinese research assistants and a long list of well-wishers in China who helped me with their objectivity, expertise, professional insight and acumen. All those persons to whom I owe a special debt are on top of this list of acknowledgements.

Long journeys, shuttling between cities and memorable talks with the Chinese helped me in comprehending the subject better. My lengthy conversations with my colleagues at Peking University were illuminating and facilitated shaping my arguments. I must admire the class interactions where intriguing questions posed by my students compelled me to dig deeper and seek answers.

With extreme humility, I submit that this book is the result of faith shown in me by all my teachers, colleagues and friends from diverse geographies. The great deal of learning, humility and tolerance I inherited from each one of them has helped me immensely.

I must thank Jabin Jacob, a classmate, friend and a fantastic colleague who lured me away from my corporate stint in Shanghai, encouraged me to remain focused on research, and write something unique and fresh. Without his guidance, this book would not have emerged.

A special mention to my Indian team supporting this publication. I must thank Subir Rana, who read the first draft and helped edit it. Reeja Nair and

Chetan Patil took care of the most treacherous work of de-cluttering the references, especially Reeja, who took out time to arrange the notes and do last-minute editing.

Besides the content and the narratives, a book is incomplete without its physical appearance and aesthetics. Pankaj Giram did yet another fabulous work on the book cover and my sincere gratitude for his dedication to the work. My publisher, Pentagon Press LLP, and Rajan Arya deserve special mention for their patience and organised efforts.

List of Graph, Figures and Maps

Graph

Figures

Maps

List of Tables

List of Acronyms

ABC	Agricultural Bank of China
ADB	Asian Development Bank
AMC	Asset Management Company
BCG	Boston Consulting Group
BOC	Bank of China
BOLT	Build-Operate-Lease-Transfer
BOO	Build-Own-Operate
BOOT	Build-Own-Operate-Transfer
BOT	Build-Operate-Transfer
BRI	Belt and Road Initiative
BRICS	Brazil, Russia, India, China, South Africa
CASS	Chinese Academy of Social Sciences
CBRC	China Banking Regulatory Commission
CCB	China Construction Bank
CCCC	China Communications Construction Company Limited
CDCC	Chaohu Dongya Cement Company
CECEP	China Energy Conservation and Environmental Protection group companies
CERCG	China Energy Reserve & Chemicals Group Co.
CEWC	Central Economic Work Conference
CFI	Central Financial Institution
CIC	China Investment Corporation
CIRC	China Insurance Regulatory Commission
CIT	Corporate Income tax

CNBM	China National Building Material Group Co. Ltd.
CNPC	China National Petroleum Corporation
CPC	Communist Party of China
CpC	China Post Corporation
CRC	China National Railway Corporation
CRS	Contract Responsibility System
CSG	China Southern Power Grid
CMEA	Council for Mutual Economic Assistance
CMG	China Merchants Group
CNTC	China National Tobacco Corporation
COFCO	China National Cereals, Oils and Foodstuffs Corporation
CPGC	China Pharmaceutical Group Corporation
CSRC	China Securities Regulatory Commission
CTIG	China Taiping Insurance Group
CWTEC	Chaohu Wastewater Treatment Engineering Company
EBRD	European Bank for Reconstruction and Development
ECC	Eleventh Central Committee
EPC	Engineering Procurement Construction
EU	European Union
FCB	foreign commercial bank
FDI	foreign direct investment
FTZ	free-trade zone
FYP	Five-Year Plan
G7	Group of Seven nations
G8	Group of Eight nations
G20	Group of Twenty nations
GDI	gross domestic investment
GDP	gross domestic product
GLF	Great Leap Forward
HCFP	Hefei Chemical Fertilizer Plant
HCRS	Household Contract Responsibility System
HCW	Hefei Chemical Works
HDPC	Hefei Development and Planning Commission
HISC	Hefei Iron and Steel Corporation
HSBC	Hongkong and Shanghai Banking Corporation

HSTC	Hefei Sewerage Treatment Company
HVAC	high voltage alternating current
HVDC	high voltage direct current
HWC	Hefei Wangxiaoying Sewage Treatment Co. Ltd.
ICBC	Industrial and Commercial Bank of China
IMF	International Monetary Fund
IWEP	Institute of World Economics and Politics
JV	joint venture
JSC	joint stock company
JSCB	joint-stock commercial bank
JLSC	joint limited stock company
LLC	limited liability company
LOT	Lease-Operate-Transfer
M&A	merger & acquisition
MBO	management buyout
MOF	Ministry of Finance
MSR	Maritime Silk Road
NDRC	National Development and Reform Commission
NPC	National People's Congress
NPL	non-performing loan
OECD	Organisation for Economic Co-operation and Development
OFDI	outward foreign direct investment
PBOC	People's Bank of China
PFI	private finance initiative
PG	Petroleum Group
PLA	People's Liberation Army
PM	particulate matter
PRC	People's Republic of China
RLOT	Reconstruction-Lease-Operation-Handover
ROA	return on assets
ROC	Republic of China (Taiwan)
ROFA	returns on fixed assets
ROT	Rehabilitate-Operate-Transfer
SAFE	State Administration of Foreign Exchange
SAR	special administrative region

SASAC	State-owned Assets Supervision and Administration Commission
SDIC	State Development Investment Corporation
SETC	State Economic and Trade Commission
SEZ	special economic zone
SGCC	State Grid Corporation of China
SHRM	strategic human resource management
SoCB	state-owned commercial bank
SOE	state-owned enterprise
SOSME	State-owned Small and Medium-sized Enterprise
SREB	Silk Road Economic Belt
SSP	subsidiary SOE in the province
SSSR	supply-side structural reform
TOT	Transfer-Operate-Transfer
TVE	township and village enterprise
UN	United Nations
UHV	ultra-high voltage
VAT	value-added tax
WNZ	Wenzhou Longwan International Airport
WB	World Bank
WTO	World Trade Organization
XXG	Xiamen Xiangyu Group
ZSERDF	Zhejiang State-owned Enterprise Reform and Development Fund

CHINA AND ITS PROVINCES

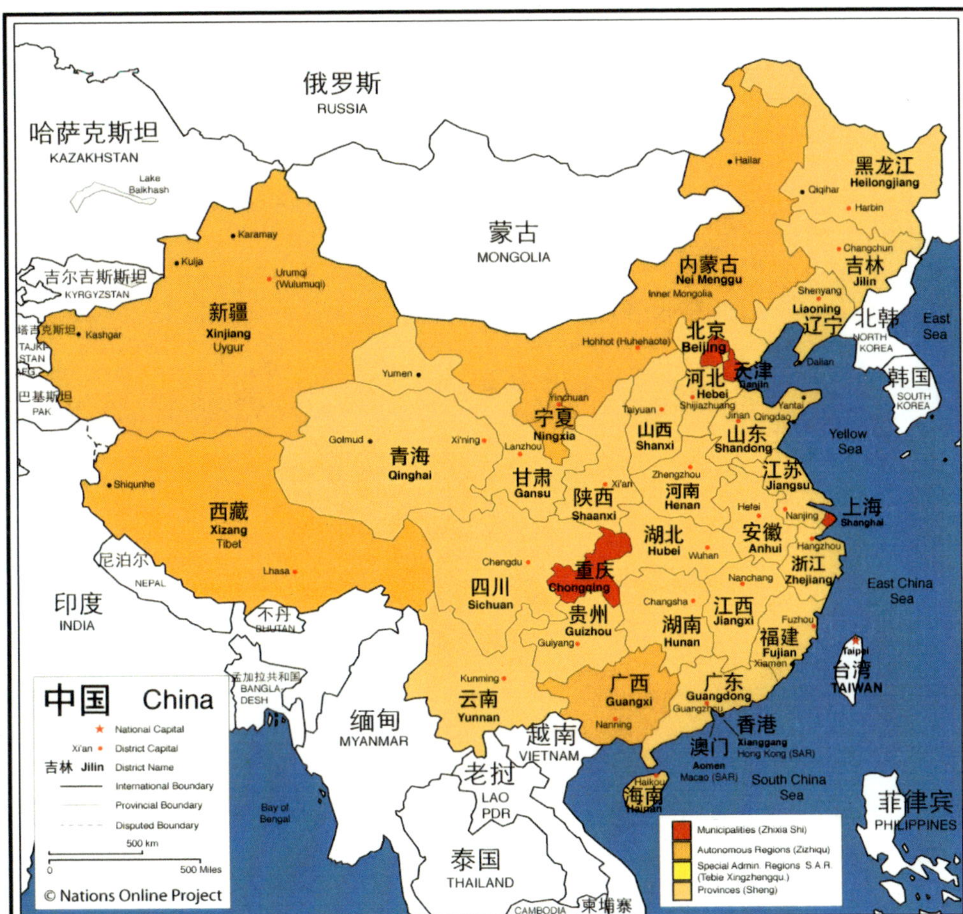

A Note on Style

This book follows the Romanisation system of the Chinese written language developed by the People's Republic of China and known as *Pinyin*.

As for the names, the surnames come first followed by the names: Deng Xiaoping is leader Deng, and Jiang Zemin is President Jiang, or Hu Jintao is President Hu.

Although, as mentioned above, the book uses the *Pinyin* system of transliteration, there are a few names, which are better known by the older system, for example, Chiang Kai-shek. A few Taiwanese names are also used as per the older system.

Prologue

The *Chinese Dream* of Superlatives

In the early years, the CPC (Communist Party of China) made strenuous efforts to overcome an inherited economy that was severely disrupted. Agricultural collectivisation and massive industrial expansions were carried out to gain control over prices, wages and unemployment. Significantly, the Party and the government were closely interlocked. For decades, SOEs (state-owned enterprises) and their socio-economic nomenclature, 'danwei' were a medium of socio-economic transaction for the CPC. For bands of youths exhausted by internal wartime political turmoil, Japanese aggression, war-ravaged industries and woeful agrarian conditions, transacting political rights and securing commune and *danwei*-led state of living were seen as prestigious. After decades, socialism persists; the state presence rises overwhelmingly, and the class divide re-emerges in newer forms. Only a few exercise political rights, while for many, accumulating wealth amounts to exercising the right to a secure future and well-being, both social and political. Ideology, party, state and class have attained formidable heights, and to protect their dispositions, the entire system is emphasising radicalisation and a greater reliance on state institutions.

After seventy years of its founding, China is a strong one-party state, and the state can pool its economic and social resources to meet critical objectives. While earlier generations of leadership attempted to make the Chinese state stronger and adaptive, each generation picked their means and goals wisely. What did not change was the greater control the Communist Party exercised over all aspects of life and what the leadership exercised over the former. This control reflects the contraction of non-Party spaces and the expansion of the Party's influence beyond tightening its grip through tiny Party units even in sparsely inhabited neighbourhoods and every possible private space. A few decades ago, no one knew how this non-distinctive mark of leadership control over the Chinese economy and society would help the state to strike back to balance its role as the sole guarantor of a *well-off society*.

This contradicts the theories spiced up about China's collapse and how institutions would get weaker to let non-Communist forces grow stronger. Many acclaimed, well-read experts and handsomely-funded institutions in the West subscribed to monochrome thoughts of China collapsing. The new leadership at the helm shattered the illusions and steered politics and economics by reasserting the dominance of the Communist Party and state control. The General Secretary of the CPC, Xi Jinping, announced extending his full control over all matters of the Party and the Chinese state. As a result, China inches fast forward towards a more muscular form of state capitalism. The state-owned sector has been pushed to take a dominant position. It is also a fact that given the series of challenges such as a slump in growth, hyper production and creaky supply lines, domestic stocks crash in 2015 and capital plight and other challenges such as trade war with the USA and the COVID-19 pandemic, the Party is convinced that the state needs to be in control, without which China may not be able to go ahead on its own. It projects its chest-thumping victory against structural anomalies within the economy, tiding over financial risks, the trade war with the USA, etc., because of state efficiency and the central role of its state firms. Consequently, the strengthening of SOEs was also seen as a step closer towards economic statecraft. It is evident that China's state capitalism has reinforced the old concept of economic statecraft among the Chinese leadership, which means China is deploying its wealth for strategic foreign policy purposes. To ensure that the Chinese state averts any risks to its economy and eventually to its nation, reorganisation, loyalty and discipline are closely watched to prevent any form of discontent and deviance.

What does this mean? It means state firms are protected and given strategic refuge. A starring role of SOEs signifies the reputation it holds for the state and Party. They are standing firm and help build invincible state capitalism.

There is no retreat, and in some respects, they have gone in the reverse direction. The SOE reforms have come far ahead and re-engineered a newer and dynamic brand of state capitalism. The total number of enterprises, numbering more than 150,000, is still owned by the central and local governments. Their share of industrial assets amounts to 40 per cent, besides their share of the pie in bank credits that cross the halfway mark. Despite strong headwinds, when the economy slows or stalls, the State Council trumpets additional spending, and by all means, the state keeps them afloat. The SOEs will continue to be the last outpost of the Chinese state, which it will never abandon, and the Party will not cease exercising control over them. In the larger scheme of statecraft, they are the most trusted players in Chinese strategies. For China, the external footprints of SOEs in securing supplies, and affecting produce and prices are noteworthy, but more than anything else, it is an important matter of statecraft.

In recent years, SOEs have been helping China build a formidable force overseas. Relatively new to their competitors, they have not only outperformed them but also surged ahead in all global tallies of wealth and might. SOEs have been serving the Chinese state to pursue ambitious geo-economic goals, and the Belt and Road scheme of things is the newest on the list. In terms of statecraft, the BRI (Belt and Road Initiative) plays a crucial role.

From the scale of research methodology, SOEs are a gigantic topic. Even for a native Chinese, it is a notoriously complex topic to engage with. Given the intricate relationship SOEs share with the political setup, many aspects are unfamiliar even to Chinese researchers. Strengthening SOEs is consistent with the political belief of tighter state control of just about every aspect of society. Hence, many aspects of SOEs are kept secret and left to speculation. Keeping such complexities in mind, this book prepared the initial wireframe that probes the form and function of these fine intricacies. Thus, one of the primary hypotheses this book started to work with was centred on the idea that SOEs are complex and rigid, and yet, there is an 'orderly chaos'. The book was motivated to bring out critical aspects of SOEs into the mainstream conversations among China experts and for those who wish to know more about Chinese SOEs from scratch.

The study that was conducted for this book shows that SOE-related research has become more focused and categorised. Advanced multidisciplinary approaches, methodologies and new techniques unveiled research domains more than just debts, assets, and performance. Chinese state firms function beyond their usual vectors and render tangible global interests. The international role of SOEs, their rise in the *Fortune 500* list, geographical expanse and closing ranks with Western players give measurable visuals of these new dynamics. Furthermore, global collaborations, mergers, incorporations and outright buying of businesses have been conceived and directed to improve the level of innovation and scientific advancement, and scale new heights of technological transformations (from bullet trains to space sciences).

This book is a small part of the whole debate revolving around China's state enterprises. SOEs are not just subjects of political interventions and corrections, or institutions to administer the entire state system, amass legacy or exercise the state's social responsibilities; they also build ambitious economic statecraft. Besides, in a Communist regime, they are not just simple binary systems as many claim but their functions need to be closely studied by looking at their rise and role in specific fields, the competition they face, and how they mitigate the internal complications concerning managerial freedom and professional outlook. SOEs, financial or industrial, have been pressured to show output, and while this economic output is measured in political leverage, it also heightens the pressure they undergo. The regulatory body, State-owned Assets Supervision and Administration Commission (SASAC), that governs the industrial enterprises, is an *open ring of wolves.* Open or general literature may give the impression that the State Council houses SASAC, and protects industrial SOEs against odds and directs them to carry out their jobs. However, in reality, the State Council uses SASAC to let the SOEs struggle for funds, space and performance. The financial and industrial enterprises have their own set of goals. In recent times, amidst the pressure to perform and reduce losses, fault lines are emerging between the types (financial and industrial) and layers (central and sub-national) of enterprises. SOEs carrying out propaganda and soft-culture aspects globally work on an independent template from the earlier two categories. Most of these aspects are unheard of when it comes to SOEs and their imperishable position in the entire Chinese system. Moreover, the SOEs know that they would never want Premier Zhu Rongji-style ruthless enterprise reforms to return and turn lethal. Therefore, consistency, performance and efficiency are set as gold standards.

SOEs are functional at the national and sub-national levels, which is how the central SOEs run the entire show by pulling strings. Their provincial subsidiaries play a crucial role in installing a grid of enterprises that are neatly connected with calibrated and well-oiled levers of finance and political appointments. The performance metrics work efficiently at the provincial level too, where 'checks and balances' within the Party and the provinces equipoise their role and output. Besides, the provinces own some enterprises that act as safety valves for the local economy. The provinces know that even if the *Emperor* is far away, he controls their finances ever since Zhu clipped their wings. The provincial enterprises, at their will, try to play a safe role to help provincial leaders and local cadres provide their own life-support system without offending the central enterprises and the rulers in Beijing. All these enterprises—central, subsidiaries and provincial—fight for bitter survival.

In addition to these aspects, the role of SOEs in public-private partnerships and wealth creation is worth exploring for more in-depth insights into state capitalism. This work is expected to help the audience that is on the lookout for an objective analysis of the state-run economy, and the categorisation and role of the SOEs. This book expects to be a step towards building a capacity in knowing how these public institutions enact the 'China Dream' flawlessly.

Aravind Yelery
Shenzhen, PR China

1

The Rise of State Capitalism in China

Back in 2008, when China planned to commemorate the 30th anniversary of China's opening up of the economy followed by economic reforms, it was none other than Xi Jinping, the then Vice-President and heir-apparent to President Hu Jintao, who was appointed the chief organiser of the celebration programs. Xi Jinping delivered his promise to arrange huge concerts, exhibitions, and endless forums celebrating the 'turning point.' He would not miss a chance to remind the Chinese of their unfinished 'project of modernity'.[1]

From 1978 until now, China underwent a series of policy reversals and breakthroughs that saved China from the verge of a major collapse and offered it a chance to turn itself into a significant force in the global economic system dynamics. Deng's disruptive Chinese economic interventions had a clear plan or strategy to restore China to its 'rightful' prosperity and power—*Fuqiang* (富強). To attain wealth, China had to show growth, which would, in turn, earn global 'respect' (尊重 *Zun zhong*) for the Chinese state. Deng strategised the economic rise and meanwhile avoided open conflict both on the domestic turf as well as on the international front. Externally, the economic flexibility shown at home paid off, building ties with near and distant neighbours with whom China had conflictual relations. Except for the 1979 Vietnam War, Deng used his energy to channel wealth and power growth.

Deng is considered to be the 'chief designer' (总设计师 *Zong sheji shi*) of Chinese reforms.[2] While the Chinese reforms were done with 'controlled' experiments and 'managed' risks, one can see them as breakthroughs that were disruptive but controlled by the state. The reforms did not let any element run out of control and threaten the Chinese state's rulebook. Reforms were achieved through low political risks and high economic rationale. We will try to examine some of these disruptions carried out most effectively and resolutely by the Chinese State, which are responsible for its rise as the leading nation in terms of wealth and experience besides GDP and FDI.

During Deng's regime, China achieved a high average economic growth (in terms of GDP) compared to any other developing and developed nation. It is during the same period that the whole economic structure was put under a complete overhaul. At the end of the century, when China launched another wave of reforms, Deng could not resist augmenting reforms in Chinese State-owned enterprises (SOEs) so that the balancing act initiated by him in 1978, could get rid of the major impediments and roadblocks to the geo-economic rise of a 'New and Globalised China'. This chapter focuses on issues related to economic development under Deng's rule, which featured in the revamping of the system, followed by economic restructuring.

Towards a Systemic Disruption

Before introducing reforms in 1978, China's economy was extremely vulnerable to the vagaries of politics and ideology; but since then, the situation has been different. Chinese leadership after 1949 translated the demands of a socialist ideology into economic processes and structures that could comfortably be labelled as 'socialist'.[3] Mao's concept of development differed from the Western perspective in the sense that it gave extraordinary importance to ideological variables. In the West, it is generally held that economic development encourages individuals to own the means of production and maximise profits. Resource allocation is determined by the price system. This also encompasses the belief that investment increases as per capita income increases and that consumerism and materialism accompany growth. Profit and efficiency are measures of economic development. In contrast to the Western view of economic growth, Mao's methods proposed economic development through a step-by-step resolution of contradictions where each answer would move

China toward a higher rate of production in the Marxian economic perspective until it reached communism. Mao finds different kinds of contradictions in the course of China's bourgeois-democratic revolution. Mao notes,

> "There exists the contradiction between all the oppressed classes in Chinese society and Imperialism, the contradiction between the great masses of the people and feudalism, the contradiction between the proletariat and the bourgeoisie, the contradiction between the peasantry and urban petty bourgeoisie on the one hand and the bourgeoisie on the other, the contradiction between the various reactionary ruling groups".[4]

The Maoist view of economic development entails the gradual elimination of 'the three great differences'—the gap between the rural and urban life, between industrial and agricultural sectors, and between mental and manual labour. While eliminating the three gaps, any distinction of material wealth or social status deriving from property or roles also had to be eliminated[5] whereby development determined the output, especially heavy industrial producer goods. This model did not entirely ignore efficiency and quality issues, but its priority was to increase production rapidly by meeting ever-larger production quotas. The path of accomplishing economic development was revolutionary, rapid, and massive. Mao believed in attaining rapid change and maintained that politically conscious masses and cadres loyal to the CPC's vision were essential. This path was too hasty since people were not familiar with this rapid mode of transformation. During the Cultural Revolution, the Red Guards' attempt to remould people's mentality and outlook can be seen as a kind of exertion to reshape people's thoughts. The belief that correct political thought could enhance production was firm, and thus, political education was introduced in the factories to make work more effective.

The revisionist line of leaders was discreetly consolidating their stand in Mao's years. In this case, it is simple to understand why the Soviet Union's rejection left Chinese leaders with two policy lines—a radical and a revisionist line.[6] After the First Five-Year Plan (1953–1957), Mao tried to accelerate the economic reforms without Soviet assistance, whereby he allowed each section of the party to contribute. Mao introduced new methods to break out of the Soviet economic development model, given China's different factor endowment.[7]

To everyone's surprise, the crisis brought a leader in Deng to the forefront who believed in economic re-modelling. An answer to the question, which is raised in the subsequent chapter as to why China did not fail after it 'opened up', lies with Deng's ability or temperament to decide meticulously upon his choices and priorities back in the 1950s. The lack of planning made pre-reform modernisation a case of failures, leading to a series of disasters. Amid such a crisis, Deng was directed to manage the policy platform and facilitate the recovery of the economy from the problems precipitated due to the Great Leap Forward (or GLF, which was a campaign with economic and social goals, covering the period between 1958 and 1962). This crisis offered a narrow window of opportunity to Deng and the revisionists a chance to prove their ability. Deng's policy provided the experience for pragmatic policy choices,[8] and since then the revisionist group earned an unwelcome appearance.

On the one hand, these policies marked a dramatic shift from the priorities of the GLF and produced greater reliance on modern inputs to pursue growth, but on the other, they re-imposed central bureaucratic controls and widened public acceptability of reforms based on material self-interest.[9] The importance of the economy shifted the balance in favour of the radicals in the party. On the contrary, the revisionists' growing importance could not keep Mao content as he struggled to assume full control of the policy flow. After the Cultural Revolution, the revisionist group's activities increased, and the flank believed that the economic transformation was forced. The revisionist line emerged in pragmatic response to the difficulties that radicalism had inadvertently precipitated.[10] The revisionist leaders were less utopian and saw increased materialism and consumerism and more significant material incentives as necessary ingredients of economic growth. Revisionists also had hoped to achieve communism in the distant future. The regime was no longer able to legitimise its rule by appealing to a vision of communist principles of exploiting contradictions and achieving a stable and assured livelihood. People had become sceptical of the party's programs and its right to rule.[11] In 1979, Deng established full control over the party at the Third Plenum of the 11th Congress of the CPC and embarked on a reform program. He offered more than stability to the Chinese people and assured livelihood with unmatchable prospects of rising for China and its masses.

Mao's hasty decisions allowed enough room for the revisionist line to emerge where efforts were made to transform the economy in a revolutionary way by freeing it from the ideological inhibitions through a paradigmatic shift into economic thinking. Deng saw this as a part of a new revolution and termed it the 'Second Revolution.'

The *Second* Long March

While defending his struggle for the second revolution, Deng said, "The reforms we are now carrying out are very daring. But if we do not carry it out, it will be hard for us to make progress. Reform is China's second revolution. It is something significant that we have to undertake, even though it involves risks".[12] Deng's concept of development varied from that of the Mao's as his ideas were based on both the actual condition and the principle of Marxism-Leninism as well as that of Mao's thoughts. Deng believed that China should also learn from foreign countries and draw on their experience in revolution and construction. He was alive to experience what he had said while opening up China for FDI-led manufacturing in 1978. However, Deng mentioned that the mechanical copying and application of foreign experience and models would get China nowhere.[13]

Deng's pragmatic economic thinking brought changes in China's development process that occurred in the 1980s. He did not negate the importance of Mao's ideology, but he wanted to limit ideology to ensure political discipline and use the economy to incentivise the domain by augmenting reforms. He established a reciprocal relationship between the two. This proved to be an outstanding contribution to Deng, where he managed to identify himself as an opponent of the cult while avoiding any Khrushchev-like explicit criticism of Mao or his thought. He did so by quoting Mao's words supporting a pragmatic rather than a dogmatic interpretation of Maoist doctrine and explicitly confronting the supposition that Mao's thoughts were infallible with reasoned counter-arguments.[14]

As far as the reform process in post-1978 China is concerned, there was a unanimous belief (among ruling elites) that the utter pragmatic style of thinking would bring economic progress. With the reforms, an attempt was made to achieve ideological flexibility with the slogan "practice is the sole criterion for testing truth". The reform era was formally inaugurated with Deng taking over the *de facto* leadership within the Politburo at the Third Plenum of the

Eleventh Central Committee (ECC) (in December 1978), But the actual pragmatic reform efforts started only after the Fifth Plenum of the ECC. The Fifth Plenum of the ECC marked the end of the transitional period from 'politics in command' for Deng's 'economics in command' hoping to turn China into an advanced nation by 2000.[15] This was the time when China's modernisation within the framework of socialist ideas began. According to Deng, this path was revolutionary. To quote Deng,

> "...modernisation does represent a great new revolution. The aim of our revolution is to liberate and expand the productive forces. Without expanding the productive forces, making our country prosperous and powerful, and improving the living standards of the people, our revolution is just empty talk. We oppose the old society and the old system because it oppressed the people and fettered the productive forces. We are clear about this problem now. The gang of four said it was better to be poor under socialism than to be rich under capitalism. This is absurd".[16]

It is important to understand the discernible drive behind Deng's initiative in introducing a 'new revolution', which would continue its business of fulfilling the dream of constructing a strong China. Based on some of the assumptions that China is strong enough to face a new round of reform, Deng did not hesitate to begin the reform process, and he could see favourable conditions for the success of reforms.

The radical's criticism of revisionists like Deng was short-term and even Deng never negated some of the amateur reform measures attempted earlier. For him, it was just like laying the foundation for industry, agriculture, science, and technology. Deng further believed that the Chinese people's intelligence was suppressed under the radical ideological drive in the past few decades. Deng thought that the mental restraints imposed by Lin Biao and the Gang of Four fettered people's thinking and restrained them from bringing their wisdom and creativity into full play. Fourth, Deng was optimistic about getting help from the outside world and believed that foreign funding was also essential. With these arguments, Chinese leaders and the people were convinced about the modernisation drive. The leadership summed up a new ideology appropriate to reform in the phrase "socialism with Chinese characteristics".

The Four Modernisations (四个现代化 *Si ge xiandaihua*) pertaining to agriculture, industry, science and technology, and defence have a special place in China's modernisation process and have been mentioned in the Party Constitution (Eleventh Congress, 18 August 1977) and the State Constitution (Fifth National People's Congress, 5 March 1978).[17] In March 1979, in his effort to solve the tension between the conservatives and reformists, Deng came up with an idea of four cardinal principles.[18] Deng, in a major speech given on 30 March 1979, at a forum on directions for the CPC's theoretical work, had declared these four as 'the basic prerequisites for achieving modernisation' and enunciated them as follows, which included keeping to the socialist road, upholding the dictatorship of the proletariat, maintaining the leadership of the Communist party and upholding Marxism-Leninism and Mao's thoughts.[19] Deng, however, made it clear that these reforms aimed to promote and not dissolve Chinese communism.

Along with the concept of four modernisations, Deng had clear thoughts over the current and future economic agenda. During his talk at a forum of the first secretaries of the provincial, municipal and autonomous regional committees of the CPC on 4 October 1979, he underlined the difficulties in pursuing the hard decisions. Deng was aware that the economic choices would have political implications too. In one of his debates, he did clarify that economic work is a political task of prime importance and that the economic question is an overriding political question.[20] He was aware that the reforms would not be complete in a decade or so, and hence he termed it another 'long march' to continue for decades to come. As a result, his primary focus was to concentrate on economic work for a long period to come.[21] The road to affluent China would begin at the centre, and therefore his frequent meetings with the provincial leaders and ground-based cadres emphasised concentration on economic work rather than petty-political issues. The local leaders and cadres spread across various party units at different geographies were preoccupied with disciplinary actions and political merits. Deng's job was to augment gradual reforms and make economic development to be the central task of party committees at all levels. In essence, economic policies were used as tools to settle political problems.[22] This was a radical thought because the political and economic sectors were never separated from each other. Deng separated economic thinking from that of ideological thinking and made it the core of the Chinese developmental process. His main emphasis was now to calm down the radicals and prevent them criticising the reforms with social achievements.

With only one bank existing and that too cash stripped and with shrinking revenue, the inflow of capital had to be generated outside of China. Without generating capital and attracting investors, China could not generate employment, manufacture, and learning. To do this, China had to break through the ideological constraints, establish free-trade zones, dismantle collective farms, and woo foreign capital. This represented a breath-taking ideological reversal, which characterised pragmatically because the party had no money to spare. The foreign capital combined with demographic dividend could do miracles and was not the only one to notice it, but certainly, was the only to make the two variables work hand in hand (see Graph 1.1).

Graph 1.1: Exploiting the Demographic Dividend

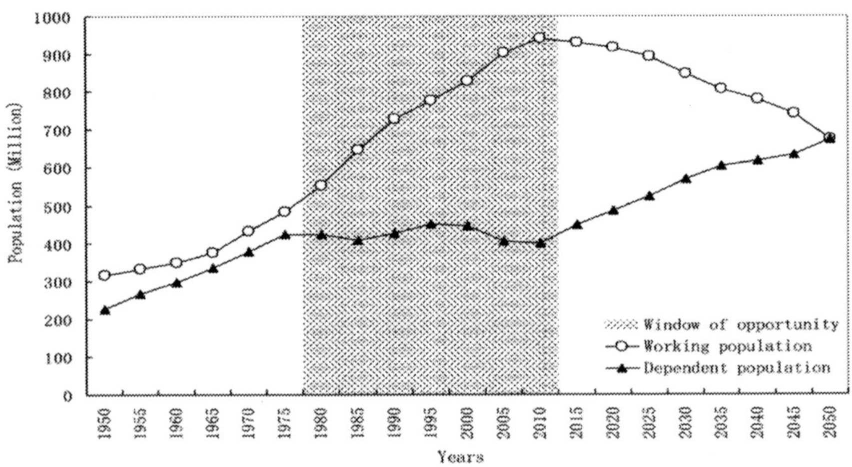

Source: United Nations Department of Economic and Social Affairs (UN DESA) (2015), *World Population Prospects: The 2015 revision*

Without hesitating, Deng accepted the use of foreign capital as he was convinced that no matter what category foreign capital belongs to, China should utilise it.[23] He often referred to the countries devastated after World War II, which developed by using loans, mainly by importing technology and patents. Besides, Deng believed that if China could make the best use of the opportunity, it would open more foreign capital avenues.[24] Interestingly firm decisions and control over the post-Mao political affairs ensured that investors look up to China for investment and higher returns. The investment, which the Chinese leadership welcomed had the potential to make fortunes, was soon made legal, and in this endeavour, overseas Chinese were ahead. The overseas Chinese, which translates as *Huaqiao* in Chinese, were the ones who were wooed by Deng and his team so that they could choose China for manufacturing-led investments. China was presented as a big magnetic pull: culturally, geographically as well as linguistically. The overseas Chinese community majorly supported the foreign-investment boom in China and concomitantly, from 1985 to 1996, two-thirds of foreign investment in China came from Hong Kong, Macau, and Taiwan.[25] With their strong link with family ties in China, the overseas Chinese could sense assured businesses. Deng knew that these investors were the ones who were looking for diversifying their firms as wages were rising steeply. By the early 1980s, Hong Kong, Macau, and Taiwan-led labour-intensive manufacturing industries for export and offers were irresistible.

The 'Red Capitalism' that China built over the next decades had its roots in Deng's reforms. If he had not initiated opening up and brought in reforms in the financial system, the rise of Chinese state capitalism would have had different results. China's rising ratings among financial groupings had a direct bearing upon its strategic projections. Deng knew how the state was far from meeting its daily expenses, as its coffers had been empty for years. China's formal financial system had shrunk to a single institution, the People's Bank of China (PBoC) and whose branches could be found only in cities but had no independence as it simply implemented the Central government's financial plans. The banking sector existed as an adjunct to the government sector. It was a ridiculously closed system where the bank performed the role of a centralised commercial bank and controlled over 93 per cent of the country's total financial assets.

Deng was well aware of China's financial system and therefore had aimed to grant more decision-making power to the enterprises and operating banks on a commercial basis. In 1979, the PBoC was separated from the MoF and given the authority of a central bank. During the same year, three state-owned specialised banks were created, namely, the Bank of China (BOC), the Agricultural Bank of China (ABC), and the China Construction Bank (CCB). In 1984, an autonomous new PBoC, the Industrial and Commercial Bank of China (ICBC) was created by the PBoC. In the following decade, the number of banks increased along with the rise of trust companies, securities firms, and pawnshops. However, China had to assume a separate cleanup task to set matters straight, which were still worrisome for the leaders. But the opening of the financial system as a gateway turned China into an economy that could look forward to a promising and stable future. To put it into context, China had more dollars within two decades of opening up of the economy than it could spend.

Beyond these goals, Deng's more extensive plans were to engage in 'economic readjustment'. He continued doing this until his last days. Fiscal reforms in the 1990s and the enterprise reforms were painful but were carried through an intensive readjustment of the policies. President Jiang Zemin and Prime Minister Zhu Rongji would not have carried out the reforms if they were not sure Deng had their back. Jiang Zemin's team was qualified to carry out Deng's readjustment plans with precision and although these changes were thoughtful, they were often brutal, and sometimes mistaken.

Restructuring of the Economy

The political sessions proved to be 'warm-up rounds' for the leaders to decide the length and scale of the reforms. Most of the leaders were consistent in avoiding the Stalinist strategy of modernisation as the borrowed Stalinist plan, and the Maoist development principles could not raise China's economy to more than average.[26] The main thrust of the reform policies was 'restructuring' the national economy,[27] which meant a fundamental reform and revamping of the entire system, which would have far-reaching implications. It was, therefore, necessary to rearrange the established procedure in a way that would introduce reforms since its success as suggested by Deng, mostly dependent upon these re-arrangements and re-alignments.

After the triumph of the socialist revolution, China gradually established a socialist economic system characterised by public ownership, which opened up for its socialist development and the well-being of its people. The change in the structure of the national economy became inevitable because of the shift in priorities. This shift in priorities from defence and heavy industry to agricultural and light industry led to a significant increase in the supply of consumer goods and the level of living[28] side by side with the restructuring of the economy aimed to speed up modernisation. China's industry, agriculture, science, and technology and national defence inevitably were in dire need of reform as the relation between production and the superstructure including forms of management and ways of thinking were not in conformity with the growth of the productive forces.[29] The complex domestic economic reform program undertaken since 1978 could be summarised in three ways: private ownership was given a free hand and made to believe to be occupying a kosher place in a socialist economy, market forces were allowed to influence the allocation of goods, and the determination of prices and material incentives turned out to be the principal mechanism for stimulating greater productivity and efficiency. These three steps allowed individuals to start or merge their businesses to enjoy greater autonomy in running their factories, less direct administrative control exercised by state officials over economic activities, and higher consumption levels of workers.[30]

The initial phase of experimenting with structural reform in the Chinese economy started during the third plenum. In both industry and agriculture, markets were opened up to handle the distribution of above-quota production. This phase saw many negative impacts on the restructuring process. Since the restructuring and reforms were new for the Chinese leaders, the success rate was relatively low. As enterprises and local government agencies retained a larger share of their profits, state revenues declined, and the national budget went into deficit. Imports, especially of capital goods, increased faster than exports, and China experienced a combined foreign trade deficit of 9.36 billion yuan (US$ 3.90 billion) in 1979-80, the largest in its history.[31] Since the local authorities and enterprises were given extended decision-making powers, they now had the capital to invest, but the big question was where to invest? The local authorities and enterprises lacked the microanalysis of the market and had no idea of what to develop. Moreover, the party-protected management and boards did not have a unified plan or necessary guidance to overcome complexities.[32] It is here that 'readjustment' was used as a tool to fix these errors as a result of which investment was slashed, the economy slowed down, budget expenditures reduced, and trade deficit put under control.

The changes in the total investment level and its allocation within the urban industrial sector demonstrated the post-Mao leadership's dramatic rejection of the Stalinist model. As a result of this restructuring of priorities for investment and production, light industrial production surpassed massive industrial output for the first time in the 1970s. It was now clear that the post-Mao leadership had rejected the 'big-push' strategies of the Stalinist model for 'balanced' growth.[33] After two years' of rethinking, new moderate economic reforms were introduced. One of the most important structural reform documents was adopted on 20 October 1984 at the Third Plenum of the 12th Central Party Committee. The guidelines[34] contained the following goals:

1. To secure a dynamic socialist economic structure
2. To invigorate enterprises as the key to restructuring the national economy
3. To devise a planning system for 'developing a socialist commodity economy'
4. To establish a 'rational price system'
5. To separate government from enterprise to allow the enterprise to perform its proper economic function
6. To create various forms of economic responsibility system and to implement the principle of distribution of reward according to one's work
7. To develop diverse economic ways to expand foreign and domestic economic and technological exchanges
8. To promote a new generation of cadres and a contingent of managerial personnel for the future economy, and finally
9. To strengthen party leadership in the reform process and its success.

The result of the restructuring was mixed in nature in which agriculture was transformed from a collective undertaking to a family enterprise. For the enterprise, the moderate reforms allocated more autonomy in decision-making, more control over the allocation of profits, and more responsibility for the outcomes of their decisions. Reforms were responsible for bringing changes in urban and rural areas and were more successful in rural areas than cities.

Rural Economic Reforms

The most critical readjustment and reforms were introduced in agriculture. These reforms were equally necessary, and most analyses miss the crucial point that the post-Mao period focused on the de-collectivising agricultural system. Agricultural policies de-emphasised collective farming and actively promoted individual farming.[35] The two main aspects of rural economic reforms were the Household Contract Responsibility System (HCRS) and changes in marketing practices introduced in the early stages of agricultural reform. These were the most notable reforms in the rural sector. Under the HCRS, introduced in 1979, individual households would enter into contracts with the state to produce agricultural products, especially grain and some cash crops, on land leased from the government. The HCRS permitted the abolition of communes, formerly the highest level of collective organisation in the countryside, and their control over agricultural land was transferred to smaller production brigades. The system successfully created the possibilities of incentive and initiative and gradually spread to various parts of the country and aroused peasant enthusiasm by giving major decision-making powers to individual peasant households.

The introduction of the HCRS was accompanied by changes in agricultural marketing and state procurement practices. The Chinese state increased procurement prices by 17.1 per cent and by 20 per cent on grain at the cost of 7.99 billion yuan (US$ 4 billion).[36] Besides, the quotas for mandatory deliveries to the state were frozen, allowing farmers to sell an increasing share of their annual output at prices higher than that paid for above-quota production.[37] In 1979, the Chinese state's budget included provisions for price increase for quota and above-quota purchases and reduction and remission of agricultural taxes.[38]The HCRS brought changes in marketing too. Increases in government procurement prices for grain and other agricultural commodities proved useful to boost production, and a kind of specialisation emerged in the agriculture sector. With the relaxation of mandatory sales to the state, peasants were relatively free to choose what they wanted to grow, depending on their expertise and natural conditions and if they wished to, alternatively they could also develop other lines of work.

Before this new policy and even after the readjustments of the early 1980s, the state monopoly over the marketing of significant crops was maintained. The new system was seen as a move towards eliminating state monopoly over purchasing and introducing supposedly voluntary state contracts with individual peasant households involving cotton, grains and oil seeds. Now peasants were allowed to receive higher than quota price for 70 per cent of their sales and the lower basic price for the remaining 30 per cent. The conditions of peasants were changing rapidly since not only were their day-to-day needs met, but they could also save. From now on, farm households took over as prominent investors in the rural economy, whereas previously, the state was virtually the only investor.

Following closely on the heels of de-collectivisation of agriculture, the Township and Village, Enterprises (TVEs) were given space to rise.[39] Post-reforms, the neglected TVEs were allowed to spread in the rural areas of China.[40] Mao's interventions had inflicted significant casualty to rural industrialisation, which delayed China's schedule in building a modern industrial network. Since the reforms of 1978, the development of the TVEs had been an integral part of rural and agricultural reforms. People started a small business in the countryside engaged in artisan production or services like hair cutting, bicycle repairing and other ancillary activities, which developed rapidly in the villages. In 1980, the proportions had changed to such an extent that over 50 per cent of the population worked in ancillary or rural industries.[41] This was followed by swift growth in its industrial enterprises. In 1987, limits on the size of private firms, which had been enforced, were lifted. These changes altered the village's previous economic structure, in which almost 90 per cent of the population were engaged in farming. In the initial stages, these industries absorbed a vast surplus of rural labour, and in their heyday (1985 to 1995), rural enterprises were creating up to 12 million new jobs a year. In the 1980s, they absorbed 80 million surplus, rural labourers.[42] Compared to the SOEs' performance, TVEs were ahead with the most considerable bulk in the total industrial output and emerged as the fastest-growing sector in the economy. In 1978, TVEs produced only 9 per cent of the industrial output in the country. From 1978 to 1995, the output value of TVEs grew at an annual average of 24.7 per cent, and its employment rose at an average yearly rate of 9.3 per cent. In 1995, TVEs produced 56 per cent of the total industrial output.[43] These developments created a rural society that was far more complex and differentiated than it had been in the Maoist period. In the Marxian sense of class, there were now several classes engaged in the sphere of production.

Urban Economic Reforms

The new economic reforms in post-1978 China focused on the agrarian sector. Deng's policies were responsible for propelling industrial reforms in 1984. When the agricultural industry was released from the state's control (administered through collective farming, known as communes—about 25,000 of them), it was easier to position raw material supply according to industrial needs and demands in urban China. Gradually, this led to a return of confidence, and the living conditions were improved so that Deng was ready to launch more effective urban economic reform plans. Deng's urban economic reforms followed his experiments in rural reforms. He allocated a more extensive land plot to each farmer, encouraged more ancillary private production activities, permitted rural free marketing, improved individual income, and enlivened light industry growth throughout rural China. Deng made rural economic revitalisation the cornerstone of urban industrial development[44] as a result of which significant policy changes took place in October 1984.

The measurers concerned with urban areas were as follows:

> (1) Reform in price systems and utilisation of all economic levers for competition in production and management efficiency; (2) Separation of government from enterprise in the latter's internal decision-making and operation through enterprise autonomy and internal collective decision making; (3) Institutionalisation of responsibility and accountability through wage differentials and salary reward; (4) Development of diverse economic forms in both domestic and foreign economic exchanges, and (5) Training of a new generation of cadres and managerial personnel for the new socialist economy.[45]

The enhancement of the market was made with the withdrawal of the state from the decision-making process. With this decentralisation, a kind of dual system emerged, where the plan and the market played similar coordinating roles in the allocations of resources and the distribution of products. Centralised planning as a means of economic regulation indeed lost its importance in Deng's era. The chance of profit maximisation through increasing output (above plan output) and selling in the open market almost led to the mandatory system's demise. The other significant measure was that the state accepted the price factor to accelerate the reform process. The economic decision-makers were aware that unless factory prices are successfully readjusted to reflect their real values, attempts to reform the economic system would achieve little success. Once the role of the market is expanded, the decontrol of prices was obvious. On the one hand, price flexibility reflected the market demand and supply relations more directly,[46] whereas, on the other hand, for the urban Chinese, inflation caused worry and with prices changing every day, they no longer felt financially secure.[47]

The control-related product priority, production and distribution and sales were left to the enterprises. The theme 'responsibility is equal to profit' became popular. With the reduction in state planning and involvement and an increase in enterprise responsibility, the scope of economic development widened. Thus, a concerted industrial reform began in 1984, giving enterprises greater power over production, pricing, and distribution of above-quota or non-planned output and over hiring, promotion, remuneration, and dismissal of their workers.[48] State enterprises were allowed to retain a share of their profits and sell a part of their output independently that exceeded mandatory state quotas. In the post-Mao period, the situation varied as reforms prescribed that the educational system be upgraded so that the content of the middle school curriculum in the cities would put stress on vocational training and meet the demands of the industrial sector.[49] Workers were allowed to change their jobs within the network of state enterprises. On the other hand, the non-state sector's employing capacity was increased. As part of voluntary initiatives by the state, workers seeking employment were allowed to apply for jobs they found attractive and refuse assignments offered to them by the state labour bureau. The workers' incentives also drastically changed since enterprises were allowed to retain the profit; they (enterprises) started granting bonuses to deserving workers from the profits.[50] This created an atmosphere for fostering economic development.

Among the urban economic reforms, the most noticeable was establishing the denominated geographies for attracting foreign investments—the Special Economic Zones or SEZs. The Chinese leaders saw the advantages of 'zones' for economic development[51] and the idea of economic zones.[52] By allowing the establishment of SEZs, Deng wished to set an example for others to emulate. That's why selected regions and locals were allowed to try their hands at experimenting with this path breaking idea. Far away from Beijing, and its notorious political interventions and meddling by party officials, the Pearl Delta Region was chosen to turn itself into a laboratory of capitalism. Moreover, Chinese provinces like Fujian and Guangdong were having strategic locations and could exploit the proximities. Principles of equity and dreams of communism were soon going to be out of fashion in this designated region. Deng knew that adjunct lands to the mainland, namely, Hongkong, Macau, and Taiwan, were prospering faster than their Chinese counterparts.

Moreover, for the overseas Chinese, these provinces were more comfortable to establish their industries. With a history of socio-cultural contact with the outside world and being strategically located near Hong Kong, provinces like Guangdong and Fujian stood the best chance. Amidst plans to provide a physical window for foreign investments, Xi Zhongxun (father of Xi Jinping) led a party delegation from the Guangdong province and presented their claim over the opportunity to open the pockets of coastal geography for foreign investment. Giving up to the provincial political pressure and geographical opportunities, Deng, within months (July 1979), declared the Southern coastal regions as 'special zones' (特殊地区 *Teshu diqu*) (Special Economic Zones—SEZs were abbreviated as 经济特区 – *Jingji tequ*). China's SEZs were defined as designated geographical areas that allow the integration of free-market principles to attract additional foreign investment. Guangdong, Shenzhen, Zhuhai, and Shantou were demarcated and declared as SEZs in 1979 and Xiamen in Fujian province in 1980.

SEZs were intended to have a 'spillover effect' where the higher volume of economic growth from the coastal regions would trickle down to the Central and Western regions. According to Deng, "A special economic zone is a medium for introducing technology, management, and knowledge. It is also a window for our foreign policy."[53] The implementation of this policy, in the real sense, opened the gates of new avenues for China's economy and bolstered the Chinese economy in competing with significant powers in the world market. The policy of 'to open not to close'[54] through SEZs proved a game-changer, and within a decade or so, the coastal regions attracted 85 per cent of foreign investment.[55] The 120,000 foreign-funded companies employing nearly 10 per cent of the urban workforce accounted for 47 per cent of their foreign trade.[56] Overall, the urban economy became the core of Deng's reform to revitalise the economy at home and open the country to foreign technology and trade.

Opening of China to the Outside World

The contradiction within the communist bloc and the failure of the development policy accepted by Chinese leaders proved hopeless. The idea of self-reliance and 'leaning to one side', proved less compatible with the changing internal and external conditions, which were later labelled as 'faults'. Under socialism, producing firms were forbidden from having direct contact with the outside world, that is, with foreign customers and suppliers. They could not engage directly in foreign trade but had to conduct such operations through the appropriate foreign corporations. In socialist countries, foreign trade corporations were given monopoly rights over the foreign trade in industry, and domestic industries were banned from taking, acquiring, and applying foreign technical know-how. In his speeches, Deng warned radicals that China should not adopt a closed-door frame of mind and refuse to learn from the good things of foreign countries.[57] However, the merger of the Chinese economy with the world economy would have benefited China in many ways.

The 'Open Door Policy' of the 1980s became a prime source of innovation in the reform efforts but would have been entirely impracticable in the domestic context of the early 1960s. The 'opening up' and concomitant reforms dramatically increased China's imports of industrial supplies and foreign technology, particularly for coal plants and expanded the exports of agricultural goods and raw materials. China decided to revise its development strategy, end isolation, open up to the outside world, increase exports, and raise the status of exporting industries. The reforms of 1978 focused on improving China's interaction with the international economy, wherein Beijing began welcoming direct foreign investment. Greater authority was granted to ministries and local-municipal governments to allow them to engage in foreign trade transactions. This system was further devolved to bring corporations, enterprises, and factories in contact with foreign firms, presumably hoping that this would expose them to the benefits of international comparative advantage and co-operation. The government started encouraging foreign trade companies to form joint operations with productive enterprises so that, for the first time, a single organisation became responsible for production and marketing.[58] The localities were allowed to retain a portion of the foreign exchange which they earned through foreign trade. To justify their proposal and welcome foreign investment in the country, the Chinese leaders described it as a form of 'State Capitalism'[59] where they hoped the foreign entrepreneurs would play a constructive role in China's economic development. Loans were negotiated, and foreign businessmen were encouraged to participate in joint investment enterprises in China.

The approach was cautious and limited the scope for foreign investment for particular organisational forms (the equity joint venture as the organisational format) and specific geographic zones.[60] These limitations were soon lifted, and investment was accepted in every sector of the economy and the list was extended along the coastal region to absorb foreign technology, introduce foreign capital, and expand Chinese exports in foreign markets. China designated four areas along the southeast coast—Shenzhen, Zhuhai, Xiamen, and Shantou—as Special Economic Zones in 1979. By the middle of 1986, "some more areas were created to attract foreign investment. Three development triangles in South-eastern and central China—the Pearl river, Min river, and Yangtze river deltas were identified, and trade and investment promotion zones. These regions were expected to do the same job, which SEZs were doing. Like the SEZs, these regions are a base for exports and a filter to digest the world's modern science and technology and advanced managerial methods...so as to discard the dross and select the essential."[61]

China's efforts to open up its economy to the world was a significant disruptor or a 'breaching experiment'[62] that turned the country into a hub for manufacturing-centred foreign investments and window for more experiments with the market economy of the West. The resulting business ventures enabled overseas Chinese investors to exploit their comparative advantages in technology, entrepreneurial ability, and culture.

Conclusion

The notion of State Capitalism introduced and experimented with by the party, faces several paradoxes and witnessed ire and backlash too as it is not all about performance. In several instances, China's state capitalism turned out to be an adverse factor in the global trading system and posed threats. The growing interventions by the state beyond a limit could not yield the expected returns always and Chinese experiments in the past decade or so witnessed some significant drawbacks. This is noticeable just as China's model of debt, massive investment, and state direction are yielding diminishing returns and growth is the worst in nearly four decades while many suspect lower figures may lead China to long-term instability.

Deng's 'Long March' resulted in turning China into a hub for global attraction, although inequality and pollution have soared, and so have living standards. The people of China thank Deng for putting money in their pockets and turning cities into global competitors. The party has presided over one of history's successes. The soaring city skylines and modern infrastructure are mainly the product of rapid growth in the past 40 years. Growth figures were maintained at a 10 per cent compound annual rate. The 'March' can better explain how a country that struggled to free itself from economic hardships and a rigid political ideology is now the world's biggest manufacturer. Combined with rapidly advancing techniques and technologies, Chinese trains and digital-payments systems are better off than developed countries elsewhere. China's 'state capitalism' is a product of hard-nosed liberal economics rather than any magic touch; yet East European and other socialist economies could not do better than the Chinese. Several other factors explain why China survived the collapse though its experiments became more radical than others.

NOTES

1. Jurgen Habermas. 1996. 'Modernity: An Unfinished Project', in Maurizio Passerin D'Entreves and Seyla Benhabib (eds.), *Habermas and the Unfinished Project of Modernity: Critical Essays on the Philosophical Discourse of Modernity* (Cambridge: Polity Press), 38-58.
2. Lowell Dittmer. 1994. *China Under Reform* (New York: Routledge), 80.
3. Suzanne Ogden. 1995. *China's Unresolved Issues: Politics, Development and Culture* (Englewood Cliffs, N.J.: Prentice Hall), 259.
4. Mao Zedong. 1967. *Selected Works of Mao Tse-Tung:* Vol. I (Peking: Foreign Languages Press), 322.
5. Ogden. *China's Unresolved Issues,* 264.
6. Dittmer. *China Under Reform,* 14.
7. Kenneth Lieberthal. 1993. 'The Great Leap Forward and the Split in the Yan'an Leadership, 1958-65,' in Roderick Macfarquhar (ed.), *The Politics of China 1949-1989* (Cambridge: Cambridge University Press), 87-147.
8. Ibid.
9. Ibid.
10. Ogden. *China's Unresolved Issues,* 14.
11. Andrew J. Nathan. 1997. *China's Transition* (New York: Columbia University Press), 59.
12. Ibid.
13. Deng Xiaoping. 1982. 'Opening Speech at the Twelfth National Congress of the Communist Party of China', in *Selected Works of Deng Xiaoping* Vol. III, 1 September, www.english. peoplesdaily.com.cn. (accessed on 24 July 2020).
14. Dittmer. *China Under Reform,* 25-26.
15. Immanuel C. Y. Hsu. 1983. *The Rise of Modern China* (New York: Oxford University Press), 799.
16. Deng Xiaoping. 1979a. 'We Can Develop a Market Economy under Socialism', *Selected Works of Deng Xiaoping* Vol. II, 26 November, www.english.peoplesdaily.com.cn (accessed on 24 July 2020).

17. Deng Xiaoping did not introduce the idea of Four Modernisations. Zhou En-Lai is generally credited with initiating the idea of the Four Modernisations. At the Third National People's Congress, December 1964, he proposed the socialist construction of a 'modernised agriculture, industry, national defence, and science and technology' to be accomplished 'within not too long period of history. However, no concrete action followed due to the onset of the Cultural Revolution. Deng, during his speech at the Fourth National Congress in January 1975, extended Zhou En-Lai's modernisation and renewed his call for an independent and relatively comprehensive industrial and economic system, by1980, an overall modernisation of the four sectors before the end of the century, which is considered as the basis of the current Four Modernisations.
18. Democracy Wall Movement shows that how in Post-Mao China, with gradual relaxation, various political demands emerged. The movement was in favour of political liberalisation, and to some extent supported by the reformers, to challenge the left. With the Four Cardinal principles, Deng Xiaoping showed his commitment to Marxism-Leninism-Mao Zedong thoughts, party leadership, socialism and the proletariat dictatorship. This step was in a way to balance the ongoing clash between the two sides.
19. Deng Xiaoping. 1979c. 'Uphold the Four Cardinal Principles', in *Selected Works of Deng Xiaoping* Vol. II, 30 March, www.english.peoplesdaily.com.cn (accessed on 8 July 2020).
20. By the political task, Deng refers to the Four Modernisations.
21. Deng Xiaoping. 1979b. 'Some Comments on Economic Work', in *Selected Works of Deng Xiaoping* Vol. II, 4 October, www.english.peoplesdaily.com.cn (accessed on 24 July 2020).
22. Ibid.
23. Earlier, Comrade Chen Yun had classified foreign capital in two categories: invested foreign currency and loans for equipment.
24. Deng Xiaoping. 1984. 'Make a success of Special Economic Zones and Open more cities to the outside world', in *Selected Works of Deng Xiaoping* Vol. II, 24 February, www.english.peoplesdaily.com.cn (accessed on 2 July 2020).
25. C. Y. Chang. 1980. 'Overseas Chinese in China's Policy', *The China Quarterly*, Vol. 82, June, 281-303.
26. Soviet model also adopted the priorities set by Stalin and his central planners, that is, heavy emphasis on the high rate of investment and rapid growth in heavy industrial production, especially the basic metals and machine building industries. And this development was attempted to be achieved at the cost of agricultural development. China has also implemented the Stalinist development strategy throughout the quarter of a century before the death of Mao.
27. The process of restructuring was different from that of readjustment. Restructuring is necessarily more difficult and time consuming than readjustment. The focus of readjustment is mainly short run. In view of existing imbalances, their correction has a special urgency and is expected to show results within a relatively short period.
28. Robert F. Dernberger. 1984. 'China's New Economic Development: Problems and Prospects', in Ginsberg, Norton and Bernard Lalor (eds.), *China: The 80s Era* (Boulder: Westview Press), 127.
29. Liu Guoguang (ed.). 1981. *Theoretical Issues in National Economic System Reform*. Beijing: Chinese Academy of Social Sciences Press. Quoted in Joseph C. H. Chai. 1997. *China: Transition to a Market Economy* (New York: Oxford University Press), 74.

30. Harry Harding. 1987. *China's Second Revolution: Reform after Mao* (Washington D.C.: Brookings Institution Press), 99-100.
31. Ibid., 71.
32. Liu Guoguang and Wang Ruisun. 1984. 'Restructuring of the Economy', in Yu Guangyuan (ed.), *China's Socialist Modernization* (Beijing: Foreign Languages Press), 135.
33. Dernberger. 'China's New Economic Development: Problems and Prospects', 125.
34. Central Committee of the Communist Party of China. 1984. 'Decision of the Central Committee of the Communist Party of China on Reform of the Economic Structure (adopted by the Twelfth Central Committee of the CPC at its Third Plenum)'. Quoted in David Wen-Wei Chang. 1988. *China Under Deng Xiaoping: Political and Economic Reform* (Basingstoke: The Macmillan Press), 162.
35. Jasper Becker has given an interesting explanation of this process. "After Mao's death almost immediately, and perhaps spontaneously, the peasants began to divide up the land and grow food as they thought fit instead of following state directives. According to the party's history, the first to do so were a group of peasants in Fengyang county in Anhui, who signed a secret compact in 1977. In 1978, Deng Xiaoping…officially endorsed the Anhui experiment and began to dissolve the communes, authorising the adoption of the Household Contract Responsibility System.
36. Collin Mackerras, Pradeep Taneja and Graham Young. 1994. '*China since 1978: Reform, Modernization, and Socialism with Chinese Characteristics* (New York: St. Martin's Press).
37. Since the early 1950s, the Chinese government had used the 'unified purchase' (*tongguo*) system as the keystone of its grain control policy, procuring grain and other agricultural commodities from the rural areas at fixed prices and then selling them to urban residents at prices lower than the procurement prices.
38. Dernberger. 'China's New Economic Development: Problems and Prospects', 126.
39. TVEs consist of collective, partnership and individually-owned enterprises in rural areas.
40. The Great Leap Forward of the late 1950s led local governments to establish numerous rural small-scale industrial firms, but most of them turned out to be unsustainable. After that, they were poorly looked after by the state.
41. Fei Xiaotong. 1988. *Chinese Village Close-Up*. Beijing: New World Press. Quoted in David Wen-Wei Chang. 1988. *China Under Deng Xiaoping: Political and Economic Reform* (Basingstoke: The Macmillan Press), 162.
42. Jasper Becker. 1999. 'Slump in countryside deepens as bubble bursts for rural enterprises' *South China Morning Post*. 27 August. Quoted in Becker, Jasper. 2000. *The Chinese* (New York: Free Press), 79-80.
43. Ma Jun. 2000. *The Chinese Economy in the 1990s* (London: Palgrave Macmillan), 114.
44. Ma Hung. 1983. *New Strategy for China's Economy*. Beijing: New World Press. Quoted in David Wen-Wei Chang. 1988. *China Under Deng Xiaoping: Political and Economic Reform* (Basingstoke: The Macmillan Press), 162.
45. Central Committee of the Communist Party of China. 'Decision of the Central Committee of the Communist Party of China on Reform of the Economic Structure (adopted by the Twelfth Central Committee of the CPC at its Third Plenum)'. Quoted in David Wen-Wei Chang. *China Under Deng Xiaoping: Political and Economic Reform*, 162.
46. Here by "price flexibility", the author means the negotiable scene in price fixing. The layers of prices are introduced for different categories. There are now four types of prices in China: Planned prices or state fixed prices, applied to materials and services covered by

the mandatory state plan; Floating prices, with upper and lower limits—another kind of planned price.; Negotiated prices, for non-staple agricultural products and some consumer goods, set through negotiations between local and provincial governments and the producers. Free-Market prices, applicable to manufactured goods not covered by state plans and to goods sold in the free market, determined by producers and retailers according to demand and supply.

47. Urban residents had received financial protection since the early 1950s by way of food subsidies and medical and social welfare facilities. Soaring prices were also one of the reasons behind the tragedy of June 1989.
48. Harding. *China's Second Revolution*, 113.
49. Ibid., 117.
50. Ibid., 119.
51. Prior to 1978, Chinese officials regarded export promotion zones in many developing countries as a manifestation of contemporary imperialism and new colonialism.
52. Wei-Wei Zhang. 1996. *Ideology and Economic Reform under Deng Xiaoping 1978-199* (London: Kegan Paul International). Quoted in Michael Weisskopf. 1984. 'China caught in cycle of reform and retreat' *The Washington Post.* 26 April, https://www.washingtonpost.com/archive/politics/1984/04/26/china-caught-in-cycle-of-reform-and-retreat/18e492ec-d5d7-4991-aa2e-1149450909c1/ (accessed on 26 July 2020), 76.
53. Deng Xiaoping. 'Make a success of Special Economic Zones and Open more cities to the outside world'.
54. Ibid.
55. Jasper Becker. 2000. *The Chinese* (Oxford: Oxford University Press), 121.
56. Ibid.
57. Harding. *China's Second Revolution*, 133.
58. Ibid., 137.
59. Ibid., 159.
60. Ibid.
61. *Ban yue tan* (Bi-Monthly Talks). 1985. No. 4, February 25. Quoted in Harry Harding. 1987. *China's Second Revolution: Reform after Mao* (Washington D.C.: Brookings), 167.
62. Breaching experiment is a form of sociological analysis and an experiment in rupture or 'breaching' introduced by the American sociologist Harold Garfinkel (1967) in his book *Studies in Ethnomethodology*. Englewoods Cliffs, NJ: Prentice Hall. The experiment seeks to examine people's reactions to violations of commonly accepted and taken for granted aspects of the social world, rules or norms.

2

Why Did China Not Collapse?

After decades of reforms, the success of China's economic policies has been widely registered. Compared to other developed and developing countries worldwide, China's GDP growth remained outstanding. It picked its battles carefully, and as a result, it recorded noticeable rates of change in the past four decades, averaging more than 10 per cent. The steady opening-up and restructuring process let the economy to adjust its goals and to remarkable changes in Chinese society. But still, Beijing faces vast challenges. Chinese reforms and opening up were kicked off when its peers in Eastern Europe pledged to reform their economies in record time and match Western Europe's developed economies. In most post-war socialist economies, market reforms were carried out with more or less similar variations. The restructuring and opening up of the domestic market failed as the leadership could not prioritise economic adjustments. Chinese fared well over Eastern European and Russian experiments.

Compared to other socialist economies, China was neither a small country with a compact population and economic challenges nor was it as gigantic as Soviet Russia, where the likes of Yegor Gaidar[1] did not realise the ground realities of broken economies and took free advice from Western financial institutions. The priorities of Chinese leaders were not sparkling growth rates or matching that of developed nations. Although heavily steeped in ideology, the Chinese state played a balancing act. Deng turned out to be the stabiliser who stabilised the inter-state hierarchies, the growth sectors, and displeasures within the Zhongnanhai and factions within the party. This was encapsulated as a strategy of *taoguang yanghui, you suo zuowei*, keeping a low profile while trying to accomplish something (韬光养晦有所作为). The periodic policy appraisal, ground visits, and low-profile interventions paid off well in the Chinese case.

The Chinese leaders' political socialisation had its life cycle, and the party maintained it deliberately to train and balance factionalism. This was not a familiar scene in Russia's case. The Soviet Union had a miscalculated national identity whereby the Soviets were disconnected from each other. The leadership had visions to fulfil the communist plan and pave the way for a Westernised economy and growth models by removing state controls and denouncing the command economy. Other socialist states carried out complete price liberalisation accompanied by rapid and free-hand privatisation of state companies and assets.

On the other hand, the alternative course was adopted by China when it launched its economic reforms carried them out without immediate full price liberalisation and privatisation of existing large-scale state-owned enterprises (SOEs). This does not mean that the Chinese experiment was clean and clear. The challenge of increasing unemployment, rising income disparity and widespread social unrest left the leadership in a dilemma. As Premier Zhu Rongji, during his speech in March 1999 at the National People's Congress (NPC), said, 'economic order is somewhat in disarray,' 'financial discipline is lax,' and 'demand in the market is feeble'.[2] China had to switch between reforms, accelerate and alienate the sectors, and there was no 'sputnik race' while this was underway.

From Eastern Europe to the Berlin Wall: Communism and 'Big Bang' Reforms

In the post-war period, Soviet Russia successfully let fellow socialist economies replicate the fundamentals of the command economy. The Soviet system, after the formation of the Council for Mutual Economic Assistance (CMEA) in 1949, incorporated the countries of Eastern Europe as well as those of the

Soviet Union itself, was based on the proposition that state commands can maximise social gain.[3] The Western society's economies were fashioned on the proposition that as individuals pursue their personal growth, the country's benefits will exceed its costs, yielding social gain.[4] The governments of socialist states accepted an economic and political system based on collective or state ownership of the 'means of production' and 'distribution'[5] whereby they did not allow prices to play a role in encouraging production and regulating goods and services.

Since the 1950s and throughout the 1960s, Eastern European economies attempted to undo the severe socio-economic setback by embracing economic reform. To avoid getting renounced as impoverished and low-income economies, and to halt the ebbing of people's living standards, which was apparent for some years, leaders in the Soviet Union and elsewhere in Eastern Europe embarked on a bold path to bring moribund and rogue economies into market systems and end the isolation of the command economies from the Western world by seeking integration into the capitalist world economy. Since the early 1960s, most Soviet-type Eastern European economies were resuscitated by the economy's reforms and the policy of 'opening up.' The post-Stalinist deliberations and discussion on the prospects of change in the functioning of the centrally planned economies were also mulled over by Chinese leaders like Lin Biao and Deng Xiaoping. The Eastern European economies showed significant interest in correcting the economies by following a pragmatic agenda. Even Soviet Russia was not an exception to the wave of reform agenda because, after the fall of Khrushchev, the 'Kosygin reform' of 1965 looked at ways and means to broaden government's legitimacy beyond its doctrinal legitimacy.

When the reforms began, the previous stages saw reform euphoria picking up and controls loosening. Still, the vector of the reforms was inadequate and untimely. However, the command economies were severely underperforming due to denial of the price factor, production efficiency, and technological innovations, which hampered modernisation efforts. Moreover, decades of centralised state planning had proved to be economically disastrous. The economic problems experienced by the command economy included a declining rate of productivity growth, shifting of managerial initiative and worker enthusiasm at the production unit level, economic sector imbalance (specifically in favour of heavy industry but at the expense of light industry), and failure to meet consumer demand.[6] The reforms in structures and institutions regulating reforms could not be introduced at a single go, but when it was facilitated, the momentum was lost, and the economies started contracting immediately. This had political implications and worsened the effects further. The reforms conflicted with the Communist state system, which held back the reforms and failed to alleviate internal conflicts and contradictions.

In addition to inconsistencies in the reform measures, the East European economies could not avoid a lucrative market in Soviet Russia and exploit the market beyond East Europe—the continent's rich Western side. Production and supplies were weak and needed quality reform measures, but pertaining to conflicting political interests, these reform measures were never considered a priority. As a result, the political obstacles led to the debacle of reforms. As Wlodzimierz Brus describes the events, "In the light of East European experience over the 1966-75 decade, one is inclined to view the political obstacles to economic reform of a Hungarian type in a less simplistic manner. They existed and played a large part in blocking change but in conjunction with genuine difficulties in implementing the reform's basic propositions. This makes the future course of institutional developments in East European economies perhaps less predictable than previously thought, if not concerning the general direction, then at least about the pace and scope of changes".[7]

The "market socialism" of socialist countries was carried out in two ways; one, as discussed above, in a rapid 'Big Bang' method (sometimes even called Shock Therapy) and another in the 'Gradualist' way. These two approaches were simultaneously developed to derive maximum benefits from both the market and socialism. The Sachs model of development was widely expected by most socialist societies to achieve rapid economic growth. This well-known American economic professor, after serving in Bolivia, arrived in Central and Eastern Europe with the panache of Francisco Pizarro to surprise the surgical operation they considered necessary for economic revival.[8] The contribution of Jeffery Sachs is worthy of understanding Shock Therapy. Sachs is widely credited with founding a new discipline—the economic theory of transition. Sachs' model was referred to with various names: 'shock treatment,' 'radical economic reform,' 'big bang,' and 'shock therapy.' Sachs formulated his model to solve one big problem: how should the entire ex-communist region of Eastern Europe and Soviet Russia be reorganised to achieve, in Sachs' words, 'a recovery of human freedom and a democratically based rise in living standards'.[9] In the Soviet Union and Eastern Europe, the ideology-based economic system failed as steadily as it tried to rise. Overall, the decade of the 1980s was full of dramatic incidents, which were already marked as historical events. The political and economic dynamic change in Central and Eastern Europe and the former Soviet Union created a new historical conjuncture. The socialist project's future was called into question.

The East European economies favoured radical reforms, as portrayed in Figure 2.1. Under the shock therapy that is path *R*, it was assumed that abrupt changes affect consumption but recover faster. The alternative or the gradualist approach shown by path *G* describes a slower fall in consumption and a slower rise to the initial level later, signifying the slower metabolism of reforms and growth. In both these approaches, once the strategies reach the initial level, which indicates the transition stage, the growth rate follows the same trajectories, i.e., the economy grows at the same rate under the two strategies.

Figure 2.1: Gradual versus Big-Bang Reform

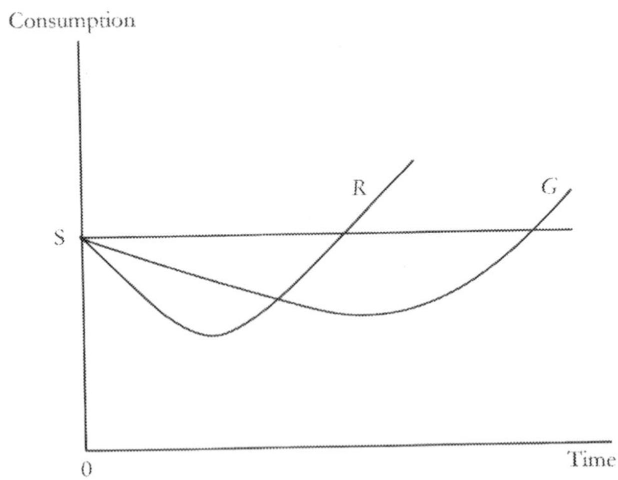

Source: Przeworski[10] (1991/95: 163)

While in Eastern Europe, there was a strong emphasis on creating irreversibility and moving fast on all fronts (Big Bang approach), China stressed on flexibility and cautious experimentation. In December 1978, the Third Party Plenum repudiated both the leftist[11] and the Soviet model of development to rapidly expand China's economy. After the Third Party Plenum, China started moving away from a centrally administered economy to a more decentralised system that allowed greater local autonomy. This radical reform process was termed 'shift to socialist modernisation'. These changes were revolutionary because they were revisionists, who were outcastes within the communist scheme of Mao's ideas. In times of crisis, outdated and moribund political ideologies may not work in an unorthodox way. However, the 1970s were still experimenting with revisionist ways and was not less than calling for a revolution. A few would claim that the 1971 Chinese rapprochement with the USA was a win for those who wanted to align with capitalism, but it was not entirely true. The Sino-USA diplomatic engagement needs to be seen from the binary of Sino-Soviet ideological conflict. Growing Soviet resistance to China was assumed to have conspired to thwart the pressure on China, isolate the Chinese state and let Chinese communism die the East European way.

The leadership, which announced 'opening up', was once purged by Mao. The new leadership was ideologically radical on party lines and believed in the party's interest and its targeted projections. It is important to remember that this leadership was criticised within party circles for its leniency towards creating property rights, allowing the masses to enjoy freedom over production and consumption, and creating wealth-based divisions, which resulted in income disparities and imbalance within provinces and cities, which turned out to be fuel for the 1989 mass pro-democracy protest in Beijing. Early years of reforms were quick and compressed in a short span of time and certainly had to pay a social cost. The reforms aimed at achieving 'Socialism with Chinese characteristics'[12] and were revolutionary and a *continuum* of the party's hold over China. And this was the first time when in China, the idea of economic transformation reached its peak, and the process of socialist modernisation began. The Chinese leaders looked up to a gradual approach to pursue opening up. Gradualism (the bottom-up approach) moved gradually from a centrally planned to a market economy by establishing a market at the decentralised level.

The efforts to restructure the economy meant acknowledging the need to allow economic institutions to follow an independent self-assessment path and market behaviour. China was not the only socialist country to start this kind of transformation in the socialist economy. In Eastern Europe and former Soviet Russia, efforts were made to transform the economy, though the means to bring about change was different from that of China. As elaborated earlier, the experiments of quick reforms in Eastern Europe were met with mixed results, and most of the efforts succumbed to institutional and planning inconsistencies. The economies of these countries stagnated, and their re-entry into the world economy proceeded at a snail's pace, whereas in China, the Communist party did not fall, and the economy was transformed not with a big bang, but incrementally and could be labelled as 'gradual economic development.' As a result, the economy grew faster, and it has been reintegrated into the world economy. China and Hungary made essential gains by introducing market reforms and opening up their societies to foreign contacts. Soviet Russia followed suit soon.

Planned Commodity Economy in China

The transformation that occurred in socialist societies imparted essential lessons to the Chinese leaders. While speaking about Chinese experiments, Overholt (1993) points out that the striking aspect of China's success was contrasting it with the economic failures of European countries that had abandoned communism. Many knowledgeable Chinese familiar with the recent developments in Eastern Europe are thankful that they live in China. Despite decades of economic loss, disasters, deaths, and undisputable control exercised by the Communist party, the masses may not like their party. Still, after seeing the results of chaos over the last two hundred years, China was prepared to accept the regime that assured them of order and allowed them to escape poverty and begin to enjoy the benefits of modern industry.[13] The Chinese had understood the importance of the market, which is why their move towards a market economy started with a conscious step. If a country decides to transform its economy, it can do so possibly because of the primitive, underdeveloped economic situation, and as a result, in most cases, the market becomes the centre of the transforming economy. Demand must play a significant role in the transition process to increase economic efficiency, realise the country's inherent potential for material prosperity, check bureaucracy and extend the initiative and responsibility among the immediate producers. How market values are introduced in the system is a different matter because the redefining and the readjustment of the market are always expected, and they differ from each other. In the initial stage, similar things happened in China whereby the leaders planned to merge the market and turn the planned economy into a 'planned commodity economy' by introducing market elements.[14] It is visible that the Chinese leaders adopted market values maintaining the designed economic structure or the bureaucratic 'socialist' economy,[15] as a result of which the World Bank said "to be efficient, enterprises must be motivated to improve their economic performance; they must have some freedom for manoeuvre; they must be faced with economically reasonable prices, and they must be subjected to competition....Besides, the state must retain the ability to direct the overall pace and pattern of development. The essence—and the difficulty—of a successful and comprehensive reform thus lies not only in bringing together the several elements of market regulation but also in combining them with an appropriately modified system of planning".[16]

Since the system was deeply accustomed to the technical and bureaucratic procedures and structured according to a bureaucratic style,[17] Chinese leaders found it difficult to follow the 'pre-planned mode' of economic development. This administrative problem of policy formulation and implementation of policy made leaders adopt a gradual implementation of progressively deeper, even more radical market reforms within the overall framework of the state-owned, state-planned economy.[18] These reforms evolved through three different stages. The first stage meant devolution of authority to enterprise managers and the introduction of enterprise sharing,[19] due to which the connection between flexible production decision and profit was established. Secondly, the gradual freeing of prices and state control over resource allocation so that newly empowered managers could respond to market demand and maximise the cost/price ratio (this step began with the institution of free-market prices for sales over-plan output in the early 1980s).[20] Thirdly, the imposition of 'hard budget constraint,' that is, capitalist-like sanctions of bankruptcy and unemployment, to force procedures to respond appropriately to market signals on failure.[21] This step probably was introduced to accept the market as the signifier of the efficiency of enterprises. It opened the enterprises to the market system. The state-sponsored economic reforms in China are doing well while planning continues in some of the state enterprises.

Enterprise Reform in East European Economies

In developing economies, the government's economic role grew dramatically in the second half of the twentieth century. In many of these countries, the state was striving to mobilise resources and direct them toward rapid economic growth rather than just stabilise the economy, as in the developed countries. Until the 1980s, the pattern of state-dominated development, which included centralised planning and state control of the economy, was widely followed. The budgets of the smaller developing states were significantly smaller. In developing countries, less government spending was possible for social services as funds were used to subsidise enterprises processing goods and processed goods. According to World Bank data, during 1986 and 1991, the low-income countries spent a 14 per cent share of their GDP on SOEs, whereas the share was 28 per cent as far as the Gross Domestic Investment (GDI) was concerned. During the same period, Western thinkers brought the idea of privatisation in the region, which became the main reason for the emergence and advancement of the private sector. Since the 1980s, many developing countries adopted privatisation programs where the pace of privatisation varied according to the intensity of market reforms. The introduction of privatisation (fully or partially) in developing economies was meant to free their budgets from the burden of subsidising loss-making enterprises.

Eastern European economies found themselves able to work for building human capital and providing for social development. However, privatisation was not the only way to pull back the economy from a deep economic crisis but the most preferred way for the underdeveloped and developing economies, including socialist countries, which wanted transformation. Enterprise reform is at the heart of transition in pre-socialist economies. As defined by the International Monetary Fund (IMF), World Bank, the Organisation for Economic Co-operation and Development (OECD), and European Bank for Reconstruction and Development (EBRD), enterprise reform suggested ownership reform and enabled enterprises to make decisions with guidance from price signals. Price signal signifies pure market behaviour. A price signal is a change in the price of goods or services, which indicates that the supply or demand should be adjusted. This required financial autonomy, with owners and managers taking responsibility for the economic costs and benefits as well as overall business decisions.

The public sector, especially state enterprises, remained a hallmark of control of the socialist economies over the country's population. The management of the SOEs proved helpful for showing state's absolute socio-economic control over the country. The enterprise reform in the East European countries and Soviet Russia started taking place in the 'shock method', where the state sector was regarded as less significant compared to the needs of the private enterprises. As the decision was made to transform the economy into market socialism, the Eastern European economies were not hesitant about opening their economy for both insiders and outsiders and the socialist countries considered this method to be the shortest to achieve success. Since economic transformation took place in socialist societies rapidly, the private sector emerged at the cost of the state enterprises. The word and concept of privatisation generated obsession among socialist countries, and in Eastern Europe, 'spontaneous privatisation' became the critical tool of enterprise reform. In Poland, spontaneous privatisation occurred under which deals were made with a partner from the outside. Recommending privatisation for public sector sicknesses has been linked to a doctor prescribing the same pill for all ailments.[22] Different measures were taken in China to make enterprises efficient, where case-by-case gradual privatisation was comparatively successful. It was not until 1999, through a constitutional amendment, that the non-state sector was upgraded to 'an essential component of a mixed economy'. In 2001, on the eightieth anniversary of the CPC, the then general secretary, Jiang Zemin, invited private entrepreneurs to join the party, leading to a substantial change in the party's membership composition.

In these countries, the abrupt shift to free pricing without first abolishing the state trading agencies turned out to be sabotaging reforms. Sachs and Lipton also clearly underestimated the valuation problem in their schemes for immediate privatisation. Even where rudimentary stock exchanges emerged in Poland and Hungary, the number of firms whose shares were traded (and thus susceptible to a kind of market valuation) was minimal. Upon examination, it was found that before privatisation, other state enterprises proved unsuitable for purchase and woefully unattractive for legitimate foreign investors. The number of scandals over exploitative privatisation by unscrupulous speculators was a prime reason for widespread disaffection in Poland and Hungary, which forced the governments to recast their privatisation strategies.[23] Full privatisation that occurred in the socialist countries was not evident in China. The pre-communist countries resisted implementing enterprise reforms and continued with their trial-and-error method of the reform process, which now seemed to be guiding the rest of the transforming economies. The World Bank, in its report *Beyond Economic Growth* (1997), says, "In some cases, reducing the economic prominence of state enterprises is even possible without extensive privatisation mainly employing market liberalisation that leads to the accelerated growth of the private sector. That was the case in the Republic of Korea in the 1970s and 1980s and China in the 1980s and 1990s".[24] The enterprise reforms in China took place incrementally with a sufficient gap.

In the past four decades, one of the most far-reaching reforms China recorded was the dismantling of tens of thousands of SOEs, although it did not take off until the late 1990s. In the case of enterprise closures, there was massive suffering as millions were left unemployed. During the time of opening up the market economy, SOEs received special attention, and they produced vast quantities of essential commodities such as iron, steel, coal, and cotton. This was achieved amidst several problems such as quality and cost, as the state sector was ill-equipped to respond to market needs. One of the most pressing issues faced by China's leadership was the enormous burden on the national budget created by increasingly inefficient SOEs. The banks were saddled with 'non-performing loans' and were technically bankrupt, and the SOEs were dragging Chinese growth backwards.[25]

The restructuring process aimed to make SOEs more efficient and improve their performance to face upcoming challenges. In the intensified process of reforming SOEs, the state gradually withdrew and relaxed control, vitalised them through reorganisation, association, merger, leasing, contract operation, joint-stock partnership, and outright sale. As part of this, Zhu Rongji, the newly elected Premier of China, at the First Plenary session of Ninth National People's Congress (NPC) in March 1998, announced a renewed effort to make the SOEs competitive, configure the banking system, and streamline the government bureaucracy by eliminating 50 per cent of the workforce.[26]

As a result, the issues of social welfare and development became a complicated matter. Since the early 1990s, more than half the workers were estimated to have lost their jobs, giving rise to spontaneous worker protests. The Chinese state attempted to appease the growing intensity of public anger by encouraging them to move to the countryside. Few cities, like Beijing and the hard-hit north-east, had begun to promote redundant workers and coal-miners to go back to farming, offering incentives such as interest-free loans, a three-year tax exemption, and free farm equipment to those who switched to full-time farming. Some had been offered posts as village officials and members of the Communist party and full retentions of the benefits as urban workers.[27] While the enterprise reforms experienced many ups and downs, and were pushed to perform or perish, and tasked with improving the competitiveness, twenty years ago, it was possible, even sensible, to imagine that China would gradually free markets and entrepreneurs would play a more prominent role. It was a timely call to address the issues that were chronic for economic survival.

Compared with the East European economies and the ex-Soviet republics, the Chinese economic performance since 1978 seemed to have delivered results. However, a few similarities could be drawn between their methods. First, the reforms lacked an exact goal-oriented model and a guiding principle. Knowledge and ideas were gradually picked and summarised by a trial-and-error approach.[28] Each time a policy decision was taken, it aimed at resolving the earlier intricacies and not a step in entirety which made the path of progress obscure. Second, the social welfare cost and infrastructure building became complicated matters, both ideologically and economically. The resource allocation process and rise in debt triggered a financial crisis in several socialist economies. Reforms of Soviet-type economies fell short of overcoming these transitional difficulties. They were bogged down due to inflation, debt crises, stagflation, or sometimes, a combination of all these.[29] In the end, due to frequent changes in economic policies and their related theoretical explanations, it was challenging to infuse the public with confidence and enthusiasm for the reforms.[30]

Despite these teething problems between Eastern European economies and China's economy, China's reforms were more cautious and planned than those attempted in other socialist societies. The Chinese reform process successfully turned state enterprises into semi-private firms without full-blown privatisation. This gradual transformation process gave enterprises greater autonomy over product decisions and allowed them to retain a more significant fraction of profits which in turn increased productivity.[31] In brief, the Chinese economy had performed on all fronts and in multiple ways since the reforms began.

The Collapse of Socialist Economies and China's Balancing Act

As discussed earlier, contrasting institutional transformation between Central and Eastern Europe and the former Soviet Union on the one hand and China on the other is often characterised as Shock Therapy versus Gradualism. Hence, the ways of introducing reform measures were different, reflected in the varying pace of change towards a 'market economy'. Because of the initial massive macro-disequilibrium existing in the former socialist economies, rapid stabilisation and price liberalisation were required. Still, these did not materialise in practice, and the system did not succeed in duplicating the efficiency of a competitive market economy. The continuing poor macro-economic performance of Central and Eastern Europe and the former Soviet Union was at least in part due to the failure to carry through the Shock Therapy logically, for example, in allowing the continuation of soft-budget constraints for large-scale SOEs and ex-SOEs; while the excellent performance of the Chinese economy is partly because, despite the continued existence of a soft-budgeted state-sector, the private and local state firms (township and village enterprises) were 'free' to respond to market forces.[32]

Market socialism is associated with the expectation that the 'marketisation' of the socialist economy would create a demand and supply equilibrium. It was a litmus test for reforms to see whether such equilibrium had been established.[33] In the Soviet-type economies like Hungary, Poland and Yugoslavia, market socialism was aborted before it could prove its abject failure. Full privatisation was out of the question for socialist economies, and hence genuine marketisation was inconceivable without large-scale privatisation. China's policy of gradualism is often contrasted with the proclaimed preference in Eastern Europe for rapid privatisation.[34] However, in practice, privatisation proceeded slowly in Eastern Europe but remained disappointing for medium and large-scale firms; inconclusive policies put these enterprises in a dilemma.

Gowan argues that Shock Therapy aimed to engineer sweeping institutional changes in the internal structures of these political economies to open them to maximum Western penetration and influence.[35] In other words, Shock Therapy proved helpless in assisting in transforming economies. Shock Therapy's consequences were hopeless and did immense and unnecessary damage to the region's economic life. It created a negative balance of trade and disturbed the region's trade relations. The 'market socialism experiments' were not successful in socialist societies because economic planning was abandoned in between without an adequate market system.[36] The experiment of market socialism with a gradual approach has possibly yielded better results (i.e., Hungary, Czechoslovakia, and China) compared to the 'big bang' approach, which proved to be less successful (Poland), or chaotic (Russian example). It is now clear that Western economic thinkers perceived the economic conditions of the socialist countries poorly. This misinterpretation was of the following kinds. Firstly, Western economic thinkers ignored the adverse outcomes of pursuing their recommended policies in both the First and Third worlds.[37] Secondly, they failed to appreciate the fundamental difference between Eastern and Western economic structure and behaviour.[38] Thirdly, in the wake of introducing reform strategies, the leaders overlooked the domestic social and political conditions persisting in the Eastern European countries, as far as the restructuring of the economy was concerned. This inevitably led to widespread dismay with the entire transformation process.[39]

The experience showed that merely theory and policies without understanding the ground reality are bound to fail. Methods, taken directly from economic theory, caused more harm than benefits.[40] With the former Soviet Union in economic chaos and many central and East European countries discovering that the market place can be cold and uncomfortable, the reasons behind their failure to achieve market socialism can be elaborated as follows:

1. In socialist societies, economic decision-making remained politicised and subject to political monopoly to ensure that market outcomes did not contradict socialist equality. These economies failed to successfully lose control over the right of ordinary citizens to access the market and allow the operation of the labour market, and encourage unique entrepreneurial initiatives.
2. The market factor did not exist, and a non-competitive atmosphere polluted the concept of market-socialism. Domestic barriers to competition assured workers' security by precluding the capital market's functioning and facilitating competitive investment.
3. In these societies, domestic products were kept outside the influence of the market and competition, which severely hampered product quality. As part of this highly protectionist policy of international trade, foreign competition was ruled out.

4. The lack of private property rights characterises the market in these countries. The absence of private entrepreneurship paralysed the progress of these markets, which was already advancing at a ridiculously slow pace. The political system, which is dominated by a single party, reduced the probability of partial privatisation. Along with privatisation, the sale of the state's assets turned into a necessary condition to achieve the aim, but in this case, too, the East European economies and the former Soviet Union failed.
5. The state did not discharge the responsibility of conserving efficient enterprises and let the inefficient ones go. These states continued to provide lifelines to state enterprises financially and allowed the government to go bankrupt. The provision of soft-budget constraints did not allow the state to emerge successfully from the economic crisis and precluded the success of macro-economic efficiency. In the absence of privatisation, no one was responsible for capital and its efficient utilisation. Even cases of rampant losses were fabricated to evoke subsidies to make higher wage payments. Later, it became challenging to accept bankruptcy and declare the state of chaos, which would have further threatened the political establishment. The sickness of enterprises in these economies spread like an epidemic, and their bankruptcy proved highly contagious. Enterprises lent each other money by accumulating arrears, thereby creating 'chain indebtedness' or what is known as the "Domino Effect" wherein the insolvency of one enterprise led to a series of bankruptcies, politically unacceptable to the government.[41]

Eastern Europe and the former Soviet Union were flooded with advice from the West on liberalising their planned economies. As pointed out earlier, this advice was, unfortunately, offered in a vacuum since no one knew how these economies would react to the proposed liberalisation measures. There existed, however, a paucity of information.

In China, gradualist reforms started in agriculture and have not yet involved the sale of state farms to private individuals. However, an essentially private sector developed in both agriculture and industry.[42] Although the sale of collective farms did not exist in China, 'private farming' was quite successful. Private farming referred to as the House Contract Responsibility System (HRS), and perhaps the most significant agricultural reform, allowed many peasants (perhaps 200 million) to escape from dire poverty.[43] Looking at the Eastern European experience, the Chinese gradualist experience was a success by any economic measure.[44] By contrast, China's reforms were not conceived as a grand plan; instead, they consisted of small step-by-step changes. No ultimate goal was announced, nor was any timetable given for the transition. Data shows that China's GDP during the years of growth was healthier than its socialist counterparts. From 1986 to 1989, the average increase was 8.6 per cent, far ahead of other transforming socialist states. In 1992, when the economic reform was at its peak, the annual GDP rate of China was 12.8 compared to Russia's 19.9 (in minus), Bulgaria's 7.7, Czechoslovakia's 5.0, Hungary's 4.6, and Poland's 1.5 (see Table 2.1).

Table 2.1: Economies in Transition: Annual Growth (% per annum)

Country	*Average*			
	1986-89	*1990*	*1991*	*1992*
China	8.7	4.1	7.7	12.8
Russia	2.4	– 2.0	– 9.0	– 19.0
Bulgaria	5.2	– 11.6	– 22.7	– 7.7
Czechoslovakia	1.6	– 3.0	– 15.5	– 5.0
Hungary	1.4	– 4.0	– 10.5	– 4.6
Poland	2.7	– 11.4	– 7.7	1.5
Romania	– 0.9	– 7.1	– 13.4	– 10.2

Source: China Statistical Yearbook 1992; *IMF, Economic Review: Russian Federation,* 1992; *World Tables 1993,* and *IMF, World Economic Outlook* 1993.

China's example shows the centrally planned system's specific characteristics that can be used to initiate a step-by-step reform process. Chinese reform moved ahead, experimenting with multiple joint ownerships, vesting separate components of the traditional, Western-style property rights in different kinds of owners. State ownership in China was traditionally divided between central and local governments. Since 1978, the course of Chinese reform has progressively broadened the range of stakeholders.

China's reforms were gradual, but their cumulative effect has been different. China's experiments provide some practical lessons on what kind of reforms can work elsewhere. For Socialist economies, it is necessary to continue the reform process. In both Eastern Europe (including the Soviet Union) and

China, there appears to be a consensus on at least two key points: No one wants a return to the years of catastrophe (as in the Soviet Union under Stalin or in China during Mao's Great Proletarian Cultural Revolution), and there is a shared desire for better material life, and a better standard of living, after decades of scarcity and living with shortages.[45] In China, the consumer revolution is probably the most potent popular force supporting the continuance of market reforms.

Compared with individual performance in other large developing nations such as Brazil and India, since they have enjoyed freer access to foreign assistance, expertise, and technology than China, China's achievements scored relatively well.[46] In this case, industrial development was remarkable, and during the same period, the growth of the country's GDP exceeded some of the advanced countries (see Table 2.2).

Table 2.2: China's Growth has been Outstanding in the Second Half of this Century Average Annual per Capita GDP Growth (per cent)

Country/Region	*Period*				
	1820-70	*1870-1900*	*1900-50*	*1950-78*	*1978-92*
China	0.1	0.7	– 1	2.6	4.8
Latin America	0.2	1.1	1.6	2.3	–
Western Europe	0.9	1.2	1.0	3.2	1.4
United States	1.2	1.6	1.6	2.1	1.0

Note: – not available

Source: Maddison 1995 cited in World Bank, 'Understanding the Present'[47] and 'Annex One: Accounting for China's Growth,' in *China 2020: Development Challenges in the New Century* (Washington DC, 1997), pp. 1-5.

During the tumultuous first half of this century, the per capita income in China fell dramatically. The period from 1949 to 1978 was a period of experiments, and experience helped shape the future face of China's economy. In some cases, efforts were made to compare the Chinese experience with the West. This explanation does not disapprove of the fundamental inefficiency and structural problems that existed during Mao's era. And as a positive step to tackle the existing issues in the economy, the reform and restructuring at various levels began after 1978. The reformist league of leaders had to keep the radical thoughts and the factions within the party on the sidelines. Deng's market reforms promised the Chinese people an end to ideological campaigns and an emphasis on consumption. This experience also provides lessons for other transitional economies.

The leadership of Deng could stall the East European shocks cast a shadow over Chinese experiments of reforms and opening up. In their downfall, the East European economies offered China a few lessons in disguise. The reforms were experimental but reflected a balance between caution and vision and eventually proved 'time tested,' and it did uphold the leadership's control. China's plan not to copy the West and not look at democracy as an alternate proved a hard fact. Moreover, the chaos and fall of economies in other socialist economies were portrayed as eye-openers for the Chinese masses. Given these facts, China did not fall but, on the contrary, developed strategies to avoid their predecessors' fate.

Conclusion

Deng accepted his failure and success for the survival of the Party and China became one of the largest global economies. He did face uncertainties, but he was practical enough to drive through. During his period in political exile, his ideas and supporters underwent harsh criticism for maligning the socialist path of progress, attempted socialist engineering by raising people's standards and, in turn, their belief in the party and ideology. He was confident that his attempts were focused on making China wealthy and strong without letting China fail. In one of his writings, he argued that it was possible to import foreign 'means of production' without importing the 'relations of production'—in other words, opening up the economy need not change China's political and social system.

In recent years, China has, in some ways, gone backwards since 2013 (President Xi assumed power), with the state tightening its grip. For example, the share of government-owned firms of new bank loans has risen from 30 per cent to 70 per cent.[48] The exuberant private sector has been stifled. The new normal to make the Chinese state immune to any possibility of collapse controls private enterprises and brings back the SOEs in the centre. Regulators have become more vital for maintaining control of currency, stock markets and capital flows. SOEs are back as the core interest of the party and the Chinese state.

NOTES

1. Yegor Timurovich Gaidar was the Acting Prime Minister of Russia from 15 June 1992 to 14 December 1992. He played a major role in Russia's economic transition out of communism, introducing a controversial program of dramatic reforms after the breakup of the USSR.
2. Susan V. Lawrence. 1999. 'Reality-Check: At least Premier Zhu isn't hiding China's problems', *Far Eastern Economic Review,* Vol. 62, No. 11, March, 26.
3. Charles W. Kegley (Jr.) and Eugene R. Wittcopf. 1993. *World Politics: Trend and Transformation* (New York: St. Martin's Press), 252.
4. Raymond Vernon. 1979. 'The Fragile Foundations of East-West Trade', *Foreign Affairs,* Vol. 57, No. 5, Summer, 1035-051.
5. Gordon Marshall (ed.). 1998. *Oxford Dictionary of Sociology* (New York: Oxford University Press), 622-23.
6. Peter Van Ness (ed.). 1989. *Market in Socialist Societies: Comparing China and Hungary* (Boulder: Lynne Rienner), 9.
7. Wlodzimierz Brus. 1979. 'The East European Reforms: What Happened to Them?' *Soviet Studies,* April, Vol. 31, No. 2, 267.
8. Laszlo Andor and Martin Summers. 1998. *Market Failure: A Guide to Eastern Europe's "Economic Miracle"* (London: Pluto Press), 22.
9. Jeffery Sachs. 1994. 'Understanding Shock Therapy', *Social Market Foundation Occasional Paper Series,* No. 7, 1-44. Sachs has given some conditions for the success of the new policy which includes:
   "(1) Open international trade; (2) currency convertibility; (3) private ownership as the main engine of economic growth; (4) cooperate ownership as the dominant organizational form for large enterprises; (5) openness to foreign investment; and (6) membership of key international economic institutions, including the IMF, the World Bank, and the GATT..."
10. Adam Przeworski. 1991. *Democracy and the Market: Political and Economic Reforms in Eastern Europe and Latin America* (Cambridge: Cambridge University Press), 163.
11. Here the Leftist way of development means the heavy emphasis on radical ideological thinking.
12. Deng Xiaoping. 'Opening Speech at the Twelfth National Congress of the Communist Party of China'.
   The 12th CPC Congress was held in September 1982 amid high expectations of economic reforms. In terms of ideology and its discursive framework, the 12th Congress was noted for themes, viz., 'Socialist Spiritual Civilization' and Deng's concept of 'Socialism with Chinese characteristics'. At this Congress, Deng put the most vital theme for future Chinese economy. One can say that this was the most important ideological concept in his political career. About building socialism with Chinese characteristics, he stated, "In carrying out our modernization program we must proceed from Chinese realities...We must integrate the universal truth of Marxism with the characteristics of China, blaze a path of our own and build a socialism with Chinese characteristics".
   Deng's effort was to find a solution to the problem created by socialism. The path was a result of Deng's exploration. And this shows how Deng was trying to deviate from the moderate Leninist approach. According to Zhang, Deng's discourse on 'Socialism with

Chinese characteristics' was to highlight the Chinese national and ideological identity and independence from both the Soviet Communist model and the Western Capitalist model.

13. William H. Overholt. 1993. *China: The Next Superpower.* London: Weidenfeld & Nicolson LPB, 2.
14. The elements of the market economy can be broadly described as follows: supply/demand pricing, competition, specialisation, economic incentives, rewards for performance, the threat of unemployment and bankruptcy for failure to reform.
15. As earlier discussed at various places the term has been understood as majority state ownership and the predominance of centralised bureaucratic planning.
16. World Bank. 1985. *China: Long Term Development Issues and Options* (Baltimore: World Bank Publication), 8.
17. Richard Smith. 1993. 'The Chinese Road to Capitalism', *New Left Review*, No. 199, May/June, 55-99.
18. Ibid.
19. Ibid.
20, Ibid.
21, Ibid.
22. Andor and Summers. *Market Failure*, 89.
23. Robert F. Miller. 1992. 'Economic Reform in Former Communist Systems: The Problems of Privatization', paper presented at the *36th Australian Agricultural and Resource Economics Society (AARES) Conference*, https://ageconsearch.umn.edu/record/146546 (accessed on 8 July 2020).
24. World Bank. 1997b. *China 2020: Sharing Rising Incomes* (Washington D.C.: World Bank). Quoted in Aart Krray. 2000. 'Household Savings in China', *The World Bank Economic Review,* Vol. 14, No. 3, September, 545-570.
25. Here social security means subsidized housing, medical care for employees, along with 'cradle to grave' policy of providing housing to retired employees until death and the policy of providing retirees the same level of medical care that current workers receive.
26. Erik Eckholm. 1998. 'New China Leader Promises Reform for Every Sector' *New York Times.* 20 March https://www.nytimes.com/1998/03/20/world/new-china-leader-promises-reforms-for-every-sector.html (accessed on 24 July 2020).
27. Becker. *The Chinese*, 104.
28. Janos Matyas Kovacs and Martori Tardos (eds.). 1992. *Reform and Transformation in Eastern Europe: Soviet type Economies on the Threshold of Change* (New York: Routledge), 197.
29. Ibid.
30. Ibid.
31. Husnu Kizilyali. 1998. *Economics of Transition: A New Methodology for Transforming a Socialist Economy to a Market-led Economy* (New York: Routledge), 210.
32. Dic Lo and Hugo Radice. 1998. 'Institutional Change and Economic Development in East-Central Europe and China: Contrasts in the light of the `East-Asian Model', in Jeffery Henderson (ed.), *Industrial Transformation in Eastern Europe in the Light of the East Asian Experience* (London: Macmillan Press Ltd.), 138.
33. Janos Kornai. 1986. 'The Hungarian Reform Process: Visions, Hopes and Reality', *Journal of Economic Literature,* Vol. 24, December, 1715.
34. Kizilyali, *Economics of Transition*, 80.

35. Peter Gowan. 1995. 'Neo-Liberal Theory and Practice for Eastern Europe', *New Left Review*, No. 213, September/October, 1-60.
36. Inadequate market system means partial price reforms affecting commodity market, absence of money and capital market, improper taxation system without private property rights and entrepreneurship.
37. Andor and Summers, *Market Failure*, 22.
38. Ibid.
39. Ibid.
40. Andras Inotai. 1998. 'The West and the Transformation of Central and Eastern Europe', in Andor and Summers. *Market Failure,* 22.
41. Kizilyali, *Economics of Transition*, 75.
42. Stanley Fischer. 1994. 'Russia and the Soviet Union: Then and Now', in Olivier Blanchard, Kenneth Froot and Jeffrey Sachs (eds.), *Transition in Eastern Europe,* Volume 1 (Chicago: University of Chicago Press), 221-58.
43. Becker. 2000. 'The good news about being fired'. Quoted by Becker, *The Chinese,* 25.
44. Fischer. 1994. 'Russia and the Soviet Union: Then and Now', 221-58.
45. Van Ness, *Market in Socialist Societies*, 19.
46. Thomas G. Rawski. 1975. 'China's Industrial System', in U.S. Congress, Joint Economic Committee (ed.), *China: A Re-assessment of the Economy* (Washington D.C.: US Government Printing Office). Reproduced in Joseph C. H. Chai (ed.). 2000. *The Economic Development of Modern China* Vol. II*: Socialist Modernization, 1949-1978* (Cheltenham: Edward Elgar), 112-135.
47. World Bank. 1997a. 'Understanding the Present', in Vikram Nehru, Aart Kraay and Xiaoqing Yu (eds.), *China 2002: Development Challenges in the New Century* (Washington D.C.: The World Bank), 1-5.
48. *The Economist.* 2019b. 'Pandas can fly: The struggle to reform China's economy', 27 February, https://www.economist.com/leaders/2019/02/21/the-struggle-to-reform-chinas-economy (accessed on 1 January 2021).

3

Almanac of China's State-owned Enterprises

State-owned Enterprises (SOEs) are the core institutions of the Chinese economic infrastructure envisaged to undertake scientific, economic, and societal (welfare, to be specific) duties. As a result, SOEs have an eternal presence in the Chinese constitution. Article 7 of the Constitution of the People's Republic of China (PRC) reads, "The State-owned economy, namely, the socialist economy under ownership by the whole people, is the leading force in the national economy. The State ensures the consolidation and growth of the State-owned economy".[1] The essential attribute of SOEs is that they are 'owned by the whole people'. In the socialist economic system, state-owned capital belongs to all.

Ever since the communist leaders founded the People's Republic of China (PRC), two engines in China have been trusted to discharge party commands and help the party gather additional thrust to fend off resistance and socio-economic crisis with integrity and precision. These engines, namely, the People's Liberation Army (PLA) and the State-owned Enterprises (SOEs), provide the wide-bodied Chinese economic statecraft with a chance to take-off, glide and land smoothly at its will. The Chinese leadership has been implicitly adding to their strength and explicitly using their weight to achieve intended results.

The Chinese leadership has been utilising State enterprises to deliver public services and legitimise the Communist rule. The SOEs were created in the early days of the PRC's founding because of the wave of nationalisation scheme that went on owning state-owned assets to prioritise the development of heavy industry and accelerate the pace of the country's industrialisation. To prioritise the development of heavy industry and accelerate the country's industrialisation, in the early days of the PRC's founding, the government, under the wave of nationalisation schemes, went on owning state-owned assets and creating SOEs. Blue-collar jobs in the factories were recognised as the most reputed during the Mao era. After the reforms were announced, SOEs were still holding their ground against increased participation. Post-1978 reform established a socialist economic system focused on consolidating the role of SOEs beyond its traditional part of owning state-owned assets and expanding the sectoral and geographical operation to maintain social stability and economic development. The reform of SOEs is a complicated systematic structural adjustment, and it is the central link in the reform of the entire economic system. In marathon rounds of reforms in SOEs, the enterprises and their boards have been questioned for their losses and assets, but they remain strong and add substantial state control over China.

Before investigating the SOEs' non-formidable roles in China and how they remain a critical part of China's statecraft and geo-economics, it is necessary to analyse some facts about them. SOEs refer to wholly state-owned enterprises, companies, and capital holding companies that the State Council and provincial governments invest on behalf of the State. They include enterprises supervised by the Central and local state-owned assets supervision and management institutions and other departments. In a SOE, the State owns or controls its capital, and the government's will and interests determine the SOE's behaviour. SOEs are the backbone of national economic development and that of 'socialism with Chinese characteristics'.[2] As a form of production and operation organisation, SOEs have commercial and public welfare features. Their commercial nature is embodied in the pursuit of maintaining and increasing the value of state-owned assets besides discharging duties of public welfare as part of the agenda of SOEs.[3]

The classification of SOEs is quite complicated due to historical reasons. Before the reform and opening up in 1978, and even until the end of the 20th century, SOEs have been the government's active intervening institutions. Most of the SOEs today are descendants of various ministries and bureaus from the planned economy era. Some SOEs emerged from original government departments such as China Telecom and China Mobile, originally the Ministry of Posts and Telecommunications, and were changed to the Bureau of Telecommunication but were reorganised in the late 1990s and early 2000s

According to the division of State-owned Assets Management Authority, administratively, SOEs are divided into 'Central enterprises' (SOEs supervised and managed by the Central government) and 'Local enterprises' (SOEs supervised and managed by local governments). The responsibilities of individual Central enterprises in the national social and economic development are relatively unique. They belong to the direct management of the State Council and function at the ministerial level.

The large SOEs are the mainstay of China's national economy, although through 'grasping the big and letting go of the small' (抓大放小 *Zhua da fang xiao*), some State-owned small and medium-sized enterprises have been prompted to diversify property rights through leasing, contracting, selling, and equity participation. State-owned and state-holding enterprises still occupy a dominant position in almost all industrial sectors. However, it is reported by the State Council that by the end of 2018, the total assets of all SOEs reached 210.4 trillion yuan (US$ 29.72 trillion), up 14.66 per cent from a year earlier. Additionally, the total debt increased to 135 trillion yuan (US$ 19.09 trillion), an annual increase of 13.92 per cent.[4]

China continues to use SOEs to build its might globally. SOEs have been strategically spread in essential sectors like energy, finance, infrastructure, and even media and entertainment. They share the responsibility of the global economy today and the significant rise of the Chinese economic might in the past four decades. In 2000, the *Fortune 500* list included 27 SOEs,[5] which increased to 102 in 2017 and 119 in 2019, a remarkable feat and a significant share in the *Fortune 500* companies. In 2019, the revenues of the Chinese *Fortune 500* list of SOEs reached a total of US$ 8.3 trillion,[6] but they still lag behind that of the US (US$ 9.8 trillion).[7] On the domestic front, Chinese leaders relate the rise of the large SOEs as a counter force against the large MNCs. This is especially evident after China acceded to the WTO, and internationally renowned large-scale global companies aggressively expanded their operations in the Chinese market. Various multinationals have been increasing their performance by tapping Chinese consumerism. However, to counter the growing expanse of the MNCs, the Chinese private enterprises have risen to the occasion along with open intervention by the State to limit the expansion of the foreign firms, and the large SOEs have been used as a force to compete against multinational companies.

The monopoly created by the SOEs was rock solid and manipulated to keep them away from any competition. The large SOEs are essential to support China's 'pillar industries' that include petroleum, chemical, machinery, electronics, metallurgy, non-ferrous metals, and building materials. SOEs top in the sale of Chinese-branded vehicles domestically and have taken over half of the domestic automobile market share and 40 per cent of the passenger vehicle market.[8] Moreover, local motorbike producers, who are provincial SOEs, have also been showing their real competitiveness vis-à-vis Central SOEs and foreign players. To name a few, the four largest motorcycle groups are China Jialing Industrial Co. Ltd. (中国嘉陵实业有限公司 *Zhongguo jialing shiye youxian gongsi*), Henan Beifang Yongsheng Motorcycle Co. Ltd. (河南北方永胜摩托车有限公司 *Henan beifang yong sheng motuo che youxian gongsi*), Jinan Qingqi Motorcycle Co. Ltd. (济南轻骑摩托车有限公司 *Jinan qingqi motuo che youxian gongsi*), and Jincheng Group Co. Ltd. (金城集团有限公司 *Jincheng jituan youxian gongsi*), who account for half of the sales in the whole of China. In the power sector, the Shanghai Electric Power Generation Equipment Co. Ltd. (上海电气 *Shanghai dianqi*), Dongfang Electric Corporation (东方电气集团 *Dongfang dianqi jituan*), and Harbin Electric Company Limited (哈尔滨电气股份有限公司 *Ha'erbin dianqi gufen youxian gongsi*), are the three power generation equipment groups that provide 70 per cent of domestic power station equipment.[9]

State-owned medium-sized enterprises and small enterprises have been at a loss, and large-scale enterprises have been struggling to organise their management, assets, and performance to recover the losses. There is a gap between China's large SOEs and large foreign companies. The SOEs have been marred by a low concentration of production, and in reality, there are few true consortia and enterprise groups. In terms of technological innovation, the sum of annual sales of China's 500 largest industrial companies does not even equal the sales of a single General Motors Corporation in the USA.

Under the powerful centralised planning management, SOEs lacked pursuit for performance and profits, and as a result, some SOEs have become *de facto* 'national factory' or 'production workshop.' In early 1981, when the Contract Responsibility System (CRS) (承包制 *Chengbao Zhi*) was extended to cities, many SOEs implemented contracting and leasing business models. SOEs became tools for contractors and tenants to maximise profits. The results were mixed, but overall the proportion of state-owned fiscal revenue from SOEs declined, and state-owned fiscal expenditures in SOEs also slowed down while they turned into 'rental factories'.[10]

The formal implementation of the socialist market economic system and the wave of marketisation, introduced in 1994, substantially influenced the operating mechanism of the SOEs and put forward new requirements for their positioning. In response to market-oriented competition needs, the Chinese government carried out a series of SOE reforms, the most important of which was the distribution of laid-off jobs, downsizing, increasing efficiency, and establishing a social security system besides SOE reorganisation and listing. The distribution of laid-offs and employee reduction to improve efficiency was meant to solve excessive staffing and inefficiency in SOEs while establishing the social security system that liberated SOEs from unreasonable social burdens.

Classification

As mentioned earlier, SOEs are divided into Central SOEs and are under the Central authority. According to industry attributes, regulators and control entities, the Central SOEs are further classified and roughly divided into four categories (given below in Table 3.1): Central Industrial SOEs, Central Financial SOEs, Central Cultural SOEs, and Central Administrative SOEs.

Table 3.1: The Classification of Central State-owned Enterprises

SOEs	*Examples*
Central Industrial SOEs	China National Nuclear Corporation, China Shipbuilding Corporation
Central Financial SOEs	China Development Bank, Bank of China Limited, China Exim Bank
Central Cultural SOEs	China Publishing Group Co. Ltd., China Radio and Television Network Co. Ltd.
Central Administrative SOEs	China National Railway Group Co. Ltd., China Post Group Co. Ltd.

Source: Author's analysis

I. Central Industrial SOEs

The first is the Central industrial enterprises. As of June 2020, there were 97 Central enterprises under the State-owned Assets Supervision and Administration Commission (SASAC) of the State Council.[11]

Many Central enterprises (the first 49 enterprises) carry an operating status of a deputy ministerial-level unit from the list (Table 3.2) below. The Central Organisation Department appoints a Bureau within the SASAC, known as the First Bureau of Enterprise Cadres (企业干部第一局 *Qiye ganbu di yi ju*) of the SASAC, and the principal positions. Five bureaus within SASAC manage everything from training and appointments to the supervision of those employed in these 97 enterprises.[12] The Central SOEs hire nearly 10 million employees at all levels.[13] SASAC, as an arm of the State Council and plays a critical role in exercising control over Central industrial enterprises and shows a keen interest in the staffing of top SOE positions. Although SOEs have been given managerial discretion and boards are free to manage executive duties, for most of the SOEs, the job of the Chairman is only fructified once the name is seconded by the Board of Directors, which plays a ceremonial role on this account. Technical posts, which need vocational background and ground experience, may escape the SASAC's habit to rotate SOE officials indiscriminately. Also, SASAC may appoint their officials on any SOE for training purposes, and those who are well connected may even take seats in government and Party bodies, especially the top enterprise groups. Moreover, not to forget that of the total number of employees, many are party members; an unorthodox number is around one-third—based on SASAC yearbooks.

Besides these ministerial-level SOEs, the other category of SOEs operates at the level of departments. Fourty-eight such enterprises with serial numbers 50-97 are managed by the SASAC with the departmental hierarchies involved. The leadership team is governed by the Second Bureau of Enterprise Management of the SASAC.

The list of Central industrial enterprises is as follows:

Table 3.2: List of Central Enterprises Managed by the State-owned Assets Supervision and Administration Commission (SASAC) of the State Council

1	China National Nuclear Corporation	中国核工业集团有限公司
2	China Aerospace Science and Technology Corporation	中国航天科技集团有限公司
3	China Aerospace Science and Industry Corporation	中国航天科工集团有限公司
4	China Aviation Industry Corporation	中国航空工业集团有限公司
5	China Shipbuilding Corporation	中国船舶集团有限公司
6	China North Industries Group Co. Ltd.	中国兵器工业集团有限公司
7	China North Industries Group Co. Ltd.	中国兵器装备集团有限公司
8	China Electronics Technology Group Co. Ltd.	中国电子科技集团有限公司
9	China Aviation Engine Group Co. Ltd.	中国航空发动机集团有限公司
10	China Rongtong Asset Management Group Co. Ltd.	中国融通资产管理集团有限公司
11	China National Petroleum Corporation	中国石油天然气集团有限公司
12	China Petroleum & Chemical Corporation	中国石油化工集团有限公司
13	China National Offshore Oil Corporation	中国海洋石油集团有限公司
14	National Petroleum and Natural Gas Network Group Co. Ltd.	国家石油天然气管网集团有限公司
15	State Grid Corporation of China	国家电网有限公司
16	China Southern Power Grid Co. Ltd.	中国南方电网有限责任公司
17	China Huaneng Group Co. Ltd.	中国华能集团有限公司
18	China Datang Group Co. Ltd.	中国大唐集团有限公司
19	China Huadian Group Co. Ltd.	中国华电集团有限公司
20	State Power Investment Group Co. Ltd.	国家电力投资集团有限公司
21	China Three Gorges Group Co. Ltd.	中国长江三峡集团有限公司
22	National Energy Investment Group Co. Ltd.	国家能源投资集团有限责任公司
23	China Telecom Group Co. Ltd.	中国电信集团有限公司
24	China United Network Communications Group Co. Ltd.	中国联合网络通信集团有限公司
25	China Mobile Communications Group Co. Ltd.	中国移动通信集团有限公司
26	China Electronics Information Industry Group Co. Ltd.	中国电子信息产业集团有限公司
27	China FAW Group Co. Ltd.	中国第一汽车集团有限公司
28	Dongfeng Motor Group Co. Ltd.	东风汽车集团有限公司
29	China First Heavy Industry Group Co. Ltd.	中国一重集团有限公司
30	China National Machinery Industry Corporation	中国机械工业集团有限公司
31	Harbin Electric Group Co. Ltd.	哈尔滨电气集团有限公司
32	China Dongfang Electric Group Co. Ltd.	中国东方电气集团有限公司
33	Angang Group Co. Ltd.	鞍钢集团有限公司
34	China Baowu Iron and Steel Group Co. Ltd.	中国宝武钢铁集团有限公司
35	China Aluminium Corporation	中国铝业集团有限公司
36	China COSCO Shipping Group Co. Ltd.	中国远洋海运集团有限公司
37	China National Aviation Corporation	中国航空集团有限公司
38	China Eastern Airlines Group Co. Ltd.	中国东方航空集团有限公司
39	China Southern Airlines Group Co. Ltd.	中国南方航空集团有限公司
40	China Sinochem Corporation	中国中化集团有限公司
41	COFCO Corporation	中粮集团有限公司
42	China Minmetals Corporation	中国五矿集团有限公司

43	China General Technology (Group) Holding Co. Ltd.	中国通用技术(集团)控股有限责任公司
44	China Construction Group Corporation	中国建筑集团有限公司
45	China Grain Reserve Management Group Co. Ltd.	中国储备粮管理集团有限公司
46	National Development Investment Group Co. Ltd.	国家开发投资集团有限公司
47	China Merchants Group Co. Ltd.	招商局集团有限公司
48	China Resources (Group) Co. Ltd.	华润（集团）有限公司
49	China Tourism Group Co. Ltd.	中国旅游集团有限公司
50	Commercial Aircraft Corporation of China	中国商用飞机有限责任公司
51	China Energy Conservation and Environmental Protection Group Co. Ltd.	中国节能环保集团有限公司
52	China International Engineering Consulting Co. Ltd.	中国国际工程咨询有限公司
53	China Chengtong Holdings Group Co. Ltd.	中国诚通控股集团有限公司
54	China Coal Energy Group Co. Ltd.	中国中煤能源集团有限公司
55	China Coal Science and Industry Group Co. Ltd.	中国煤炭科工集团有限公司
56	Mechanical Research Institute Group Co. Ltd.	机械科学研究总院集团有限公司
57	China National Steel Corporation	中国中钢集团有限公司
58	China Iron and Steel Research Institute Technology Group Co. Ltd.	中国钢研科技集团有限公司
59	China National Chemical Corporation	中国化工集团有限公司
60	China National Chemical Engineering Group Co. Ltd.	中国化学工程集团有限公司
61	China National Salt Industry Group Co. Ltd.	中国盐业集团有限公司
62	China National Building Materials Group Co. Ltd.	中国建材集团有限公司
63	China Nonferrous Mining Group Co. Ltd.	中国有色矿业集团有限公司
64	Youyan Technology Group Co. Ltd.	有研科技集团有限公司
65	Mining and Metallurgical Technology Group Co. Ltd.	矿冶科技集团有限公司
66	China International Technology Intelligence Cooperation Co. Ltd.	中国国际技术智力合作有限公司
67	China Academy of Building Research Co. Ltd.	中国建筑科学研究院有限公司
68	CRRC Corporation Limited	中国中车集团有限公司
69	China Railway Communication Signal Group Co. Ltd.	中国铁路通信信号集团有限公司
70	China Railway Engineering Group Co. Ltd.	中国铁路工程集团有限公司
71	China Railway Construction Group Co. Ltd.	中国铁道建筑集团有限公司
72	China Communications Construction Group Co. Ltd.	中国交通建设集团有限公司
73	China Putian Information Industry Group Co. Ltd.	中国普天信息产业集团有限公司
74	China Information and Communication Technology Group Co. Ltd.	中国信息通信科技集团有限公司
75	China Agricultural Development Group Co. Ltd.	中国农业发展集团有限公司
76	China Forestry Corporation	中国林业集团有限公司
77	China National Pharmaceutical Group Co. Ltd.	中国医药集团有限公司
78	China Poly Group Co. Ltd.	中国保利集团有限公司
79	China Construction Technology Co. Ltd.	中国建设科技有限公司
80	China Metallurgical Geology Administration	中国冶金地质总局
81	China Coal Geology Administration	中国煤炭地质总局
82	Xinxing Jihua Group Co. Ltd.	新兴际华集团有限公司
83	China Civil Aviation Information Group Co. Ltd.	中国民航信息集团有限公司
84	China National Aviation Fuel Group Co. Ltd.	中国航空油料集团有限公司

85	China Aviation Equipment Group Co. Ltd.	中国航空器材集团有限公司
86	China Power Construction Group Co. Ltd.	中国电力建设集团有限公司
87	China Energy Construction Group Co. Ltd.	中国能源建设集团有限公司
88	China Aneng Construction Group Co. Ltd.	中国安能建设集团有限公司
89	China National Gold Group Corporation	中国黄金集团有限公司
90	China General Nuclear Power Corporation	中国广核集团有限公司
91	China Hualu Group Co. Ltd.	中国华录集团有限公司
92	Overseas Chinese Town Group Co. Ltd.	华侨城集团有限公司
93	China Nanguang Group Co. Ltd.	中国南光集团有限公司
94	China Xidian Group Co. Ltd.	中国西电集团有限公司
95	China Railway Materials Group Co. Ltd.	中国铁路物资集团有限公司
96	China Guoxin Holdings Co. Ltd.	中国国新控股有限责任公司
97	China Certification & Inspection (Group) Co. Ltd.	中国检验认证(集团)有限公司

Source: State-owned Assets Supervision and Administration Commission.

II. Central Financial Enterprises

As China carries out restructuring, the role of Central Financial Institutions (CFIs) in the economic rebalancing is a critical one and has been used by the Chinese government to manage many crises since the 1990s. They are not only big but also act as an arm of the treasury. One could connect the CFIs' sensitivities when the SOE restructuring exposed a massive pile of non-performing loans (NPLs) that the financial SOEs had offered. Amidst the crisis, Premier Zhu Rongji had written off the estimated 3.3 trillion yuan (US$ 400 billion) in NPLs to prevent the most acute national crisis, but that did not lead to substantial changes in financial enterprises compared to the Central industrial enterprises as the reform-oriented central bureaucrats had centralised financial power without liberalising the banking sector.[14] To deal with the assets and capitalisation crisis, the State Council needed a centralised unit to coordinate the financial agencies. This had to be done efficiently and by overriding the institutional differences and hierarchies. The Chinese banks, within themselves, and ministries have had differences over financial irregularities.

In 2003, the State Council approved the establishment of the Central Huijin Investment Co. Ltd. (中央汇金投资有限责任公司 *Zhongyang huijin touzi youxian zeren gongsi*), commonly referred to as Huijin (汇金), an SOE capitalised by the Central bank and Ministry of Finance, that put money into the banks and also monitored them by having controlling stakes.[15] Huijin owns controlling stakes in the four major banks, namely, Agricultural Bank of

Figure 3.1: Investment by Huijin and Ministry of Finance in China's top Central Financial SOEs

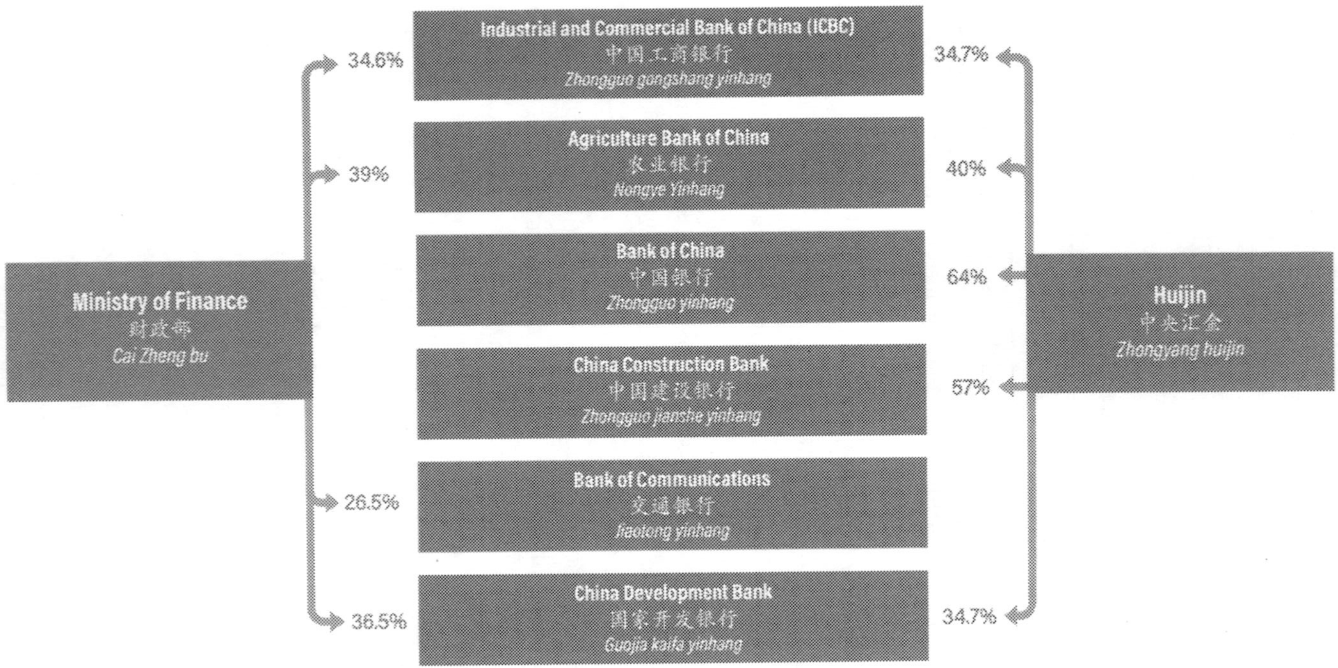

Source: Author's analysis based on the data from annual reports, quarterly reports and official websites.

China (ABC), Bank of China (BOC), China Construction Bank (CCB), and Industrial and Commercial Bank of China (ICBC), by initiating shareholding reform. Huijin is also currently the largest financial investment company in China. For instance, as the absolute controlling shareholder of BoC and CCB and the largest shareholder of ICBC, Huijin dominates the dividend policy of the three banks. In the past few years, Huijin received 37.085 billion yuan (US$ 5.29 billion) in dividends from the three banks.

Huijin has been growing as big as SASAC or even the PBoC. In September 2007, the Ministry of Finance issued special treasury bonds and acquired all the shares of Central Huijin from the PBoC.[16] The Finance Ministry has been using Huijin to control state funds. It is a well-known fact that Ministry of Finance officials have been at odds with the PBoC for years over the management of state funds.[17] In 2007, the Central bank lost a battle for Huijin, a government company that holds stakes in China's leading commercial lenders, and the sovereign-wealth fund came under the control of the finance ministry. Although Huijin is called a company, it is solely a government agency. Since the SASAC is not responsible for managing financial state-owned assets, Huijin is regarded as a 'financial SASAC.' In terms of procedures, Huijin has to obtain authorisation from the Finance and Economics Committee of the National People's Congress (NPC). Huijin does not carry out any other commercial activities and does not interfere with the daily operations of key state-owned financial enterprises that it controls. In general, the Ministry of Finance and Huijin are in charge of 'finance.' After the national institutional reform in 2018, the Central Organisation Department and the China Banking Regulatory Commission (CBRC) became in charge of 'people.' The PBoC, China Securities Regulatory Commission (CSRC), and China Insurance Regulatory Commission (CIRC) are responsible for business supervision.

Therefore, the Chinese financial system's giants are controlled by the Ministry of Finance and Huijin as investors. In China's increasingly monetised economy, fiscal institutions become even more crucial in the elite political calculus. Huijin has been systematically turned into a giant regulator as finances determine China's rise and fall.

Table 3.3 gives the list of CFEs controlled by Central Huijin.

Table 3.3: List of Central Financial Enterprises

1	Agricultural Development Bank of China	中国农业发展银行
2	China Exim Bank	中国进出口银行
3	China Development Bank	国家开发银行
4	Industrial and Commercial Bank of China Limited	中国工商银行股份有限公司
5	Agricultural Bank of China Co. Ltd.	中国农业银行股份有限公司
6	Bank of China Limited	中国银行股份有限公司
7	China Construction Bank Corporation	中国建设银行股份有限公司
8	Bank of Communications Co. Ltd.	交通银行股份有限公司
9	China Export & Credit Insurance Corporation	中国出口信用保险公司
10	The People's Insurance Company of China	中国人民保险集团股份有限公司
11	China Life Insurance (Group) Company	中国人寿保险(集团)公司
12	China Reinsurance (Group) Co. Ltd.	中国再保险(集团)股份有限公司
13	China Taiping Insurance Group Co. Ltd.	中国太平保险集团有限责任公司
14	China Huarong Asset Management Co. Ltd.	中国华融资产管理股份有限公司
15	China Great Wall Asset Management Co. Ltd.	中国长城资产管理股份有限公司
16	China Orient Asset Management Co. Ltd.	中国东方资产管理股份有限公司
17	China Cinda Asset Management Co. Ltd.	中国信达资产管理股份有限公司
18	China CITIC Group Co. Ltd.	中国中信集团有限公司
19	China Everbright Group Corporation	中国光大集团股份公司
20	China Galaxy Financial Holdings Co. Ltd.	中国银河金融控股有限责任公司
21	China Construction Bank Investment Co. Ltd.	中国建银投资有限责任公司
22	China Central Government Securities Depository and Clearing Co. Ltd.	中央国债登记结算有限责任公司
23	China Investment Corporation	中国投资有限责任公司

Sources: The Ministry of Finance of the People's Republic of China

III. Central Cultural SOEs

The Central Cultural SOEs form a critical part of China's influence in the cultural sphere, including propaganda. There are three prominent Central Cultural SOEs: China Publishing Group Co. Ltd., China Foreign Culture Group Co. Ltd., and China Radio and Television Network Co. Ltd.[18] Besides, there are 98 publishing organisations where the Ministry of Finance performs the responsibilities of investors on behalf of the State Council. On 28 November 2018, the Ministry of Finance injected 1.5 billion yuan (US$ 215 million) into these SOEs to implement key national cultural strategy programs.

A few examples of the Central Cultural SOE's mandate are given on text page:

Note: *Common Destiny,* a promotional documentary produced by Silk Road Culture Communication and Xindingming Film and Television Investment, is the best example of how Cultural SOEs use political contexts to publicise. This documentary talks about the demography, history, civilisation; links along China's Silk Road Economic Belt and Maritime Silk Road under the overarching Belt and Road Initiative (BRI).

The reorganisation of publishing and communication enterprises into SOEs started in 2009 when the China Oriental Performing Arts Group Co. Ltd., China Culture Media Group Co. Ltd., and China Animation Group Co. became the first batch of Central cultural enterprises that were directly transformed from operational, cultural institutions into wholly state-owned companies. The Chinese Council planned to fund and use these enterprises to publish, communicate, and document China's culture. In China, when culture is the denominator of news and publications, it not difficult to imagine the extent of the industry's workload. The mandate of these SOEs is to 'correct the orientation of public opinion' (正确的 舆论导向 *Zhengque de yulun daoxiang*).[19]

Table 3.4: List of Central Cultural Enterprises Financed by Ministry of Finance

1	China Publishing Group Corporation	中国出版集团公司
2	China Foreign Culture Group Corporation	中国对外文化集团公司
3	China Radio and Television Press	中国广播电视出版社
4	China Industry and Information Technology Publishing and Media Group Co. Ltd.	中国工信出版传媒集团有限责任公司
5	China Human Resources and Social Security Publishing Group Co. Ltd.	中国人力资源和社会保障出版集团有限公司
6	China Culture Media Group Co. Ltd.	中国文化传媒集团有限公司
7	China Oriental Performing Arts Group Co. Ltd.	中国东方演艺集团有限公司
8	China Digital Culture Group Co. Ltd.	中国数字文化集团有限公司
9	China Animation Group Co. Ltd.	中国动漫集团有限公司
10	China Press, Publication and Media Group Co. Ltd.	中国新闻出版传媒集团有限公司
11	China Broadcasting Communications Group Co. Ltd.	中广传播集团有限公司
12	Chinese Literature and History Publishing House	中国文史出版社
13	China Founder Publishing House	中国方正出版社
14	Party Building Books Publishing House	党建读物出版社
15	Learning Press	学习出版社
16	Contemporary World Press	当代世界出版社
17	Wuzhou Communication Publishing House	五洲传播出版社
18	Jincheng Publishing House	金城出版社
19	World Knowledge Publishing House	世界知识出版社
20	China Planning Press	中国计划出版社
21	China Market Press	中国市场出版社
22	Educational Science Press	教育科学出版社
23	Science and Technology Literature Press	科学技术文献出版社
24	China National Photography Art Publishing House	中国民族摄影艺术出版社
25	China Social Publishing House	中国社会出版社
26	Law Publisher	法律出版社
27	China Financial and Economic Publishing House	中国财政经济出版社
28	Economic Science Press	经济科学出版社
29	China Land Publishing House	中国大地出版社
30	Geological Publishing House	地质出版社
31	China Environmental Publishing Co. Ltd.	中国环境出版有限责任公司
32	China Construction Industry Press	中国建筑工业出版社
33	China City Publishing House	中国城市出版社
34	China Communications Press	人民交通出版社
35	China Water Conservancy and Hydropower Press	中国水利水电出版社
36	China Agriculture Press	中国农业出版社
37	China Agricultural Science and Technology Press	中国农业科学技术出版社
38	China Business Press	中国商务出版社
39	Culture and Art Publishing House	文化艺术出版社
40	Forbidden City Publishing House	故宫出版社
41	National Library Press	国家图书馆出版社
42	People's Medical Publishing House Co. Ltd.	人民卫生出版社有限公司

43	China Population Press	中国人口出版社
44	China Finance Press	中国金融出版社
45	China Times Economic Press	中国时代经济出版社
46	China Business Press	中国商业出版社
47	China Light Industry Press	中国轻工业出版社
48	China Fortune Press	中国财富出版社
49	China Textile Publishing House	中国纺织出版社
50	Chemical Industry Press	化学工业出版社
51	Enterprise Management Press	企业管理出版社
52	China Customs Press	中国海关出版社
53	China Taxation Press	中国税务出版社
54	China Industry and Commerce Press	中国工商出版社
55	China Quality Inspection Press	中国质检出版社
56	China International Broadcasting Press	中国国际广播出版社
57	China Education Publishing Media Group Co. Ltd.	中国教育出版传媒集团有限公司
58	China Book Publishing House	中国书籍出版社
59	Wire-bound Bookstore	线装书局
60	China Sports Press	中国体育报业总社
61	Coal Industry Press	煤炭工业出版社
62	China Medical Science and Technology Press	中国医药科技出版社
63	Chinese Medicine Ancient Books Publishing House	中医古籍出版社
64	China Statistics Press	中国统计出版社
65	Intellectual Property Publishing House	知识产权出版社
66	China Tourism Publishing House	中国旅游出版社
67	Religious Culture Press	宗教文化出版社
68	China Overseas Chinese Press	中国华侨出版社
69	China Legal Publishing House	中国法制出版社
70	China Yanshi Publishing House	中国言实出版社
71	Ocean Press	海洋出版社
72	China Map Publishing House	中国地图出版社
73	Surveying and Mapping Publishing House	测绘出版社
74	China Cartography Society	中华地图学社
75	Xi'an Map Publishing House	西安地图出版社
76	Harbin Map Publishing House	哈尔滨地图出版社
77	Chengdu Map Publishing House	成都地图出版社
78	China Civil Aviation Publishing House	中国民航出版社
79	Cultural Relics Publishing House	文物出版社
80	China Traditional Chinese Medicine Press	中国中医药出版社
81	People's Court Press	人民法院出版社
82	China Procuratorate Press	中国检察出版社
83	China Youth Publishing Corporation	中国青年出版总社
84	China Children's Press and Publication Corporation	中国少年儿童新闻出版总社
85	China Women's Publishing House	中国妇女出版社
86	Writers Publishing House	作家出版社
87	China Film Publishing House	中国电影出版社

88	China Photography Publishing House	中国摄影出版社
89	Huaxia Publishing House	华夏出版社
90	China Railway Press	中国铁道出版社
91	Science Popularisation Press	科学普及出版社
92	Unity Press	团结出版社
93	Qunyan Publishing House	群言出版社
94	Democracy and Construction Press	民主与建设出版社
95	Kaiming Publishing House	开明出版社
96	China Zhigong Publishing House	中国致公出版社
97	Academy Press	学苑出版社
98	Taiwan Strait Publishing House	台海出版社

Sources: Ministry of Finance; Ministry of information and Culture, PRC

IV. Central Administrative SOEs

The Central SOEs comprise China National Railway Corporation (CRC), China National Tobacco Corporation (CNTC), and China Post Corporation (CPC). The three legendary enterprises are more extensive and have thousands of subsidiaries that are incorporated as SOEs. Looking at the network's scale, national integration of services and labour division, the Railways, Post, and Tobacco sectors have been directly put under the State Council. The State Council has separated China Post and CRC's administration from their business, making them a corporate entity responsible for its assets and profits. In all these Central SOEs, the administration of these enterprises is separated from their businesses like the State Post Bureau, where the Ministry of Finance performs the responsibilities of investors on behalf of the State Council.

CRC is quite large and incorporates everything from hospitals to schools. The system was created after China's former railway ministry was dissolved in 2013 and since then has been central to Beijing's efforts to use infrastructure investment to support a slowing economy. The China Railway Group holds its status at the ministerial level. The CRC has 18 Railway Bureaus, 2.04 million employees, and total assets of 4.6 trillion yuan (US$ 657 billion).[20] In 2018, the CRC had revenue of 1.1 trillion yuan (US$ 157 billion) and a net profit of 2.045 billion yuan (US$ 292 million).[21]

After the restructuring, China Post Group Co. Ltd. is managed by the Central government and is a wholly state-owned company with the Ministry of Finance as the state-owned asset management department of the CPC. The CPG is a Central SOE at the deputy ministerial level but is not an SOE managed by the SASAC. It is an investment institution authorised by the State Council to maintain and increase the value of state-owned assets. It has established postal companies in all provinces, autonomous regions and, municipalities across the country and has a long history and role that goes beyond a company.

The CNTC is a Central SOE at the deputy ministerial level. It is a nationally integrated agricultural, industrial, the social-economic entity with a legal personality.

Table 3.5: List Central Enterprises of Culture

1	China National Railway Group Co. Ltd.	中国国家铁路集团有限公司
2	China National Tobacco Corporation	中国烟草总公司
3	China Post Group Co. Ltd.	中国邮政集团有限公司

Sources: From the Company and group profiles available online

Major Restructuring Decisions of Central Enterprises under SASAC

Restructuring the Central SOEs into efficient corporate entities and improving their competitiveness has been the regulators' chief goals that include SASAC, Huijin, Ministry of Finance, and the State Council. From 2010, the purpose of reforms and development in SOEs was to complete the strategic adjustment and reorganisation and form a more reasonable state-owned economic layout and structure.

Here are some of the critical decisions made to restructure the Central SOEs under SASAC:

Year 2010

- On 2 February 2010, China National Packaging Corporation merged with China Chengtong Holding Group Co. Ltd. and became its wholly-owned subsidiary.
- On 15 March 2010, China New Era Holdings (Group) Company and China Energy Conservation Investment Corporation were merged and reorganised.
- On 12 April 2010, Shanghai Pharmaceutical Industry Research Institute was merged with China National Pharmaceutical Group Corporation and became its wholly-owned subsidiary.

- On 14 April 2010, China South Locomotive and Rolling Stock Industry Corporation changed its name to China South Locomotive Group.
- On 26 May 2010, Anshan Iron and Steel Group Co. Ltd. and Pangang Group Co. Ltd. carried out a joint reorganisation. After the restructuring, the Ansteel Group Corporation was newly established as the parent company, with the SASAC to continue to perform its investor responsibilities on behalf of the State Council; Anshan Iron and Steel Group Corporation and Pangang Group Co. Ltd. are both wholly-owned subsidiaries of Anshan Iron and Steel Group Corporation and no longer serve as enterprises under SASAC supervision.
- On 5 August 2010, China National Real Estate Development Corporation was merged with China Communications Construction Group Co. Ltd. as a wholly-owned subsidiary; Shanghai Shipping Research Institute was incorporated into China Shipping (Group) Corporation as a wholly-owned subsidiary.
- On 18 October 2010, China National Service Corporation for Personnel Abroad was merged with China National Pharmaceutical Group Corporation and became its wholly-owned subsidiary.
- On 23 December 2010, China High-tech Investment Corporation was incorporated into the State Development and Investment Corporation as a wholly-owned subsidiary.

Year 2011

- On 31 January 2011, China Merchants Enterprise Group Corporation merged with China Chengtong Holdings Group Co. Ltd. and became its wholly-owned subsidiary.
- On 25 May 2011, China Huaxing Group Corporation was put under China Guoxin Holdings Co. Ltd. and became its wholly-owned subsidiary.
- On 7 September 2011, the SASAC of the State Council issued a 'Notice on the Reorganisation of China Aerospace Science and Technology Corporation and China Lucky Film Group' on September 5. According to the document's spirit, Lucky Group was integrated with China Aerospace Science and Technology Corporation as its wholly-owned subsidiary.

Year 2012

- In May 2012, with the State Council's approval, China Printing Group Corporation was put under China Guoxin Holdings Co. Ltd. and became its wholly-owned subsidiary.

Year 2013

- In March 2013, China Hualiang Logistics Group Corporation merged into COFCO Group Co. Ltd. and became its wholly-owned subsidiary.
- In June 2013, following the bankruptcy of Huacheng Investment Management Co. Ltd. It ceased to be an enterprise that fulfilled investors' responsibilities.
- On 18 July 2013, China Second Heavy Machinery Group Corporation (also known as China Erzhong) and China National Machinery Industry Corporation carried out a joint reorganisation. After the restructuring, the new group changed its name to 'China National Machinery Industry Corporation'.[22]

Year 2014

- On 26 November 2014, China Huafu Trade Development Group Corporation was merged with COFCO Group Co. Ltd., and the number of Central enterprises under the supervision of SASAC was reduced to 112.[23]

Year 2015

- In June 2015, China Power Investment Corporation and State Nuclear Power Technology Co. Ltd. carried out a joint reorganisation.[24]
- In August 2015, China North Locomotive and Rolling Stock Industry Group Corporation and China South Locomotive Group Corporation carried out a joint reorganisation.[25]
- In December 2015, China Metallurgical Corporation was merged with China Minmetals Corporation as a wholly-owned subsidiary.[26]

Year 2016

- On 18 February 2016, the former COSCO Group and the former China Shipping Group reorganised and established as China COSCO Shipping Group Co. Ltd.[27]

- On 11 July 2016, China International Travel Service Group Co. Ltd. was merged with China Hong Kong and China Travel Service Group Corporation as a wholly-owned subsidiary. China International Travel Service Group Co. Ltd. ceases to be an enterprise under the supervision of the SASAC.
- On 15 July 2016, China National Textile and Apparel Corporation was merged with COFCO Corporation as a wholly-owned subsidiary. China Textile Group no longer directly supervises the enterprise as the SASAC.
- In July 2016, the newly established China Aviation Engine Group Co. Ltd. was included in the list of companies performing investor responsibilities by the SASAC after China Electronics Technology Group Corporation.[28]
- On 26 August 2016, China National Building Materials Group Co. Ltd. and China National Materials Group Co. Ltd. held a reorganisation meeting in Beijing. China National Building Materials Group Co. Ltd. became the officially announced organisation. This reorganisation marked the restructuring model for large SOEs in China's building materials industry.[29]
- On 22 September 2016, after being reporting to the State Council for approval, Baosteel Group Co. Ltd. and Wuhan Iron and Steel (Group) Company carried out a joint reorganisation.[30]
- On 23 November 2016, China Cotton Reserve Management Corporation was merged with China Grain Reserve Management Corporation as a wholly-owned subsidiary. China Cotton Reserve Management Corporation does not remain under SASAC listed enterprises.[31]
- On 1 December 2016, the SASAC announced the reorganisation of Nanguang (Group) Co. Ltd. and Zhuhai Zhenrong Company. Zhuhai Zhenrong merged with Nanguang Group and became a subsidiary of Nanguang Group in the mainland.[32]

Year 2017

- In August 2017, China Light Industry Corporation and China National Arts & Crafts (Group) Corporation were merged with China Poly Group Corporation as a wholly-owned subsidiary. The SASAC no longer supervises China Light Industry Corporation and China National Arts & Crafts (Group) Corporation.[33]

- In August 2017, China Guodian Corporation and Shenhua Group Co. Ltd. were merged and reorganised as the State Energy Investment Group Co. Ltd.[34]

Year 2018

- In January 2018, China National Nuclear Corporation and China Nuclear Industry Construction Group Co. Ltd. were reorganised. China National Nuclear Industry Construction Group Co. Ltd. was merged with China National Nuclear Corporation and no longer remained under the SASAC list.[35]
- In June 2018, Wuhan Research Institute of Posts and Telecommunications Co. Ltd. and Telecommunication Science and Technology Research Institute Co. Ltd. carried out a joint reorganisation.[36]

Year 2019

- In March 2019, the corporate reform of Central enterprises was completed whereby 83 Central enterprises established standardised boards of directors, and 46 Central enterprises implemented contractual management of more than 3,300 managers and implemented the control of 81 listed companies.[37]
- In April 2019, the Armed Police Hydropower Unit was declared an SOE, and the name was changed to 'China Aneng Construction Corporation Group Co. Ltd'.[38]
- In July 2019, China Poly Group Co. Ltd. and China Silk Group Co. Ltd. were reorganised. China Silk Group Co. Ltd. was merged with the China Poly Group Co. Ltd., and the SASAC no longer supervised it.[39]
- In October 2019, China State Shipbuilding Corporation and China Shipbuilding Industry Corporation carried out joint reorganisation.[40]
- On 26 November 2019, China State Shipbuilding Corporation (China State Shipbuilding Corporation) was officially inaugurated and established in Beijing.[41]
- On the morning of 9 December 2019, the long-awaited National Petroleum and Natural Gas Pipeline Network Group Co. Ltd. was formally established.[42]

Year 2020

- Not a significant restructuring decision, but SOEs were put into service to help the Hubei province (the epicentre of China's COVID-19 outbreak), until 18 February 2020. Central SOEs supplied 181,700 tons of gasoline, 38,600 tons of diesel, 461 million cubic metres of natural gas, 11.279 billion kilowatt-hours of electricity, 7,721 tons of grain and oil, and 257 4G/5G base stations to Hubei. Aviation companies carried out 159 special charter flights to Hubei.[43]
- On 2 June 2020, Shanghai Nokia Bell Co. Ltd. was removed from the SASAC and was allowed to be managed by the relevant Central enterprises according to the equity relationship.[44]
- On 5 June 2020, China Certification & Inspection (Group) Co. Ltd. was brought under SASAC's control to discharge the investors' responsibilities.[45]

SASAC being in charge of regulating the SOEs' performance, managing the assets and human resource, have been busy with multifarious and painstaking tasks. Without a doubt, the duties, which SASAC delivers on behalf of the State Council, are subject to scrutiny and influence. Party members and top bureaucrats do have vested interests in certain SOEs. Hence, merging them or striking off their names from the privileged list has directly impacted the functioning of the SASAC. Nearly 800+ members manage SASAC's in-house bureaucracy, which engages in passing the buck. SASAC appoints top officials and managers to these SOEs, which are politically influenced. In many instances, SASAC rotates the SOEs' bosses within an industry with the airlines, energy units and banks being recent examples—even though these firms are supposed to be commercial rivals. There does not exist any competition in the past few years; most airlines are managing their businesses under the wings of big players and often concede to their demands. Still, when competitiveness is not improving the SOEs' restructuring, the monopoly created by the SOEs are also not being brought under the ambit of investigations by anti-trust authorities.

Central SOEs in Business

In the past three decades, the SOEs' restructuring remained oriented around performance and reducing risks. The gross revenue and the net profit were

Table 3.6: Chinese SOEs in the *Fortune Global 500* (2020)

Chinese Rank	*Overall Rank*	*Name*	*Chinese Name*	*Region*	*Ownership*	*Sector*	*Revenue ($ millions)*	*Profits ($ millions)*	*Assets ($ millions)*	*Employees*
1	2	SINOPEC Group	中国石油化工集团有限公司	Beijing	Central SOE	Energy	407,009	6,793	317,516	582,648
2	3	State Grid	国家电网有限公司	Beijing	Central SOE	Energy	383,906	7,970	596,616	907,677
3	4	China National Petroleum	中国石油天然气集团有限公司	Beijing	Central SOE	Energy	379,130	4,443	608,086	1,344,410
4	18	China State Construction Engineering	中国建筑集团有限公司	Beijing	Central SOE	Engineering & Construction	205,839	3,333	294,070	335,038
6	24	Industrial & Commercial Bank of China	中国工商银行股份有限公司	Beijing	Central SOE	Financials	177,069	45,195	4,322,528	445,106
7	30	China Construction Bank	中国建设银行股份有限公司	Beijing	Central SOE	Financials	158,884	38,610	3,651,645	370,169
8	35	Agricultural Bank of China	中国农业银行股份有限公司	Beijing	Central SOE	Financials	147,313	30,701	3,571,542	467,631
9	43	Bank of China	中国银行股份有限公司	Beijing	Central SOE	Financials	135,091	27,127	3,268,838	309,384
10	45	China Life Insurance	中国人寿保险(集团)公司	Beijing	Central SOE	Financials	131,244	4,660	648,393	180,401
12	50	China Railway Engineering Group	中国铁路工程集团有限公司	Beijing	Central SOE	Engineering & Construction	123,324	1,535	152,983	302,394
13	52	SAIC Motor	上海汽车集团股份有限公司	Shanghai	SOE	Motor Vehicles & Parts	122,071	3,706	121,931	151,785
14	54	China Railway Construction	中国铁道建筑集团有限公司	Beijing	Central SOE	Engineering & Construction	120,302	1,359	155,598	364,907
15	64	China National Offshore Oil	中国海洋石油集团有限公司	Beijing	Central SOE	Energy	108,687	6,957	184,922	92,080
16	65	China Mobile Communications	中国移动通信集团有限公司	Beijing	Central SOE	Telecommunications	108,527	12,145	266,190	457,565
18	78	China Communications Construction	中国交通建设集团有限公司	Beijing	Central SOE	Engineering & Construction	95,096	1,333	232,053	197,309
19	79	China Resources	中国华润有限公司	Hong Kong	Central SOE	Health Care	94,758	3,572	232,277	396,456
20	89	China Faw Group	中国第一汽车集团有限公司	Jilin	Central SOE	Motor Vehicles & Parts	89,417	2,848	70,354	129,580
21	90	China Post Group	中国邮政集团有限公司	Beijing	Central SOE	Transportation	89,347	4,441	1,518,543	927,171

Chinese Rank	Overall Rank	Name	Chinese Name	Region	Ownership	Sector	Revenue ($ millions)	Profits ($ millions)	Assets ($ millions)	Employees
23	92	China Minmetals	中国五矿集团有限公司	Beijing	Central SOE	Materials	88,357	230	133,442	199,486
24	100	Dongfeng Motor	东风汽车集团有限公司	Hubei	Central SOE	Motor Vehicles & Parts	84,049	1,328	71,423	154,641
26	105	China Southern Power Grid	中国南方电网有限责任公司	Guangdong	Central SOE	Energy	81,978	1,833	134,036	283,639
28	108	China Energy Investment	国家能源投资集团有限责任公司	Beijing	Central SOE	Energy	80,498	4,264	251,272	331,373
29	109	Sinochem Group	中国中化集团有限公司	Beijing	Central SOE	Wholesalers	80,376	473	78,799	60,049
30	111	China Baowu Steel Group	中国宝武钢铁集团有限公司	Shanghai	Central SOE	Materials	79,932	2,901	123,777	196,378
31	112	People's Insurance Co. of China	中国人民保险集团股份有限公司	Beijing	Central SOE	Financials	79,788	3,204	162,687	198,951
32	126	CITIC Group	中国中信集团有限公司	Beijing	Central SOE	Financials	75,115	3,647	1,074,806	304,260
34	134	Beijing Automotive Group	北京汽车集团有限公司	Beijing	SOE	Motor Vehicles & Parts	72,554	747	71,909	114,315
35	136	COFCO	中粮集团有限公司	Beijing	Central SOE	Wholesalers	72,149	414	85,847	110,896
36	145	Sinopharm	中国医药集团有限公司	Beijing	Central SOE	Health Care	70,690	912	56,506	155,622
39	154	China North Industries Group	中国兵器工业集团有限公司	Beijing	Central SOE	Aerospace & Defence	68,714	1,284	61,502	204,378
40	157	Power China	中国电力建设集团有限公司	Beijing	Central SOE	Engineering & Construction	67,371	773	139,084	180,416
41	158	China Telecommunications	中国电信集团有限公司	Beijing	Central SOE	Telecommuni-cations	67,365	1,803	129,343	401,965
42	162	Bank of Communications	交通银行股份有限公司	Shanghai	Central SOE	Financials	66,564	11,186	1,422,054	87,828
43	163	Aviation Industry Corp. of China	中国航空工业集团有限公司	Beijing	Central SOE	Aerospace & Defence	65,909	578	144,798	417,798
44	164	ChemChina	中国化工集团有限公司	Beijing	Central SOE	Chemicals	65,767	-1,251	121,160	145,526
46	187	China National Building Material Group	中国建材集团有限公司	Beijing	Central SOE	Materials	57,626	-105	85,590	204,936
48	191	China Poly Group	中国保利集团有限公司	Beijing	Central SOE	Financials	57,147	2,031	188,479	100,393
49	193	China Pacific Insurance (Group)	中国太平洋保险(集团)股份有限公司	Shanghai	Central SOE	Financials	55,800	4,016	219,408	111,247

Chinese Rank	Overall Rank	Name	Chinese Name	Region	Ownership	Sector	Revenue ($ millions)	Profits ($ millions)	Assets ($ millions)	Employees
51	206	Guangzhou Automobile Industry Group	广州汽车工业集团有限公司	Guangdong	SOE	Motor Vehicles & Parts	53,662	565	43,838	105,780
53	210	Wuchan Zhongda Group	物产中大集团股份有限公司	Zhejiang	SOE	Wholesalers	51,954	396	13,399	20,332
54	212	Shandong Energy Group	山东能源集团有限公司	Shandong	SOE	Energy	51,893	730	44,552	153,545
55	217	Aluminum Corp. of China	中国铝业集团有限公司	Beijing	Central SOE	Materials	51,649	273	93,948	156,286
56	218	HBIS Group	河钢集团有限公司	Hebei	SOE	Materials	51,345	-94	66,333	127,116
57	220	Shanghai Pudong Development Bank	上海浦东发展银行股份有限公司	Shanghai	SOE	Financials	51,313	8,507	1,006,833	58,253
58	222	Industrial Bank	兴业银行股份有限公司	Fujian	SOE	Financials	50,945	9,534	1,025,838	60,455
60	234	XIAMEN C&D	厦门建发集团有限公司	Fujian	SOE	Financials	49,170	667	49,004	26,732
61	235	China Merchants Group	招商局集团有限公司	Hong Kong	Central SOE	Wholesalers	49,126	5,233	277,918	157,635
65	253	China Everbright Group	中国光大集团股份公司	Beijing	Central SOE	Financials	46,957	1,990	748,020	79,800
66	264	China Cosco Shipping	中国远洋海运集团有限公司	Shanghai	Central SOE	Transportation	44,655	1,087	125,906	118,243
67	265	Shaanxi Yanchang Petroleum (Group)	陕西延长石油(集团)有限责任公司	Shaanxi	SOE	Energy	44,564	215	57,549	129,920
68	266	China Huaneng Group	中国华能集团有限公司	Beijing	Central SOE	Energy	44,502	187	161,663	130,764
69	273	Shaanxi Coal & Chemical Industry	陕西煤业化工集团有限责任公司	Shaanxi	SOE	Energy	43,798	120	78,757	120,802
70	281	Sinomach	中国机械工业集团有限公司	Beijing	Central SOE	Industrials	43,122	452	55,071	146,792
71	284	Xiamen ITG Holding group	厦门国贸控股集团有限公司	Fujian	SOE	Wholesalers	42,790	42	14,656	15,178
72	290	China United Network Communications	中国联合网络通信股份有限公司	Beijing	Central SOE	Telecommunications	42,052	721	81,001	243,790
73	295	Yankuang Group	兖矿集团有限公司	Shandong	SOE	Energy	41,323	275	45,731	101,166
75	298	XMXYG	厦门象屿集团有限公司	Fujian	SOE	Wholesalers	41,135	220	20,008	11,635
77	305	China National Aviation Fuel Group	中国航空油料集团有限公司	Beijing	Central SOE	Wholesalers	40,487	569	9,712	13,705
80	316	State Power Investment	国家电力投资集团有限公司	Beijing	Central SOE	Energy	39,407	180	171,460	123,010

Chinese Rank	Overall Rank	Name	Chinese Name	Region	Ownership	Sector	Revenue ($ millions)	Profits ($ millions)	Assets ($ millions)	Employees
84	332	China Aerospace Science & Industry	中国航天科工集团有限公司	Beijing	Central SOE	Aerospace & Defence	37,604	1,959	50,065	147,712
85	343	Jiangxi Copper	江西铜业集团有限公司	Jiangxi	SOE	Materials	36,980	170	22,646	25,333
87	352	China Aerospace Science & Technology	中国航天科技集团有限公司	Beijing	Central SOE	Aerospace & Defence	36,209	2,628	68,555	177,905
88	353	China Energy Engineering Group	中国能源建设集团有限公司	Beijing	Central SOE	Engineering & Construction	36,111	395	61,054	122,560
90	361	CRRC Group	中国中车集团有限公司	Beijing	Central SOE	Industrials	34,704	523	61,803	176,348
91	367	Anhui Conch Group	安徽海螺集团有限责任公司	Anhui	SOE	Materials	33,916	1,773	31,609	55,952
92	369	Jinchuan Group	金川集团股份有限公司	Gansu	SOE	Materials	33,824	298	16,570	29,291
93	370	China Huadian	中国华电集团有限公司	Beijing	Central SOE	Energy	33,808	310	118,038	94,790
94	381	China Electronics Technology Group	中国电子科技集团有限公司	Beijing	Central SOE	Aerospace & Defence	32,948	1,743	57,865	177,443
95	386	China Electronics	中国电子信息产业集团有限公司	Beijing	Central SOE	Technology	32,447	138	47,019	138,603
96	392	China Taiping Insurance Group	中国太平保险集团有限责任公司	Hong Kong	Central SOE	Financials	31,912	586	118,439	65,957
97	401	Ansteel Group	鞍钢集团有限公司	Liaoning	Central SOE	Materials	31,469	-209	47,781	126,909
98	406	Jizhong Energy Group	冀中能源集团有限责任公司	Hebei	SOE	Energy	30,666	-114	33,149	107,359
100	423	Shanghai Construction Group	上海建工(集团)总公司	Shanghai	SOE	Engineering & Construction	29,746	569	36,935	42,762
102	429	Shougang Group	首钢集团有限公司	Beijing	SOE	Materials	29,274	40	71,543	97,903
103	434	China South Industries Group	中国兵器装备集团有限公司	Beijing	Central SOE	Aerospace & Defence	29,063	988	48,802	176,326
105	436	Gree Electric Appliances	珠海格力电器股份有限公司	Guangdong	SOE	Industrials	29,024	3,575	40,624	88,846
106	442	Shenzhen Investment Holdings	深圳控股有限公司	Guangdong	SOE	Financials	28,855	1,594	100,422	67,518

Chinese Rank	Overall Rank	Name	Chinese Name	Region	Ownership	Sector	Revenue ($ millions)	Profits ($ millions)	Assets ($ millions)	Employees
110	456	Tongling Nonferrous Metals Group	铜陵有色金属集团	Anhui	SOE	Materials	27,819	-65	12,549	22,860
111	459	Shandong Iron & Steel Group	山东钢铁集团有限公司	Shandong	SOE	Materials	27,755	22	51,265	51,300
112	463	Datong Coal Mine Group	大同煤矿集团有限责任公司	Shanxi	SOE	Energy	27,557	-159	53,030	152,733
113	465	China Datang	中国大唐集团有限公司	Beijing	Central SOE	Energy	27,464	427	108,896	95,748
115	473	Shanghai Pharmaceuticals Holding	上海医药集团股份有限公司	Shanghai	SOE	Health Care	27,005	591	19,672	47,778
116	477	China General Technology	中国通用技术(集团)控股有限责任公司	Beijing	Central SOE	Engineering & Construction	26,559	490	28,310	43,197
117	485	Shanxi Coking Coal Group	山西焦煤集团有限责任公司	Shanxi	SOE	Energy	26,179	212	48,744	196,034
118	486	Henan Energy & Chemical	河南能源化工集团有限公司	Henan	SOE	Energy	26,163	-306	39,364	164,236
119	489	Shanxi Luan Mining Group	山西潞安矿业 (集团)有限责任公司	Shanxi	SOE	Energy	26,078	105	35,870	106,188
120	490	Guangxi Investment Group	广西投资集团有限公司	Guangxi	SOE	Financials	26,060	78	70,591	30,605
121	493	China National Nuclear	中国核工业集团有限公司	Beijing	Central SOE	Energy	25,975	1,105	119,401	156,300
122	496	China National Coal Group	中国中煤能源集团有限公司	Beijing	Central SOE	Energy	25,846	308	56,841	122,827
123	499	Yangquan Coal Industry Group	阳泉煤业(集团)有限责任公司	Shanxi	SOE	Energy	25,491	-82	35,409	101,817
124	500	Shanxi Jincheng Anthracite Coal Mining Group	山西晋城无烟煤矿业集团有限责任公司	Shanxi	SOE	Energy	25,386	22	42,257	127,336

Source: Author's Analysis

met to mitigate the returns on assets. Some of the SOEs continued building assets in strategic areas, but the SASAC and the State Council periodically warned those who were engaged in building a substantial amount of dead assets.

There lies the importance of SOEs in China's past and future economic success. Although the SOEs have not turned into profit-generating systems, they have steadily performed well in sales and assets. In 2018, Central SOEs achieved a cumulative operating income of 29.1 trillion yuan (US$ 415 billion), a year-on-year increase of 10.1 per cent, realised total profits of 1.7 trillion yuan (US$ 243 billion), a year-on-year increase of 16.7 per cent, a record high.[46] In the following year (2019), the Central enterprises achieved a total of 30.8 trillion yuan (US$ 440 billion) in operating income, a year-on-year increase of 5.6 per cent, and a cumulative net profit of 1.3 trillion yuan (US$ 185 billion), a year-on-year increase of 10.8 per cent, besides completing various goals.[47]

On a different scale, the Chinese Central SOEs have been carrying out state capitalism beyond borders. We will discuss the details of Central SOEs' 'going out', internationalisation and its nomadic nature in the following chapters separately. Table 3.6 shows how seriously Red Chip SOEs are sitting on the nation's wealth. The intention is to give readers a bird's eye view of how these SOEs manage vast pools of capital, assets, and the sector they dominate.

Conclusion

Most of the giant SOEs fulfil the Chinese leaders' dream to be on top of the global chart, be in any field—banking, infrastructure, energy, telecommunications, engineering, newer technical areas, or even health. This serves the purpose of the Chinese state amplifying its strategic role on a worldwide scale. Chinese presence in the *Fortune 500* list of companies is dominant, and the list is an indicator of the growth of Chinese businesses. The list of Chinese SOEs indicates that although they may look like middle and lower-rung companies in the Chinese list of *Fortune 500* companies, they come in the first 125. One can also note that not all of these Chinese SOEs, which are part of the global list, operate out of Beijing and under SASAC, but come from tiers of provinces and varied sectors. This indicates that the rise of SOEs is not just about a template which the Chinese adopted and lined up for the SOEs, but that they have been able to isolate their priorities, streamline strategies and deliver the goods set forth by Chinese statecraft.

Four decades after the death of Mao, the first Chairman, the SOEs stand firm and stable. Mao had crushed the private sector and protected the state enterprises, and helped them grow and turn into giants. Communist Party officials have mixed opinions to sell off what they see as jewels in the crown. Today, China still has around 150,000 SOEs (including the Central SOEs, their subsidiaries, and provincial SOEs). Despite reforms being launched in the mid-1990s and backed by Deng and continued for the past 25 years, many resist reforms that would loosen their grip on the economy. Many of the best-known companies, from China Mobile to CITIC, are Red Chip firms. Many even do not know the numbers, scale, and expanse of the SOEs. It is a dichotomy that the private enterprises are surviving at the mercy of the State and limiting themselves not to fall out of line. Despite resisting heavily to the restructuring and letting small enterprises go and merge with larger ones, the restructuring task remained the most arduous and shaky for the Chinese leaders.

NOTES

1. National People's Congress of the PRC. 2004. 'Constitution of the People's Republic of China', 14 March, http://www.npc.gov.cn/zgrdw/englishnpc/Constitution/2007-11/15/content_ 1372963.htm (accessed on 8 August 2020).
2. Amir Guluzade. 2019. 'The role of China's State-owned companies explained' *World Economic Forum.* 7 May, https://www.weforum.org/agenda/2019/05/why-chinas-state-owned-companies-still-have-a-key-role-to-play/ (accessed on 20 July 2020).
3. *Xinhua News Agency.* 2019. 'Zhongguo youzheng jituan youxian gongsi jiepai chengli' (中国邮政集团有限公司揭牌成立) [China Post Group Co. Ltd. was inaugurated and established], 28 December, https://baijiahao.baidu.com/s?id=1654156682908150058&wfr=spider&for=pc (accessed on 13 June 2020).
4. Chen Jia and Zhong Nan. 2019. 'Debt burden of State-owned enterprises decreases in 2018' *China Daily.* 24 October, https://www.chinadaily.com.cn/a/201910/24/WS5db10417 a310cf3e355723dd.html (accessed on 18 July 2020).
5. Scott Cendrowski. 2015. 'China's Global 500 Companies are bigger than ever – and mostly State-owned Enterprises' *Fortune.* 22 July, https://fortune.com/2015/07/22/china-global-500-government-owned/ (accessed on 18 July 2020).
6. Brand Finance Global Forum. 2019. 'Global 500: The annual report on the world's most valuable and strongest brands', *Brand Finance*, February, https://www2.deloitte.com/content/dam/Deloitte/cn/Documents/about-deloitte/deloitte-cn-global-500-2019-en-190215.pdf (accessed on 17 July 2020).
7. Scott Kennedy. 2020. 'The biggest but not the strongest: China's place in the Fortune Global 500' *CSIS Blogs.* 18 August, https://www.csis.org/blogs/trustee-china-hand/biggest-not-strongest-chinas-place-fortune-global-500 (accessed on 20 August 2020).

8. *China Daily*. 2020. 'Chinese brands grab half of domestic auto market share', 17 August, https://www.chinadaily.com.cn/a/202008/17/WS5f39f97aa310834817260c21.html (accessed on 20 Aug 2020).
9. *Sohu.com*. 2016. 'Dongfang Electric and Harbin Electric switch coaches during the trough period, power equipment giants may encounter huge losses', 13 June, https://www.sohu.com/a/82811936_109478 (accessed on 18 July 2020).
10. The Contract Responsibility System (CRS) was patterned after successful experiments in the province of Sichuan. Under the system, peasants entered into a contract to produce and sell certain commodities at low official prices to the state. They are then free to sell on the open market anything produced over the contracted amount. The system amounted to a lump-sum tax on farm produce or a zero-marginal tax on the incremental yield. While the farmers responded enthusiastically, the system also worked satisfactorily for small industrial enterprises. Koo, Anthony Y. C. 1990. 'The Contract Responsibility System: Transition from a Planned to a Market Economy', *Economic Development and Cultural Change,* Vol. 38, No. 4, July, 797.
11. List of Central enterprises of the SASAC (State-owned Assets Supervision and Administration Commission).
12. There are five bureaus within SASAC's Central Organisation Department which looks after the management of personnel being hired, trained and managed for their duties. It is Party's Human Resource Department that SASAC created specifically for central industrial enterprises.

    The First Bureau Department is the Cadre Deployment Bureau. This bureau is mainly responsible for the macro management of cadres, designated cadre policy, management of civil servants in the party-mass system. Some specific tasks carried out by this bureau includes— in accordance with the policy guidelines and instructions of the Party Central Committee, study and solve the party's organisational work issues, and put forward specific requirements for the party's organisational line. Inspect, select and promote party cadres. The other four bureaus carry out different divisions of labour and are respectively responsible for the appointment and management of cadres in certain systems. The Second Bureau Department is the Bureau of Party and Foreign Affairs Cadres, which is mainly responsible for the training, inspection, allocation, adjustment, appointment, and management of cadres in the Party, government and foreign affairs departments. The first bureau and the second bureau of the Central Organisation Department have the same power level as the third, fourth and the fifth bureau.

    The third bureau of the organisation department is the Bureau of Economics, Science, Technology and Education; the fourth bureau of the organisation department is the Bureau of Central and State Organs, and the fifth bureau of the organisation department is the Bureau of Enterprise Cadres.
13. Paul Hubbard. 2014. 'SOEs are the Champions' *A Natural History of Chinese State-owned Enterprises.* 8 September, https://chinasoe.wordpress.com/tag/sasac/ (accessed on 14 July 2020).
14. Victor Shih. 2004. 'Dealing with Non-Performing Loans: Political Constraints and Financial Policies in China', *The China Quarterly*, Vol. 180, December, 922.
15. Central Huijin Investment Ltd. 2008. 'Company Profile', http://www.huijininv.cn/huijineng/About_Us/index.shtml (accessed on 17 July 2020).
16. Ibid.
17. Chriss Gill. 2020. 'China's bureaucrats tussle over control of the treasury' *Asia Financial*

Times. 3 September, https://www.asiatimesfinancial.com/china-s-bureaucrats-tussle-over-control-of-the-treasury (accessed on 9 September 2020).

18. *China Daily*. 2010. 'Sanjia wenhua "yangqi" chengli wei shou pi zhuanzhi de zhongyang wenhua qiye' (三家文化"央企"成立为首批转制的中央文化企业) [Three Cultural Central Enterprise were established as the first batch of central cultural enterprises to be transformed], 11 August, http://www.chinadaily.com.cn/dfpd/whtzgg/2010-08/11/content_11137762.htm (accessed on 22 July 2020).
19. Ibid.
20. *163.com*. 2020. 'Zhongguo zui "juewujinyou" de yangqi! Zhangguan 14 wan gongli tielu, ceng zi dai "gongjianfa"' (中国最"绝无仅有"的央企！ 掌管 14 万公里铁路曾自带"公检法") [China's most "unique" central enterprise! In charge of 140,000 kilometres of railways, once brought its own "Public Security Law"], 14 September, https://baijiahao.baidu.com/s?id=1677528086760256102&wfr=spider&for=pc(accessed on 8 December 2020).
21. Ibid.
22. China National Machinery Industry Corporation (SINOMACH). 2013. 'Zhongguo er chong yu guo ji jituan shishi lianhe chongzu' (中国二重与国机集团实施联合重组) [China Erzhong and SINOMACH to carry out the reorganisation], 25 July, http://www.sinomach.com.cn/xwzx/zgsdt/2013zgsdt/201412/t20141218_41384.html (accessed on 11 March 2021).
23. *People's Daily*. 2014. 'China Huafu Trade Development Group Corporation was merged into COFCO corporation', 26 November, http://politics.people.com.cn/BIG5/n/2014/1126/c70731-26100059.html (accessed on 14 July 2020).
24. State-owned Assets Supervision and Administration Commission (SASAC). 2015b. 'Zhongguo dianli touzi jituan gongsi he guojia hedian jishu youxian gongsi shishi lianhe chongzu' (国电力投资集团公司和国家核电技术有限公司实施联合重组) [China Power Investment Corporation and State Nuclear Power Technology Co. Ltd. implement joint reorganisation], 1 June, http://www.sasac.gov.cn/n2588035/n2641579/n2641660/c3753547/content.html (accessed on 24 July 2020).
25. Ibid.
26. Ibid.
27. *cnafc.com*. 2019. 'Dazao "yi zong, yi fen, si de" jiagou, zhuli jituan shixian "san ge pao ying" ——relie zhuhe zhongyuan hai cai beijing fen gongsi zhengshi kaiye' (打造"一总、一分、四地"架构，助力集团实现"三个跑赢" ——热烈祝贺中远海财北京分公司正式开业) [Create a structure of "one headquarters, one branch, and four locations" to help the group realise the "three outperforms" —Congratulations on the official opening of COSCO SHIPPING Beijing Branch], 4 June, http://www.cnafc.org/cnafc/front/detail.action?id=0FF8C1EDDCF 84C6E8F69B8B0A101341C (accessed on 12 August 2020).
28. State-owned Assets Supervision and Administration Commission (SASAC). 2016. 'Guozi wei guanyu zujian zhongguo hangkong fadongji jituan youxian gongsi de gonggao' (国资委关于 组建中国航空发动机集团有限公司的公告) [State-owned Assets Supervision and Administration Commission on the establishment of China's aviation engine Group Co. Ltd. announcement], 13 July, http://www.sasac.gov.cn/n2588035/n2641579/n2641660/c3753618/content.html (accessed on 12 July 2020).
29. *China Enterprise News*. 2016. 'Zhongguo jiancai jituan youxian gongsi xuanbu chengli' (中国建材集团有限公司宣布成立) [China National Building Materials Group Co. Ltd. announced its establishment], 30 August, https://money.163.com/16/0830/00/BVM54OA9002580S6.html(accessed on 8 December 2020).

30. *Xinhua News Agency*. 2016. 'Baogang yu wugang lianhe chongzu huo pi' (宝钢与武钢联合重组获批) [The joint reorganisation of Baosteel and WISCO was approved], 22 September, http://www.gov.cn/xinwen/2016-09/22/content_5110905.htm (accessed on 13 June 2020).
31. *Sina Finance*. 2016a. 'Zhongguo chubei liang guanli zong gongsi yu zhongguo chubei mian guanli zong gongsi shishi chongzu' (中国储备粮管理总公司与中国储备棉管理总公司实施重组) [China Grain Reserve Management Corporation and China Cotton Reserve Management Corporation reorganised], 23 November, http://finance.sina.com.cn/roll/2016-11-23/doc-ifxyasmv1622811.shtml.
32. State-owned Assets Supervision and Administration Commission (SASAC). 2015a. 'Nanguang (jituan) youxian gongsi he zhuhai zhen rong gongsi shishi chongzu' (南光（集团）有限公司和珠海振戎公司实施重组) [Nanguang (Group) Co. Ltd. and Zhuhai Zhenrong Company reorganized], 1 December, http://www.gov.cn/xinwen/2015-12/01/content_5018604.htm (accessed on 14 August 2020).
33. State-owned Assets Supervision and Administration Commission (SASAC). 2017b. 'Zhongguo baoli jituan gongsi yu zhongguo qing gong jituan gongsi, zhongguo gongyi (jituan) gongsi shishi chongzu' (中国保利集团公司与中国轻工集团公司、中国工艺（集团）公司实施重组) [China Poly Group Corporation, China Light Industry Corporation and China National Arts & Crafts (Group) Corporation reorganized], 21 August, http://www.sasac.gov.cn/n2588025/n2588119/c7768396/content.html (accessed on 14 August 2020).
34. State-owned Assets Supervision and Administration Commission (SASAC). 2017a. 'Zhongguo guodian jituan gongsi yu shenhua jituan youxian zeren gongsi shishi lianhe chongzu' (中国国电集团公司与神华集团有限责任公司实施联合重组) [China Guodian Corporation and Shenhua Group Co. Ltd. implement joint reorganization], 28 August, http://www.sasac.gov.cn/n2588035/c7795367/content.html (accessed on 14 August 2020).
35. State-owned Assets Supervision and Administration Commission (SASAC). 2018b. 'Zhongguo he gongye jituan youxian gongsi yu zhongguo he gongye jianshe jituan youxian gongsi shishi chongzu' (中国核工业集团有限公司与中国核工业建设集团有限公司实施重组) [China National Nuclear Corporation and China Nuclear Industry Construction Group Co. Ltd. reorganised], 31 January, http://www.sasac.gov.cn/n2588035/n2641579/n2641660/c8551590/content.html (accessed on 14 August 2020).
36. State-owned Assets Supervision and Administration Commission (SASAC). 2018a. 'Wuhan youdian kexue yan jiu yuan youxian gongsi yu dianxin kexue jishu yan jiu yuan youxian gongsi shishi lianhe chongzu' (武汉邮电科学研究院有限公司与电信科学技术研究院有限公司实施联合重组) [Wuhan Post and Telecommunications Research Institute Co. Ltd. and Telecommunication Science and Technology Research Institute Co. Ltd. implement joint reorganisation], 27 June, http://www.sasac.gov.cn/n2588025/n2588119/c9175370/content.html (accessed on 14 August 2020).
37. *Sina*. 2019. 'Xiaoyaqing: Yangqi gongsi zhi gaige quanmian wancheng' (肖亚庆：央企公司制改革全面完成) [Xiao Yaqing: The reform of the state-owned enterprise system is fully completed], 27 March, http://news.sina.com.cn/o/2019-03-27/doc-ihtxyzsm0948191.shtml (accessed on 7 August 2020).
38. State-owned Assets Supervision and Administration Commission (SASAC). 2019d. 'Guowuyuan guoyou zichan jiandu guanli weiyuanhui gonggao)' (国务院国有资产监督管理委员会公告) [Announcement of the State-owned Assets Supervision and Administration Commission of the State Council], 4 April, http://www.sasac.gov.cn/n2588035/n2641579/n2641660/c10885879/content.html (accessed on 24 August 2020).

39. State-owned Assets Supervision and Administration Commission (SASAC). 2019c. 'Zhongguo baoli jituan youxian gongsi yu zhongguo zhong si jituan youxian gongsi shishi chongzu' (中国保利集团有限公司与中国中丝集团有限公司实施重组) [China Poly Group Co. Ltd. and China Silk Group Co. Ltd. reorganised], 8 July, http://www.sasac.gov.cn/n2588035/n2641579/n2641660/c11679355/content.html (accessed on 24 August 2020).
40. State-owned Assets Supervision and Administration Commission (SASAC). 2019b. 'Zhongguo chuanbo gongye jituan youxian gongsi yu zhongguo chuanbo zhonggong jituan youxian gongsi shishi lianhe chongzu' (中国船舶工业集团有限公司与中国船舶重工集团有限公司实施联合重组) [China State Shipbuilding Corporation and China Shipbuilding Industry Corporation implement joint reorganisation], 25 October, http://www.sasac.gov.cn/n2588035/n2641579/n2641660/c12397252/content.html (accessed on 24 August 2020).
41. *Xinhua*. 2019. '"Liang chuan" zhengshi heti zhongguo chuanbo jituan youxian gongsi jiepai chengli' ("两船"正式合体中国船舶集团有限公司揭牌成立) ["Two ships" officially merged China State Shipbuilding Corporation Limited was inaugurated and established], 26 November, http://www.xinhuanet.com//fortune/2019-11/26/c_1125277030.htm (accessed on 12 August 2020).
42. *Sina Finance*. 2019. 'Guojia youqi guan wang gongsi zhengshi chengli xin ju wu ba dansheng' (国家油气管网公司正式成立新巨无霸诞生) [The National Oil and Gas Pipeline Company was formally established, the new giant was born], 9 December, http://finance.sina.com.cn/wm/2019-12-09/doc-iihnzahi6271079.shtml (accessed on 14 July 2020).
43. *Xinhua*. 2020. 'Kai zu mali bao fang kong fugong fu chan wen jingji——zhongyang qiye quanli yi fu kangji yiqing' (开足马力保防控复工复产稳经济——中央企业全力以赴抗击疫情) [Strive to ensure prevention and control, resume work and resume production to stabilise the economy-central enterprises go all out to fight the epidemic], 18 February, http://www.xinhuanet.com/politics/2020-02/18/c_1125593316.htm (accessed on 22 July 2020).
44. State-owned Assets Supervision and Administration Commission (SASAC). 2020e. 'Guanyu shanghai nuojiya bei'er gufen youxian gongsi bu zai lie ru guowuyuan guoyou zichan jiandu guanli weiyuanhui lu hang chuzi ren zhize qiye mingdan de gonggao' (关于上海诺基亚贝尔 股份有限公司不再列入国务院国有资产监督管理委员会履行出资人职责企业名单的公告) [About Shanghai Nokia Bell Co. Ltd. No longer listed in the State-owned Assets Supervision and Administration Commission of the State Council Announcement on the list of companies performing the duties of investors], 3 June, http://www.sasac.gov.cn/n2588035/n2641579/n2641660/c14770605/content.html (accessed on 22 July 2020).
45. State-owned Assets Supervision and Administration Commission (SASAC). 2020d. 'Guanyu jiang zhongguo jianyan renzheng (jituan) youxian gongsi lie ru guowuyuan guoyou zichan jiandu guanli weiyuanhui lu hang chuzi ren zhize qiye mingdan de gonggao' (关于将中国检验认证(集团)有限公司列入国务院国有资产监督管理委员会履行出资人职责企业名单的公告) [About China Certification & Inspection (Group) Co. Ltd. Listed in the State-owned Assets Supervision and Administration Commission of the State Council Announcement on the list of companies performing the duties of investors], 5 June, http://www.sasac.gov.cn/n2588035/n2641579/n2641660/c14787870/content.html (accessed on 22 July 2020).
46. *CNR News*. 2019. '2018 Nian yangqi shixian lirun zong'e 1.7 Wan yi yuan chuang lishi zui hao shuiping' (2018 年央企实现利润总额 1.7 万亿元创历史最好水平) [In 2018, the

total profit of central enterprises reached 1.7 trillion yuan, the best level in history], 17 January, http://news.cnr.cn/native/gd/20190117/t20190117_524485815.shtml (accessed on 16 July 2020).

47. State-owned Assets Supervision and Administration Commission (SASAC). 2020c. '2019 Nian zhongyang qiye jingji yun hang qingkuang' (2019 年中央企业经济运行情况) [Economic performance of central enterprises in 2019], 16 January, http://www.sasac.gov.cn/n2588035/n2588330/n2588360/c13551779/content.html (accessed on 20 July 2020).

4

Fall of the Titans?

All the major industries in China are owned, controlled and dependent upon the State. Hundreds of millions of Chinese are reported to work in these State-owned Enterprises (SOEs) where the Chinese state, in the name of collective ownership, controls the SOEs that produce a wide variety of industrial goods. In 1978, with Deng's rise to power, the Chinese economy witnessed a growth spurt with innovations in SOEs. These economic institutions worked for the fulfilment of political, social, and financial goals. They occupied an important place in the PRC's economic experiments during the post-49 period. In the early days of nation-building, the role of the SOEs was critical for China. All-round inefficiency and the need to shift from the Soviet-style extensive growth to intensive growth based on improved resource allocation contributed to the emergence of Chinese economic reforms in the late 1970s. However, the fundamental weakness lay with the inefficient use of labour, capital, energy and raw materials and a mismatch between the composition and quality production and demand. In December 1978, the Third Plenary session of the Eleventh Party Congress adopted a 'new adjustment and reform program'.[1] In the quest to increase economic development, it became indispensable to take strong measures. Soon the plight of the SOEs turned into a bone of contention between the State and workers. Several steps were taken to revitalise the enterprises. However, given the nature of the role of

SOEs and their complicated operation in China's economic development, a thorough restructuring process of the enterprises is yet to be completed and take shape.

It is ironic that even after the commencement of economic reforms, the condition of these enterprises continued to deteriorate. After 1978, market-based managerial relations were created throughout the SOE sector, transforming China's industrial sector into a market-oriented enterprise. The following discussion pertains to review reforms and structural changes concerning SOEs and highlights some crucial achievements and problems.

SOEs in the Pre-reform Period

The nature of the SOEs in Mao's era was too politicised and complex in its structure. The SOEs were merely a production unit, and more than that, those who were engaged in providing social stability through the role of social security providers were used as a tool to strengthen the party's rule. The functions of the SOEs were intertwined with each other. It is essential to understand the nature of these institutions in the pre-reform period. There are three shades of the performance of SOEs in the pre-reform period, i.e., political dimension, economic dimension, and social size.

SOEs played a political role in establishing state control throughout China. Institutions like *danwei* (单位 meant 'work unit'. The term *Danwei* used to refer to a place of employment) were created to sow and spread the ideological seeds. The Chinese leadership used decentralisation as an instrument to put central policy into effect under local conditions more swiftly and diligently.[2] But the control over the profits of these decentralised state-enterprises remained with the Central government. In the name of socialism, the government could control the country's economic nerves and this was a significant political step. For the first time, decision-making power pertaining to social security was passed on to the *danwei*,[3] with the SOEs as caretakers. The Central government had a firm grip on the *danwei* as a unit delegating important tasks of social control and implementing central policies. Under the *danwei* system, individual initiative, autonomy of social organisations and market mechanism were non-existent. From the top to the grassroots, the vertical chain of the state administrative power brought every *danwei* and thus every individual, through his *danwei*, under state and party control.[4] The control on SOEs was 'systemic'[5] and was often supported to consolidate the party's rule. Thomas Rawski explained this phenomenon as "the firm's chief obligation, and the managers and party personnel occupying key posts were to carry out annual economic plans issued by the State Council and other organs of the central government".[6] The *danwei* net spread over the enterprises helped the State to reach the bottom-most level of the system. Ideologically speaking, the State was engaged in socialising people politically by controlling enterprises. The SOEs worked for political integration and further education. Under the planned economy, SOEs played a significant role in the interaction between the State and members of society.

Along with political performance, the SOEs were also a fundamental economic unit meant to strengthen their financial health. Before 1979, China's SOEs were typical production units in a centrally planned economy. The interlocked market system eroded the vitality of enterprises. Since profit retention and incentives were not thought of, the functions of enterprises were too technical, causing stagnation of innovative ideas. According to Rawski (1975), "Despite periodic changes in the list of norms and their relative importance, plan targets have always included figures of sales value and physical output of major commodities, financial quotas involving wages, costs and profit, and subsidiary requirements concerning input coefficients, research, and innovation".[7] SOEs transferred all their surplus funds to the state budget and relied on the State for subsidies to cover losses and grants for investment. According to government plans, the investment and working capital were mostly financed through assistance provided by the government budget or loans from the banking system.[8] Under this system, SOEs had minimal autonomy in decision-making to set prices and decide investment priorities.

The SOEs had a social face too. SOEs, as a guarantee of social security, worked as an institution of control, as mentioned earlier, which in Mainland China operated as a working unit, *danwei*. This *danwei* was supposed to integrate social functions.[9] By absorbing almost all social parts, the *danwei* controlled the distribution of resources among its members. The Central power could not provide such facilities directly to the people since it was a centralised State. By allocating SOEs or *danweis* to perform the role of the guarantor of social security, the Central power bifurcated the responsibility of providing social security to its citizens. Concepts like 'eating from a big pot' and an 'iron rice bowl' emerged from providing basic amenities to the ordinary Chinese.

The *danwei* had controlled the distribution of food and consumer goods.[10] From a social perspective, the enterprises had become 'cells of society,' or 'small societies within themselves' that were interwoven and interlinked with each other in many different ways. For many people, apart from their immediate families, *danwei* were the only social institutions that they knew. Childcare, pensions, education, and health care were organised and provided by these *danweis,* thus encouraging the phenomena of an 'enterprise run society'.[11]

Towards Restructuring the SOEs: Epicentre of Economic Imbalance and Political Crisis

Soon after establishment of the PRC, the lack of infrastructure and entrepreneurship had posed a big problem for the Chinese economy. Under the direction of the CPC, the experiment with the Soviet structure in China was chosen for further development. SOEs proved successful in producing vast quantities of infrastructural commodities such as iron, steel, coal, of which China became the world's largest producer. To make SOEs an efficient economic institution, Mao had applied some of the Japanese management measures to the Chinese economy, like 'raise rational suggestions' (*ti hei hua jianyi*) or the *danwei* system that was familiar to the Japanese 'workplace family system'. Unfortunately, these steps failed in yielding the desired results.

The so-called progress was achieved in the face of disregard for quality or cost. Subjugation to the party's interests meant that industrial enterprises under Mao were run by the party, which discouraged the managers of government-owned enterprises. Managers were forced to focus on numerical measures of output rather than on quality or customer needs, making large-scale production of inferior goods that could not be sold outside the country. Politically, these institutions were conservative and allowed to perform only a social role in the country but performed at the cost of economic efficiency.

The problem was deep-rooted, and therefore in 1978, some measures (discussed in the next section) were taken to cure the problem, which proved insufficient. The doors were widely opened, and foreign investment played a massive role in this with other gradualist economic policies. Before investment came, only the State-controlled large industries and competitions within the boundaries were low. The opening brought new foreign ventures to the country, as a result of which the State started losing its control over the domestic market.

With increasing FDI, private and joint ventures flourished in China, something that was unheard of during the pre-reform period. Later, this sector, with improved management skills and sophisticated technology, started competing with SOEs, which eventually led to complications within China's economic structure, resulting in the failure of SOEs. However, the SOEs remained dominant in China's economy and consumed about 70 per cent of the total labour and capital employed in Chinese industry. However, the SOE sector only generates about 40 per cent of the output,[12] signifying the inefficiency of SOE management. Factories failed to adopt updated and contemporary technology, as a result of which the problems of relative inefficiency attained embarrassingly high levels.

Too much government-control of SOEs led to its slow-paced transformation, mostly due to the highly hierarchical structure and parallel decision-making, which rendered matters slow and inflexible.[13] Therefore, the enterprises were inhibited from responding quickly to the changing market and technological conditions[14] as a result of which, in 1978, Sichuan Chengdu Measuring and Cutting Tool Plant, desperately in need of special machine tools, had to pass through the process of getting approval from ten different administrative bureaus and wasted about two years in the process.[15] This happened because of the culture of subordination to many administrative supervisors. An enterprise was very often subject to many immediate superiors and usually received targets not only from its parent bureau, that is, the respective industrial bureau or corporation, but also from a specialised supporting functional bureau.[16] For example, the finance bureau in charge of a group of enterprises for financing always directed the management of a particular enterprise. The enterprises were obliged for clearance by the industrial bureau and financial bureau, resulting in a blurring of a hierarchy of command and time-consuming process even for trivial matters. Also, there was a lack of proper coordination due to a plethora of intervening agencies and bodies with their varied interests that exerted their influence. Furthermore, the lack of responsibility resulted in inconsistency and inflexibility in enterprises.

In the past few years, Chinese economic growth has recorded positive growth with an increased per capita income, which is more than four-fold compared to pre-1978 records, and millions have moved from the dying state industrial sector to the non-state commercial sector. However, more severe and tenacious issues remain unresolved, particularly in the financial service industry. This includes continued monopolising scarce capital allocation by four large state-owned banks besides restricting the flow of funds earmarked for the non-state sector. Further, it was largely political and not efficiency and profitability, which determined and dictated the disbursement of available funds. Indeed, all these actions and inactions led to extremely poor outputs despite the fact that SOEs received more than two-thirds of the funds but accounted for less than one-third of the industrial output value.

The inefficiency of SOEs also created a problem for state-owned banks as the Central government had put more than 80 per cent of the state banks' financial assets into the SOEs to encourage and boost growth, which was also seen as socially and politically essential at that point in time.[17] The feeding of loss-making SOEs was an open secret, but most banks were technically bankrupt and held non-performing loans (25 per cent or more of all loans). This rendered recapitalising of the banks a non-solution. It was feared that the cheaper credit flow to favour SOEs would waste scarce capital on low-quality pet projects that had little net value to consumers.[18] The complete undermining of the entire banking system by the State made SOEs a burgeoning 'Black hole' on the State's resources. Financial information was corrupt to the extent that neither firms nor banks nor anyone else knew the proper financial health of borrowers or lenders.[19] This kind of favouritism and corruption in the financial system caused havoc for long-term growth.[20]

Some of the services provided to the employees like health care facilities, housing, medical care, and pensions were always defended in the name of the social welfare system, and funds were made available for these requirements. To some extent, these practices were justifiable. However, the over-burden of expenses was enough to show the 'rational necessity' of restructuring as surplus expenditure could not be justified if profits were possible. Bringing down the subsidy rate was necessary. The over-concentration on the SOEs led to negligence of other aspects pertaining to society and the economy. Rural sector policies were treated as subordinate to the industrial systems concerned with urban areas. The urban area, which was closely related to the enterprises and state-owned industry, enjoyed more benefits than the interior and non-urban area. Subsidies for urban industry can also be seen as a massive transfer of resources from the countryside, where most of the population reside. This shift deprived the rural economy, especially the poorer interior provinces, of many economic growth benefits, even though agriculture powered much of its development.[21]

In China, agriculture was given little attention during the reform years as compared to its industrial sector. The surety of economic security often varied from village to town. Since the State was engaged in paying more attention to SOEs, its subsidies and social facilities to SOE employees, the job atmosphere, and economic security compelled a large section of the population to leave villages and agriculture and migrate to urban areas.

Corruption, one of the most inseparable and integral parts of the Chinese economy, was also the result of the centralised economy. The CPC's interest and nepotism created by high-ranking party members in the industries changed the social face of the state enterprises. The PLA was also one of the front runners to seize the opportunity. The State proposed a-political body with its links established through various management of SOEs. The monopolisation of SOEs by the CPC and the PLA gave birth to redtapism and corruption in the recent past, and this phenomenon continues unabated. To give one example, about 400 PLA pharmaceutical companies produce 10 per cent of China's drugs, and the army's factories make about 20 per cent of its cars, trucks, and half of its motorcycles.[22] The involvement of these influencing bodies in some enterprises made it compulsory for the State to provide funds and infrastructure facilities to firms without consideration, which was also one reason behind the collapse of China's financial system.

The SOEs lacked credible strategies with regard to managerial aspects and technology, the two critical variables responsible for China's success story. To begin with, organisational activities were not efficient and authorised to adopt such steps. Due to lack of freedom at the managerial level and constraints over importing new technology, SOEs were transformed into technically functioning industrial units. Since the State outlined the boundaries of executive functions, enterprises could not develop new ideas. Those running the enterprise never felt possessive and responsible for their functioning. Even in the Maoist era, as discussed earlier, introducing the Chinese version of the Japanese style of democratic participation in enterprises had failed. According to this system, "workers were asked to 'raise rational suggestion' (*ti hei hua jianyi*)",[23] yet these Chinese practices became formalistic rituals and never achieved the intended results. The value of workers and their hidden entrepreneurial qualities were never recognised. This was the prime reason that made the managerial activities passive and affected the performance of enterprises while turning them into loss-making enterprises. Moreover, the authoritarian control of the enterprises crushed the innovative mindset of the workers.

The poor performance of the SOEs sent ripples throughout the Chinese economy, affecting every facet of the developmental processes. The interconnection of debts and losses among state enterprises also contributed to aggravating their worsening condition. Since the enterprises were allowed or made to lend to other SOEs, the chain of indebted enterprises grew in numbers creating a line of 'failed' enterprises. Even lending was not refused as it was necessary to keep the enterprises in working mode. Along with this, lack of cooperation and specialisation between enterprises[24] highlighted China's industrial and administrative structure. Property rights over the enterprises were distributed to different supervising administrative units that controlled these enterprises, beginning with decision-making and income rights to sharing the revenues generated by the enterprises. The sense of 'belonging' towards the enterprises created a favourable environment for the breeding of departmentalism, localism, and autarky[25] and which in turn signified dysfunctional behaviour on the part of the administrative units that aimed at maximising their group interests at the expense of social interests. Autarky resulted from a variety of factors that included departmentalism or localism in combination and also from the weakness of Chinese central planning, which was under constant attack by Maoist ideologues. Autarky resulted in duplicate investment and production,[26] where most of the factories produced commodities for their administrative units.[27] This resulted in a gap between the reality that existed on the ground and that reflected through data.

For these reasons, it is apt to say that the SOEs have been the epicentre of all the economic tremors that the Chinese economy has faced in the past. The rebuilding of the economy was necessary by taking appropriate steps to avoid other malpractices, which would creep into other sectors of the economy.

Restructuring of the SOEs

Restructuring of the SOEs was the only way to tackle this hydra-headed problem. China's opening provided an option without any delay, along with the emergence of reformist or revisionist ideas. The emergence of Deng at the centre of this reformist enterprise only accelerated this transformation. The impetus for enterprise reforms was derived from a combination of problems in the economy, an open intellectual atmosphere that prevailed in the wake of the campaign for 'practice as the sole criterion of truth,'[28] and competition for political power.[29]

The tug of war and skirmishes between the radicals (Status Quoists) and reformists fostered the restructuring of the economy and the SOEs. By accepting reorganisation, the State aimed to increase the efficiency and performance of the SOEs to face challenges. The restructuring state had various options. It gradually withdrew and relaxed control, thus revitalising SOEs through reorganisation, association, merger, leasing, contract operation, joint-stock partnership, and outright sale. The decision to open the economy and other economic restructuring was not decided abruptly. The evolution of the idea of a holistic restructuring is essential to analyse the performance and reform measures of the SOEs.

In 1975, Zhao Ziyang, a reformist, was appointed as the party's first secretary to Sichuan province.[30] He took a personal interest in the research activities of the Sichuan Academy of Social Sciences. In 1977, with Hua Guofeng, Zhao went to Eastern Europe and was impressed by Yugoslavia's experiment with self-managing enterprises. This left a profound impact on Zhao's thinking, and he decided to implement these policies in Sichuan as an innovation to the existing situation.[31] These experiments got underway in the fourth quarter of 1978 when the Sichuan provincial government granted authority to six enterprises. At the time, the experiments were quite limited, while profit targets were fixed, and the factories were allowed to keep a certain amount of their profits above their quotas.[32] The results of these early experiments in the enterprises proved helpful for leadership to get critical feedback.

During the same period in China, the discussion about enterprise restructuring was taking place at the political level, and the need for a restructuring process was felt necessary. The Wuxi Conference and the role played by Yu Qiuli, Hu Xiaomu, and Xue Muqiao proved significant in deciding the enterprise reforms, which had focused on the restructuring process.

The 'Petroleum Group' (PG), guided by Yu Qiuli, was a powerful economic and political category in pre-1978 China. It was composed of officials who had made their careers and rose to the top of the Chinese political system by developing China's petroleum industry, particularly the Daqing oil field.[33] During the 1960s, when intensive efforts to explore new oil fields began, the then Minister of Petroleum, Yu Qiuli, had moved to Daqing, where he initiated efforts of direct development of its oil fields. In 1964, Mao invited Yu Qiuli and his associates to draw up plans for faster growth in China's interior or the so-called "third front".[34] But the plans drawn by Yu could not be implemented.[35] After the rise of Deng in 1978, the PG again came to the forefront. Policies like import of foreign technology and equipment were given attention along with the suggestions made by Chen Yun,[36] like the expansion of market forces in the economy, greater autonomy for enterprises, and the restoration of 'balance' in the economy through a policy of 'readjustment.'

The genealogy of enterprise reforms can be traced back to Hu Qiaomu's now well-known report to the State Council in July 1978, entitled *'Act in Accordance with Economic Lens',* and which stepped up four modernisations. The report functioned as a 'catalyst' to generate debates across the country. These discussions and talks concentrated on issues related to reform, particularly to the "Law of Value".[37] As Stuart Schram writes, "Although the communique of the fourth meeting of the Politburo placed stability and reform in that order, as had Li Peng, it also decided that the law of value was the key to solving the major problem of inflation".[38] These meetings culminated in the Wuxi Conference, held in April 1979, where the State Planning Commission's Economic Research Office, the State Statistical Bureau, and the Chinese Academy of Social Sciences (CASS) attacked the planning system as it had existed in China over the past three decades. The crux of their critique was that excessive concentration of authority in the party shifted constantly, stifling the initiative of enterprises. This resulted in enterprises producing for the plan, not for market needs, whereby unwanted products piled up in warehouses while much-needed goods were out of the production loop.[39] The Wuxi Conference emphasised a blend of both plan and market whilst concentrating on enterprise reforms.

The systematic criticism of the orthodox Marxist economy was the main feature of the Wuxi Conference. During the same period, Xue Muqiao's[40] work *Studies on China's Socialist Economy* caught Deng's attention and underpinned his reformist ideas. The book was an effort to articulate a theory of socialist economics most systematically and authoritatively.[41] Xue condemned the Cultural Revolution period because it undermined the plans and the economy, which were anarchic, according to him. Xue argued in favour of increasing both planned management and the decision-making authority of localities and enterprises.[42]

These developments regarding the restructuring of the economy paved the way for the commencement of the reform era. The main thrust of these reforms was to stress the importance of redefining state-enterprise relations and provide autonomy to them. The Wuxi Conference and Xue Muqiao's research marked significant efforts at a systematic conceptualisation of the errors and wrongdoings of China's economic management system and the direction of the reform program. In this sense, they can be taken as the political-intellectual baseline from which economic reform proceeded.[43] Meanwhile, the restructuring process progressed in stages.

The Stages of SOE Restructuring

The efforts to restructure the SOEs that began in 1978 took place in a phased manner. These phases were not planned and demarcated, but to study and critically analyse their functionality, reorientation and their complex phenomena, it is necessary to divide them into different periods as given below:

The First Stage (1978-1983)

The increasing costs of industrial growth prompted the Chinese government to decentralise China's state industrial system in the late 1970s. The decision to decentralise was initiated at the third plenary session of the 11th Central Committee of the CPC held in late 1978. This initial stage focused on increasing the operational autonomy accorded to enterprise managers, mainly by allowing them increased authority over allocating their profits.[44] The experiments were conducted in Sichuan province, where six enterprises were chosen for this purpose and in 1979, it was extended to the entire country. During the experiment, the behaviour of the authorities and the functioning of the enterprise were closely scrutinised against the results observed during the experiments in Sichuan. The State Council accelerated the pace of issuing more decrees, thus widening the independent managerial authority of SOEs.[45] The gist of the policies can be summarised as follows:

1. Greater decision-making autonomy for enterprises in production and to a lesser extent in investment.
2. The reinstitution of financial incentives for enterprises and individuals.
3. Expansion of the role of the market in the allocation of industrial goods and corresponding reductions on the part of the planning and administrative allocation,
4. Enterprises were allowed to retain profits at a fixed proportion of total profits determined by the Ministry of Finance and Local Finance Bureau.
5. Enterprises, after fulfilling their production quotas, were allowed to produce extra-plan products.
6. Enterprises were required to pay a charge on their fixed assets, and
7. Working capital was financed by bank loans rather than by grants from the Ministry of Finance and Local Finance Bureaux.

Prior to 1979, such enterprises operated as part of a planned and highly centralised Soviet-style system, which had been introduced in China during the Fifties, the heyday of Sino-Soviet friendship. For example, a factory producing drive shafts in Liaoning province, for instance, would be allotted a certain amount of raw material and told to produce a certain number of units by the appropriate Ministry in Beijing. Any profit had to be remitted to the Central government. It was then up to the Ministry to determine how much of that profit should be returned to the drive-shaft plant, in the form of subsidies for repairs, retooling, or expansion. Factory managers were essentially cogs in a machine controlled from above; workers were goaded by moral exhortations and political pressure rather than material incentives. But following the decisions of the Third Plenum, at the end of 1978, this system began to change radically. Centralised control was relaxed and state enterprises all across China were thrown back on their resources, thus becoming more like privately owned factories in a capitalist economy. Under the new *zeren zhi* (责任制), or "responsibility system", the Liaoning drive-shaft factory was responsible for finding its raw materials, setting its production targets, and hiring and firing its labour force instead of having to accept workers assigned by state labour bureaus. It no longer remitted its profits to a Ministry but retained them after paying taxes and made its own decisions about how those profits were reinvested or spent. It also became responsible for its losses. For the first time in decades, a factory worker had the opportunity for advancement, like his/her counterpart in the private entrepreneurial world. If he/she worked overtime, he/she received extra compensation and received a bonus if the factory did well; he/she was also made to feel more custodial towards his/her job, because if the factory was unprofitable—say, through the laziness of its workforce or the incompetence of its managers—the government was no longer obligated to rescue it from bankruptcy with subsidies.

By the end of the first half of 1980, over 6,000 enterprises accounting for 60 per cent of the gross output value and 70 per cent of the profits of China's key industrial enterprises',[46] comprising 15 per cent of China's 42,000 industrial enterprises, followed the above instructions. The firms were allowed to opt for their choices in the decentralised, semi-market transactions, while earlier enterprises had to work according to the number of product groups' index and the number and detail of obligatory targets. Measured in terms of the first index, Chinese state industrial enterprises gained increased discretion in output decisions as both the number of products and shares of their industrial output reduced substantially. The former fell from 120 in 1979 to 60 in 1987, while the latter declined from 40 per cent in 1984 to 17 per cent in 1987.[47] Earlier, funds allocation to the enterprises was linked to fulfilling some requirements, such as output, quality, variety, and profit, together with the delivery contract. The culmination of these requisites used to affect how an enterprise could subtract money for enterprise funds.[48] But after the commencement of reforms, the enterprise fund system was replaced by the 'profit retention scheme', thus reducing the number of earlier plan targets. The price reform during the first five years was significant. At this stage, reform measures centred on improvements in cost calculations and adjustment of controlled prices. The objective of the reform was to make steady prices reflect the actual costs of production.

The industrial hierarchy was rearranged to cut administrative costs and accommodate the economy's growing liberalisation and marketisation. Reforms were flattening the industrial hierarchy, eliminating intermediate administrative units, namely, the industrial ministries or bureaus and the central departments. An idea of placing enterprises directly under the administration of a single body, namely, the Economic Commission, was accepted, which was supposed to replace the old four-level hierarchy (Economic Planning Commission, ministries, departments, and enterprises). The simplification was carried out through the following ways:

1. The reduction of the number of units at the bottom of the industrial hierarchy
2. The formation of branch associations
3. The removal of the number of levels in the order and
4. The transfer of supervision from the top government economic organs to the branch administration.[49]

The reforms, which took place in the late 1970s, and early 1980s, were prepared and implemented at a macro-level. With more experience, conscious planning headed by micro-level reforms was introduced in the next stage.

The Second Stage, 1984-1989

In the past, the economic package generated a need for specific reforms and included two significant reforms, namely, 'Price Reform' and 'Contract Responsibility System (CRS)'. Price reforms were needed so that market prices would reflect scarcity values in the economy. In contrast, labour reforms were required to determine wages, bonuses, and labour allocation and provide credible incentives to workers. Under price reforms, the focus was on price decontrol. In the industrial producer goods sector, price reforms featured in the dual price system under which two sets of the processes—fixed and uncontrolled market prices—co-existed for the same product. In 1984, the State Council allowed enterprises to enter the market with their own surplus output over and above the mandatory quotas at prices within the 20 per cent limit fixed by the State. Later in 1985, the limit of 20 per cent was removed, and since then, most industrial producer goods were sold without being influenced by dual pricing.[50]

Dual pricing divided supplies of industrial products into plans and market components. Under the dual pricing regime, most state enterprises transacted marginal sales and purchases, and markets prices responded increasingly to the forces of supply and demand.[51] The contract system's objective was to increase productivity within the framework of continued state ownership by further separating the State's ownership of assets from the management of the enterprises. The contracts were made mainly between state and various (state as well as collective) enterprises, and the duration of the contracts varied between three and five years. The arrangements were finalised after consultations and fixing the amount payable to the State. During the contract period, the State promised that the enterprises could retain any profit over and above the obligatory delivery,[52] and the enterprises would guarantee three things to the State, namely:

1. Obligatory delivery of a certain amount of profit;
2. Completion of the planned tasks of the technical renovation of the enterprise and
3. Link-up of the wage bill with that of its efficiency indicators.

During this period, smaller State and urban collective enterprises instituted more radical measures. Small firms were sold outright to individuals, others to their workers or a group of employees. Another practice, like 'leasing', became widely accepted, according to which the lessee paid a fee to the government and was allowed to keep most of the financial proceeds from improved performance during the lease period. The government attempted to reduce the burden by bringing specific structural changes to the SOEs. Pensions of state enterprise employees, which had been paid directly by their employers, were pooled at the municipal level. Efforts to reduce the responsibility of enterprise for the heavily subsidised housing system also got underway slowly.[53]

The survey of SOEs, covering the period from 1980 to 1989, shows that the share of material inputs purchased through the market rose from 32 to 59 per cent. In another research by Zou and Wang, the number rose from 12 to 66 per cent. In the case of the share of output sold on the market, the number shown is 49 to 60 per cent and 13 to 66 per cent, respectively (with reference to the survey)[54] besides a consistent reform package compared to the first stage of reform. During these years, the reform package was compatible with progressive follow-up plans of opening, which further enhanced the role of the market.

After the second round of reforms, the autonomy of the SOEs increased significantly. The year 1989 witnessed the Tiananmen Square incident; the waged reforms were cautious at a policy level and ground level after the experience. Despite the widening circle of the autonomy of enterprises, the growing losses of the state factories had posed a challenge and an area of prime concern in forthcoming reforms.

The Third Stage, 1991-2000

The 1990s witnessed unprecedented changes within the SOEs. The new round of restructuring started taking shape immediately after the CPC's Central Committee meeting on 23 September 1991. The Central Work Conference's main agenda was to investigate how to improve state-owned large and medium-sized enterprises. During his speech at the meeting, Premier Li Peng directly held large and medium-sized state-run enterprises responsible for the economy's breakdown and problems. According to him, "the downturn in economic efficiency has not been reversed. The profits of enterprises have been declining, while stockpiles of finished products keep on growing. Debt defaults remain unsolved as no sooner has one debt default been settled than another one is incurred".[55] Second, rising deficits, and third, "some significant economic relations have yet to be straightened out. The more prominent ones are the irrational economic structure and the heavy tilt towards individuals distributing national income. Both the share of state revenue in the national income and the proportion of state revenue at the disposal of the Central authorities are too low".[56] On the eve of the 1991 restructuring process, the loss of the SOEs had reached a record high since the reform process began in China, which provoked a drastic change in the economy's restructuring. In 1979, the total loss of SOEs was 3.638 billion yuan (US$ 2.27 billion), which reached 8.192 billion yuan (US$ 2.202 billion) in 1988, after which the figure doubled every year. For example, in 1990, losses were recorded at 18.019 billion yuan (US$ 3.35 billion) and 34.880 billion yuan (US$ 6.49 billion) in 1991 (see Table 4.1).

Table 4.1: Increasing Losses of SOEs

Year	*Loss (billion yuan)*
1979	3.638
1980	3.430
1981	4.596
1982	4.757
1983	3.211
1984	2.661
1985	3.244
1986	5.449
1987	6.104
1988	8.192
1989	18.019
1990	34.880
1991	36.700

Source: Statistic Year Book of China's Industry Economy, 1994, p. 56.

The contradictions in the economic management system and economic operations made the leadership conscious. Fresh restructuring measures were based on the following issues:

1. The macroeconomic structure was irrational
2. Prices had not been rationalised
3. Neither the egalitarian practice of sharing food from the same big pot nor the iron rice bowl changed fundamentally
4. The increase in workers and the income of staff members was higher than the production growth rate, and distribution favours individuals
5. Enterprise management did not have sufficient awareness of the commodity economy and market mechanisms
6. SOEs had a heavier tax burden and social burden than the other enterprises
7. An impact of a weak market.[57]

Amidst rising chaos, Premier Li Peng concluded that to enhance the vigour of enterprises and raise their economic efficiency, China should rely on efforts to deepen reforms, improve management, carry out technological transformation and make enterprises gradually turn into socialist commodity producers and dealers who assume sole responsibility for their profits and losses and could transform, develop and restrain themselves.[58] Based on these suggestions, the State Council prepared a list of measures to be implemented. During the Third Plenum of the 14th Congress of the CPC, 1993, leaders vowed to create a modern enterprise system that approved the following measures:

1. Allocating more funds for technical transformation;
2. Reducing mandatory plan quotas for selected enterprises;
3. Increasing depreciation rates for selected enterprises;
4. Increasing funds for product development;
5. Providing additional working capital for certain enterprises;
6. Appropriately lowering interest rates;
7. Granting external trading rights to some enterprises;
8. Implementing a policy of double-guarantee for 234 key enterprises;
9. Clearing inter-enterprise debt;
10. Establishing 100-enterprise groups;

11. Reducing the burdens of enterprises by eliminating ad-hoc levies and charges from local authorities, and
12. Reducing the income tax rate of enterprises from 55 per cent to 33 per cent.[59]

Along with these reforms, 'Corporatisation' also began, which was the most significant among other reforms introduced during this period. Renowned economist You Ji called this effort *de-statisation.*[60] The *de-statisation* here means the withdrawal of the State from all levels. The *de-statisation* was seen as necessary to revitalise the state industry through the nourishment of private industries. Corporatisation in state factories was a further step towards transforming the state ownership system. This was the reversal of the nationalisation movement in China in the 1950s, which eliminated private concerns. Corporatisation was the necessary gateway for privatisation; a Chinese strategy for ownership reform antithetical to the Soviet Shock approach prescribed to the former Soviet bloc, where the political authorities issued public decrees for privatising state factories.[61] This included both stock reform and share reform, whereby stock reform was supposed to create corporations of four major types. This included:

1. Corporate Stock Companies of limited liability,
2. 'Internal shares,' companies issuing non-transferable shares to staff,
3. Joint Stock Companies that can issue public offerings but cannot trade shares on the stock exchanges; and
4. Joint Stock Companies, which can trade shares on the stock exchanges.

Along with this, the State Commission for the Restructuring of the Economic System (SCRES) established four categories of shares: state shares, corporate, private and foreign shares. In 1993, SCRES prepared a comprehensive program for Corporatisation reform,[62] which practically dealt with the means of conversion and prescribed a timeframe for the same. The program contained fourteen mechanisms for the conversion,

1. A new firm created by multiple investors may be made a limited liability company (LLC), and each investor may hold stock certificates to express his or her limited liabilities,
2. Existing joint ventures may be converted to LLCs,
3. A joint stock company (JSC) may be established through promotion,

4. A factory may be converted into a joint limited stock company (JLSC) through specific offerings, with its existing stock capital turned into share subscriptions,
5. A factory may be converted into JLSC through specific offerings, with its current stock turned into share subscription,
6. A factory may be converted into a limited JSC through private placement, with its stock capital turned into share subscriptions,
7. Several factories may merge to form an LLC. With the assets of each party evaluated, determine the allocation of investment certificates,
8. A factory may establish a JSC in its subsidiaries through specific or public offerings,
9. Several factories may merge to form a JSC with their fixed assets, patents, and marketing networks, etc., serving as shares,
10. A factory may be converted into LLC with the rights of its creditors as share subscriptions, while its fixed assets were transformed into shares,
11. A factory may be converted into LLC with investment from various philanthropic foundations or insurance firms turned into stockholdings, while its fixed assets were transformed into shares,
12. A factory may be converted into an LLC by absorbing foreign capital,
13. A factory may be converted into an LLC by absorbing capital from the domestic non-state sectors,
14. A factory may be converted into JSC by issuing 'B-shares abroad.'[63]

As a result of these recommendations, a number of measures were taken to implement the programme. Some of the essential steps were:

1. A large number of enterprise groups were formed and granted full property management responsibilities. The ambiguity in the state-enterprise property relationship was to end. Under the 1994 Regulation on Supervision of Property of State-Owned Enterprises, these assets are managed by "organisations specialising in the control of state-owned assets".[64]
2. Under Company Law, SOEs either transformed into a limited liability company, possibly wholly state-owned, or a majority state-owned joint-stock limited company.
3. Laws and regulations regarding Corporatisation reform were

promulgated to regularise the conversion process. The most significant was the Corporation Law promulgated in 1993 as "Company Law of the People's Republic of China 1993".[65]

4. The inability of SOEs to provide an investment outlet for Chinese citizens had to be quickly addressed too, and a few other investment outlets such as Stock Exchanges have to be brought under the ambit of SOE reforms. The improvement of the existing two stock exchanges in Shenzhen and Shanghai were given priority to accelerate the shares reform. This improvement was both technological and institutional, with the establishment of legal and administrative surveillance. The trading was utterly popular and caused riots, and the reforms were a quite serious matter for the State leaders.[66]
5. With the SOE profit rate (returns on fixed assets, or ROFA) declining from 18 per cent in 1985 to below 6 per cent in the early 1990s,[67] in 1993 the State Council launched a national project to re-evaluate all state-owned fixed assets.
6. Since 1 July 1993, the state sector started implementing a new accounting system designed according to international practices as it was essential for a transition from a state plan and control oriented system to a capital market oriented system.[68]
7. China also ensured that to maintain the right pace of SOE reforms and the aligned institutional reforms, instituting intermediate organisations such as accounting and law firms and independent investment bodies were developed.

Table 4.2: Number of Industrial Enterprises

Year	*1995*	*1996*	*1997*	*1998*	*1999*
Number of Industrial Enterprises (10000 units) of the Total	734.15	798.65	792.29	797.46	792.99
State-owned Enterprises (including enterprises with controlling shareholding by the State)	11.80	12.76	11.00	6.47	6.13
Collective-owned Enterprises	147.50	159.18	177.23	179.78	165.92
Individually-owned Enterprises	568.82	621.07	597.47	603.38	612.68
Enterprises of other Types of Ownership	6.03	7.02	7.73	8.57	9.18
Share-holding Corporations	0.59	0.83	1.31	1.14	1.42
Enterprises Funded by Foreigners	5.40	4.43	4.38	6.25	6.23

Source: http://www.allchinadata.com/english/industrial%20economy/table1.htm

Table 4.2 shows that between 1995 and 1999, the numbers of SOEs were substantially reduced. At the same time, share-holding, foreign-funded, individual, and collective enterprises rose significantly, highlighting the intensity of the privatisation measures.

This new round of reforms could not reduce the deficits and social security burdens of the SOEs which ended with the least successful reforms. The number of loss-making enterprises increased along with unemployment, and numbers had a different story to tell. It was estimated that the total fiscal and monetary subsidies to industrial SOEs grew from 6.3 billion yuan (1.4 per cent of gross national product, or GNP) in 1980 to 268 billion yuan (10 per cent of GNP) in 1992.[69] By the end of 1997, of the 16,784 large and medium-sized SOEs, 6,599 reported negative earnings, with losses of 66.6 billion yuan (US$ 802 million).[70] The total assets of the SOEs also rose substantially. The value of fixed assets of industrial SOEs as a whole steadily increased between 1995 and 1999. In 1995, the fixed assets of industrial SOEs totalled 2,541 billion yuan (US$ 306.14 billion) and reached 4,354 billion yuan (US$ 524.57 billion) in 1999 [1996: 2,832 billion yuan (US$ 341.20 billion); 1997: 3,141 billion yuan (US$ 378.43 billion); 1998: 3,873 billion yuan (US$ 466.62 billion)].[71] The debt also grew from 5.8 trillion yuan (US$ 698 billion) to 6.7 trillion yuan (US$ 805 billion) in the respective years, yielding a higher debt-equity ratio of 60.79 per cent. The *China Statistical Year Book* in 1996 stated that in 1995, among 87,905 industrial SOEs, the debt-equity ratio for large SOEs was 62.3 per cent, for medium SOEs it was 71.6 per cent and for small SOEs it was 71.5 per cent.[72] The *China Statistical Year Book* (1995 and 1998) gives further details about real financial profits and losses for SOEs between 1978 and 1998.

New Phase, since 1998

In the 'Year of the Tiger', Chinese officials were determined to intensify enterprise reforms. The main thrust was on cracking down on loss-making enterprises. The effort was legitimised by the concept, 'building a modern enterprise system.'

The fourth session of the 15th Congress of the CPC made decisions on significant SOEs reform and development issues. It emphasised that China will try its best to realise the target and carry out overall arrangements for reform and development of the SOEs spanning the millennium and adopted a series of drastic policies and measures in this regard.[73] The decisions taken in the fourth session of the 15th Party Congress resulted from the errors neglected earlier during the third stage of the reform years. The targets of the 15th Party Congress for restructuring SOEs included: 1. Enabling the majority of loss-making medium-to-large-sized SOEs, escape from the current difficulties within three years. 2. Enabling the majority of large and medium-sized state-owned backbone enterprises to initially adopt a modern enterprise system by restructuring, regrouping, carrying out renovations, and reinforcing management. While marching towards a more mature market and economic globalisation, it was challenging to keep a soft approach towards loss-making enterprises. A time came when hindrances posed by the SOEs had to be eliminated permanently, and a favourable domestic and international situation made the process inevitable. The focus of intensified restructuring included the following tasks:

1. Intensifying mergers and perfecting the mechanisms of the SOEs.[74] The environment of 'survival of the fittest' was accepted in the case of state enterprises. The enterprises that had no hope of getting out of their loss-making plight were to be eliminated.
2. Further regulate and perfect the enterprises that completed the reform to a corporate system. These enterprises were expected to establish a unique legal management structure and deepen the internal three-system reform covering labour, personnel, and distribution.[75] The need and effort to construct a Modern Enterprise system was strongly felt and articulated.
3. Speeding up implementation of transferring debt to equity shares.[76] The effort was constructive for enterprises as well as for banks. 'Equity Rights' was the safest way to prevent enterprises from the debt making habit.
4. It was said that further reorganising of the enterprises needed to be intensified. The large enterprises occupied by the central position, the policy *Zhua da fang Xiao* (*Grasping the big and releasing the small*) became the guiding line. The policy of 'walking out' was accepted. According to this policy, profit-making industries were allowed to move to developing countries.[77]
5. The Congress also stressed the need to speed up enterprise technical transformation.

The need for improvement in management operations—costs, capital, quality and security production, expenditures, and competitive capacity, was strongly felt.

The reforms were still on, and taking major steps like selling SOEs and laying-off workers were not appropriate given the ideological legacy of the Communist Party. On the other hand, the efforts proved successful in pushing China towards its newly defined development.

Methods of Restructuring

Regarding the methodology, China's state officials and political leaders applied a mixed methodology to reform the SOEs. These hybrid methods can be divided into three categories: decentralisation of management, restructuring of management and property rights, and privatisation.

1. Decentralisation of Management

This included an increase in managerial autonomy, followed by establishing the contract management responsibility system. It also meant simplifying administration, reducing taxes and mandatory planning, apart from practising the profit incentive system. The central theme of the enterprise reform policies between 1979 and 1993 was decentralisation from the government to enterprises under 'expanding enterprise autonomy' and 'increasing retained profits' to improve incentives. The SOEs received more authority over autonomy in production decisions and wage discretion. They were allowed increased control over wages and benefits, expansion in market activity, changes in investment patterns, and increased competition, which helped improve the productivity of firms. The so-called 'managerial benefits' are shown in Table 4.3:

This strategy was prompted in no small measure by the over-centralisation of authority in the past, the successful experience of the contracting system in agriculture; the slowness in the progress of fiscal, financial, and price reforms; and the political constraint on privatisation. Between 1985 and 1992, the restructuring category of decentralisation of management methods was introduced for all SOEs.

Table 4.3: Increased Autonomy of SOEs

Year	*Retention Rate*		*Autonomy in Production Decisions*	*Wage Discretion#*	*Management Responsibility System#*	*New Management Appointed after 1980#*
	Bases$	*Marginal@*				
1980	7	11	7	1	0	9
1981	19	12	8	1	0	9
1982	22	11	10	1	0	15
1983	30	14	14	2	1	25
1984	34	17	25	9	4	40
1985	37	17	35	9	4	40
1986	39	19	40	12	8	61
1987	38	23	53	20	42	75
1988	39	26	64	32	83	85
1989	39	27	67	35	88	94

@ Portion of profits that could be retained if profits exceeded the base level.
$ Portion of profits that could be retained if profits did not exceed a specified base level.
# Share of firms in the sample.

Notes: Based on a 1991 retrospective sample survey of SOEs by the Chinese Academy of Social Sciences (CASS).

Source: Xu Yi-Chong (1996)[78]

2. Restructuring of Management and Property Rights

The release of property rights was a significant step taken by the Chinese government to restructure the SOEs. The management sector also experienced restructuring. The Chinese government adopted the following measures: setting up of national enterprise groups by purchasing assets and stocks of subsidiaries; merging SOEs and operating cooperatives; leasing arrangements; spin-offs; and turning debt into shareholders' equity.

3. Privatisation

The third category of reform method was privatisation, and efforts to privatise were most common in small SOEs. The State Economic and Trade Commission (SETC) Report categorically recommended the privatisation of small SOEs.[79] SETC defended its argument that small state firms should be privatised to generate money to finance development in the priority sectors, a state social welfare system, and relocation of state staff.[80] This method, popularly known as *Zhua da Fang Xiao*, or "grasp the large and let go the small", represented the State's plan and came in different forms. It included outright sale or auction, bankruptcy, creation of public companies with listed stocks, mergers and acquisitions, formation of share-holding enterprises (companies limited by shares or companies with limited liability), shares of cooperation, and joint ventures. The reason for setting up joint ventures was to attract foreign capital. It was also hoped that setting up experimental joint-stock companies would raise funds to circumvent credit quota regulations imposed on banks. In all limited liability companies and most joint-stock companies, new funds were raised by private placement, often through closed subscriptions by employees and institutional investors.

To know the results of privatisation efforts, one can see the developments in Zhuchen county of Shandong province, the Chinese government's exemplar for privatisation efforts where reforms took place in 274 small SOEs. The local government carried out its complete overhaul between 1992 and 1995 by applying aggressive privatisation methods. Nine of these small SOEs became limited liability companies; 204 converted into a company limited by shares; 18 were auctioned off; 35 were leased out; mergers and acquisitions transformed five; the remaining three appeared in court for bankruptcy.[81] The effects of privatisation can be seen in Tables 4.3 and 4.4, which clearly shows the decrease in the number of state industries. With the growth of private enterprises, the share of SOEs was affected dramatically. In 1978, the output share of the SOEs (compared total industrial output) was 77.6 per cent. The periodical structural changes in the state industries, and increasing competition from the emerging non-state enterprises, based on quality and service, started occupying the market. After ten years, during the concluding years of the second stage reforms, the industrial output share of each sector was 56.8 per cent and 24.4 per cent, respectively. In the form of individually-owned, private industries had also occupied their share, which was 4.6 per cent. With the new phase of reforms in 1998, the three types of industries were 28.2 per cent, 35.3 per cent, and 18.1 percent, respectively. The structural reforms in the state enterprises adversely affected its performance in the market. This led to an increase in the number of impoverished enterprises, which later created various social problems.

In a way, this struggle for restructuring was a struggle for a 'decisive victory' for economic development. The reform process that started in 1978 seems to be an unending process of growth and emerging crisis. In the quest to achieve a development path, China faces monetary problems and societal issues. The prime concern of the Chinese government was towards the societal concerns of the reforms. The emergence of the economic interests in China was a prominent historical event of Deng's Second Revolution. Still, along with that, various other social problems soon cropped up in China.

Table 4.4: Performance of State-owned Enterprises during the Reform Period (share of the total value of Industrial Output, 1978-1999)

Year	*State-owned Enterprises*	*Collectively-owned Enterprises*	*Individual-owned Enterprises/Private*
1978	77.6	18.5	...
1980	75.1	19.8	0.0
1981	74.3	20.0	0.0
1982	73.3	20.3	0.1
1983	73.8	20.7	0.1
1984	67.6	23.6	0.2
1985	64.9	23.7	1.8
1986	62.3	23.9	2.9
1987	59.7	23.9	3.9
1988	56.8	24.4	4.6
1989	56.1	n.a.	n.a.
1990	54.6	35.7	5.4
1991	52.2	n.a.	n.a.
1992	48.4	38.0	6.8
1993	46.9	34.0	7.9
1994	37.3	37.7	10.0
1995	33.9	36.5	12.8
1996	28.7	39.5	15.4
1997	31.6	38.1	17.9
1998	28.2	38.4	17.1
1999	28.2	35.3	18.1

Note: "..." Negligible

Collective Enterprises includes Urban as well as Township enterprise

Sources: PRC National Bureau of Statistics, China Statistical Yearbook, China Data Centre, and Foreign Broadcast International Service (various issues).

Conclusion

SOE reform was cautious but alert and adopted the 'trial and error' approach to "cross the river by feeling the stones". The reform process was the product of the Central government's promotion of the integration of local practices.

In the first phase of SOE reforms, the interaction between productivity and production relations was essentially put at the centre. At the same time, the leadership focused on addressing the objective needs of building a socialist market economy. Traditional SOEs reformed their systems, mechanisms and management systems to adapt to the socialist market economy. The central link and core content established a modern enterprise system, enhancing the vitality of the SOEs and improving their economic benefit. China wanted to use the SOE reform to build formidable statecraft. Hence the reforms in SOEs—whether seen in terms of restructuring, layoffs or losing bureaucracy—were not causing tensions as much as the scheme of economic statecraft was concerned. Hence, for China's top leadership, SOE reform was not about profits or theoretical reasoning to promote privatisation. Moreover, SOE restrictions were not to invite trouble, but, as explained at the outset, the aim was not to reduce State control over key sectors of the economy but to make that control more effective. Beyond effectiveness, the SOEs were forced to embrace technology, expertise, and discipline to help the government further strengthen its control.

NOTES

1. Adjustment was to achieve five main objectives. First, it would reverse the traditional order to priority given to heavy industry, light industry, and agriculture. Second, it would increase the share of consumption in national income. Third, it would reduce the consumption of energy. Fourth, it would increase exports, especially of manufactured goods. Fifth, it would emphasise plant modernisation and improved efficiency in existing enterprises rather than economic development through new capital construction
2. Manfred F. Romich. 1994. 'Decentralization and the Danwei System: Economic Reform and Its Impact on Social Development in Chinese Cities', *China Report,* Vol. 30, No. 4, October-December, 447-56.
3. *Danwei* constitutes the basic work unit of contemporary Chinese society.
4. Romich. 1994. 'Decentralization and the *Danwei* System'.
5. In the post-1949 period, the establishment of government control over SOEs was generalised under the rule of law. The phenomenon was so frequent that later it became less objectionable and widely acceptable. In spite of having an independent economic entity, it was overshadowed by government control and became part of that machinery.
6. Thomas G. Rawski. 1975. 'China's Industrial System', in U.S. Congress, Joint Economic Committee (ed.), *China: A Re-assessment of the Economy* (Washington D.C.: US Government Printing Office). Reproduced in Joseph C. H. Chai (ed.). 2000. *The Economic Development of Modern China* Vol. II: *Socialist Modernization, 1949-1978* (Cheltenham: Edward Elgar), 112-135.
7. Ibid.

8. Qimiao Fan and Peter Nolan (eds.). 1994. *China Economic Reforms: The Costs and Benefits of Incrementalism* (New York: Palgrave), 139.
9. Romich. 'Decentralization and the *Danwei* System', 447-456.
10. Ibid.
11. The term such as 'Cells of Society', 'Small societies within themselves', 'Enterprise-run Society' have been exclusively taken from the work done by Chien-Min Chao and Bruce J. Dickson (eds.). 2001. *Remaking the Chinese State: Strategies, Society, and Security* (London: Routledge), 221-238.
12. Satya J. Gabriel. 1998. 'Restructuring State-owned Enterprises in China', https://www.mtholyoke.edu/courses/sgabriel/soe.htm (accessed on 22 July 2020).
13. Joseph C. H. Chai. 1997. *China: Transition to a Market Economy* (New York: Oxford University Press), 34.
14. Ibid.
15. Liu Guoguang (ed.). 1981. *Theoretical Issues in National Economic System Reform* (Beijing: Chinese Academy of Social Sciences Press), 59. Quoted in Joseph C. H. Chai. 1997. *China: Transition to a Market Economy* (New York: Oxford University Press), 34.
16. Chai. *China: Transition to a Market Economy*, 34.
17. Deng Xiaoping. 1979b. 'Some Comments on Economic Work', in *Selected Works of Deng Xiaoping* Vol. II, 4 October, www.english.peoplesdaily.com.cn (accessed on 24 July 2020).
18. James Dorn. 2000. 'State-owned Enterprises continue to hinder Chinese growth' *Japan Times*. 21 September, https://www.cato.org/commentary/state-owned-enterprises-continue-hinder-chinese-growth (accessed on 24 July 2020).
19. Elizabeth C. Economy. 1999. 'Reforming China', *Survival*, Vol. 41, No. 3, Autumn, 21-42.
20. Because bank savings have been moving from high-growth sectors to low-growth sectors, which is unnecessarily affecting the mode of development.
21. Strategic Comments (Indian Institute for Strategic Studies). 1999. 'The End of China's Era of Growth' *The Hindu*. 9 March.
22. M. V. Rappai. 1999. The PLA (People's Liberation Army) sheds its business interests', *The Hindu* (Hyderabad). 10 February.
23. Barrett L. McCormick and Jonathan Unger (eds.). 1996. *China Under Socialism: In the Footsteps of Eastern Europe or East Asia* (New York: Routledge), 190.
24. Chai. *China: Transition to a Market Economy*, 35.
25. Ibid.
26. Ibid.
27. Liu Guoguang. *Theoretical Issues in National Economic System Reform*. Quoted in Chai. *China: Transition to a Market Economy*, 36.
28. After the end of the Cultural Revolution, many Chinese intellectuals who had fled, came back to the country. The establishment of the Chinese Academy of Social Sciences further fostered unprecedented openness.
29. Joseph Fewsmith. 1994. *Dilemmas of Reform in China: Political Conflict and Economic Debate* (New York: M.E. Sharpe), 57.
30. He became the Premier of the People's Republic of China from 1980 to 1987 and the General Secretary of the Chinese Communist Party from 1987 to 1989. Zhao Ziyang was the leading Dengist reformer in post-Mao China.

31. In 1975, when Sichuan province was facing agricultural difficulties, Zhao was reassigned there as a governor and party leader with full authority. In Sichuan, Zhao made his reputation as a daring innovator who disbanded Mao's Commune system. He personally visited the fields to inspire farmers to work for their own material betterment. His effort resulted in a miraculous increase in agricultural productivity. The prosperity of Sichuan's rural population earned Zhao a nationwide reputation.
32. Fewsmith. *Dilemmas of Reform in China,* 56.
33. Ibid., 57.
34. Kam Wing Chan, J. Vernon Henderson and Kai Yuan Tsui. 2008. 'Spatial Dimensions of Chinese Economic Development' in Loren Brandt and Thomas Rawski (eds.), *China's Great Economic Transformation* (Cambridge: Cambridge University Press), 819.
35. Since Yu Qiuli advocated the need to import foreign technology and equipment, he came under sharp criticism in the early part of the Cultural Revolution. Those reform policies were called 'three poisonous weeds' and were criticised for 'selling out' China's interests.
36. During the 1960s, the policies for the Third Five-Year Plan were drawn under the supervision of Chen Yun. But the plan was never pursued as Mao labelled it irrelevant.
37. Sung Yun-wing and Thomas M. H. Chan. 1987. 'China's Economic Reforms: The Debates in China', *The Australian Journal of Chinese Affairs,* No. 17, January, 29-51.
38. Stuart R. Schram. 1988. 'China after the 13th Congress', *The China Quarterly,* Vol. 114, June, 177-97.
39. Fewsmith. *Dilemmas of Reform in China,* 64-65.
40. Xue had been Vice Minister of the State Planning Commission and Head of the State Statistical Bureau in the 1950s. Later, following the arrest of the Gang of Four, he was appointed an advisor to the Economic Research Office (*Jianji yanjiu suo*) of the State Planning Commission.
41. Xue Muqiao. 2010. *Chinese Economists on Economic Reform - Collected Works of Xue Muqiao* (New York: Routledge).
42. Ibid.
43. Ibid.
44. Nicholas R. Lardy. 1998. *China's Unfinished Economic Revolution* (Washington D.C.: Brookings Institution), 22.
45. During this time, the regulations issued by the State Council were as follows: (a) 'Several Rules concerning the Expansion of Managerial and Marketing Autonomy in State-owned Industrial Enterprises'; (b) 'The Regulation on Profit Retention in State-owned Enterprises'; (c) 'The Provincial Regulation on a Fixed-assets Tax in State-owned Enterprises'; (d) 'The Regulation on the Increase in the Depreciation rate and Improvement in the Use of Depreciation Funds in State-owned Enterprises'; (e) 'The Provisional Regulation Concerning the Use of Bank Loans for the Total Amount of Working Capital in State-owned Enterprises'. See Qimiao and Nolan (eds.). *China Economic Reforms,* 154.
46. Robert Michael Field. 1983. 'Slow Growth of Labour Productivity in Chinese Industry, 1952-81', *The China Quarterly,* Vol. 96, December, 641-64.
47. Mengan Xie and Yuanmin Luo. 1990. *China's Economic Development During Last 40 Years* (Beijing: Chinese Academy of Social Sciences Press). Quoted in Joseph C. H. Chai. 1997. *China: Transition to a Market Economy* (New York: Oxford University Press), 53.
48. Chai. *China: Transition to a Market Economy,* 53.

49. Ibid., 36.
50. The gap between market and fixed prices for selected producer goods became quite large with the market price being higher than the fixed price. Later, efforts were made to correct the dysfunctional mechanism by imposing a ceiling on market prices, an upward adjustment of the state fixed prices (an upward adjustment was, under which the fixed prices of crude oil, coal, steel products, ferrous and non-ferrous metals, chemical industrial raw materials, plate glass and cotton textiles were adjusted upwards by 10 to 40 per cent) and an attempt was also made to eliminate the dual price system altogether by phasing out the fixed prices through decontrol of prices of most industrial producer goods). See Hu Bangding. 1989. *Zhongguo wujia nianjian 1989 (China Price Yearbook 1989)* (Beijing: China Price Publishing House), 144 and Hu Bangding. 1990. *Zhongguo wujia nianjian 1990 (China Price Yearbook 1989)* (Beijing: China Price Publishing House), 37. Quoted in Joseph C. H. Chai. 1997. *China: Transition to a Market Economy* (New York: Oxford University Press), 53.
51. Gary H. Jefferson and Thomas G. Rawski. 1994. 'Enterprise Reform in Chinese Industry', *Journal of Economic Perspectives*, Vol. 8, No. 2, 47-70.
52. Chai. 1997. *China: Transition to a Market Economy*, 76.
53. William A. Byrd. 1992. *Chinese Industrial Firms under Reform* (Washington D.C: Oxford University Press), p. 12.
54. Jefferson and Rawski. 'Enterprise Reform in Chinese Industry'.
55. Li Peng. 1991. 'The Current Economic Situation and the Issues of further Improving State-owned Large and Medium-sized Enterprises (CCP Committee Work Meeting, 23 September)', reproduced by *China Report,* Vol. 27, No. 4, April-June 2000, 329-348.
56. Ibid.
57. Ibid., 338.
58. Ibid.
59. Zhu Rongji. 2013. *Zhu Rongji on the Record: The Road to Reform 1991- 1997* (Washington D.C.: Brookings Institution Press).
60. You Ji. 1998. *China's Enterprise Reform: Changing State/Society Relations after Mao (Routledge Studies on China in Transition)* (London: Routledge), 166.
61. Ibid.
62. Fang Liufang. 1995. 'China's Corporatization Experiment', *Duke Journal of Comparative and International Law,* Vol.5, 149-269.
63. The shares other than the 'Voting shares' (Equity shares entitling holders to vote in the election of directors of a company).
64. Wu Zengxian. 1997. 'How Successful Has State-Owned Enterprise Reform Been in China?', *Europe-Asia Studies*, Vol. 49, No. 7, 1237-1262.
65. Ministry of Commerce of the People's Republic of China. 1993. 'Company Law of the People's Republic of China', 29 December, http://english.mofcom.gov.cn/article/lawsdata/chineselaw/200211/20021100053539.shtml (accessed on 26 July 2020).
66. Even prior to the opening of the Shanghai and Shenzhen Exchanges in 1990 and 1991, respectively, trading occurred on the street, and such trades continued immediately after the openings because few companies at the time were listed on the exchanges.
67. Ligang Song. 2018. 'State-Owned Enterprise Reform in China: Past, Present and Prospects', in Ross Garnaut, Ligang Song and Cai Fang (eds.),*China's 40 Years of Reform and Development: 1978–2018* (Acton ACT, Australia: ANU Press), 350.

68. Tang Qingliang and Amy Lau. 2000. 'Accounting Reforms in China: A Transition from a State Plan and Control oriented System to Capital Market oriented System', *Managerial Finance,* Vol. 26, No. 5, May, 80-98.
69. Huang Yiping. 1999. 'State-owned enterprise reform' in Ross Garnaut, Jane Golley and Ligang Song (eds.), *China: Twenty Years of Reform*, Canberra: Asia Pacific Press, 113.
70. Karen Lin, Xiaoyan Lu, Junsheng Zhang and Ying Zheng. 2020. 'State-owned Enterprises in China: A Review of 40 Years of Research and Practice', *China Journal of Accounting Research*, Vol. 13, 31-55.
71. Harry G. Broadman. 2001. 'The Business(es) of the Chinese State', *The World Economy*, Vol. 24, No. 7, July, 849-875.
72. Ji Wei. 1999. *The Great Tendency of the Chinese SOEs,* Unpublished Master's Thesis, Tung Hai University.
73. Sheng Huaren. 2001. 'Striving to Realize the Three-Year Target of State-owned Enterprises Reform and separation of losses', in Laurence J. Bhahm (ed.), *China's Century: The Awakening of the Next Economic Powerhouse.* Singapore: Wiley, 175-183.
74. Ibid., 180.
75. Ibid., 182-83.
76. Ibid., 181.
77. Ibid., 182.
78. Xu Yi-Chong. 1996. 'Deepening and Widening the Economic Reform in China: From Enterprise Reform to Macroeconomic Stability', *The Journal of Developing Areas,* Vol. 30, No. 3, 361-84, in World Bank. 1997c. *China 2020: Development Challenges in the New Century*. Washington D.C.: World Bank. Reproduced Singh, Surjit. 1998. 'Economic Reforms and State Enterprises in China', *China Report*, Vol. 34, No. 2, 199-212.
79. State Economic and Trade Commission (SETC). 'Creating a Modern Enterprise Mechanisms that suits the Market'. Quoted in You Ji. 1998. *China's Enterprise Reform: Changing State/Society Relations After Mao (Routledge Studies on China in Transition)*. London: Routledge, 163.
80. Ibid.
81. Economic Research Centre of Academic School of Chinese Communist Party. 1996. *Research of Reforming the Small SOEs*. Beijing: Economic Science Press.

5

Fixing China Inc.

China, which believes in superlatives, has witnessed SOEs turning into global titans that have met energy requirements, followed by the technology and services sector for a growing and new China. SOEs, after several rounds of reforms, are taking on global business and heterogeneous market needs. Domestically, despite reforms and restructuring, it was a herculean task to break a vicious loop of non-performance, corruption, and debt. The reforms, which were carried out in the 1990s, intended to break this loop and, at the same time, dent the political and bureaucratic might that the enterprises had created. The leadership had to deliver the reform promises without letting any of them turn ugly. SOEs were soon coming forward to turn the mega-scale projects into a reality. The Chinese state continued to make strategic changes in the SOEs, mainly merging them and asking assets management companies to take care of the non-performing assets (NPA).[1] The SOEs were reduced into strategically organised categories and brought under an umbrella formation called State-owned Assets Supervision and Administration Commission (SASAC), established in March 2003.

The restructuring, which resulted in mass layoffs and downsizing of the Chinese bureaucracy, was stringent for the whole nation as protests grew and demands for freedom of the press and democracy started finding more takers within the system. This was more threatening for the existence of the party. In this sense, the transitory period between 2000 and 2001 was precarious for the political setup. The SOE reforms triggered a new storm and presented the reality that the critical restructuring and closure of thousands of SOEs could not put a lid on controversial issues. SOEs were still settling down, and with the policy of further privatisation and letting the foreign direct investment (FDI) drive-in, the problems of the SOEs multiplied. As a result, the second phase of fine-tuning these reforms was introduced by the Chinese leaders at regular intervals. The SOEs continuing reform turned out to be a major strategic step for the Chinese government to implement the strengthening and expansion of the SOEs. The deepening of reforms aimed at maintaining and increasing the value of state-owned capital, besides improving the competitiveness of the state-owned economy and boosting the function of state-owned capital.

It is evident that China lacks market-supporting institutions, and often economic affairs are characterised by indiscriminating government interventions, however, it still tops the growth rate in the world. Chinese economy consistently relied on SOEs and restructured them. While the SOEs have been termed as a drag and liability on any economy and have low production efficiency in the world, they, however, have been realigned and restructured to play a strategic role in China.

The Global Quest of Chinese Enterprises

The reforms of the SOEs were so far internal and limited to adjusting policies to the whole range of industrial recycling. These reforms focused on 'decentralising powers and giving up profits' (1978-1986) and 'separating control from ownership' (1987-1992). In November 1993, the Third Plenary Session of the 14th Congress of the CPC debated the need to adjust the industrial layout and structure of the state-owned economy to promote more state-owned capital, concentrate on essential industries and critical areas of national security, and enhance the control of the state-owned economy as the lifeline of the national economy. The reforms launched early in 1990 were seen as vital for the launch of modern enterprises.[2] After the launch of modern enterprise reforms in 1993, the focus shifted to 'establish a modern enterprise system,' the first step to transform the enterprise dynamic. In September 1999, the Fourth Session of the 15th Congress of the CPC adopted several significant decisions concerning the reform and development of SOEs,[3] which further emphasised the need to strengthen the state-owned economy's control over the national economy. The session deliberated and sketched 'important industries and key areas' that were to be retained in the state-owned economy and kept out of restructuring. This included sensitive and important industries involving national security and those providing critical public products and services, pillar and high-tech industries as well as sectors that were naturally monopolised.

Moreover, the session also agreed to go ahead with the state-owned economy layout's strategic adjustment to combine optimisation and upgrading the industrial structure by adjusting and improving ownership structure. This was a significant shift, as China was openly gearing up for the WTO. Before the Fourth Session, Jiang Zemin and Bill Clinton had agreed to resume the WTO discussion at the Auckland APEC summit meeting.[4] After the Fourth Session was over, China and the USA announced a WTO pact where China agreed to open a wide range of markets, from agriculture to telecommunications. Within a year, in May 2000, the European Union (EU) signed a WTO accession pact with China.[5] By October 2000, Clinton succeeded in getting Congress approval to give China normal trade status with the USA,[6] thereby keeping pressure on the Chinese leadership.

In concurrence with the entry into the WTO, China enacted "grasp the big and let the small go" (抓大放小 *zhua da fang xiao*), the development of mixed ownership economy, and "going out" policy to forward the overall position of SOEs. The "going out" policy was aimed to turn Chinese enterprises into global players. To prepare for its accession to the WTO, China replaced its previous goal of reforming SOEs with a new one—building the world's first-class enterprises and groups to deal with the competition in the international market.

Against these new changes in the domestic and international environment, SOEs were now facing urgencies as soon as China embarked on the WTO bandwagon. It was feared that foreign competition would uproot farmers and upend rusty SOEs.[7] Post-WTO accession, China augmented vertical screening of SOEs, i.e., performance and relevance for each sector. The functions of SASAC as the central supervisory agency had a significant impact on the reform outcomes of the SOEs, where substantial reforms carried out by it focused on preserving and increasing their state-owned assets. Globalised and consolidated

SOEs were going global, internationalising their operations, getting bigger, and displacing their competitors. The transition of SOEs into the global Chinese Inc. was now a reality.

The Long March Ahead

The reform of SOEs was a gradual process and a costly affair for the leaders and the economy. For most Chinese people, it was a new and 'unseen' phenomenon where 'Blue-collar jobs' were still considered secure and well-respected. Despite stellar growth in the 1980s, ordinary Chinese would have never thought that social tensions would arise out of reforms and especially centred on SOEs. The performance of SOEs was never judged and evaluated publicly and hence the restructuring came as a shock for urban China. For leaders, it was difficult to follow the historical experiences of other countries as it had little chances to offer economic respite to the commune-led Chinese economy. China had to devise its own methods to deal with the menace of underperformance. In the 1990s, China's SOEs underwent historical changes in an enterprise system, which included industrial configuration, state-owned assets supervision, and corporate leadership. By 2000, the SOE reforms were still far from their final goals. For the Chinese state, the aftershocks of the restructuring, which were the party's *raison d 'être*, were severe—politically, socially, and economically. As the government established a strategy to invigorate the state-owned economy, SOEs experienced an unprecedented and violent industrial restructuring process during this period. They witnessed the rise of collective and private enterprises, and this process continued until the establishment of the SASAC in 2003.

The original management system of SOEs featured multilevel-management, which involved several levels of authority to manage people, businesses, assets, and different government departments that directly controlled the SOEs. Such a power structure made it difficult to distinguish between the enterprise's business responsibility and its responsibility towards the government's regulatory bodies and framework. In November 2002, the report of the 16th Congress of the CPC was directed to adjust the state-owned economy's layout and structure.[8] Besides, the directives were focused on carrying out reforms in the state-owned asset management system, which were pointed at the reforms in the economic system and the redistribution of power.

It involved the reforms of the political system and government institutions. So far, the difficulties and resistance faced by the establishment were noticeable, and sometimes the reforms were kept cryptic to benefit the vested interests in buying time and delaying reforms. As a result, some of the big and adamant enterprises carried out restructuring over ten years. Restructuring limited to mergers, closing small SOEs, managerial reforms, and layoffs were relatively doable compared to more drastic asset management reforms. The Central and local governments were expected to perform a stakeholder's role and not just limit investors and pass the responsibilities to SOEs alone. Being prime investors, the government agencies, be it central or local, were enterprise owners and were responsible for fulfilling obligations and not just extend them. The central and provincial, municipal, autonomous regions, and the Special Administrative Regions (SARs) were directed to establish special state-owned assets management agencies, which were combined with personnel and business management. Except for a small number of SOEs solely owned by the State, the local governments were now expected to promote the shareholding system, develop a mixed-ownership economy, implement standardised company system reforms, and improve the corporate governance structure. In March 2003, central and local state-owned assets supervision and management committees were established separately to unify the powers of managers, enterprise affairs, and assets.[9] After the 16th Congress of the CPC in 2002, the continuous deepening of constructing modern enterprise systems, changes in the management of state-owned assets, and capital market reforms heralded a new stage in China's SOE reforms.

The SASAC was established in April 2003, symbolising the systematic transition of SOEs towards a unified, independent and regulatory managed body. After the SASAC's establishment, it was clear that large SOEs under its jurisdiction were supposed to attract foreign capital and social funds, implement property rights diversification and raise funds through listings. In October 2003, the Third Plenary Session of the 16th Congress of the CPC proposed developing a mixed-ownership economy involving state-owned capital, collective capital, and non-public capital.[10] This was new to China as the SOEs were asked to pursue the diversification of investment entities and make the shareholding system a form of public ownership. In 2004, in the aftermath of these reforms, more than fifty per cent of large-scale backbone SOEs completed shareholding reforms. As per the National Development and Reform

Commission (NDRC) data in 2004, there were 2,903 large-scale state-owned backbone enterprises, which accounted for 66.9 per cent of the net assets of SOEs (including state-owned holding enterprises) while 1,464 were restructured into companies with multiple shareholders, with a restructuring coverage of 50.4 per cent.[11] This percentage further increased to 72 per cent in 2011.[12] By the beginning of 2012, more than 90 per cent of SOEs across the country had completed the corporate shareholding reform. Most of them had established shareholder meetings, boards of directors, managers, and boards of supervisors.

The establishment of the SASAC meant that an extra official stamp separated the functions of owners and managers of the SOE. The governments' role shifted from managing enterprises to capital management, focusing on implementing corporate property rights and operational autonomy. In specific operations, the forms of shareholding reforms were also diversified, allowing the sale of state-owned assets, introducing strategic investors, management buyouts (MBO), stock options, employee stock ownership, and listings. However, the imperfect operating system of corporate governance, investors' irregular performance and lack of adequate management supervision caused by the owners' absence led to a profound loss of state-owned assets in the reform process.

The establishment of a modern enterprise system and the fulfilment of the state-owned economy's strategic reorganisation required the capital market to provide substantial financial support and effective financial services. The capital market was crucial for the reform of SOEs. On the one hand, the opening up and deepening of reform, development of non-public economy, and the flow of international capital promoted by economic globalisation allowed the private sector to accumulate a large fortune. On the other hand, after loan allocation, the direct financing channels of the SOEs turned narrower, and the capital market emerged as an alternate financing platform for them. The capital market was also conducive to improving the SOEs' governance structure and establishing a modern enterprise system. However, the congenital disabilities of equity split in China's capital market severely restricted its development. The functions of investment, financing, pricing, and resource allocation gradually weakened, and they were soon overwhelmed with a marginalisation crisis. The reform of the congenital disabilities of the capital market hence became a priority area for reforms in the state-owned economy, of which the most important was the reform of non-tradable shares. In April 2005, the China Securities Regulatory Commission (CSRC) launched a pilot program for the reform of equity splitting.

By the end of 2006, with the completion of share-trading reforms, the capital market's function gradually returned and attracted a large amount of fixed private capital. The investment demand was expected to attract more high-quality assets and companies to enter the capital market to obtain wealth and realise capital appreciation. Therefore, after the share-trading reform's success, with the gradual improvement of the capital market system, the capital market was destined to entice high-quality assets across the country, providing a nationwide resource allocation platform for the reform of SOEs and large exchanges between enterprises. All these reforms and 'fixes' enabled stock mergers and acquisitions to have a positive impact on the state-owned economy's strategic structural adjustment, leading to non-public capital participation in the restructuring of SOEs, industrial integration, and the improvement and strengthening of listed companies. Moreover, state-owned capital market value and the market price could be moderately priced in the capital market. Stock prices proved to be the new indicators of performance evaluation, a market standard at par with global markets. So far, whether it is to assess the preservation and appreciation of state-owned assets or to transfer state-owned assets, the net assets were referred to as the critical reference index of efficiency. But this indicator did not reflect the real value of state-owned assets. Therefore, the capital market changes were termed conducive to the deepening of SOE reform, and new technocrats within the party could not delay it further.

In 2006, the State Council finalised the listing of enterprises into a crucial area.[13] After the Fourth Session of the 15th Congress of the CPC (September 1999), several decisions were taken to identify 'important industries and key areas' to continue controlling and dominating specific sectors. These sectors included high technology, non-renewable natural resources, public utilities and infrastructure services, as well as national security. Table 5.1 illustrates the lists of industries, along with their goals.

Table 5.1: The Industrial Dominance of SOEs
(based on the approved list issued by the State Council in 2006)

Industry group	*Industries included*	*Ownership Goal*
Strategic and key industries	Defence, power generation and distribution, oil and petro-chemicals, telecommunication, coal, civil aviation, shipping	Maintaining 100 per cent state ownership or absolute control; increasing state-owned assets in these industries
Basic and pillar industries	Machinery, automobiles, IT, construction, steel, base metals, chemicals, land surveying, research, and development	Absolute or conditional, relative controlling stake; enhancing the influence of state ownership even as the ownership share is reduced, wherever appropriate
Other industries	Trading, investment, medicine, construction materials, geological exploration	Maintaining necessary influence by controlling stakes in key companies, state ownership will be reduced in non-key companies.

Source: Extracted from Mattlin (2007: Table 1, p. 16), cited in Ross et al. (2018) p. 357.[14]

After 2008, the operation of SOEs was gradually integrated with the market and accepted the golden rule of *survival of the fittest*. With the improvement of business autonomy, SOEs could not just report losses and but had to aggressively bring losses under control. The reforms and measures announced at the 18th Congress of the CPC in 2012 were implemented broadly based upon experience and experiments carried out by the SASAC. The prime motive behind the reforms was to make SOEs more competent and additionally internationalise the industry. SOEs could not be mere workplaces taking work orders of the government and growing at an abysmal rate. But these gains were short-lived as increasing market competition, asset loss, ambiguous rights and responsibilities, and rising liabilities deterred the reform of the state-owned asset management system. Few SOEs, which had turned around losses into recovery, began suffering losses again. As a result, SOEs had to look at the structural reforms to reduce leverage, lower debt, and control operational risks.

Reforming the state-owned capital authorised operation system, reorganising state-owned capital investment companies, and establishing state-owned capital operating companies, further clarified the relationship between the government and the market. Since 2014, eight central enterprises, including State Development & Investment Corporation (SDIC) and China Oil and Foodstuffs Corporation (COFCO), successively carried out pilot projects for state-owned capital investment companies.[15] Further, two central enterprises, namely, Chengtong and Guoxin, launched pilot projects for state-owned capital operating companies.[16]

State-owned capital investment companies aim to serve the national strategy, optimise state-owned capital distribution, enhance industrial competitiveness, and promote industrial structure in significant areas and industries concerning national security and economy.[17] In continuation, in September 2015, the CPC Central Committee and the State Council issued a guideline to deepen Chinese SOE reforms as crucial to stimulating state-controlled industries and their struggling management to keep the balance sheet in order. After the reform and opening up, with the rapid development of private enterprises and entry of foreign-funded enterprises into the domestic market, China's SOEs started facing increasing market competition pressure.

In February 2016, the SASAC issued an implementation plan for the "Ten Pilot Reforms of State-owned Enterprises".[18] The reform pilots included exploring comprehensive listings for SOE groups, cooperation between multiple government social capital, and employee shareholding in mixed-ownership enterprises. In 2017, SOEs carried out mixed pilot reforms in power, oil, natural gas, civil aviation, telecommunications, and military industry. As of 2017, three SOEs, including China Unicom, Shanghai Bell, and Hualu Group, explored mixed reforms at the group level.[19] In 2017, the company's corporate restructuring was further accelerated when the corporate restructuring plan was unveiled at the central enterprise group level.[20] In short, the reforms aimed to improve various state-owned asset management systems, promote more investment of state-owned capital in essential industries and key areas related to national security and core areas of the national economy and ensure China's vital state-owned economy.

The performance index measures the impact of reforms carried out by State Council devices.[21] The award emphasises rewards for innovative enterprises and talent and, in a way, encourages enterprises to become leaders in breakthrough technologies. From 2000 to 2018, China awarded the State Natural Science Award to 636 projects, the State Technological Invention Award to 946 projects, and the State Scientific and Technological Progress Award to 4,246 projects. The awarded projects included high-temperature superconducting materials, a manned space program, Qinghai-Tibet Railway, supercomputers and hybrid rice.[22] In the case of SOEs, between 2000 and

2007, Central SOEs won 19 first prizes and 154-second position prizes for National Science and Technology Progress, accounting for 47.5 per cent and 27.1 per cent of the awards.[23] In 2017, in the National Science and Technology Awards tally, SOEs won awards beyond a normal count. Among the general projects awarded by central enterprises, there were more than ten technological invention awards and more than 40 technological progress awards given to SOEs.[24] SOEs received special attention for their research and inventions. The awards gave everyone the impression that it is done to foster competition, stay ahead and win prizes, and pride for political managers and other stakeholders.

While the SOEs continue to win awards, one must also note that Chinese SOEs have been displacing Western enterprises from the *Fortune 500* list of top enterprises. While SOEs claim prizes and bag higher capital infusion and permission to increase assets, what is the level of profitability of these SOEs compared to other global enterprises on the list? Compared with the world's top 500 companies, China's SOEs have relatively low profits.[25] In the list in 2017, the same year when the SOEs were ahead in bagging awards, the sales yield of SOEs and return on net assets were lower than the average level of the *Fortune 500*. In 2018, with average sales revenue of US$ 61 billion, a moderate net asset of US$ 35 billion, and an average profit of US$ 3.1 billion, the average sales yield of Chinese companies on the list and the average return on net assets were 5.1 per cent and 8.9 per cent, respectively.[26] In the same year, with an average sales revenue of US$ 70.5 billion, a moderate net asset of US$ 38.1 billion, and an average profit of US$ 5.2 billion, the US companies' (those in the *Fortune 500* list) average sales yield reached 7.4 per cent, and the average return on net assets gained 13.6 per cent.[27] The latest list in 2020 indicates that China's *Fortune 500*-listed companies averaged a return on assets (ROA) of 1.9 per cent, still just ahead of France (1.7 per cent), but once again substantially behind Switzerland (4.2 per cent) and the USA (4.9 per cent).[28] The difference is noticeable, and challenges for Chinese SOEs are ever growing.

The overall impact of 'grasp the big and let the small go' asset management was not to kill the importance of SOEs but to make them healthy (see Table 5.2). For instance, although the number of SOEs, as well as their assets, was declining, it does not mean that SOEs were less potent than before. There could be fewer small SOEs and more extensive and medium ones. It could also mean that SOE assets and capital were concentrated in particular sectors to apply absolute control over them. For example, in 2009, Shandong Iron and Steel Group, which was the largest company solely invested by the State within Shandong Province and also a massive loss-making SOE, swallowed up a promising profit-making private company, Rizhao Steel, by purchasing 67 per cent of its shares at a low price.[29] In 2008, Shandong Iron and Steel Group was formed by combing several steel SOEs in Shandong Province, including Laigang Group, Jigang Group, and their subsidiaries, which means a decline in the number of steel SOEs in Shandong Province, which means a decrease in their total number. But after taking over Rizhao Steel, Shandong Iron and Steel Group became the third largest steel enterprise in China, controlling the steel production in Shandong Province.[30] This case is, in fact, a sign of state advance and private retreat in mining and processing of ferrous metal ores. In terms of industrial output, one can certainly argue that decreasing proportions of SOEs did not match the assets or the investments, but that does not mean SOEs were losing their central standing. The low efficiency of SOEs and other entrenched problems were at the heart of these problems (Table 5.2).

For the manufacture of tobacco, the proportion of SOEs rose from 96.93 per cent in 2002 to 99.04 per cent in 2012,[31] indicating that their degree of monopoly was growing continuously during those ten years. As for the extraction of petroleum and natural gas, the trend of state advance and private retreat is also undeniable. From 2004, the proportion of SOEs began to rise from 95.37 per cent to 99.01 per cent in 2012,[32] even more than their balance in 2000, which was 98.53 per cent.[33] This means that after reforming SOEs for more than ten years, the degree of their monopoly was even higher than before. A similar phenomenon occurred in the production and supply of electric and thermal power where the State Grid Corporation of China (SGCC), the behemoth SOE, transmits and supplies nearly 90 per cent of electricity.[34]

As Table 5.2 below indicates, SOEs were getting particular focus internally when everyone thought that the rising number of private enterprises would affect them, which is reinforced by the indices. The liabilities of the SOEs increased at the rate equivalent to its assets. Additionally, the sales also increased by 5.6 times, and net income shot up 31.34 times. A closer look at the data set explains that the ratio of net income to total assets in 2016 stood nearly the same as in 1997 (2.70 and 2.30 per cent, respectively), which describes how SOEs amassed assets and remained the core business for the State Council. On the other hand, the ratio of net income to shareholder equity decelerated substantially from 12.10 per cent in 2007 to 4.80 per cent in 2016 and higher than the 1.70 per cent in 1997. On the sales front, the net income had increased by more than 4.58 times. These statistics demonstrate a significant improvement in SOE operational efficiency but not an up-to-the-mark performance.

Table 5.2: SOE Performance Amidst Restructuring (1997-2016)

Year	*No. of SOEs (Thousand)*	*Total Assets (Billion)*	*Total Liabilities (Billion)*	*Sales (Billion)*	*Net Income (Billion)*	*Lev* (%)*	*ROA (%)*	*ROE (%)*	*ROS (%)*
1997	262	12,497.5	7881.06	6813.20	79.12	67.10	2.30	1.70	1.20
1998	238	13,478.0	8440.93	6468.51	21.37	65.50	2.10	0.40	0.30
1999	217	14,528.8	9147.49	6913.66	114.58	65.40	2.70	2.10	1.70
2000	191	16,006.8	10,209.24	7508.19	283.38	66.00	3.30	4.90	3.80
2001	174	16,671.0	10,527.33	7635.55	281.12	65.00	3.30	4.60	3.70
2002	159	18,021.9	11,367.58	8532.60	378.63	64.80	3.60	5.70	4.40
2003	146	19,971.0	12,871.89	10,016.09	476.94	65.90	3.50	6.70	3.00
2004	136	21,560.2	13,883.91	12,072.20	736.88	65.70	4.50	9.60	6.10
2005	126	24,256.0	15,517.32	14,072.66	957.99	65.10	5.00	11.00	6.80
2006	117	27,730.8	17,929.37	16,239.03	1219.35	67.40	5.50	12.40	7.50
2007	112	34,706.8	20,247.25	19,483.53	1744.18	68.70	6.40	12.10	9.00
2008	110	41,621.9	25,000.84	22,939.79	1333.52	61.60	4.60	8.00	6.00
2009	111	51,413.7	31,541.69	24,301.54	1560.68	62.80	4.20	7.90	6.60
2010	113	64,021.4	40,604.32	31,499.39	2142.82	63.40	4.60	9.20	7.00
2011	135	75,908.2	48,609.08	38,634.14	2466.98	64.00	4.60	9.00	6.60
2012	147	89,489.0	57,513.54	42,535.65	2427.73	64.30	4.10	7.60	5.90
2013	156	104,094.7	67,097.46	47,112.51	2557.39	64.50	3.80	6.90	5.60
2014	160	118,471.5	76,595.59	48,909.91	2644.40	64.70	3.50	6.30	5.50
2015	167	140,683.2	92,441.72	45,735.20	2497.04	65.70	2.90	5.20	5.60
2016	173	154,914.2	101,521.49	47,439.16	2555.87	65.50	2.70	4.80	5.50

Note: This table presents the primary performance measures for SOEs and different ratios for the 1997–2016 period. The data comes from the Ministry of Finance of China.

*Lev is measured as the ratio of total liabilities to total assets;

ROA is the ratio of net income to total assets; ROE is the ratio of net income to shareholder equity; ROS is the ratio of net income to sales.

Source: Lin *et al.*, p. 34.[35]

Based on the decisions taken at the Third Plenum of the 18th Congress of the CPC (November 2013), the government identified SOE reforms as a central pillar of its reform efforts.[36] The structural reforms were imminent and urgent against the backdrop of falling growth numbers. The impact of the global financial crisis and the overall slowdown in the international market assured a prolonged spell of economic recovery for Chinese enterprises. This forced the new Chinese leaders, at the helm of power and authority, to accept the fact that growth would remain slow and that the SOEs needed to balance their debt load, assets, and net profits. In May 2014, President Xi, while describing China's subsequent economic growth stage, used the phrase 'new normal.'[37] In December 2014, the Central Economic Work Conference (CEWC) laid stress on promoting SOE reform. It emphasised dealing with problems, focus on enhancing enterprise vitality and improving efficiency, improving SOE core competitiveness, and establishing clear property rights, clear rights and responsibilities, separation of government and enterprises, and scientific management.[38] As the pace picked up to reform and streamline the scattered reform measures, President Xi introduced China to 'supply-side structural reform' to foster new growth engines, and the SOEs became the trusted agencies.[39]

After its first appearance in 2015, the supply-side structural reform (SSSR) evolved into a significant component of the Chinese government's economic policy framework. This suite of policies focuses on reducing distortions in the supply side of the economy and upgrading the industrial sector.[40] While the 'new normal' and 'supply-side structural reform' found ways in immeasurable policy statements and documents, the ultimate place was to include the same in the 13th Five-Year Plan (2016–20) (13th FYP). The 13th FYP further reiterated the urgencies.[41] The CEWC core objectives were put together in a series of guidelines and announcements throughout China's 13th FYP and several reform proposals (Table 5.3).

Table 5.3: Strategic Principles of Current SOE Reforms

Strategic Principles	*Measures*	*Recent Developments and Progress*
1. Classifying SOEs for respective reforms	– SOEs to be classified into commercial competitive, commercial strategic and social functions.	About 20 provinces identified SOEs into various categories for respective reforms. All central SOEs were to be incorporated by 2017.
2. Improving SOE efficiency		
• Mixed-ownership reform	– Encourage private capital participation	A pilot program initiated; about two-thirds of SOEs plan to diversify their equity base but few strategic industries.
	– Allow employee stock ownership	A pilot program initiated but without details.
• State asset management	– Focus on ownership rather than management	About 11 SOEs were chosen as pilot state capital management/operation companies.
• Professional management	– Link remuneration to management performance; salary cap; professional recruitment, and board of directors	Salary structure reviewed for 72 central SOEs, while pilot programs on corporate governance rolled out.
• Separate social functions	– Separate fringe benefits for employees (utilities and other public services) from SOEs	Social functions on utilities and real estate management fees to be separated from SOEs by 2018, while other public services will be gradually phased out.
3. Resolving overcapacity and meeting national strategies	– Eliminate excess capacity	Reduce coal and steel capacity by 10–15 per cent over 3–5 years [meeting 38–47 per cent of 2016 target as at the end of July). A restructuring fund established to minimise social costs.
	– Exit of non-viable "zombie" firms	About 345 central SOEs identified as zombies (about 7,000 at the local level) to be resolved in 2–3 years. However, the focus appears to be on mergers and consolidation of SOEs.
	– Prepare broad guiding principles on resolving over-indebtedness	Guidelines made available on the creditor committee and debt-equity swaps to advance debt restructuring.
	– Encourage strategic SOEs to "go global"	An SOE Adjustment Fund was established to facilitate the restructuring and facilitate investment.
4. Institutionalising the Communist Party's control of SOEs	– Prevent the loss of state assets	A pilot program initiated, but details not disclosed.

Source: Cited in Lam and Schipke (2017), p. 319.[42]

Besides, SASAC set up four special teams to look into the problems faced by state enterprises. This was also known as the 'four reform' pilot program or *Si xiang gaige* (四项改革).[43] The *first* focus was to restructure SOEs themselves and capital assets; *second*, to introduce mixed-ownership in SOEs on a pilot basis; *third*, to do a microanalysis of managerial boards, monitoring of senior management personnel, performance appraisal, and compensation model; and *lastly*, to establish discipline inspection groups in the pilot state enterprises.[44]

To carry out these reforms, SASAC listed six enterprises: the State Development Investment Corporation (SDIC), China National Cereals, Oils and Foodstuffs Corporation (COFCO), China Pharmaceutical Group Corporation (CPGC), China National Building Material Group Co. Ltd. (CNBM), China Energy Conservation and Environmental Protection Group companies (CECEP), and the Jihua Group Co.[45] These companies were further categorised as per the reforms intended to be introduced. COFCO and SDIC were listed as the State Capital Investment Corporation pilot units; CNBM and CPGC were nominated to undergo the mixed-ownership reform models; CECEP, CPGC, CNBM, and Jihua Group were identified as pilot units to undertake experiments with managerial and board level configuration. A few more enterprises are being considered from among the centrally-owned enterprises under SASAC for the pilot discipline inspection group.[46]

Among other SOE reforms, mixed ownership is gaining more attention due to access to capital and sectors owned and controlled by state enterprises. Chinese Premier Li Keqiang underlined SOE reforms as crucial and noted the importance of mixed-ownership reforms. The six significant enterprises chosen for the pilot program represented varied sectors. Additionally, with each of them having many subsidiaries, they are expected to create a wide impact area. For instance, COFCO has COFCO Biochemical, COFCO Property, and COFCO Tunhe as its mainland subsidiaries apart from other Hong Kong subsidiaries, in addition to its core expertise in industrial investment. SDIC also has a presence in power, coal, transportation, fertiliser, and infrastructure with interests even in resource industries, strategic and defence industries, and financial investments. The reforms underway are certainly aimed at creating momentum along the industry chain in China.

Major Roadblocks

The State Council of China seems to be determined not to let the dominance of SOEs wane. The list of strategic sectors controlled by the SOEs (refer to Table 5.1) has established a monopoly over several critical sectors in China, like energy, telecommunications, or the primary sector but the SOEs do not like competition. Moreover, even since the restrictions started, the State resolutely protected the SOEs and allowed them more room to outplay domestic and global competitors. Figure 5.1 highlights that State guarantees make benefit the borrowing of the SOEs as they earn consistent global ratings. Chinese SOEs use their State links to secure guarantees, claim higher credit ratings, and lay their hands over a swathe of cheaper and more massive loans. These trends highlight two pathologies. First, private firms struggle to get financing, while banks are willing to fund SOEs more, and secondly, the bank cheques offered to SOEs involve domestic investors, and foreign investors are shocked when some of these SOEs report losses. The State backup may not be a reality in times of crisis,[47] which indicates a vicious cycle of funding, done without or little due diligence. Chinese investors are not the only ones who fall prey to this kind of discrimination. South Korean brokerage firms[48] were exposed to chain losses after a unit of China Energy Reserve & Chemicals Group Co. (CERCG) failed to meet the US$ 350 million bond that matured,[49] which triggered cross-defaults[50] on other bonds, although Barclays, a British bank, was one of its underwriters.[51] The way SOEs continue to keep their monopoly is questionable.

Since the 1990s, China introduced market competition mechanisms in traditional monopolistic industries such as telecommunications, aviation, electric power, railways, banking, and insurance and encouraged private enterprises to lend additional support. The purpose of the reform was to improve the operational efficiency of SOEs in monopolistic industries and meet growing diversified needs. After 2000, against the backdrop of the Central government's strategy of 'grasping the big and letting go of the small' and implementing the goal of the SOEs to maintain and increase the asset value, many small SOEs were closed, and medium enterprises began to withdraw from competitive fields. These policy arrangements inflicted losses on state-owned assets. Moreover, the shrinking of competitive areas forced the SOEs to focus on the monopoly industries. The steep rise in the monopoly of the

Figure 5.1: Monopolistic Dominance of SOEs

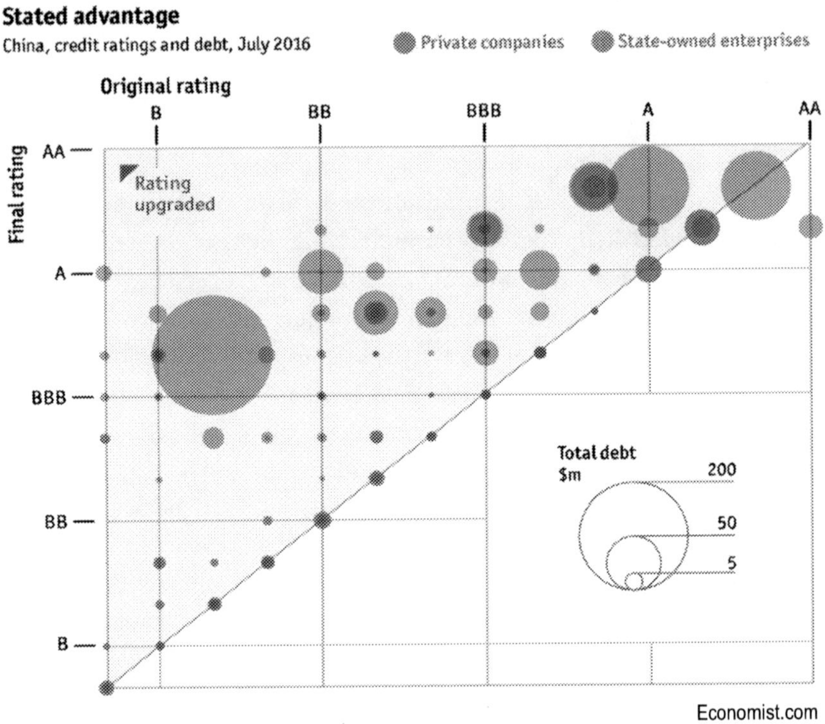

Note: As the Economist explains, the horizontal axis is their original rating. The vertical axis is their final rating after state support is added to the equation. The size of the bubble indicates the size of their debt. When ratings are unchanged, as is the case for most private companies, the bubbles incline upwards along a 45-degree angle. But when ratings are boosted, the bubbles migrate above the 45-degree line: virtually all SOEs are in this category.[52]

Sources: Moody's; Standard & Poor's; Fitch Ratings.

SOEs was a natural consequence of restructuring as well as their urgency to multiply corporate profits. Monopoly was key to attain efficiency and insulate them from further losses.

In 2019, the total revenue of China's top 500 private enterprises was 30.17 trillion yuan (US$ 4.4 trillion).[53] In contrast, the total income of the State Grid Corporation alone was 2.7 trillion yuan (US$ 394.16 billion),[54] which was one-tenth of the revenue earned by the top 500 Chinese private enterprises. Although the reforms did prompt a few non-public enterprises to join SOE monopolised industries such as power, telecommunications, railways, and civil aviation, the overall situation of 'natural monopoly' did not change significantly, and comprehensive market competition is yet to be formed in the mainland. Especially after the 2008 Global Financial Crisis, the high monopoly profits of the SOEs contrasted with the ecosystem's gradual deterioration needed to thrive in private enterprises. While natural monopoly is a reality and SOEs are becoming habitual, it may have severe implications. This will discourage entrepreneurs from growing ambitious and working in a non-competitive market. On the other hand, the market dominance of the SOEs can serve national interests by providing affordable and efficient public services and products instead of using a monopoly to earn profits. Moreover, maximising sales and profits to maintain and increase value may turn precarious. For industries that do not have natural monopoly attributes, such as commerce, communications and automobiles, China can afford to break the monopoly, encourage more business entities to enter the market, and improve resource utilisation efficiency.

Followed by the challenges to end the dominance of the SOEs, operational autonomy remains the key to efficiency and performance. For many years, the reform of SOEs in China failed to break the power relationship between the State and enterprises. Since China pledged to reform the SOEs, a diverging set of policy measures was centred around two key themes: to expand decision autonomy for enterprises and increase their market role. Operational independence is a significant roadblock for the SOEs and the experiments of other Chinese regulators. For example, if the SOEs are not allowed to make independent decisions over mixed-ownership, the so-called operational autonomy is just a policy jig. Dividing managerial and party roles cannot resolve more profound tension between firm autonomy and party control and will be a critical step for *yangqi* to pursue mixed-ownership reforms.[55]

There exists a complicated explanation over the dubious operational autonomy of the SOEs. The "separation of two powers" in management is biased towards the State and not the enterprises. The operational independence of the SOEs is not fully accomplished as multiple government departments still impact decision-making in SOEs' operation. The multi-head leadership increased the operating costs of SOEs and affected the management's efficiency on the operational level. It affected stable development of the SOEs at the strategic level, resulting in their fuzzy and vacillating direction. From the perspective of organisational structure, SOEs are treated to play the role of non-operating units.[56] Moreover, as an extended arm of the party and the State, setting up many sister departments add up to ordinary business operations to deal with political and social activities such as meetings, inspections and awards of various higher-level departments that cause an additional burden.

In addition to the institutional tangle, financial subsidies also affected the autonomy of the SOEs. Although financial subsidies are closely related to the country's economic and industrial adjustments, it also reflects the preference for the SOEs to operating and manage mechanisms to withstand market competition and price fluctuations and rely on financial subsidies. The Chinese government continues to maintain subsidies to SOEs; this, in turn, resulted in SOEs ignoring cost control, reduced enthusiasm for improving efficiency, and rely on subsidies instead.

Another factor that regressively affected the autonomy of SOEs is the restrictions faced by managers despite having the right to operate independently. Additionally, they are politically appointed, and their restraint and need for incentive are influencing their accountability. The granular definition of these relations would need substantial time to come into effect as it involves questions related to integrity and party discipline. Anything which distantly digresses from the party's principles and cadre's integrity is cast aside. Issues concerning the corporate governance structure's effectiveness is an important aspect that has raised questions over the whole restructuring process. Although most SOEs have established a governance structure that meets the requirements of 'Company Law,'[57] in reality, China's corporate governance structure differed drastically. Because the laws were meant to serve the State's interest, the 'form' of corporate governance was subject to the functions of the so-called Boards of Directors. Perhaps one can describe this reform in corporate governance as reflective of the paradoxes. During Hu Jintao's time, the SASAC did try to introduce radical reforms in corporate governance structure by directing SOEs to involve fifty per cent external directors.

Corporate governance did evolve after China opened up its economy, especially after SOEs were asked to mind their business, even partly. Jiang Zemin's call to establish a "modern enterprise system", the 1994 Company Law, and SOE entry into equity markets, catalysed the initial but superficial adoption of corporate governance institutions.[58] A historical overview reveals that greater SOE autonomy from the State has always come with Party participation in SOE governance (Table 5.4). But eventually, the thrust on corporate governance began to witness its natural death as the formal restructuring of SOEs and board formation mirrored party interests. SASAC and Party organs urged to retain many vital powers that undermined the effectiveness of the boards despite their existence on paper. With Xi Jinping radicalising China's business, corporate governance will be a thing of the past. The SOEs that get the best corporate governance award are the ones that would accept the autonomy defined by the states and not from the State, meaning thereby some degree of Party participation in the governance of SOEs. After Xi took power, SASAC and CSRC focused more on 'Party building work and the Party committee's role in corporate governance.'[59]

Table 5.4: Key Corporate Governance Developments in China's State Sector

The 1970s-1980s	• SOEs transition from production units to enterprises with limited autonomy and accountability for performance
The 1990s	• 1994 Company Law and SOEs' entry into equity markets catalyse superficial adoption of corporate governance institutions. • Early national pilots on SOE restructuring and governance at the group company level are largely unsuccessful. • CSRC outlines the first corporate governance framework for listed firms. • Weak oversight and insider control result in the loss of state assets during the downsizing of the state sector and SOE public listing. • State Council establishes a "special inspectors" system to strengthen group-level oversight of largest SOEs.
The 2000s	• SASAC experiments with establishing boards of directors and external directors at the group company level. • CSRC announces code of corporate governance for listed firms, implements an independent director system, issues regulations on tunnelling, related party transactions, M&A, and insider trading.
The 2010s	• SASAC establishes boards of directors at the group company level for most central SOEs but slows corporate governance policy efforts. • CSRC updates and expands existing regulations to prevent shareholder abuses and draft a new version of the corporate governance code for listed firms.

Source: Author's analysis based on SASAC news briefs and Organisation for Economic Co-operation and Development (OECD) Report[60]

A prominent issue causing SOE underperformance is the inherent defect of property rights held by them. The State owns SOEs, but the State cannot truly exercise ownership, so SOEs cannot build corresponding governance mechanisms based on the control of their interests by the owners of the enterprise. The undefined property rights invite all associated problems to seek their justification plugged in ownership rights. The absence of owners leads to a lack of interest of stakeholders in the assessment, supervision, and incentives of managers and property rights agents. This can be used to explain almost all management problems in SOEs. When resources are shared and have no defined ownership, anyone who can access them will act independently according to their interests. As a result, property rights reform remained the core content of the reform of SOEs.

After the reforms and opening up, every aspect of SOE reforms was inseparable from property rights. The initial decentralisation of power and profit did not reform the property rights of SOEs. The SASAC was recognised as the main body of SOE property rights by the Enterprise State-owned Assets Law. But the property rights reform of China's SOEs deviated from Western the property rights theory. After the Third Plenary Session of the 18th Congress of the CPC, the property rights-related problems were seen as needing immediate attention in the wake of mixed-ownership reforms. The Chinese State, with its traditional mindset of leaving ownership rights undefined, raised troubling questions over the basic economic system. Under the pretext of ownership reforms, the pace of property rights reform continued at an accelerated rate. The essential changes concerning SOE property rights management included gradual surrendering of the controlling powers of SOEs in competitive fields, re-adjusting their role as one of the shareholders, and replacing SOEs with state-owned capital management activities to the property. The intention was to increase the rate of return of state-owned capital. Mixed ownership reforms were seen as essential for the SOEs in monopoly industries to introduce private capital and, at the same time, explore corporate employee shareholding to improve the corporate governance structures and implement professional management systems to optimise property rights and governance structures.

Further, reorganising and optimal allocation of state-owned capital plays a qualitative role in reforms. At the 19th National Congress of the CPC, emphasis was placed on the real economy. The new directions indicated that commercial SOEs undertake further restructuring, use market-oriented means such as financing, transfers, mergers, and acquisitions, and introduce strategic investments of various ownership capital types related to the industrial chain. The real economy was an attempt to let SOEs reorganise their priorities as per the global competition, which required SOEs to focus on forward-looking, strategic industries and core technology areas of the industrial chain. SOEs had to get over the traditional plug-and-play industries, which hardly challenged them to remain competitive by innovating and making more room for expansion. Chinese SOEs are yet to firmly grasp significant opportunities in the global technological revolution and industrial transformation. In particular, emerging strategic industries such as the Internet along with traditional industries, new-generation information technology, intelligent manufacturing, new materials, new energy vehicles, and digital creativity, which are closely related to the development and growth of the digital economy, promote new technologies, new products, and new business formats at a broader level. In the recent rounds of deliberations, SOEs focusing on public welfare were set to synchronise their goals with non-commercial policy goals. While strengthening policy guidance, supervision, and management, these SOEs have been directed to increase financial and policy capital investment so that state-owned capital could cushion the national economy by ensuring stable growth.

In addition to technological innovation, Chinese SOEs have led China's 'going out' strategy and the Belt and Road Initiative (BRI). Chinese SOEs have strong merger and acquisition capabilities and are familiarising themselves with international operating rules. Chinese SOEs have adopted asymmetric strategies to enhance their influence globally. On the one hand, these SOEs are engaged in transferring technology to relatively backward countries and regions and occupying the international market, while on the domestic front, SOEs are promoting supply-side reforms, industrial transformation and upgrading. Simultaneously, through technological innovation and international mergers and acquisitions, Chinese SOEs are entering the markets of developed countries. The main goal of these SOEs has been to leverage from learning, absorb advanced international technology and operational experience while using the same to drive domestic industrial innovation and enterprises to go global. As of August 2018, central SOEs and enterprises from countries along the BRI routes built 3,116 projects.[61]

Conclusion: 2020 and Emergence of SOEs as China's Poster-Child

The 19th Congress of the CPC emphasised the need to firmly implement the innovation-driven development strategy, and the strategic objectives of the reform of SOEs, especially central enterprises, have also begun to shift to innovation-driven development. In recent years, China's large SOEs have given full freedom to their resources and talents, using collaborative innovation platforms, industry-university-research, and collaborative innovation alliances to promote necessary technology research and development in scientific research institutes. Amidst trade wars and economic slowdown, small and medium-sized enterprises have also been closely monitoring the research and development of new industrial technologies. The innovation strategy of SOEs is also expected to cause spill over effects.

On 30 June 2020, Xi Jinping presided over the Central Committee's 14th meeting specially convened to finalise the "comprehensive deepening" of the reform plan.[62] Li Keqiang and Wang Huning, both members of the Standing Committee of the Political Bureau of the CPC Central Committee and deputy heads of the central committee responsible for deepening overall reform, also attended the meeting, signifying the gravity of the next round of reforms. A three-year action plan on the reform of SOEs is expected to optimise the use of state-owned assets and spur innovation. Taking the lead from Xi Jinping's speech, the party openly accepted that while going ahead, "state-owned enterprises are important material and political basis for socialism with Chinese characteristics, and an important pillar and force for the party to govern and rejuvenate the country".[63] This means State-owned capital and the SOEs were the material and political basis to fulfil greater aspirations and these two bases are irreplaceable. The Chinese leadership has been using twin-spin to vitalise the importance of SOEs in 2020 and going ahead. The SOEs are given extraordinary significance, which means they remain the core of the communist philosophy of political rule and economic well-being. By doing so, the State would want the SOEs to strictly remain an affair of the Chinese state and party. In response to the COVID-19 pandemic, SOEs were pressed into a variety of services. They shouldered the burden of providing emergency supplies, medical support, resumption of production, and stabilising the industrial chain supply chain.[64] Amidst the crisis, SOEs have emerged as a poster-child of China's new round of opening up and reforms. However, the central task of the SOEs will be further streamlined during China's 14th Five-Year Plan.

China is all set to re-introduce "red capitalism"[65] in China, which is more radical than the one introduced during the late 1970s. If one supposes that the growth rates of the 1980s and 1990s were all about terminating the inefficient SOEs and replacing them with competitive private players, then the present scenario indicates that the SOEs are no more shrinking in number, and the 'affordability' of retaining SOEs has gone up monetarily as well as politically. The SOEs are not going anywhere but will stay and play as per the party's script. Active state interventions stabilise the volatilities related to assets, capital, and performance. In the past couple of years, the crisis has made the leaders stick to the original plan to make SOEs big and unbreakable. The 19th Congress of the CPC report in 2017 clearly stated that the goal of SOE reforms is to cultivate world-class enterprises with global competitiveness. The task of reforming SOEs will remain unresolved. As the 19th Party Congress maintained, the "great rejuvenation of the Chinese nation is inseparable from the strategic support and leading role of state-owned enterprises",[66] and the State will not let its control over SOEs weaken. The number and size of the SOEs are massive, impacting their role in domestic and international markets, leaving little doubt that SOEs will continue to remain one of the strategic polemics of Chinese capitalism.

NOTES

1. Ben Fung, Jason George, Stefan Hohl and Guonan Ma. 2011. 'Public asset management companies in East Asia Case studies 1', *Financial Stability Institute (FSI) Papers*, Bank for International Settlements, https://www.bis.org/fsi/publications.htm?m=1%7C17%7C161 (accessed on 21 August 2019).
2. Dong Zhang and Owen Freestone. 2013. 'China's Unfinished State-owned Enterprise Reforms', *Economic Roundup,* The Treasury, Australian Government, No. 2, December, 79-102.
3. Ministry of Commerce of the People's Republic of China. 1999. 'The Decision of the Central Committee of the Communist Party of China on major issues concerning The Reform and Development of State-Owned Enterprises (Adopted at the Fourth Plenum of the 15th CPC Central Committee on 22 September 1999)', 22 September, http://english.mofcom.gov.cn/aarticle/lawsdata/chineselaw/200211/20021100053897.html (accessed on 21 October 2018).
4. Joseph Fewsmith. 1999. 'China and the WTO: The Politics behind the Agreement', *The National Bureau of Asian Research,* November, https://www.iatp.org/sites/default/files/China_and_the_WTO_The_Politics_Behind_the_Agre.htm) (accessed on 26 July 2020).

5. Embassy of the PRC in the USA. 2000. 'China, EU sign bilateral agreement on China's WTO entry', 19 May, http://www.china-embassy.org/eng/zt/wto/t36884.htm (accessed on 26 July 2020).
6. Matt Smith. 2000. 'Clinton signs China trade bill' *CNN*. 10 October, https://edition.cnn.com/2000/ALLPOLITICS/stories/10/10/clinton.pntr/ (accessed on 2 August 2000).
7. *The Economist*. 2011. 'China's economy and the WTO - All Change'. 10 December, https://www.economist.com/asia/2011/12/10/all-change (accessed on 28 January 2021).
8. *China.org*. 2002. 'Full Text of Jiang Zemin's Report at the 16th Party Congress', 17 November, http://www.china.org.cn/english/2002/Nov/49107.htm (accessed on 12 October 2019).
9. *Gov.cn*. 2003. 'Guowuyuan guoyou zichan jiandu guanli weiyuanhui zhuyao zhize nei she jigou he renyuan bianzhi guiding' (国务院国有资产监督管理委员会主要职责内设机构和人 员编制规定) [State-owned Assets Supervision and Administration Commission of the State Council, Main Responsibilities, Internal Institutions and Staffing Regulations], 15 April, http://www.gov.cn/zhengce/content/2005-08/12/content_8164.htm (accessed on 12 October 2019).
10. *Sina*. 2003. 'Shiliu jie san zhong quanhui jingshen jiedu: Guoqi gaige bu ru shizhi neirong' (十六届三中全会精神解读：国企改革步入实质内容) [Interpretation of the spirit of the Third Plenary Session of the 16th Central Committee: State-owned enterprise reform has entered crucial stage]. 24 October, http://news.sina.com.cn/c/2003-10-24/0610978283s.shtml (accessed on 12 October 2019).
11. *Gov.cn*. 2006. 'Shiwu qijian guoyou qiye gufenzhi gaige qude zhongda jinzhan' (十五"期间国有 企业股份制改革取得重大进展) [Significant progress has been made in state-owned enterprise shareholding reform during the Tenth Five-Year Plan], October 24, http://www.gov.cn:8080/jrzg/2006-01/06/content_149150.htm) (accessed on 12 October 2019).
12. National People's Congress of the PRC. 2012. 'Jiu cheng guoqi wancheng gongsi zhi gufenzhi gaige' (九成国企完成公司制股份制改革) [90% of state-owned enterprises have completed the reform of the company system and shareholding system], 25 October, http://www.npc.gov.cn/zgrdw/huiyi/cwh/1129/2012-10/25/content_1740654.htm (accessed on 12 October 2019).
13. OECD. 2009. 'State-Owned Enterprises in China: Reviewing the Evidence', *OECD Working Group on Privatisation and Corporate Governance of State-Owned Assets*, 26 January, https://www.oecd.org/corporate/ca/corporategovernanceofstate-ownedenterprises/42095493.pdf (accessed on 12 October 2019).
14. Ligang Song. 2018. 'State-Owned Enterprise Reform in China: Past, Present and Prospects', in Ross Garnaut, Ligang Song and Cai Fang (eds.), *China's 40 Years of Reform and Development: 1978–2018* (Acton ACT, Australia: ANU Press), 345-73.
15. Zhang Shasha 2018. 'State-Owned Capital Guideline' *Beijing Review*. No. 51, 20 December, http://www.bjreview.com/Special_Reports/2018/2018_in_Retrospect/Top_10_Business_ News_Stories/201812/t20181227_800152646.html (accessed on 15 September 2019).
16. Xiaobin Lin, Jianhui Liao, Haiyun Song and Xiaodong Li. 2019. 'Analysis of State-owned Capital Investment and Operating Companies Experimental Units', *2019 3rd International*

Conference on Informatization in Education, Management and Business Conference Proceedings (unpublished), 28-29 January, https://www.clausiuspress.com/conferences/AETP/IEMB%202019/IEMB51.pdf (accessed on 15 September 2020).

17. *English.gov.cn*. 2018. 'Pilot reform of State-owned capital investing, operating companies', 30 July, http://english.www.gov.cn/policies/latest_releases/2018/07/30/content_281476242 418612.htm (accessed on 15 September 2020).
18. *Xinhua Finance Agency*. 2016. 'SOEs reform to deepen as ten pilots reforms unveiled'. 26 February, http://en.xfafinance.com/html/In_depth/2016/199753.shtml (accessed on 15 September 2020).
19. *China Banking News*. 2017. 'Mixed-ownership Reforms of 19 State-owned Enterprises Expected to Draw 300bn Yuan', 4 December, http://www.chinabankingnews.com/2017/12/04/mixed-ownership-reforms-19-state-owned-enterprises-expected-draw-300bn-yuan/ (accessed on 15 September 2020).
20. Ibid.
21. China has enriched its national science and technology award system by setting up the State Preeminent Science and Technology Award, the State Natural Science Award, the State Technological Invention Award, the State Scientific and Technological Progress Award and the China International Science and Technology Cooperation Award.
22. *Xinhua*. 2020c. 'China improves S&T award system to spur innovation', 9 January, http://www.xinhuanet.com/english/2020-01/09/c_138691824.htm (accessed on 2 August 2020).
23. Li Rongrong. 2008. 'Wu nianlai guoyou qiye gaige fazhan qude zhongda jinzhan' (五年来国有企业改革发展取得重大进展) [Significant progress has been made in the reform and development of state-owned enterprises in the past five years], 29 March, http://paper.ce.cn/jjrb/html/2008-03/29/content_8361.htm (accessed on 2 August 2020).
24. *Peoples' Daily*. 2018c. 'Yi da pi yangqi xiangmu ronghuo 2017 niandu guojia kexue jishu jiangli' (一大批央企项目荣获 2017 年度国家科学技术奖励) [A large number of central enterprise projects won the 2017 National Science and Technology Awards], 10 January, http://ccnews.people.com.cn/n1/2018/0110/c141677-29756353.html (accessed on 6 August 2020).
25. Scott Kennedy. 2020. 'The biggest but not the strongest: China's place in the Fortune Global 500', *CSIS Blogs*, 18 August. Retrieved from https://www.csis.org/blogs/trustee-china-hand/biggest-not-strongest-chinas-place-fortune-global-500 (accessed on 20 August 2020).
26. Ibid.
27. Ibid.
28. Scott Kennedy. 2020. 'The biggest but not the strongest: China's place in the Fortune Global 500' *CSIS Blogs*. 18 August, https://www.csis.org/blogs/trustee-china-hand/biggest-not-strongest-chinas-place-fortune-global-500 (accessed on 20 August 2020).
29. Lu Fuming and Yang Ye. 2010. 'Shandong Iron and Steel Group to acquire Rizhao Iron and Steel Company', 3 November, http://www.eeo.com.cn/ens/homepage/briefs/2010/11/05/184970.shtml (accessed on 26 July 2020).
30. Hou Qingyang. 2010. 'New steel firm melting pot of consolidation' *China Daily*. 25 February, http://www.chinadaily.com.cn/bizchina//2010-02/25/content_9501486.htm (accessed on 27 August 2020).

31. Hui Zhang. 2015. *China's SOE Reforms in the 2000 and 2010s,* Unpublished Post-Graduate Thesis, University of British Columbia.
32. Ibid.
33. Ibid.
34. Chen Xuewan and Lu Yutong. 2020. 'State Grid's profit collapses on Covid-19 fallout' *Caixin.* 5 August, https://www.caixinglobal.com/2020-08-05/exclusive-state-grids-profit-collapses-on-covid-19-fallout-101589230.html (accessed on 26 August 2020).
35. Karen Lin, Xiaoyan Lu, Junsheng Zhang and Ying Zheng. 2020. 'State-owned Enterprises in China: A Review of 40 Years of Research and Practice', *China Journal of Accounting Research,* Vol. 13, 31-55.
36. The US-China Business Council. 2013. 'Third Plenum outcomes settle Top-line Reform Themes, but debate on specifics to continue', https://www.uschina.org/third-plenum-outcomes-settle-top-line-reform-themes-debate-specifics-expected-continue (accessed on 24 July 2020).
37. *China Daily.* 2017b. 'New Normal in Economic Development', 5 October, https://www.chinadaily.com.cn/china/19thcpcnationalcongress/2017-10/05/content_32869258.htm (accessed on 2 August 2020).
38. Zheng Xinli. 2014. 'Renmin ribao: Jinyibu shenhua guoyou qiye gaige' (人民日报：进一步深化国有企业改革) [People's Daily: Further deepen the reform of state-owned enterprises] *People's Daily,* 25 December, http://opinion.people.com.cn/n/2014/1225/c1003-26275490.html (accessed on 19 August 2020).
39. *Xinhua.* 2017. 'Economic Watch: Supply-side structural reform gears up for high-quality development', 30 December, http://www.xinhuanet.com/english/2017-12/30/c_136861755.htm (accessed on 27 July 2020).
40. John Boulter. 2018. 'China's Supply-side Structural Reform' *Reserve Bank of Australia Bulletin.* December, https://www.rba.gov.au/publications/bulletin/2018/dec/chinas-supply-side-structural-reform.html (accessed on 24 August 2020).
41. Central Committee of the Communist Party of China. 2016. '13th Five-Year Plan for Economic and Social Development of The People's Republic of China (2016-20)', Central Compilation and Translation Bureau, 17 March, https://en.ndrc.gov.cn/newsrelease_8232/201612/P020191101481868235378.pdf (accessed on 24 August 2020).
42. Lam, W. Raphael; Markus Rodlauer and Alfred Schipke. 2017. 'State-Owned Enterprise Reform', in W. Raphael Lam, Markus Rodlauer and Alfred Schipke, (eds.), *Modernizing China: Investing in Soft Infrastructure. USA: International Monetary Fund,* https://www.elibrary.imf.org/view/IMF071/23209-9781513539942/23209978151353942/ch11.xml?language= en&redirect=true#Rch11tab3 (accessed on 21 August 2019).
43. State-owned Assets Supervision and Administration Commission (SASAC). 2014. 'Guowuyuan guozi wei juban "si xiang gaige shidian xinwen fabu huì' (国务院国资委举办"四项改革" 试点新闻发布会) [State-owned Assets Supervision and Administration Commission of the State Council held a press conference on the "four reforms" pilot]. 15 July, http://www.sasac.gov.cn/n2588025/n2588119/c2668690/content.html (accessed on 23 September 2020).
44. *Fenghuang Wang Caijing.* 2014. 'Guoziwei 'si xiang gaige' shidian neirong' (国资委'四项改革' 试点内容) [SASAC 'four reform' pilot content]. 15 July, http://finance.ifeng.com/a/20140715/12725003_0.shtml (accessed on 23 September 2020).

45. *China Daily.* 2014. 'China names Six SOEs for pilot reforms', 15 July, http://www.chinadaily.com.cn/business/2014-07/15/content_17787248.htm (accessed on 23 September 2020).
46. SASAC. 'Guowuyuan guozi wei juban "si xiang gaige shidian xinwen fabu huì'.
47. *The Economist.* 2019a. 'Some Chinese firms turned out to have lied about their state pedigree', 14 November, https://www.economist.com/finance-and-economics/2019/11/14/some-chinese-firms-turn-out-to-have-lied-about-their-state-pedigree (accessed on 26 July 2020).
48. The Korean securities firms and credit rating agencies which were exposed to risks included: Hanwha Investment & Securities, eBest Investment & Securities - the two were the underwriters; Hyundai Motor Investment & Securities, BNK Securities, KB Securities, Yuanta Securities and Shinyoung Securities suffered insolvency of asset-backed commercial papers, following a Chinese firm's default on payments due for bonds.
49. *Pulsenews.co.kr.* 2018. 'Most of the allegations of preferential treatment such as luge and hotel in Tongyeong have been closed', 4 June, https://pulsenews.co.kr/view.php?year=2018&no= 354111 (accessed on 11 August 2020).
50. A clause which operates by automatically defaulting a borrower under Agreement A when it defaults under Agreement B. Cross-default is basically a provision in a loan agreement that puts the borrower in default if the borrower defaults on another loan. In other words, if the borrower defaults on one loan, he/she will be deemed to be in default on his/her other loans and the debts arising from other loans will become immediately due and payable even if there is no breach of other loans. Based on Ilayda Anaç. 2020. "Turkey: Cross-Default Clauses in Loan Agreements' *Mondaq.* 13 March, https://www.mondaq.com/turkey/financial-services/903472/cross-default-clauses-in-loan-agreements(accessed on 14 March 2021) and Thomson Reuters Practical Law. 2021. 'Practical Law - Glossary', https://uk.practicallaw.thomsonreuters. com/1-382-3377?transitionType=Default&contextData=(sc.Default)&firstPage=true (accessed on 14 March 2021).
51. *The Economist.* 'Some Chinese firms turned out to have lied about their state pedigree'.
52. *The Economist.* 2016. 'China's state firms borrow cheaply'. 23 November, https://www.economist.com/graphic-detail/2016/11/23/chinas-state-firms-borrow-cheaply (accessed on 23 September 2020).
53. *Statista.* 2020. 'Revenue of State Grid Corporation in China from 2010 to 2019', March, https://www.statista.com/statistics/302451/china-state-grid-corporation-revenue/ (accessed on 26 July 2020).
54. Cheng Yu. 2020. 'Private firms step up innovation investment' *China Daily.* 15 September, https://www.chinadaily.com.cn/a/202009/15/WS5f601a3ba3101ccd0bee0606.html (accessed on 23 September 2020).
55. Wendy Leutert. 2016. 'Challenges ahead in China's Reform of State-owned Enterprises', *Asia Policy*, No. 21, January, 83-99, https://www.brookings.edu/wp-content/uploads/2016/07/Wendy-Leutert-Challenges-ahead-in-Chinas-reform-of-stateowned-enterprises.pdf (accessed on 12 August 2020), 95.
56. A company or department that does not manage any assets or directly conduct any business, whatsoever. Rather, a non-operating unit collects money and distributes it to the appropriate parties. For example, a non-operating unit may own an asset but lease it to another company.
57. The Company Law, which was promulgated in December 1993, provided legal support

to the establishment of a modern enterprise system and laid the groundwork for China's corporate governance framework. Some SOEs were restructured into limited liability companies or limited joint-stock companies.

58. Daniel H. Rosen, Wendy Leutert, and Shan Guo. 2018. 'Missing Link: Corporate Governance in China's State Sector. Rhodium Group' *Rhodium Group.* 5 November, https://rhg.com/research/missing-link-corporate-governance-in-chinas-state-sector/ (accessed on 15 September 2020).
59. On April 27, 2017, the board of directors of Sinopec's Hong Kong-listed subsidiary, China Petroleum and Chemical Corporation approved the following revisions to its articles of association:
New clause added as Article 9 in Chapter 1 (General Provisions):
"In accordance with the Company Law and the Constitution of the Communist Party of China (the "Party"), the Company hereby set up Party organizations and related working organs and maintain (sic) an adequate level of staffing to handle Party affairs as well as sufficient funding necessary for the activities of the Party organizations. The Party organizations play the role of the leadership core and the political core in the Company."
New clause added as Article 109 in Chapter 10 (Board of Directors):
"When making decisions on significant matters such as direction of reform and development, key objectives, and priority operational arrangements of the Company, the board of directors should seek advice from the Party organization. When the board of directors appoints the management personnel of the Company, the Party organization shall consider and provide comments on the candidates for management positions nominated by the board of directors or the president or recommend candidates to the board of directors and/or the president."
60. OECD. 2009. 'State-Owned Enterprises in China: Reviewing the Evidence', *OECD Working Group on Privatisation and Corporate Governance of State-Owned Assets,* 26 January, https://www.oecd.org/corporate/ca/corporategovernanceofstate-ownedenterprises/42095493.pdf (accessed on 12 October 2019).
61. Philipp Galkin, Dongmei Chen and Junyuang Ke. 2020. 'China's Energy Investment Through the Lens of the Belt and Road Initiative' *King Abdullah Petroleum Studies and Research Centre Papers.* 12 January, https://www.kapsarc.org/research/publications/chinas-energy-investment-through-the-lens-of-the-belt-and-road-initiative/ (accessed on 12 August 2020).
62. *Xinhua.* 2020a. 'Xi Focus: Xi stresses breaking new ground amid changes through reforms', 1 July, http://www.xinhuanet.com/english/2020-07/01/c_139178782.htm (accessed 24 July 2020).
63. *People's Daily.com.* 2020. 'Wei guoyou qiye qiang "gen" zhu "hun"' (为国有企业强"根"铸"魂") [To build the "soul" for the strong "root" of state-owned enterprises], 6 January, http://paper.people.com.cn/rmrb/html/2020-01/06/nw.D110000renmrb_20200106_2-04.htm (accessed on 26 July 2020).
64. The general literature from various sources claims that the SOEs contributed to China's recovery on a war footing. A few examples are: China Construction Group was the group that built the Huoshenshan and Leishenshan hospitals in just 10 days; Sinopec and Xinxing Jihua Group increased the daily output of masks from zero to nearly 10 million in a few weeks; the daily output of protective clothing (PPE) was increased to nearly 200,000 sets;

Sinopharm, General Technology Group and China Resources Group provided frontline medical staff with sufficient medical kits.

65. Carl Walter and Fraser Howie. 2012. *Red Capitalism: The Fragile Financial Foundation of China's Extraordinary Rise* (Singapore: John Wiley and Sons).
66. *China Daily*. 2017a. 'Full Text of Xi Jinping's Report at 19th CPC National Congress', 18 October, https://www.chinadaily.com.cn/china/19thcpcnationalcongress/2017-11/04/content_34115212.htm (accessed on 20 August 2020).

6

'The Wealth of Nations' and SOEs

China's middle class is expanding rapidly. Especially, the growing affluence of urban China appears to be striking evidence that a middle class is already fast emerging. Soon after the economy unleashed the cross-market forces to flourish and get richer, the millions, including households, individuals and enterprises, took Deng Xiaoping's dictum "to get rich is glorious"[1] so much to heart that the Chinese aspire *wealth* dearly. After China's opening up, reforms and the sloganeering for *wealth* creation, at least three generations missioned to amass extraordinary *wealth*. China's reform and openness have now been ongoing for more than 40 years. During this critical period, China's economy has developed rapidly, and personal incomes have increased steeply. This is not only the case of individuals, households and private enterprises, but the Chinese State also seems to have taken a lead role in the polarisation of wealth, and State enterprises played a critical role in this. Deng applied pragmatic policies to liberalise the Chinese economy gradually while maintaining the power of the Communist state. In hindsight, by allowing ordinary Chinese to accrue capital and making the party the sole owner of such breakthroughs, Deng controlled China's historic transition.

Over the past four decades, *wealth* has made every Chinese work hard and follow the thoughts and ideologies that the leaders would profess. The earliest signs that made the Chinese begin a spree of amassing *wealth* were squatting on the sidewalk or standing along Dongsixi Street in Beijing with a tray slung around their necks. Post-78 reforms, the state-owned restaurants were soon going to be history. Private managers leasing state-owned restaurants were the first to benefit from the giving over of social life of ordinary Chinese. They set the course to create opportunities for social and, eventually, national *wealth*. These were the early signs of petty businesses that sprung the economy into action and that are still unfolding. *Wealth*, once a target for revolutionaries and Red Guards, eclipsed the ordinary Chinese imagination amidst economic hard times. Inhibitions towards *wealth* witnessed a major loss in Communist China as it no more remained a dividing line revisionists and radicals. Surprisingly, Deng issued notices to communist cadres to desist threatening ordinary people accumulating private wealth. After the dreadful years of revolution and struggle, when China opened up in 1978, the reminisces of capitalism were to be seen on the streets, the first visible sign of how Adam Smith was already living in the basement of every Chinese household.

In his *Selected Works,* Deng writes that it was now ideologically correct "to make some people rich first, to lead all the people to wealth".[2] Deng's *new wealth* was the *new opium,* which kept the Chinese exasperating for surpluses or, in other words, money or *wealth*. Before SOEs could swing into action and play a central role in restructuring their assets, the belief of accruing *wealth* became the real motivation. Public display of private wealth was banished, but after reforms, the Beijing municipality listed those households which were earning a few extra thousands more income than their neighbours and others to be nominated as 'model households'. *Wealth*, household or public (state), turned out to be the primary booster for the moribund economy. Soon *wealth* was on display, and *wealth management* became the core function of Chinese state agencies, and enterprises, leave alone households and private entities. According to the *China National Balance Sheet 2018*,[3] today China is the second wealthiest country in the world.

In the long run, State-owned industrial and financial enterprises have influenced China's accumulation of *wealth*. While state-owned industrial enterprises holding on to huge assets allowed the Chinese state to lay its hands on a large portion of the *national wealth*, this practice declined substantially when restructuring was introduced. The wealthier Chinese and private enterprises increased their share in wealth creation, reducing the share of the

SOEs. But prosperous China needed activism from the state-owned financial institutions, too, as they influenced wealth. As managing wealth does not remain limited to output and income, more stocks of assets and liabilities, especially Central financial institutions like the Chinese State-owned Commercial Banks (SoCBs), see their role as indispensable.[4] In 1995, the Chinese government introduced the Commercial Bank Law[5] to commercialise the operations of the four state-owned banks, the Bank of China (BOC), the China Construction Bank (CCB), the Agricultural Bank of China (ABC), and the Industrial and Commercial Bank of China (ICBC). Eventually, two more banks, Postal Savings Bank and Bank of Communications, were included in this list, taking the total number of big state-owned banks to six.

As China Accumulates Wealth

Trust and risk are critical factors in shaping the economic dynamics across global economies. Like developed economies, the developing and small economies eventually pay growing attention to these issues when they aspire to grow in size. Economic growth is the increase in what a country produces over time. Growth has multiple reflections, like countries attaching importance to sustainable growth and consider strengthening their national gross domestic product (GDP). The gross domestic product is the logical extension of measuring economic growth in terms of monetary expenditure. While expenditure and production influence the GDP statistics, the distribution, accumulation, and management of national wealth also affect the aspirations and trajectory of a country's growth. There are competing approaches about the position of wealth in bolstering inclusive national economic growth, both in nominal and real terms. For developing countries, unlike developed countries, managing wealth is not accruing the premiums but maintaining and distributing wealth and, at the same time, creating favourable conditions for its value appreciation. Wealth management is an approach that can elaborate on two kinds of growth approaches. One, the circulation of wealth (money/capital) from economic growth flow to poor people, rather than the rich, feeding to lift the rate of economic growth and lower unemployment, is considered as the most effective method to decrease income inequalities and address issues of receding growth rate. The increase in income inequality also leads to dragging the potentials. The efficient management of wealth gives better choices to governments to prosper more inclusively. Second, when the income distribution is seen from applied governance, the efficient management of the income and wealth would also lead to the access of low-income people to increased liquidity resulting in higher aggregate spending, more jobs, and a more robust economy.

In the past 70 years, since the PRC's founding, the wealth of society has snowballed, and ordinary Chinese lives have changed significantly. At present, China pursues the "two centenary goals" (两个一百年 *Liang ge yi bai nian*)[6] using the force of wealth that it has created in the recent past. However, China needs to improve its national wealth management capacity and enhance the scope of the national wealth management governance system. To know China's wealth in detail, one needs to consider the market value of all the non-financial and financial assets and liabilities held by each sector of the economy (households, government, and corporations). These can be used to measure the stocks of private and national wealth at the current market value. Interestingly, growing China produced a vast amount of wealth—both private and public or national—but it also reflects another side of economic disparity.

National wealth represents the wealth of a country and indicates a country's economic strength and is an essential basis for the government to formulate guidelines and policies. The concept of national wealth changes with the different development stages of a country, leading to the transformation of its development model. For example, when in the 1930s, the concept of GDP came into being; its purpose was to reflect the economic status. Gradually, GDP became the primary indicator of national economic statistics and the measurement of national wealth. However, GDP cannot measure a country's prosperity, and it remained an inaccurate method to measure national wealth in many respects. National wealth contains the prospect of achieving long-term growth of wealth based on the stock of wealth. GDP reflects the increase in flow and wealth, and part of the production activities included in GDP may not necessarily generate wealth. Therefore, one needs to deploy a new definition of national wealth. To strengthen the capacity and enhance the national wealth management capacity, wealth needs to be measured more practically. This is more relevant in the Chinese case, especially when *Socialism with Chinese characteristics* enters a new era. The ordinary Chinese have more expectations for a better life. Their understanding of national wealth demands a rigorous recalibration since it is not equality but the control over wealth that rules Chinese growth. With China growing wealthier and affluent, the Chinese are opting for wealthier prospects of life and earnings. Therefore, Chinese wealth dynamics are also swaying majorly towards new trends that are away from socialist principles. This, therefore, necessitates a new method to measure national wealth more accurately. Amidst all this confusion between 'conservatism and modernity,' while measuring national wealth, Central financial institutions are excited and moving forward to manage Chinese wealth.

The United Nations (UN) and the World Bank (WB) have tried to put forward comprehensive indicators that can measure a country's wealth more scientifically, changing the old concept of replacing wealth with income and measuring wealth only in material terms, and assessing a country's real wealth from the perspective of sustainable development. According to the UN report titled *Inclusive Wealth Report 2012*[7] and the WB report *The Wealth of a Changing Country: A Measurement of Sustainable Development Capability*,[8] the indicators for measuring national wealth should include productive capital (material wealth created by production and life), natural capital (natural resources) and intangible capital (human capital, social capital, institutional capital). The UN's and the WB's national wealth measurement method aimed at sustainable development and a move from a conventional GDP indicator to a comprehensive economic, social, environmental, and other aspects as soon as possible. Moreover, China has also agreed to abide by the *G20/OECD Corporate Governance Principles*[9] on shareholder rights, corporate decision-making, internal control management, and complementary external supervision.[10] The People's Bank of China (PBoC) and the China Banking and Insurance Regulatory Commission (CBIRC) stand united over improving corporate governance as the top priority of financial enterprise reform without which the wealth aspects of growth will remain shaky. As a result, enhancing corporate governance is critical to deepen financial enterprise reform and achieve quality performance beyond just GDP numbers.

Riding the Rich and China's way towards Wealth Management

The enhanced definition of national wealth also includes serious attention to the national balance sheet. The stock of national wealth is the basis for carrying out production activities. To find out the stock, one needs to use the national balance sheet, which can reflect the accumulation of the country's material wealth (including intangible assets) at any particular point in time. In contrast to GDP, it can more clearly reflect structural contradictions and the accumulation of macro risks, if any, which help to grasp the reality of the national economy more precisely. The health of the economy and the direction of future development provides a reliable basis for the country's macroeconomic decision-making and management. From the perspective of preventing and resolving risks, China pays more attention to the debt side, focusing on debt stock, and emphasises reducing leverage.[11] The liabilities of the Chinese government have their characteristics, which often correspond to assets. Therefore, it is necessary to analyse the assets side of Chinese government departments and include balance sheets.

China attached importance to the role of investment in economic growth. Since the reforms and opening up, investment has snowballed, especially in fixed assets, maintaining a relatively high contribution rate in growth dynamics.[12] So far, China fell short of paying enough attention to the management of the asset stock formed after spot investment, and there is a widespread phenomenon of accumulating wealth and negligence in its management. China's accumulated wealth has not generated sufficient production capacity.[13] The growth rate of social net wealth is faster than that of GDP, and the output efficiency is lower than most countries and regions in the world, basically due to flawed investments in the financial enterprise sector and large asset stocks. As a result, at present, China struggles to pay attention to the creation and management of wealth while at the same time, improve the ability to transform wealth flow into stock, promote incremental innovation with stock optimisation, drive stock optimisation with incremental innovation, change the increment flow, and increment transferring to stock.

The wealth China has accumulated needs to be probed vis-à-vis its resilience. The wealth-to-income ratio does reflect the strength of the economy. The higher the wealth-to-income ratio, the lower the income generated per unit of wealth and the lower the relative output efficiency. This rapid increase in the wealth-to-income ratio of non-financial companies can be understood from two perspectives—ineffective investment and the manner of wealth accumulation. Historical data and patterns indicate that there have been substantial increases in the ratios for Russia and China, which have tripled and quadrupled, respectively, following their transition from a communist to a capitalist-oriented economy.[14] In China's case, the attempt is not to know more about the growth rates and only assets or only flows but a cumulative assessment of all of these put together. Until recently, national accounts were mostly about flows, not stocks. The upward trend in national wealth-to-income ratios has exclusively been the result of private wealth accumulation. In China, people became rich, and enterprises turned to diversify their returns. When China's wealth was taken into account, it was generally calculated based on flows of output, income, and consumption but limited data on stocks of assets and liabilities were taken into account. Research shows that the national wealth-income ratio had increased from 350 per cent in 1978 to 700 per cent in 2015.[15] This increase is mainly driven by the rise of private wealth, which went up from 115 per cent to 487 per cent of national income during the same period. While personal wealth was accumulating, public wealth was hit by the recession. The share of public property in national wealth has declined from about 70 per cent in 1978 to about 30 per cent in 2015.[16] It can be seen that the key to reducing the wealth-to-income ratio lies in improving the production efficiency of non-financial enterprises, reducing ineffective investment, and changing the growth model driven by investment.

From 2000 to 2016, the household and inventory of China's assets, liabilities, and wealth increased manifold. At the end of 2016, China's social net wealth,[17] which ranked second in the world, totalled 437 trillion yuan (US$ 62.42 trillion). During the same period, China's GDP was 74.4 trillion yuan (US$ 10.62 trillion), ranked second in the world.[18] The growth rate of financial assets was significantly higher than that of non-financial assets, leading to a rapid increase in the financial industry's value-added ratio to GDP. China's external net financial assets have grown by an average of 1 trillion yuan per year (US$ 148 billion), of which investment contributed 171 per cent.[19]

Two opposite forces affect the distribution of net wealth between residents and the government. First is the continuous advancement of ownership reform, which reduced the proportion of government wealth. The other is that the assets held by government departments experienced a greater degree of revaluation, especially since a large number of SOEs were listed after 2000. From the perspective of risk, the large number of net assets owned by government departments was seen as an essential manifestation of national capabilities. However, from the standpoint of efficiency, the Chinese government directly owns and allocates a large number of assets, which also reduces the overall efficiency of the economy. In the long run, China needs to revitalise and reset the stock of government assets.

National Wealth Management and the 14th Five-Year Plan (2021-25)

The 14th Five-Year Plan[20] (14th FYP) kicks off under extremely difficult situations with many uphill tasks and responsibilities that the Chinese state needs to take up. More wealth in China sounds like good news, but it could also mean economic trouble. China seems to be gearing up to manage wealth accumulation and its disparities in the long run. In the process of adopting the 14th FYP, Central financial institutions need to achieve an essential breakthrough in China's national wealth management, which is a change from incremental management of wealth to focus on stock management, implement high-quality development requirements in all aspects, and improve national wealth management ability.

The comprehensive health of the Chinese economy can only be assessed by incorporating the new indicators (measuring wealth management capabilities) and including 'national wealth appreciation rate,' 'national wealth conversion rate,' and 'national wealth investment efficiency,' which will be a challenging task. Going forward, the Central financial institutions and SoCBs set out to use added indicators for measuring wealth management capabilities. The new indicators cannot be just created but would need a national wealth statistics system to be in place. This would mean populating and improving the national balance sheet and the natural resource balance sheet, further strengthening the statistical accounting of human capital, clearing the internal structure of national wealth, revitalising the stock of state-owned capital, and most importantly, improving the efficiency of state-owned capital. The Chinese state would also need to work diligently towards strengthening infrastructure statistics so that it becomes easier to isolate the scale and quality of productive capital.

Financial planning needs a clear and stringent stand on both wealth accumulation and distribution. The party-led government may blame the asymmetries in income and wealth as a result of market forces. Still, it is a fact that wealth accumulation is the direct result of a disproportionate concentration of wealth, income gap, and profits over wealth production. The data indicates that the mistrust in the financial system makes the rich and moderately affluent Chinese wary of their wealth. The fact is that only 2 per cent of the Chinese pay any income tax,[21] and the figure indicates apathy in managing wealth on income flows.[22] On a more serious note, China is already running late to manage wealth and offer its citizens more alternatives and better prospects to let them secure their wealth. It is a fact that the Chinese are looking to migrate to other countries and regions to live a quality life where their wealth and wealthy life is unquestioned and not politically driven. Chinese seek the American "EB-5" scheme; about 75 per cent of those who qualify are Chinese. This indicates the "spaghetti bowl effect" questioning the role of the Chinese authorities and institutions that worry the wealthy Chinese and also a deep-rooted contradiction in the story of China's development. With ideology occupying more limelight and centre stage in China, one can see a more reasonable attempt being made by the leaders to make national wealth accumulation more equitable to benefit the people.

Income distribution is not the main reason for the growing polarisation between rich and poor Chinese. It can be said that the imbalance in China's wealth distribution is far more significant than the inequality in income distribution. Those who hold monopolistic privileges and resources quickly amass considerable amounts of wealth, especially real estate that relies on land, resources, and capital, which has exerted enormous pressure on wealth adjustment.[23] For example, housing, unlike all other commodities, is a commodity that has dual consumption and investment attributes. When housing is used as a consumer product, the supply and significant demand for housing in the consumer-oriented housing market become the basis for determining market prices; while when housing is treated as an investment product, housing investment demand as a form of wealth holding mainly depends on personal wealth thus indicating that China's social wealth distribution is severely unbalanced. As a result, besides assessing and managing the national wealth, Chinese planners need to look into the wealth distribution system and address the wealth gap. The 'rich and the rest' is increasingly becoming a problem in China, reflecting the uneven and biased approach. Central financial institutions need to promote the coexistence of multiple distribution methods and improve the primary distribution system. The ways to regulate wealth and its distribution methods may include tax leverage, levying more taxes on the rich and less on the poor, levying more taxes on profiteering industries, and levying fewer taxes on low-profit sectors and people's livelihood industries. Adjusting the wage structure is another way that wealth accumulation can be effectively dealt with. Social subsidies and relief can also be used to regulate wealth and manage the effects. The redistribution of wealth does worry many interest groups in China, and hence it may not be as clean as it looks to implement.

Central Financial Institutions and the Role of SoCBs in National Wealth Management

The Chinese commercial banking system consists of three major players: state-owned commercial banks (SoCBs), joint-stock commercial banks (JSCBs),[24] and foreign commercial banks (FCBs). As the main body of the Chinese commercial banking system, SoCBs have maintained their status as a state-owned holding company.

In short, before we head to elaborate on the unique role of banks in wealth management, it should also be noted here that surgical methods were also deployed by the Chinese state to quickly take off the pressure created by accumulating non-performing assets from the Central financial institutions. In 1999, the Chinese government established four asset management companies: Cinda, Huarong, Dongfang, and the Great Wall. As the Central industrial enterprises were restructured, along with the Central financial enterprises, the asset management companies virtually disposed of non-performing assets, promoting the reform and development of SOEs and SoCBs to maintain social credit order.[25] To make positive contributions, financial risks were to be resolved on a priority basis. As a specialised agency for the large-scale centralised disposal of SOE non-performing assets, asset management companies performed a dual role of administering and functioning as an enterprise and not serve only as a transitional institution.

The reforms directed by the China Banking and Insurance Regulatory Commission (CBIRC) in SoCBs has played a vital role in maintaining and increasing the value of the national wealth of commercial banks. Besides, in recent years, the reform of China's SoCBs remained out-of-pace with the structural reforms in the industrial enterprises owned by the state. In contrast, the list of reforms that the SoCBs are supposed to introduce include banks to have sufficient capital, stricter internal control and firm competitiveness. While the Central financial institutions attempt to carry out the above-listed reforms, it is essential for these banks to effectively maintain and increase the value of state-owned capital in the process. Capital adequacy is a manifestation of the preservation and appreciation of state-owned capital. The protection and appreciation of state-owned capital is the basis for maintaining China's financial lifeline, although maintaining and increasing the value of state-owned capital is also an essential goal of the reform of SoCBs.

However, the reform of the state-owned financial asset management, supervision, and operation system needs further deepening and acceleration along the axes of excellence and time. In the context of increasingly complex risks in domestic and foreign financial markets, commercial banks face severe challenges in maintaining and increasing the value of state-owned capital. The corporate governance structure of commercial banks remains in a state of reforms and questions the role of strategic investors. The introduction of foreign strategic investment holds tremendous promise for the on-going reform of the Chinese banking system, where international investors and Chinese banks were expected to learn and build capacities. From a macro perspective, the introduction of strategic investors was a crucial strategic decision to promote the reforms and opening up and internationalise the SoCBs. From a micro level, this was a sales strategy to enter the international financial market, but banks have been losing patience over keeping their doors open for strategic investors. Strategic investors are not long-term investors as most of these investments in China were driven by short-term interests. Several SoCBs in China have had a similar experience. Most foreign strategic investors sell off and withdraw as soon as the "locking period" is over. The withdrawal of the Union Bank of Switzerland (UBS)[26] from the Bank of China (BOC) stocks is one example.[27] Maintaining and increasing the value of state-owned capital is an important goal of the reform of SoCBs, and the preservation and increase of the value of capital owned by the SoCBs depend on the deepening of reform and accelerated development of SoCBs.

Central financial institutions increasingly face pressure to maintain the overall stability of asset quality. The SoCBs shoulder social responsibilities and undertake major national construction projects, while medium and long-term assets account hold high proportions in their loan preferences. From the perspective of changes in the loan term structure, SoCBs are showing signs of gradually reducing the balance of short-term loans. However, there is still a peculiar gap in the loan maturity ratio between the SoCBs and joint-stock banks. Among them, in terms of the medium and long-term loans of the

SoCBs, many banks accounted for a relatively high proportion, accounting for more than 60 per cent.

Regarding the proportion of medium and long-term loans, the China Construction Bank (CCB) topped the list with a figure of nearly 70 per cent, while the share of joint-stock banks was only about half. The SoCBs have a relatively high proportion of medium and long-term loans, mainly because these banks are responsible for investing in state-directed projects. The SoCBs need to issue medium and long-term loan projects, and at the same time, take advantage of their own 'economies of scale' through the deployment of funds within the system to ease the pressure of short-term capital demand. Due to liquidity and interest rate risk considerations, JSCBs invest more credit assets in short-term loans with higher yields in small and micro-loans and bill businesses to ease the term structure's pressure.

In terms of investment strategy, SoCBs strategically choose to hold government bonds and policy bank[28] bonds with higher long-term yield returns, while JSCBs are relatively flexible, based on their institutional mechanisms. During periods of low capital interest rates, they are responding to the regulatory market. Due to the environment's impact, SoCBs continue to use innovative tools to enrich their investment portfolios and aggressively invest in credit assets or non-standard bonds with higher comprehensive yields to achieve continuous growth in asset scale and income. Long-term strategic holdings dominate investment allocation. More than half of SoCB investments are 'held-to-maturity investments,' although the proportion dropped year by year; they are transferred to 'available-for-sale financial assets.' On the contrary, the rival JSCBs are more biased towards underlying assets with higher liquidity. The JSCBs have, since the 1980s, proved to be the emerging force in the banking system and have provided a real and lively challenge to other established entities. JSCBs account for 14–15 per cent of total banking assets.[29]

The SoCBs are favouring those assets that attract higher returns. Assets with high-interest rates account for a high proportion, making the investments immune to the impact of narrowing interest margins on performance. The classification of assets held by the SoCBs indicates that the asset distribution structure of the SoCBs is similar to each other. The prevailing trend is a decline in liquid assets and an increase in the proportion of investment assets. Among them, the proportion of the Agriculture Bank of China's (ABC) liquid assets exceeds that of its peers, ranking first, while the proportion of loan assets is the lowest amongst SoCBs. Data analysis shows that loan assets, which are highly sensitive to interest rates, account for about 50 per cent of the total assets of the SoCBs, and they are increasing year by year.[30] It can be seen that the SoCBs still rely mainly on interest income generated by credit assets in obtaining operating profits. The asset matching strategy of JSCBs is significantly different. To alleviate the impact of narrowing interest margins on performance, the China Merchant Bank and the Industrial and Commercial Bank of China (ICBC) have reduced the proportion of credit assets in total assets year by year and significantly increased investment assets. Among the duo, the ICBC's expansion strategy for investment assets is more radical. In 2016, its investment assets accounted for 54.13 per cent, which exceeded loan assets by more than 20 percentage points and became the highest proportion of assets.[31]

In the end, the sluggish growth in the economy has been affecting patterns in wealth management. This has been the reality of both the demand and supply of the type of wealth product. Influenced by the macroeconomy's overall downward trend in recent years, the banks have noticed significant growth of personal credit assets. The banks are caught up with new challenges and perform a balancing act to maintain overall stability in the quality of credit assets and national wealth.

According to the classification and analysis of loan assets, there has been an upward trend in corporate loans and personal loans in the past five years. Still, the compound growth rate of personal loans has accelerated significantly, exceeding 15 per cent, almost twice the compound growth rate of corporate loans, thus highlighting the continued strengthening of loan asset allocation to personal credit. From the perspective of asset classification and distribution of the SoCBs, the share of personal loans and corporate loans has gradually adjusted from 37 per cent in 2012 to 46 per cent in 2016. ICBC had the highest corporate loan ratio, exceeding 60 per cent, and CCB had the highest personal loan ratio, slightly over 40 per cent.

Despite attempts by the SoCBs and Central financial enterprises, the number of challenges is ever-growing. For example, the state-owned assets management system is not sound, and the management consciousness of senior managers seems disoriented. Due to the traditional management model's influence, SOEs have always used the old management model in terms of internal management systems as the dominant state-owned assets in enterprises that are mostly imperfect and irregular fixed asset management systems. As discussed in Chapter Three, the senior managers turn out to be political appointees and sometimes lack proficient knowledge of the concerned SOEs. They do not qualify to make an objective and dynamic call concerning aspects of investments and assets, as a result of which the weak management awareness leads to a series of defaults. This makes the internal asset management of SOEs confused and cannot meet the requirements of enterprise development.

Strengthening the management of fixed assets and improving the asset management system are necessary conditions for ensuring the safety and integrity of state-owned banks. At present, SOEs generally suffer from incomplete asset management systems. Most senior managers are appointed by investors and are not the real owners of state-owned assets. In the assessment mechanism for senior managers, investors only pay attention to assessing business performance indicators rather than determining asset management indicators. Therefore, most senior managers have a weak awareness of asset management, which is also a big reason for the irregular asset management of SOEs.

Unclear department responsibilities and chaotic asset management are significant drawbacks of the flawless picture. The duties of various departments in some SOEs are not divided and lack a chain of command because of which, at times, the management authority is directionless. Additionally, there are multiple departments with asset management authority, asset purchase authority, and maintenance authority. For example, in a highway construction company, the asset management department is responsible for the management and daily maintenance of office vehicles and mechanical equipment. Other assets, such as office equipment, monitoring equipment, computers, water purification equipment, etc., are managed by the office, and the laboratory manages its equipment. Unclear division of responsibilities has led to wrangling and shirking responsibilities on some issues. Asset purchase lacks budget management, and there are temporary and sudden purchases. In the annual asset inventory, inconsistency between the accounts and the actual accounts is common. Some assets have accounts but no records, some have existing accounts but are not accounted for, and some assets are stored with inconsistent records. Due to loopholes in the management, responsibilities and accountabilities are not clear, work coordination among various departments is poor, resulting in a weak sense of responsibility. The financial department is responsible for asset registration and accounting, and depreciation, but the relevant vouchers of the purchased equipment are not reported in time, resulting in inconsistent registration time between the financial department and the asset management department.

At present, China's macro leverage ratio looks to be under control, but it still faces structural risks. Further, it is necessary to increase the total size of government assets and increase the flexibility of dealing with risks. In this regard, industrial SOEs can undoubtedly play a crucial role in managing assets, losses, and promoting national wealth to rise steadily. But compared with other SOEs, commercial banks can optimise resource allocation more effectively. To achieve good performance and greater profits, a commercial bank attempts to manage its capital situation and provide financial support for companies with good development trends and poor credit. To optimise the allocation of bank assets, some commercial banks have been given the task to help the government issue bonds, improve the stability of assets, and help the government do infrastructure projects and extend social benefits to the people. Moreover, commercial banks are also devising ways to formulate different development strategies for various industries and support the development of local small and medium-sized enterprises and emerging industries as per the government's regulatory needs, which will provide more impetus for economic diversification.

Central financial institutions and the active participation of SoCBs in macroeconomic policies make it the most potent executor of the national monetary system and an important contributor to fiscal revenue. The Central bank responds to the changing internal and external economic and financial situations by employing a mix of monetary policy instruments, including rediscount operations, to stabilise the financial market, boost domestic demand and promote economic growth. For example, commercial banks are the active party in rediscounting. Rediscount can refer to financing provided by the Central bank to commercial banks. In China, banks like the ICBC use this benefit extended by the Central bank where PBoC discounts a promissory note that has already been overlooked. This helps commercial banks to generate liquidity; it could be used to spark new demand or raise the spirit in an otherwise pessimistic market. Whether the Central bank's policy can achieve the corresponding effect depends on how the commercial bank adjusts the related operating behaviours to achieve the expected goal of the rediscount policy. When the economy overheats, the Central bank often proposes a monetary policy to curb or restrain the economy's overheating and then implement it indirectly through commercial banks. Besides, the Central bank uses measures like interest rates and open business to regulate and monitor commercial banks.

Commercial banks also play a vital role in generating wealth by contributing to financial profits. Part of the profits of state-owned banks is turned over to the shareholders, i.e., the Ministry of Finance, as an essential part of fiscal revenue. While the bank's profit is shrinking, the division of the profits internally has also become crucial. The banks' undistributed profits are an essential part of core capital. Against the backdrop of the COVID-19 pandemic, banks in developed countries have generally suspended dividend distribution and repurchase in 2020. However, China's finance is highly dependent on bank dividends to supplement income. It is expected that the dividend rate of banks, mainly state-owned ones, will not be lowered despite its average or even lower performance. With the highest proportion of total profits and the most considerable tax contribution, the banking industry remains crucial. State-owned banks contribute two-thirds of the net profits of listed banks. According to the 2019 data, among the listed companies as a whole, the total yield of a single bank sector accounted for as high as 13 per cent, while the contribution of income tax accounted for 11 per cent. State-owned banks contributed 67 per cent of the net profit of listed banks. The support point of fiscal revenue in 2019 is mainly non-tax revenue, which plays the most critical role in the profit paid by Central financial institutions and Central enterprises. In 2019, this profit increased by 360 billion yuan (US$ 52.2 billion) year-on-year to 610 billion yuan (US$ 88.5 billion). The increase in non-tax revenue across the country reached 13 per cent. As the profit of banks declines, its pressure to replenish capital will eventually rise to a dangerous level if the dividend rate is not lowered.

Conclusion

Total national power is a manifestation of the national wealth of a country. Besides, the scale of accumulation and quality of national wealth reflects the strength of a country's might by non-traditional dynamics. China knows well that strengthening national wealth management is necessary to enhance the country's comprehensive national power. Since the reforms and opening-up, China's economy has developed rapidly. The country's wealth has accumulated over the past 40 years, which, in turn, impacted China's international status and perception. With the deepening of industrialisation and urbanisation, the economic growth rate has changed from a high to a medium-high rate. Correspondingly, the probability of an explosive increase in national wealth is also reduced. As a result, both these extreme standpoints of development—concentration of wealth and depletion of wealth—only affects the country's ability to manage national wealth.

The need for high-quality development prompts China's focus on strengthening national wealth management. As discussed earlier in this chapter, the problem is about getting rid of dead weight in a pile of non-performing and often massive economic operations. The restructuring may address only one aspect of these inherited inefficiencies. Going forward, the structural problems continue to persist and do not address the larger question of quality performance, which is an inevitable choice to adapt to the new normal of economic development. China's economic development model has already shifted from 'extensive growth' based on scale and speed to 'intensive growth' based on quality and efficiency. The economic structure is shifting from incremental capacity expansion to inventory adjustment and simultaneous optimisation of total growth. For China, achieving high-quality development requires high-quality wealth creation and high-quality wealth management so that the accumulation of wealth is synchronised with social development, and the composition of wealth is consistent with the stage of national development.

Theoretically, Deng contradicted the ideological premises of Communist China when he flagged off reforms and encouraged the accumulation of wealth and wanted it to be displayed. *Elitisms* and *wealth voyeurisms* were rampant in post-Mao's China. Against this backdrop, the contradictions were toned down and made part of the post-Mao quest to turn China into a prosperous society. President Xi also wants to make Chinese society prosperous, but moderately—the term China is vividly using amidst slowing down of the national economic growth. Still, the larger question regarding the prevailing contradictions remains unanswered. As a result, strengthening national wealth management needs China to address major social contradictions. After China sustained rapid economic growth for thirty years, most Chinese were socialised to possess a certain sense of 'richness' which turned almost every Chinese ignorant of prodding social and economic contradictions. The core contradiction in Chinese society has been transformed into the contradiction between the people's growing need for a better life and unbalanced and inadequate development. China may boast about its ability to create, but it must realise that the national wealth creation depends on the compound growth of its people and national wealth. And to achieve it, the Chinese leadership must focus on strengthening national wealth management to enhance people's sense of gain, happiness, and security.

NOTES

1. Although there is no evidence of Deng saying it but "to get rich is glorious" is a translation of the Chinese expression, "致富光荣" (*Zhifu guangrong*), which Deng believed to have used in his speeches frequently.
2. Michael Weisskopf. 1984. 'China caught in cycle of reform and retreat' *The Washington Post*. 26 April, https://www.washingtonpost.com/archive/politics/1984/04/26/china-caught-in-cycle-of-reform-and-retreat/18e492ec-d5d7-4991-aa2e-1149450909c1/ (accessed on 26 July 2020).
3. *China Social Science Research Network*. 2018. ' "Zhongguo guojia zichan fuzhai biao 2018" zaijing fabu' ("中国国家资产负债表2018" 在京发布) ["China National Balance Sheet 2018" released in Beijing], 27 December, http://ex.cssn.cn/ts/bwdj/201812/t20181227_4801366. shtml (accessed on 24 August 2020).
4. The SoCBs include the 'Big Six'—The "big state-owned commercial bank" (国有大型商业银行).
5. *Hexun.com*. 2019. 'Yinhang fa de lishi yu weilai' (银行法的历史与未来) [The history and future of banking law], 4 November, https://bank.hexun.com/2019-11-04/199126104.html?from=rss (accessed on 6 August 2020).
6. The Two Centenaries (两个一百年 *Liang ge yi bai nian*) - espoused in 2012, at the 18th National Congress of the Communist Party of China, Xi set out two targets for China: *one*, growth target to make a 'moderately prosperous society' by 2021, the 100th anniversary of the party's founding; *two*, to make China 'prosperous and strong' by 2049, the 100th anniversary of Communist rule.
7. United Nations. 2012. *Inclusive Wealth Report 2012: Measuring Progress toward Sustainability* (Cambridge: Cambridge University Press), https://digitallibrary.un.org/record/784798?ln=en (accessed on 23 July 2020).
8. World Bank. 2011a. *The Changing Wealth of Nations: Measuring Sustainable Development in the New Millennium (Environment and Development)* (Washington D.C.: World Bank).
9. OECD. 2015. *G20/OECD Principles of Corporate Governance*. Paris: OECD Publishing.
10. *Global Times*. 2019. 'Party Leadership helps improve corporate governance', 26 May, https://www.globaltimes.cn/content/1151631.shtml (accessed on 4 August 2020).
11. *The Wall Street Journal*. 2019. 'China intends to continue debt-reduction efforts', 25 February, https://www.wsj.com/articles/china-intends-to-continue-debt-reduction-efforts-11551126582 (accessed on 26 July 2020).

12. John Knight and Sai Ding. 2010. 'Why does China invest so much?' *Asian Economic Papers,* MIT Press, Vol. 9, No. 3, Fall, 87-117.
13. Katina Stefanova. 2017. 'China's Rising Wealth Gap and Implications to Markets and the World' *Forbes.* 19 December, https://www.forbes.com/sites/katinastefanova/2017/12/19/chinas-rising-wealth-gap-and-implications-to-markets-and-the-world/#628bbf642311 (accessed on 30 July 2020).
14. *WID.world.* 2017. *World Inequality Report 2018,* https://wir2018.wid.world (accessed on 30 July 2020), 156.
15. Thomas Piketty, Li Yang and Gabriel Zucman. 2019. 'Income inequality is growing fast in China and making it look more like the US', *LSE Business Review,* 1 April, https://blogs.lse.ac.uk/usappblog/2019/04/06/income-inequality-is-growing-fast-in-china-and-making-it-look-more-like-the-us/ (accessed on 26 July 2020).
16. Ibid.
17. The sum of non-financial assets and external net assets.
18. *China Social Science Research Network.* ' "Zhongguo guojia zichan fu zhai biao 2018" zai jing fabu'.
19. Ibid.
20. *CGTN News.* 2020. '19th CPC Central Committee to hold 5th Plenary Session', 28 September, https://news.cgtn.com/news/2020-09-28/19th-CPC-Central-Committee-to-hold-5th-plenary-session-Oct-26-to-29-U9HMnelwwE/index.html (accessed on 1 October 2020).
21. *The Economist.* 2018. 'Why only 2% of Chinese pay any income tax', 1 December, https://www.economist.com/china/2018/12/01/why-only-2-of-chinese-pay-any-income-tax (accessed on 24 August 2020).
22. Tax dodging is something which the Chinese had difficulty in dealing with. Of the total number of taxpayers, the actual taxpayers is tiny in number. Citizens do not like the way the Chinese government has been charging their wealth lately by means of taxes. While levying taxes, China also has been struggling to make the tax system more transparent, progressive and less threatening. In October 2018, the Chinese government increased the tax-free threshold for monthly personal income from US$ 520 to US$ 745 (3,500 to 5,000 yuan). A second reform of the tax law came in January 2019, which allowed further tax deductions for a range of household expenses such as school fees, healthcare and care for the elderly. It also included an element of mortgage interest relief. These attempts are aimed at making the entire tax regime look tax-payer friendly.
23. Peijun Duan and Tony Saich. 2014. 'Reforming China's Monopolies', *Ash Centre Occasional Papers.* No. RWP14-023, May, 34.
24. The 13 JSCBS include the Bank of Communications (BoComm), China Merchants Bank (Merchants), CITIC Industrial Bank (CITIC), Shanghai Pudong Development Bank (Pudong), China Minsheng Banking Corporation (Minsheng), Industrial Bank, formerly Fujian Industrial Bank (Industrial), China Everbright Bank (Everbright), Guangdong Development Bank (GDB), Huaxia Bank (Huaxia), Hengfeng Bank (Hengfeng), Shenzhen Development Bank (SDB) as well as the two JSCBs established at the end of 2005, Huishang Bank (from a merger of some CCBs in Anhui province) and Bohai Bank (with support from Standard Chartered).

25. Kumiko Okazaki. 2007. 'Banking System Reform in China', *RAND Occasional Papers*, No. 194, 20.
26. UBS became the first foreign strategic investor to quit.
27. Zhu Chuanrui. 2018. 'The Impact of Foreign Strategic Investors' Shareholding Changes on China's Commercial Banks under the Impact of International Liquidity Crisis—Targeting at Bank of China and its Foreign Strategic Investors in Financial Crisis', paper presented at the *2018 International Conference on Economics, Politics and Business Management (ICEPBM 2018),* 23-25 March, https://webofproceedings.org/proceedings_series/ECOM/ICEPBM%202018/ICEPBM029.pdf (accessed on 13 August 2020).
28. Three new 'policy' banks, the Agricultural Development Bank of China (ADBC), China Development Bank (CDB), and the Export-Import Bank of China (Chexim), were established in 1994 to take over the government-directed spending functions of the four state-owned commercial banks.
29. Violaine Cousin. 2007. *Banking in China* (London: Palgrave Macmillan), 128.
30. *Sohu.com.* 2019. 'Guonei yinhang xinyong daikuan, zhizao ye daikuan, zhong changqi daikuan bili shi duoshao? Zhiliang you ruhe?' (国内银行信用贷款、制造业贷款、中长期贷款比例是多少?质量又如何?) [What is the ratio of domestic bank credit loans, manufacturing loans, and medium and long-term loans? How about the quality?], 2 July, https://www.sohu.com/a/324257480_100003691 (accessed on 20 August 2020).
31. Ibid.

7

Survival of the Fittest

In May 2016, when President Xi spoke with officials from Heilongjiang, one of China's poorest provinces, the locals were hastily putting up their problems in front of the President. Expressing hardship explicitly is not permitted as per party etiquette; any reservations over the party and political decisions are extinguished in its early stages. Though some may paint the well-rehearsed trips to provinces by the President, Premier, Politburo Standing Committee members, and other politburo members' ground supervision, the meetings hardly provide enough room for helpless provincial party workers to put forth the reality of the provinces, leave alone the ordinary Chinese who make up an obedient crowd to get a glimpse of their supreme leader. Party cadres function within demarcated and curated watertight compartments of political affiliations, and hence local questions, if unheard at the origins, will hardly have any audience elsewhere. Sometimes, administrative and complex fiscal reasons fail to resolve the worries of provincial delegates and are left unheard in highly secretive and hierarchical Beijing circles. The tenets of Chinese communism—*resistance and contradictions*—have seen newer subscribers. The party has created steep power struggles within. Even for party workers in provinces, linkages come in handy to break the barriers and make the point. Meeting with President Xi is often exploited by the locals from the party organisation as an opportunity to explain their problems and get heard but *benignly*.

Back to Xi's visit to Heilongjiang, when officials from Heilongjiang used a party card, one could have indeed fetched an answer. While one of the officials was explaining the local grievances of decreasing revenue and adverse climatic conditions in this north-eastern province of China, which borders Far Eastern Russia and North Korea, Xi cut them short and counter-argued that neighbouring provinces like Hebei and Inner Mongolia are developing snow projects despite the equally adverse environment! President Xi reminded the officials to remember that the socialist economy's new principle is *to compete and survive*. The best performers are visible, and the Party awards them and helps them rise in party ranks. He further said, "Fierce competition is like sailing against the current" (激烈的竞争就像逆流而上 *Jilie de jingzheng jiu xiang niliu er shang*).[1] The then governor of the province, Lu Hao, who was caught in a dilemma, was instead thinking how "some provincial state-owned enterprises could survive such cruel competition without reform".[2] Competition is seen as a booster dose and widely used by the central leadership to let cadres, officials, institutions, universities, provinces, and even the SOEs perform to the best of their abilities. For a socialist market economy like China, everything goes by the Darwinian dictum of survival of the fittest. For leaders, SOEs, provinces, and common Chinese, competition is the golden rule to out-survive pressure and prove ability.

The Inter-SOE competition between provincial enterprises (省级企业 *Sheng ji qiye*), Subsidiary SOEs at provinces (SSP) (地方国企 *di fang guo qi*) and Central SOEs (中央企 *Zhong yang qi*) is central to debates surrounding the competitive dynamics and survival of the enterprises under central authorities and beyond. China's Central SOEs comprise a headquarter and several subsidiaries. Subsidiary SOEs—the SSP—are subsidiaries of Central SOEs and are directly controlled by the parent Central SOE. Under planned economy, the government's administrative jurisdiction was divided into four levels: Central enterprises, provincial and autonomous region-level enterprises, prefecture-level enterprises, and county-level enterprises. Each enterprise was managed centrally by an industry. After the reforms and opening up, several adjustments were made, where the management of the Central government (ministries and commissions) was delegated to local governments. The remaining Central enterprises were unified under the State-owned Assets Supervision and Administration Commission (SASAC). After the restructuring of SOEs, the state-controlled enterprises are managed by the SASAC of local governments at all levels. Regardless of their size, other enterprises are governed according to their respective regions, which are categorised as provincial enterprises.

Central SOEs (中央企 *Zhong yang qi*) versus Subsidiary SOEs in Provinces (SSP) (地方国企 *Di fang guo qi*)

The SOEs have a specific administrative nature. Due to historical reasons, the classification of SOEs is quite complicated. China's SOEs are those with investments in state assets or holding more than 50 per cent of their shares. According to the division of the state-owned assets management authority, SOEs are divided into Central enterprises (state-owned enterprises supervised and managed by the Central government) (中央企 *Zhong yang qi*) and Subsidiary SOEs in the provinces (SSP), supervised and managed by local governments (地方国企 *Di fang guo qi*). The responsibilities of individual Central enterprises in the process of national social and economic development are relatively unique, and they are under the direct management of the State Council. As we have seen in Chapter Three, the Central SOEs are at the ministerial level, and their subsidiaries, which they can establish, can vary in types. The Company Law of the PRC, under Article 14 A, allows companies to set up branches.[3] To set up a branch, one needs to apply to the Company Registration Authority and obtain a business licence. There are three types of subordinate units of Central SOEs—wholly-owned subsidiaries like China Railways, which has hundreds of such subsidiary enterprises. It is followed by enterprises owned and controlled by those who hold 50 per cent of the shares of enterprises or hold the largest shareholding to exercise controlling rights. The third type includes those enterprises where the Central SOEs hold some shares, sometimes even less than 10 per cent, and is called the state-owned shareholding company.

The SASAC funds the three-tier subsidiaries of Central enterprises and has the right to participate in important decision-making and management of personnel. The provincial enterprises (省级企业 *Sheng ji qiye*) are generally under the direct jurisdiction of the provincial SASAC. The provincial SASAC appoints managers and supervises and assesses production. Besides, significant issues related to the enterprise's sustainability, such as operation management, finance and reform, are reported and approved by the provincial SASAC.

Many Central SOEs' projects are operated by Subsidiary SOEs in the provinces (the SSP), i.e., high-speed rail construction subsidiary companies.

The parent company, similar to the banking structure, mainly undertakes overall national planning and large-scale national projects. Simultaneously, the head office is responsible for coordinating and undertaking a few large-scale projects and local branches responsible for delegated affairs. Therefore, in China's case, when one discusses issues related to Central SOEs, it often represents the performance contributed by the SSP as well. The performance of the Central SOEs and their budgetary infusions into SSP are treated as integrated operations of the parent SOE. In other words, SSP refers to enterprises established or listed by Central State agencies and locally managed by the provincial authorities as supervisors. Generally, it is directly under the jurisdiction of the provincial SASAC. SOEs have a particular administrative nature, while Provincial enterprises are directly affiliated with local governments.

A Case Study—State Grid Corporation of China (SGCC)

Let us look at power generation and supply to better explain the relationship between Central SOEs and their subsidiaries in the provinces (SSPs). The State Grid Corporation of China (SGCC) and China Southern Power Grid (CSG) are the two largest transmission monopolies in China. In numbers, by 2017, SGCC had a customer base of over 1.1 billion, while CSG served a population of over 230 million and the combined customer basis totalled 1.33 billion.[4] As per statistics from the National Energy Administration, in 2019, the share of the SGCCs in the total national electricity consumption (7.2255 trillion kWh) was 4.45 trillion kWh (62 per cent), and China Southern Grid's share reached 1.0518 trillion kWh (15 per cent).[5] Moreover, SGCC and CSG ranked No. 2 and No. 105, respectively, in the 2020 *Fortune Global 500* list.[6] Of course, the might of the SGCC is unmatchable as explained earlier. The State Grid, the behemoth SOE, transmits and supplies nearly 88 per cent of electricity to China's territory[7] (Map 7.1). It is an extra-large Central key SOE related to the lifeline of the Chinese economy and critical infrastructure. The enterprise undertakes investment in the construction and operation of power grids as its core business. In short, the duo is the sole investor, owner, builder, and operator of the nation's electricity transmission and distribution infrastructures.[8]

The SGCC commands electricity supplies across China except for a few geographical pockets. Besides the two Central SOEs directly under the SASAC—SGCC and CSG—there is also a regional power company—Mengxi

Power Company, in the Inner Mongolia Autonomous Region, which is into power transmission and electricity grid management at a sub-national level. These three power companies cover the maximum power supply in China. The operation area of SGCC involves all provinces except Guangdong, Guangxi, Yunnan, Guizhou, Hainan, and parts of West Inner Mongolia (see Map 7.1 and Table 7.1).[9]

Map 7.1: Central SOEs' Duopoly* in Power Transmission

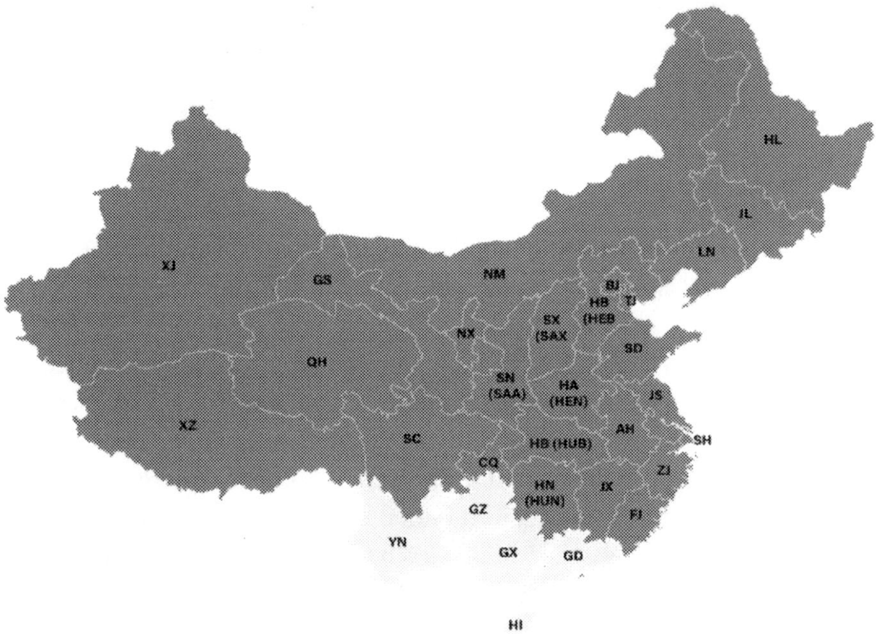

State Grid Corporation of China (SGCC)

AH (Anhui); **BJ** (Beijing); **CQ** (Chongqing); **FJ** (Fujian); **GS** (Gansu); **HA** (HEN) (Henan); **HB** (HEB) (Hebei); **HN** (HUN) (Hunan); **HB** (HUB) (Hubei); **HL** (Heilongjiang); **JL** (Jilin); **JS** (Jiangsu); **JX** (Jiangxi); **LN** (Liaoning); **NM** (Inner Mongolia Autonomous Region); **NX** (Ningxia Autonomous Region); **QH** (Qinghai); **SC** (Sichuan); **SD** (Shandong); **SX** (SAX) (Shanxi); **SN** (SAA) (Shaanxi); **SH** (Shanghai); **TJ** (Tianjin); **XJ** (Xinjiang); **XZ** (Tibet); **ZJ** (Zhejiang).

China Southern Power Grid (CSG)

GD (Guangdong); **GX** (Guangxi); **GZ** (Guizhou); **HI** (Hainan); **YN** (Yunnan).

*Except for the west of Inner Mongolia province, which is covered by Mengxi Power Company.

Note: Despite the extensive geographical cover, the duopoly covers only 88 per cent of China's physical landmass because the Central SOEs do include Taiwan (TW), Hong Kong SAR (HK), and Macao SAR (MO).

Source: Map populated by the author based on SGCC and CSG websites.

Generally, each province has its own power supply company, which means each province or municipality owns and controls one provincial/municipal level power supply company, i.e., Mengdong Electric Power Company in the Inner Mongolia Autonomous Region. Hebei province is an exception where there are two provincial-level power companies, namely, Hebei Electric Power and Jibei Electric Power. As per the local laws, the local power can be set up and may function under the aegis of the local administration.

Table 7.1: The State Grid Corporations of China's (SGCC) Provincial/ Municipal Subsidiaries (State Grid SSPs)

State Grid Beijing Electric Power Company
State Grid Tianjin Electric Power Company
State Grid Hebei Electric Power Company
State Grid Jibei Electric Power Company
State Grid Shanxi Electric Power Company
State Grid Shandong Electric Power Company
State Grid Shanghai Electric Power Company
State Grid Jiangsu Electric Power Company
State Grid Zhejiang Electric Power Company
State Grid Anhui Electric Power Company
State Grid Fujian Electric Power Company
State Grid Hubei Electric Power Company
State Grid Hunan Electric Power Company
State Grid Henan Electric Power Company
State Grid Jiangxi Electric Power Company
State Grid Sichuan Electric Power Company
State Grid Chongqing Electric Power Company
State Grid Liaoning Electric Power Company
State Grid Jilin Electric Power Company
State Grid Heilongjiang Electric Power Company
State Grid Inner Mongolia Eastern Electric Power Company
State Grid Shaanxi Electric Power Company
State Grid Gansu Electric Power Company
State Grid Qinghai Electric Power Company
State Grid Ningxia Electric Power Company
State Grid Xinjiang Electric Power Company
State Grid Tibet Electric Power Company

Source: State Grid Corporation of China (SGCC) online portal, 2020.

The SGCC includes dozens of subsidiaries (see Table 7.1). The provincial power company is a wholly-owned subsidiary of the SGCC and an independent legal entity. These subsidiaries involve all aspects of the power grid and are responsible for the operation of each province. Essentially, the data concerning power generation and consumption of SGCC reflects the sum of the operating levels of the provincial and municipal subsidiaries of the Central SOE.

The SGCC follows a standard hierarchical organisational structure. The Central SOE has several SSPs operating under the Beijing headquarters and includes the Provincial Electric Power Research Institute, the Provincial Economic Research Institute, the Provincial Power Supply Bureau and the maintenance company. The flow of organisational structure is straightforward where the SGCC has six divisional/regional headquarters, 27 subsidiary companies (as SSPs), and each provincial company has several prefecture-level power supply companies, the control centre of prefecture-level power supply companies, maintenance centre, metering centre, and county-level power supply company.[10] The 27 subsidiaries of the SGCC are organised into six different regional divisions (see Table 7.2 below).[11]

Table 7.2: Divisional/Regional Grouping of SGCC's Provincial SOEs (SSPs)

Geographic region	*Entity*	*Member Provincial SOEs*
The North China Branch of State Grid Corporation	North China Power Grid Co. Ltd.	Beijing Electric Power Company; Tianjin Electric Power Company; Hebei Electric Power Company; Shanxi Electric Power Company; Shandong Electric Power Group; and Jibei Electric Power Company
Central China Branch of State Grid Corporation	Central China Power Grid Co. Ltd.	Hubei Electric Power Company; Hunan Electric Power Company; Jiangxi Electric Power Company; and Henan Electric Power Company
East China Branch of State Grid Corporation	East China Grid Co. Ltd.	Shanghai Electric Power Company; Jiangsu Electric Power Company; Zhejiang Electric Power Company; Anhui Electric Power Company; and Fujian Electric Power Company

Geographic region	*Entity*	*Member Provincial SOEs*
Northwest Branch of State Grid Corporation	Northwest Power Grid Co. Ltd.	Shaanxi Electric Power Company; Gansu Electric Power Company; Ningxia Electric Power Company; Qinghai Electric Power Company; and Xinjiang Electric Power Company
Northeast Branch of State Grid Corporation	Northeast Grid Co. Ltd.	Liaoning Electric Power Company; Jilin Electric Power Company; Heilongjiang Electric Power Company; and Inner Mongolia Eastern Electric Power Company
Southwest Branch of State Grid Corporation	Southwest Power Grid Co. Ltd.	Sichuan Electric Power Company; Chongqing Electric Power Company; and Tibet Electric Power Company

Source: Author's Analysis based on State Grid Corporation (SGCC) online portal, 2020 and various reports by SGCC.

Inter-SSP Competitive Dynamics (Subsidiary SOEs in the Provinces)

After looking at the SOE hierarchical nature in China, it is natural to conceive Central SOEs as the leading players in Chinese growth and their subsidiaries as equal shareholder in profits and incentives. Being a subsidiary of the Central SOEs, their subsidiary SOEs – SSPs acquire a lot of value addition and easier manoeuvrability in the provincial bureaucratic set-up. Still, it is not what the provinces look for. Besides hosting the increasing number of SSPs and value addition, provinces expect a considerable share in the SSP's profits, infuse employment opportunities, and improve the overall excellence in performance. The local SOEs of a particular Central SOE work hard to bag projects and pilot programs to be introduced in their respective provinces or divisions. Within the hierarchical structure, any SSP establishes a subsidiary role with the parent SOEs. The SSP would follow what the parent Central SOEs would assign to them, as the Central SOEs work under the State Council's directions, although this practice leads to many entanglements.

The relationship between the three, i.e., Central SOEs, divisional/regional grid company, and the provincial power company (an SSP), is defined through delegated work and coordination among a group of provincial power companies under a divisional/regional set-up. As mentioned above, the provincial power company is a wholly-owned subsidiary of the SGCC with an independent legal entity. The divisional/regional power grid company comprises several provincial power companies that are its member units. The external power transmission, especially the cross-regional and inter-provincial transmission of electric energy, is organised by the divisional/regional grid company and is uniformly dispatched by the divisional/regional grid company. The provincial company's general manager is a member of the divisional/regional grid company's board of directors.

At times, the divisional/regional companies fall short of bringing SSPs together and coordinating them. The inter-regional competition is even intense as regional growth zones have been formed across three delta regions. The SSPs make enormous investments for enhancing the infrastructure and expect higher returns, which transform the local enterprises into commercial entities forcing them to adapt to competitive dynamics. These SSPs of the SGCC tie up with the neighbouring SSPs covering the entire development zone or the division for efficient performance. This is evident when a unit's performance and profits are linked to a budding local political leadership's ability. The inter-SSPs continue to compete and outperform other subsidiaries from neighbouring provinces leading to an implicit competition.

Within a regional division, SSPs, besides competing with neighbouring provinces, also cut across regional competitions. How does this happen? The SSPs invest in expanding the infrastructure of the Central SOEs in their respective provinces. Let us take a few examples to explain this case in detail. While the Chinese state modernises its infrastructure, it employs supercritical *ultra-high voltage* electricity transmission (*UHV* electricity transmission) lines for fast, long-distance power transmission and smart grids to boost end-use efficiency. State-owned power transmission utilities, viz., SGCC and CSG, will be owners and developers of these UHV projects. The two utilities had identified 14 projects for development in 2020,[12] which shall employ High Voltage Alternating Current (HVAC) and High Voltage Direct Current (HVDC) technologies. SGCC announced investments for a total of 450 billion yuan in 2020 (US$ 65 billion), with UHV projects accounting for 40 per cent of total investment.[13]

UHV refers to the transmission technology with voltage levels of AC 1000 kV and above and DC ±800 kV and above. The technical advantages of UHV are large transmission capacity, long-distance, high efficiency, and low loss. Since 2004, the SGCC integrated its efforts to achieve comprehensive innovation breakthroughs in UHV theory, technology, standards, equipment, engineering construction and operation. It has deployed UHV transmission technology with independent intellectual property rights and integrated UHV. The export of technology and equipment abroad were put forward under the tag of 'Made in China' and projected as the leader in cutting-edge technologies. Key UHV direct current transmission projects, including the ±800 *kV* Qinghai-Henan and ±800 *kV* Yazhong-Jiangxi projects, and the Shaanbei-Wuhan link started construction in February 2020.[14] In March 2020, the Standing Committee of the Central Political Bureau of the CPC chaired by Xi Jinping decided that the country should accelerate investment in this "new infrastructure".[15] By the end of March 2020, there were 25 operating UHV transmission lines in China, with seven more lines being constructed and seven other lines in the process of obtaining administrative approvals.[16]

The UHV projects that have been put into operation have a cumulative length of transmission lines of 35,583 km and a cumulative power transformation (conversion) capacity of 396.67 million kilowatts. The design capacity of cross-provincial and cross-regional transmission channels in the company's operating areas reached 210 million kilowatts, and the project is designed to transport 40 billion kilowatt-hours of clean power a year.[17] This helped improve the grid resource allocation capacity, ensure power supply, promote clean energy development, improve the environment, and upgrade grid safety levels. As having experienced four development stages, China is the only country in the UHV transmission field that has achieved large-scale commercial operations.

The cumulative investment scale of the previous three stages is believed to have reached 501.2 billion yuan (US$ 78.90 billion).[18] Not to underestimate that, the SSPs rely on the SGCC's spending on UHV power transmission projects to bring in revenue. In addition to the SSPs of the SGCC, the subordinate units (Table 7.3) also count on the SGCC's announcements and megaprojects and await to reap the benefits. These SGCC subordinate units that produce power equipment, including Henan Pinggao Electric Co. Ltd. (#17 in Table 7.3) and XJ Electric (#16 in Table 7.3), have been going through hard times in keeping their share of profits for the past few years.[19] This certainly casts its impact on the performance of the SSPs and provincial economies. Besides, the SGCC's geographical distribution of the overall budget also impacts the progress of employment driving some of the significant economic indicators. The SGCC's preliminary plan to invest 450 billion yuan

(US$ 67.16 billion) in power grid construction in 2020 was expected to lead to a social investment of more than 900 billion yuan (US$ 134.32 billion).[20]

Table 7.3: The State Grid Corporations of China's (SGCC) Subordinate Units

1	Global Energy Internet Group Co. Ltd.
2	State Grid International Development Co. Ltd.
3	Luneng Group Co. Ltd. (Ducheng Weiye Group Co. Ltd.)
4	NARI Group Co. Ltd. (State Grid Electric Power Research Institute)
5	State Grid Information and Communication Industry Group Co. Ltd.
6	State Grid Electric Vehicle Service Co. Ltd.
7	State Grid E-Commerce Co. Ltd. (State Grid Xiong'an Financial Technology Group Co. Ltd.)
8	China Power Technology Equipment Co. Ltd.
9	State Grid Xinyuan Holdings Co. Ltd. (State Grid Xinyuan Hydropower Co. Ltd.)
10	State Grid General Aviation Co. Ltd.
11	State Grid Materials Co. Ltd.
12	Yingda Media Investment Group Co. Ltd.
13	State Grid Integrated Energy Service Group Co. Ltd.
14	State Grid Zhongxing Co. Ltd.
15	Interchina Health Group Co. Ltd.
16	Xu Ji Group Co. Ltd.
17	Pinggao Group Co. Ltd.
18	Shandong Electric Group Co. Ltd.
19	State Grid Corporation of China DC Technology Centre
20	State Grid Corporation of China DC Construction Branch
21	State Grid Corporation of China AC Construction Branch
22	Information and Communication Branch of State Grid Corporation of China
23	State Grid Corporation of China Customer Service Centre
24	State Grid Corporation of China Big Data Centre
25	China Electric Power Research Institute Co. Ltd. (State Grid Corporation of China Energy Internet Technology Research Institute)
26	State Grid Economic and Technology Research Institute Co. Ltd.
27	State Grid Energy Research Institute Co. Ltd. (State Grid Corporation of China Energy Internet Economic Research Institute)
28	Global Energy Internet Research Institute Co. Ltd.
29	Party School of the State Grid Corporation of China(State Grid Management Institute)
30	State Grid University(Advanced Training Centre of State Grid Corporation of China)
31	National Grid Corporation of China Technical College Branch
32	State Grid Yingda International Holdings Group Co. Ltd.
33	China Power Finance Co. Ltd.
34	Yingda Taihe Property Insurance Co. Ltd.
35	Yingda Taihe Life Insurance Co. Ltd.
36	Yingda Changan Insurance Brokers Group Co. Ltd.
37	Yingda International Trust Co. Ltd.
38	Yingda Securities Co. Ltd.
39	State Grid International Financial Leasing Co. Ltd.
40	State Grid Overseas Investment Co. Ltd.

Source: State Grid Corporation of China (SGCC) online portal, 2020.

The construction of UHV lines in the past few years have yielded profits and various SSPs and their local budgetary bodies (provincial governments) have also invested handsomely. Although the SSPs have taken the lead in supplementing some of these investments, most of the fund sources have not been clarified anywhere in their declarations. During the interviews and field visits, it was noticed that a major part of the investments into UHV lines have come from provincial budgetary interventions. The UHV line-laying is centralised, and the provinces use SSPs to facilitate the aroused interests of the provinces.

On 12 February 2020, the State Grid Hangzhou Power Supply Company declared the first batch of power grid infrastructure investment of 4.1 billion yuan (US$ 611.94 million) and kick started the ±800 kV Baihetan-Zhejiang preliminary work of the UHV DC line.[21] Guangdong, the prosperous hub of Chinese manufacturing industries, also took the lead in construction project plans involving key energy projects such as offshore wind power, power transmission and transformation projects, UHV, waste incineration power generation, hydropower, and nuclear power. Among them, the power grid projects involved the second interconnection project of the southern main grid and the Hainan power grid (Guangdong section), 550kv, 220kv power transmission and transformation projects, 110kv and below distribution network projects, Wudongde Power Station to Guangdong Guangxi (Kunliulong DC power transmission project (UHV multi-terminal DC demonstration project) Guangdong section. The planned investment in power grid projects in 2019 exceeded 44.5 billion yuan (US$ 6.64 billion).[22] Among other provinces, Anhui also showed keen interest in claiming its share of the pie in the futuristic UHV scheme of projects. According to the State Grid Anhui Electric Power Company, the 1000 kV Wuhu substation main transformer expansion project was approved by the Anhui Provincial Development and Reform Commission. This is the first UHV project approved in the entire SGCC network, as Anhui's publicity department claims. An official provincial news release proudly highlights Anhui's destiny by reasserting that Anhui bagged the first nationally approved UHV project after the accelerated implementation of the new infrastructure strategy was deployed by the Chinese state. The claim turns cognisable when each of these provinces put investment to gain an edge over each other.[23]

However, the gestation period for profits is longer. A UHV transmission line absorbs tens of billions in investments, and it is expected that the payback time is three to five years; moreover, the provincial leaders do want to question the prospects as well because the present functional UHV lines are not even optimally used. Besides, while on the one hand, the SSPs (Table 7.1) struggle to adjust their profit to the investment ratio on the other, the regional divisions weigh in to support their respective SSPs' developmental schemes. Another factor influencing the SSPs' responses is the regionally integrated development schemes and geographical zones of experiments and reforms (Map 7.2). The SGCC sees high consumption with soaring profits and demand surge from these areas. For example, China's major electricity-consuming provinces are concentrated in North China, East China, and middle China, with a massive shortfall of electricity in places like Jiangsu, Zhejiang, Shanghai, and Beijing. The transmission of surplus electricity to mitigate shortfall deficiency is seen as essential and driving UHV construction. The regionally integrated economic zones (Map 7.2) such as the Yangtze River Delta, Beijing-Tianjin-Hebei-Shandong peninsula, Central Plains Economic Zones, Chengyu Economic Zone, and Guangdong-Hong Kong-Macao Pearl River Delta regions are the prime areas of electricity consumption, and areas with a more developed digital economy. Provincial SGCC subsidiaries are doing better, given the provincial economy's condition. But not all the SGCC subsidiaries are earning enough profits to cover their operating costs and reduce the ratio between assets and returns, thus impacting the parent Central SOE's performance—the SGCC. Competition does not always bring efficiency, and the present leadership and team face the challenge of dealing with these internal paradoxes.

The emerging situation does not create a sound balance sheet and generates tension in employment creation and efficient use of the capital of local financial institutions. This creates unsustainable opportunities for the SGCC's provincial subsidiaries leading to greater variations in profits, employment, salaries, assets, and perks of the SSPs. For example, the wages of the SGCC's SSPs differ from province to province for the same employment position. This is because of the local economic level and electricity consumption, and various historical factors, including share transfer, equipment assets, collective employee restructuring, placement,

Map 7.2: Regional Economic/Growth Zones

Source: Map customised by the author based on primary sources

etc. During interactions with officials from the provincial SGCC, it was revealed that the power grid company's local income level falls in the category of the upper-middle class.[24] The power grid's salary structure is still admirable in the second and third-tier cities, but in the first-tier cities, it still lacks competitiveness.[25]

Performance of Central and SSPs (Subsidiary SOEs in the Provinces)

The role of Central SOE has been streamlined to manage the assets, increase revenue, and therein improve the ratio of profits and pay sizable taxes in which the subsidiaries of the Central SOEs play a critical role. The provincial governments in China balance between hosting the giant subsidiaries of Central enterprises and promoting the Provincial enterprises. But the role of SSPs is beyond the reach of Provincial enterprises. Although the Central administrative bureau controls the revenue-sharing model, the provinces are also given due share in the profits of the local enterprises. In its October 2019 order, the State Council directed value-added tax (VAT) revenue to be shared 50:50 with the local governments.[26] As far as the Corporate income tax (CIT) is concerned, the part paid by the China Railway Corporation (formerly the Ministry of Railways), bank head offices, and offshore oil companies belong to the Central government, whereby the Central and local governments share 60 per cent and 40 per cent respectively.[27] It so happens that the local government retains 40 per cent of the CIT collected and forwards the remaining 60 per cent to the Central government.

The performance of the Central SOEs and their local subsidiaries (SSPs) need to be analysed based on their assets, liability ratio, revenue, profits, and taxes. In 2018, the total assets of China's SOEs were 178.75 trillion yuan (US$ 26.67 trillion) (Figure 7.1), an increase of 27.04 trillion yuan over 2017

Figure 7.1: The Assets and Growth Rate of SOEs (2014-2018)

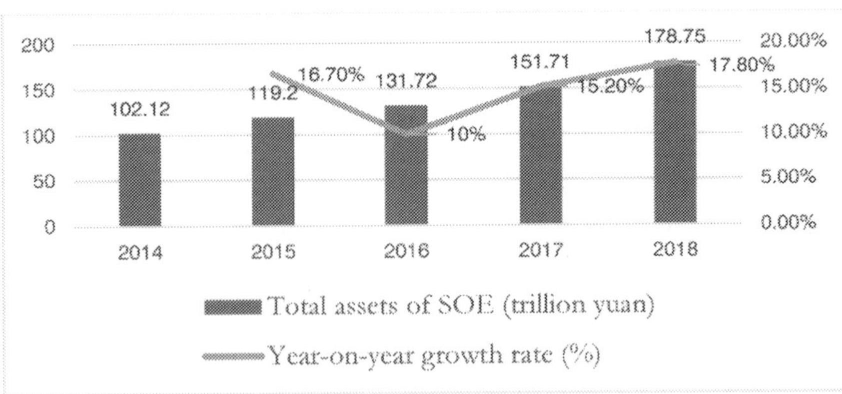

Source: Author's analysis (based on inputs from the Ministry of Finance and SASAC's periodic press releases and statements)

(US$ 4.03 trillion) and a year-on-year increase of 17.8 per cent. Further separation indicates that during the same year (2018), the total assets of China's Central SOEs were 80.34 trillion yuan (US$ 12 trillion), while the total assets of local SOEs (SSPs) were 98.41 trillion yuan (Figure 7.2) (US$ 14.68 trillion).

Figure 7.2: Total Assets of Central Enterprises and Local SOEs (Subsidiary SOEs in the Provinces) from 2014 to 2018

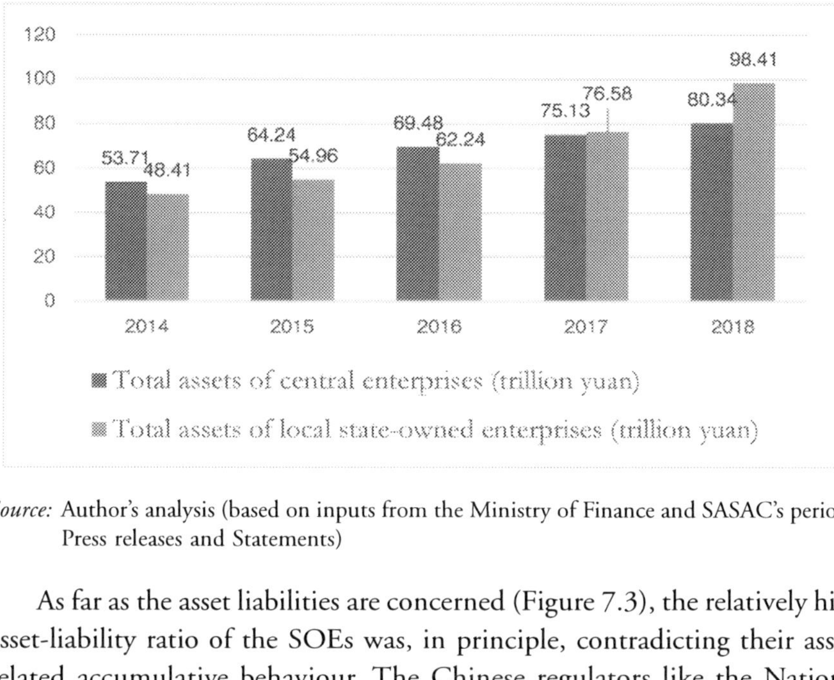

Source: Author's analysis (based on inputs from the Ministry of Finance and SASAC's periodic Press releases and Statements)

As far as the asset liabilities are concerned (Figure 7.3), the relatively high asset-liability ratio of the SOEs was, in principle, contradicting their asset-related accumulative behaviour. The Chinese regulators like the National Development and Reform Commission (NDRC) and Ministry of Finance require SOEs to reduce leverage by optimising their governance structure and market-oriented debt-to-equity swaps to reduce the average asset-liability ratio. There is a nominal reduction compared to the year 2018 (Figure 7.3), but it is not yet substantial (an expected drop by 2-3 per cent). The fundamental problem lies in the intricate connection between state-owned financial institutions and SOEs, determining the latter's high leverage. The high leverage is reflected in a high debt ratio. As a result, China's financial risks are mainly concentrated in the SOEs with high leverage, and there is an acute need for SOEs to de-leverage. As per official figures, in 2018, the asset-liability ratio of

Chinese SOEs was 64.7 per cent. In 2019, the asset-liability ratio of Chinese SOEs was 63.9 per cent, a decrease of 0.8 per cent from 2018. But the picture is far from reality, and the press releases often deflect the severe facts. As per independent statistical research data,[28] the ratio is much higher than the official data. Fourty to 60 per cent of SOEs have an asset-liability ratio of more than 90 per cent; 5 to 15 per cent have more than 95 per cent debt ratio. Some enterprises even have a debt ratio of more than 100 per cent. Information about liabilities is not made public fearing financial risks. The debt-to-asset ratio, which is higher than 40 per cent, is termed a high debt ratio, which is alarming.

Figure 7.3: SOEs' Asset-Liability Ratio

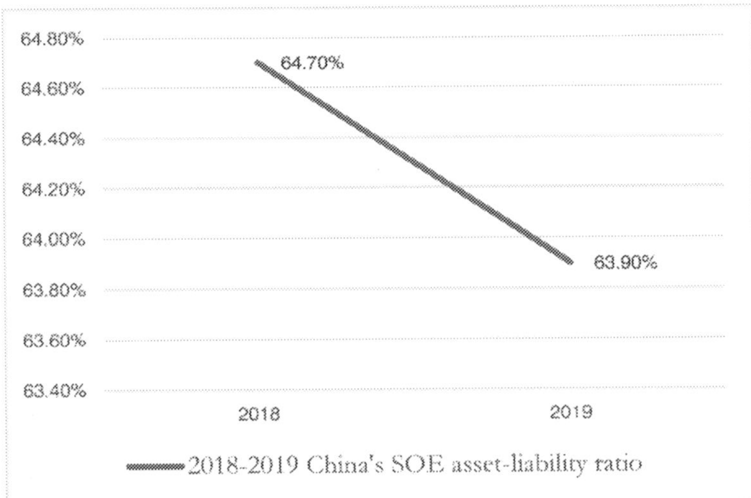

Source: Author's analysis (based on inputs from the Ministry of Finance and SASAC's periodic press releases and statements)

From 2016 to 2019, the total operating income or revenue of Central SOEs increased every year and gradually declined. Compared to 2015, the revenue in 2019 grew by more than 30 per cent. In 2018, the operating income of Chinese Central SOEs was 33.88 trillion yuan (US$ 5.05 trillion), an increase of 9.9 per cent year-on-year (Figure 7.4). In 2019, the operating income reached 35.9 trillion yuan (US$ 5.35 trillion), an increase of 6.0 per cent year-on-year. The revenue of China's Central SOEs was higher than the revenue of local SOEs (SSPs). In 2018, the revenue of China's Central SOEs was 33.88 trillion yuan (US$ 5.05 trillion), and the revenue of local SOEs (SSPs) was 24.87 trillion yuan (US$ 3.71 trillion) (Figure 7.5); the revenue of Central SOEs reached 35.9 trillion yuan (US$ 5.35 trillion) in 2019, while the local SOEs (SSPs) registered 26.65 trillion yuan in revenue (US$ 3.97 trillion) (Figure 7.5).

Figure 7.4: Revenue and Growth Rate of Central Enterprises from 2014 to 2019

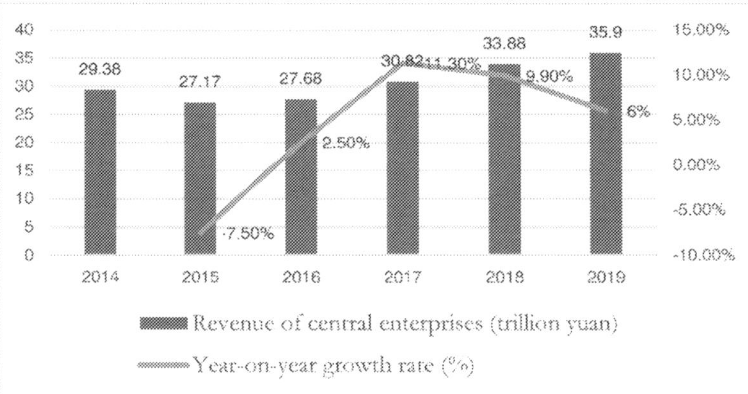

Source: Author's analysis (based on inputs from the Ministry of Finance and SASAC's periodic press releases and statements)

Figure 7.5: Revenue of Central Enterprises and Local SOEs (Subsidiary SOEs in the Provinces) from 2014 to 2019

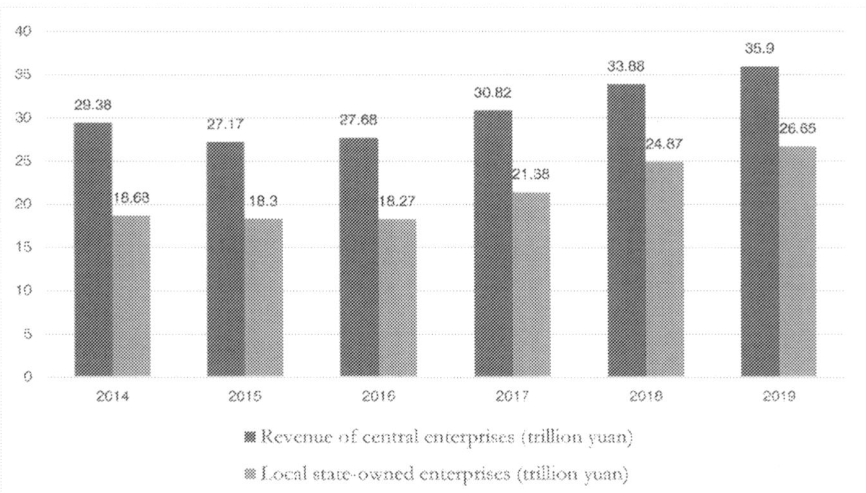

Source: Author's analysis (based on inputs from the Ministry of Finance and SASAC's periodic press releases and statements)

On the profit front (Figure 7.6), in 2018 the Central SOEs recorded a profit of 2.04 trillion yuan (US$ 299 billion), and in 2019 it increased by 0.23 trillion yuan, reaching 2.27 trillion yuan (US$ 34.32 billion). In the same period, in 2018, the total profit of local SOEs was 1.35 trillion yuan (US$ 201.49 billion), but in 2019 it decreased by 0.02 trillion yuan (US$ 2.98 billion) (compared to 2018), registering a lower number of 1.33 trillion yuan (US$ 198.50 billion). The profits of local SOEs (SSPs) do influence the overall profits of their parent Central SOEs. The earnings of the Central SOEs (Figure 7.6) indicate the same tendencies (upward and downward) as the local SOEs (SSPs). The profits of the Central and local SOEs (SSPs) have a causal relationship with assets and taxes paid (Figures 7.7 and 7.8). While the management paid extra attention to assets and the returns over assets, the taxes and fees of SOEs also witnessed a decline. After-taxation, the net profit of SOEs was 263.184 billion yuan (US$ 39.28 billion), a year-on-year increase of 5.2 per cent, and net profit attributable to owners of the parent company was 154.96 billion yuan (US$ 23.12 billion).[29]

The profit rate of costs and expenses of SOEs was 6.0 per cent, a decrease of 0.1 per cent.[30]

Figure 7.6: Total Profits of China's Central Enterprises and Local SOEs (Subsidiary SOEs at Provinces)

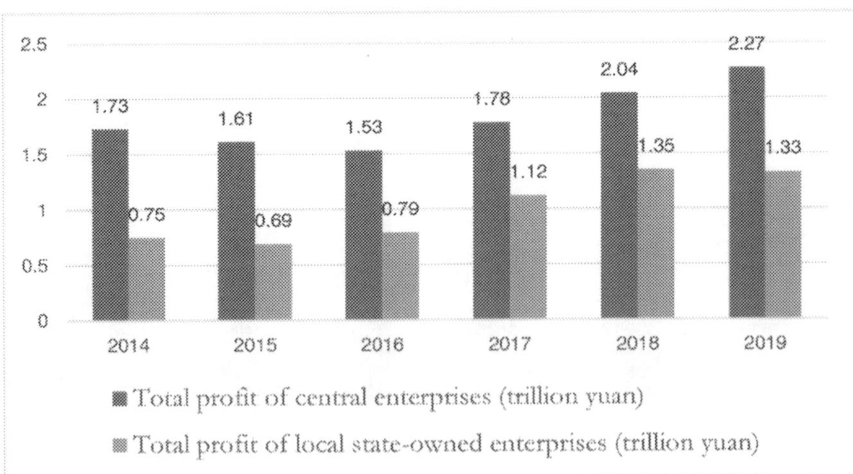

Source: Author's analysis (based on inputs from the Ministry of Finance and SASAC's periodic press releases and statements)

Figure 7.7: Taxes Payable by Chinese SOEs and their Growth Rates from 2014 to 2019

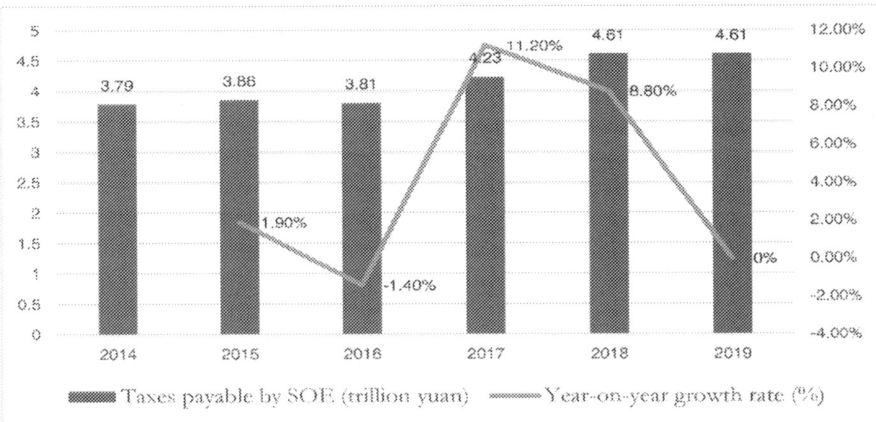

Source: Author's analysis (based on inputs from the Ministry of Finance and SASAC's periodic press releases and statements)

Figure 7.8: Taxes Payable by China's Central Enterprises and Local SOEs (Subsidiary SOEs in the Provinces) from 2014 to 2019

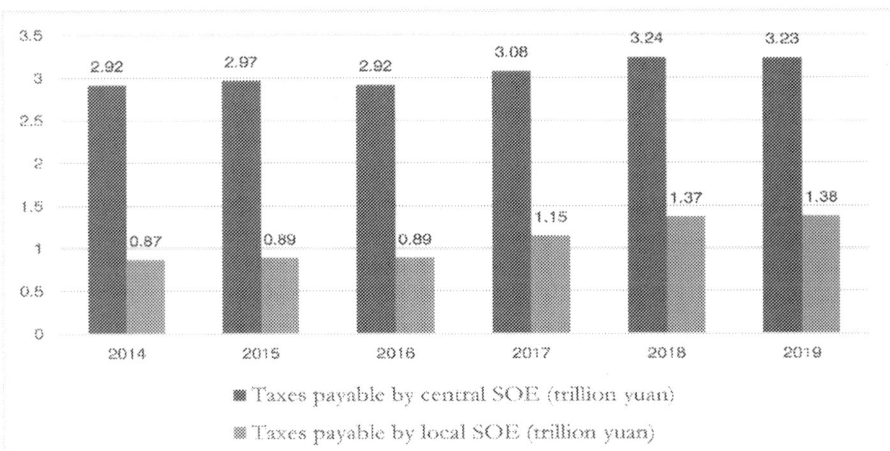

Source: Author's analysis (based on the Ministry of Finance and SASAC's periodic press releases and statements)

In 2018, the tax payable by Chinese SOEs was 4.61 trillion yuan (US$ 688 billion), a year-on-year increase of 8.8 per cent, but in the following year, the number does not reflect any changes. The tax payable by SOEs in 2019 was the same as in 2018, i.e., 4.51 trillion yuan (US$ 673.13 billion). Out of 4.41 trillion yuan (US$ 458.20 billion), the Central SOEs paid twice the tax of local SOEs (SSPs). In 2019, the tax payable by Central SOEs was 3.23 trillion yuan (US$ 482 billion), a year-on-year decrease of 0.01 trillion yuan (US$ 1.49 million) from 2018. In contrast, the tax payable by local SOEs (SSPs) was 1.38 trillion yuan (US$ 205.97 billion), a year-on-year increase of 9.98 million yuan (US$ 1.49 million) from 2018.

China is relatively sensitive to let the Central large-scale enterprises become independent and manage their businesses. While in the rest of the world, the state balances the role of large-scale enterprises, it is non-existent in China. Central enterprises are managed to exert control over various political and economic institutions. This exercise of authority does intend to serve administrative purposes as well. The local enterprises (SSPs) are created with a dual purpose; to shape provincial economies and reinforce Central enterprises.

On the one hand, the local enterprises (SSPs) have been directed by the central administrators and synced with national production and supply goals and do not choose to challenge the Central SOEs' interest and, at times, blindly follow the 'guidelines' of 'notice'. Deferring of implementations has its own economic and political costs for the provincial managers of the local enterprises (SSPs). The competing local enterprises (SSPs) from the other provinces make matters worse, and the liability to the debt ratio widens, creating political risks. Moreover, provinces have to look for alternative sources to keep funding local enterprises with the hope that they perform. The performance of the local SOEs (SSPs) has seen something that cannot be compromised. The provincial leadership does not want to declare non-performance and also resents liquidation. Except for the brand of Central SOEs and its monopolistic hold over provincial trade (performing an essential part in supplying produce and managing supplies itself), the local SOEs (SSPs) do not see Central SOEs taking the burden of funds and investments off the shoulders of local SOEs (SSPs). The parent Central SOEs do not come forward to rescue the local SOEs (SSPs) of their debt and assets built up over decades.

Moreover, property rights of state-owned assets are another critical matter. The SOEs' reforms do not address the relationship between Central and local SOEs (SSPs). The whole debate is caught between the market versus the state-led federal division of political incentives. The property rights relationship between the Central and local governments is away from any resolution, making matters worse. While most of the local SOEs (SSPs) of the same CSOE struggle to perform and compete with their cousin branches in other provinces, there are a few exceptions to this golden rule of competing, survive and rise. For example, the provinces from West China have less costs for the Chinese state as they stand no chance to out-compete coastal and central provinces in debt accumulation. The SOEs from Xinjiang, Shanxi, and Qinghai have a poor record in profits, and operating costs are met with difficulty. The Organisation for Economic Co-operation and Development's (OECD) study report indicates that the SOEs in the three provinces of Xinjiang, Shanxi, and Qinghai rank among the top five in all three indicators of debt to revenue, leverage, and debt service burden. Overall, the SOEs (Central and local) act in tandem, and in many cases, the local SOEs (SSPs) run into a competitive mode to establish their significance. The OECD study further reflects that the assets grew by a negligible level in those industries where the enterprises monopolise. But in the competitive industries, State assets grew rapidly, while in public utilities/ public welfare enterprises, assets grew even faster.[31]

Not all the partnerships between Central SOEs and local SOEs (SSPs) share a pleasant experience, but the functional and political nature of this relationship keeps them mutually interested in each other.

The SSPs carry a mandate of the Central enterprises and sync their priorities as guided by the SASAC under the State Council. But being under the jurisdiction of the provinces, the provincial SASAC includes SSPs and provincial enterprises. Revenue and tax are shared as per the regulations of the State Council. Given such an intricate nature of fiscal sharing, provinces end up having stakes in SSPs too. The SOEs in the provinces, either operating as SSPs or Provincial enterprises, are not small or weak. These enterprises hold a significant position and say over the Chinese State's economic statecraft. Chapter Three has already covered how Chinese enterprises were listed in the *Fortune Global 500* list and how they expanded their global footprint every year. To take a reference from the same list and further analytics of non-central SOEs in the *Fortune Global 500* list gives readers an idea of how critical the role of these non-central SOEs has become.

In 2020, the *Fortune Global 500* list included 48 Central SOEs funded by the SASAC of the State Council, and 32 enterprises, which were financed by the local SASAC (Table 7.4). The difference between the numbers of central and non-central SOEs in the list is not substantial; rather the number of non-central SOEs is significantly high. The Chinese provinces count on these global players to shape the provincial economy and, at the same time, use them as their trump card to push forward the provincial agenda and shift their weight around.

Table 7.4: Fortune Global 500 Ranking of Enterprise Funded by Local SASAC (non-Central SOEs)

Sr. No.	*Rank in Fortune 500*	*Enterprise funded by local SASAC (non-Central SOEs)*	*Chinese*
1	52	SAIC Motor	上海汽车集团股份有限公司
2	134	Beijing Automotive Group	北京汽车集团
3	176	Greenland Holding Group	绿地控股集团有限公司
4	193	China Pacific Insurance (Group)	中国太平洋保险（集团）公司
5	206	Guangzhou Automobile Industry Group	广州汽车工业集团
6	210	Wuchan Zhongda Group	物产中大集团
7	212	Shangdong Energy Group	山东能源集团有限公司
8	218	HBIS Group	河钢集团
9	220	Shanghai Pudong Development Bank	上海浦东发展银行
10	234	XIAMEN C&D	厦门建发集团有限公司
11	265	Shaanxi Yanchang Petroleum (Group)	陕西延长石油（集团）公司
12	273	Shaanxi Coal & Chemical Industry	陕西煤业化工集团
13	284	Xiamen Itg Holding Group	厦门国贸控股集团有限公司
14	295	Yankuang Group	兖矿集团
15	298	XMXYG	象屿集团
16	343	Jiangxi Copper	江西铜业集团公司
17	367	Anhui Conch Group	安徽海螺集团
18	369	Jinchuan Group	金川集团
19	406	Jizhong Energy Group	冀中能源集团
20	423	Shanghai Construction Group	上海建工集团股份有限公司
21	429	Shougang Group	首钢集团
22	442	Shenzhen Investment Holdings	深圳市投资控股有限公司
23	456	Tongling Nonferrous Metals Group	铜陵有色金属集团
24	459	Shandong Iron & Steel Group	山东钢铁集团有限公司
25	463	Datong Coal Mine Group	大同煤矿集团有限责任公司
26	473	Shanghai Pharmaceuticals Holding	上海医药集团股份有限公司
27	485	Shanxi Coking Coal Group	山西焦煤集团有限责任公司
28	486	Henan Energy & Chemical	河南能源化工集团
29	489	Shanxi Luan Mining Group	潞安集团
30	490	Guangxi Investment Group	广西投资集团有限公司
31	499	Yangquan Coal Industry Group	山西阳泉煤业（集团）有限责任公司
32	500	Shanxi Jincheng Anthracite Coal Mining Group	山西晋城无烟煤矿业集团

Source: Author's analysis based on *Fortune Global 500 (2020)* and *SASAC News Briefings*[32]

Provincial Enterprises (省级企业 *Sheng ji qiye*) *Hidden Cost of Market and Competition*

The Chinese state is proud of the federal system it has experimented with, and this includes some illustrative case of its socialist federal character like Autonomous Regions, more prosperous provinces, Special administrative regions and influential municipalities. Throughout the reform years and until now, they have pushed the idea of federalism as an ineffective mechanism. The experience indicates that China represents a substantive degree of fiscal unionism. China is still a transition economy and exhibits a centralised command system. The 1994 reform established a new tax-sharing system wherein it gave local governments more control over local tax administration but no significant tax autonomy and no substantial expenditure assignments. The decentralisation—administratively and fiscal—provided local government with incentives to build a friendly environment of competition for people and capital and help local economies prosper. In practice, China has a unitary fiscal system, and the fiscal revenue sharing schemes limit inter-governmental budget transfers, and eventually, every government level faces hard budget constraints.

The inter-governmental fiscal system was highly redistributive, operated by sharing revenues and produced by government-owned enterprises. During the pre-reform period in China, all the provinces shared the revenues equally despite being a unitary fiscal system. Most of these revenues were generated by the urban industry and transferred to rural areas. The financial flows and remittance were equitably redistributed. However, this fiscal structure had an adverse impact on China, with many problems having their roots in these institutional flaws. While reforms aggravated the competition and experimentation, poor provinces fell short in coping with them and were lagging far behind compared to the prosperous and politically powerful provinces. One can notice how this vicious competition, introduced by the leadership among provinces under decentralisation, let efficiency take over equity and produce "race-to-the-bottom". This is evident in several provinces when, in the 1990s, the Chinese economy transitioned from marathon to sprint, with inland provinces such as Ningxia, Gansu, and Heilongjiang lagging far behind the prosperous coast. Poorer provinces had fewer resources and had to fulfil their socialist promises by employing and protecting specific industries and keep their faith in their provincial enterprises. In comparison, more prosperous provinces had access, reserves, and structures. Fiscal decentralisation encouraged local officials to protect the local markets of their industries. Interestingly, as China's economy retards, provinces are told to be innovative and competitive, and mandatory SOE restructuring guidelines are issued. The slower growth puts pressure on the provincial enterprise to fulfil its welfare deliverables, ensure provincial growth, and persist and compete with Central SOEs.

The provincial-level enterprise can operate in the entire province. Since most of the provincial SOEs and provincial enterprises are not listed companies, and a lot of information is not public and difficult to obtain, only a few studies in China help reflect various aspects of provincial enterprises. In the following section, based on its primary literature, meetings, and discussion, takes this discussion ahead.

A Case—Provincial Enterprises of Zhejiang

Map 7.3: Zhejiang Province

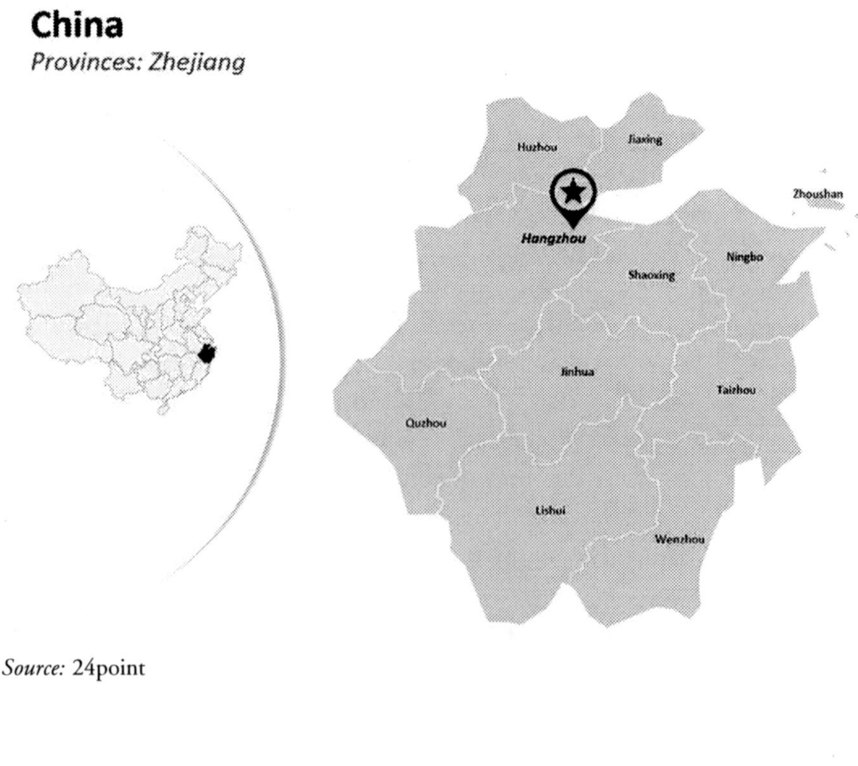

Source: 24point

During the long years of the planned economy, nearby Fujian and Zhejiang province were at the forefront of reforms and opening up. It scaled up quickly with a few heavy industries and large-scale projects in a short period. Also, Zhejiang has a fragile agriculture system owing largely to its mountainous terrain that also makes it challenging to build better connections with the string of ports and transport hubs in the region. The provincial enterprises faced an uphill task to overcome these barriers and also compete better than enterprises in neighbouring provinces. Despite their locations in the Yangtze River Delta Region (see Map 7.2), there has historically been a large gap between Zhejiang and the neighbouring province, Jiangsu, home to the ancient capital of Nanjing. In 1978, Zhejiang ranked 12th nationally in terms of GDP and 16th in per capita GDP. At that time, the economy was only half the size of Jiangsu, which ranked fifth. Zhejiang has been one of China's fastest-growing provinces. Over the past 40 years, the total GDP of the province jumped from 12.4 billion yuan (US$ 1.8 billion) in 1978 to 5.17 trillion yuan (US$ 739.5 billion) in 2020, which is comparable to a country like the Netherlands.[33] As of 2017, Zhejiang's GDP ranked fourth nationally for 22 consecutive years, and its GDP ranks fifth only after Shanghai, Beijing, Tianjin, and Jiangsu.

The provincial enterprises are crucial for the Party to mobilise party committees and reorganise itself internally. Apart from the socio-economic goals of provincial enterprises, their performance is essential for attracting enough political attention and let the provincial leadership use the same to strengthen its role compared to other provincial party organisations. Provincial party factions do use provincial enterprises to manage relations with their competitors regionally and nationally. As discussed earlier, the State-owned Assets Supervision and Administration Commission (SASAC) is directly handled by the Party for its interests. This is true about appointments, management structures, promotions, and even a way to get into the party apparatus. The present General Secretary of the Party also rose to high ranks after serving in Zhejiang. In 2002, Xi Jinping served as Deputy Secretary of the CPC Zhejiang Provincial Committee and Acting Governor of the province. From 2002 to 2003, he was Secretary of the CPC Zhejiang Provincial Committee and Acting Governor of Zhejiang Province. From 2003 to 2007, he was secretary of the CPC Zhejiang Provincial Committee and Chairman of the Zhejiang Provincial People's Congress. During his tenure in Zhejiang, the provincial economy contributed substantially to the employment of migrant workers and transfer payments of fiscal revenue to the Central Government.

Xi Jinping's encouragement to provincial enterprises in Zhejiang, when he was the party secretary between 2003 and 2007, is evident in how Xi and his office prioritised these enterprises by strategising provincial economic interests. While in office, Xi promoted private enterprises like Geely and Alibaba; he also knew the gravity of provincial enterprises. In the challenging environment for private businesses to build, provincial enterprises were supposed to fill in the widening gap with well-performing provinces. The significant subsidiaries of the Central enterprises knew little less than the provincial enterprises. By letting provincial enterprises perform, Xi also made them feel consequential and special. This was also an opportunity for him to deploy an old strategy of using provincial enterprises to mobilise party members, enhance his popularity and build his factions in provinces through enterprises cultivating the inner-party support groups; it would have been difficult for the leadership to handle bold schemes. Like his other support group from Fujian and Shaanxi, the Zhejiang group was the most influential, affluent and helped Xi's rise to power.

From a political perspective, the local enterprises were crucial in delivering political promises. Through provincial enterprises, the leadership keeps the party organisation as the core focus and helps strengthen the party's management away from political centres. The role of local enterprises is limited to the province itself, and they perform similar duties as the Central SOEs. The SASAC regulates China's industry associations and has counterparts at provincial and local government levels that administer locally-owned SOEs. The provincial SASAC party committee included 23 provincial enterprises and 54 party organisations from across Zhejiang province.[34] There are 9,516 primary party organisations managed by the provincial SASAC party committee, with 151,000 party members.[35] This helps the provincial party apparatus to implement the requirements for party-building work without fail. Party members are actively involved in the decision-making mechanism for major corporate issues, leadership systems and facilitate the promotion of the integration of party leaders into corporate governance.

As of 2018, 11,000 SOEs at all levels in Zhejiang province, with total assets of 10.44 trillion yuan (US$ 1.55 trillion), had an annual operating income of 1.8 trillion yuan (US$ 268.65 billion), and profits of 142.4 billion yuan (US$ 21.25 billion).[36] In 2018, the assets of state-owned enterprises in Zhejiang province ranked second in the country. Among them, the provincial-owned enterprises under the supervision of the local SASAC had total assets of 1.2 trillion yuan (US$ 179.10 billion) at the end of the year and achieved an annual operating income of 866.4 billion yuan (US$ 129.31 billion) and profits of 37 billion yuan (US$ 5.52 billion).[37] At present, there are five "100-billion-level" enterprises in the province, and another six selected as top 500 Chinese enterprises. Among them, the Zhongda Group has been chosen as one of the world's top 500 for ten consecutive years.[38]

Chinese provincial growth rate performers used provincial enterprises to drive the ranking up and reduce the gap with the more prosperous provinces. Over the years, Zhejiang SOEs played a critical role in building landmark projects, necessary infrastructure, and vital industrial projects. Serving effective strategies and guaranteeing substantial activities, provincial enterprises are the backbone of the province's significant projects. The 145-kilometre-long Hangzhou-Ningbo Expressway is one such landmark that connected Hangzhou, Shaoxing and Ningbo. Since its establishment in 2001, the Provincial Transportation Group of Zhejiang has built 22 expressways such as the Hangzhou-Jinan-Qu Expressway and Zhoushan Cross-sea Bridge and invested in and constructed 16 railway lines.[39]

Among the provincial infrastructure enterprises, the Zhejiang airport group can be acknowledged as one of the top performers. To out-compete neighbouring provinces, infrastructure like connectivity is crucial for the flow of resources. With this agenda, Zhejiang Airport Group was established in 2017. Zhejiang was the first to have three significant airports ranked among the "ten million club",[40] and the construction pace has accelerated. The ability to have three airports with passenger traffic exceeding 10 million in a year certainly reflects the prosperity of the regional economy and the improvement of people's living standards, economic development, and the driving force for the rapid growth of the Zhejiang civil aviation industry. According to the statistics of the Zhejiang Airport Group, between January and October 2018, seven transportation airports in Zhejiang province, including Hangzhou, Ningbo, Wenzhou, Zhoushan, Quzhou, Taizhou, and Yiwu, recorded total traffic of 5,461,400 passengers, 683,700 tons of cargo and mail, and 41,900 flights—an increase of 13.85 per cent, 6.69 per cent, and 9.55 per cent, respectively.[41] The airports of Zhejiang compete with those in the neighbouring provinces. The provincial enterprises are tasked to keep expanding the airport infrastructure by increasing the number of terminals and constructing new small airports all around Zhejiang. With airport investment, construction and operation management as its core function, the Zhejiang Airport Group has been performing better than in the past due to an advantage to integrate the province's airport resources. With the 2022 Asian Games approaching, the group is busy constructing new terminals and other transportation hubs with a total investment of more than 27 billion yuan (US$ 4 billion).[42] At present, the group has been competing fiercely to make Zhejiang as China's leading civil aviation province by 2035. It aims to turn Zhejiang into a leader in aviation service coverage, aviation network global access, and industry layout. The airports of Zhejiang province have opened more than 590 international and domestic routes, including 75 international and regional routes.

Hangzhou airport opened regular direct passenger routes to Moscow and three intercontinental routes to New York (via Anchorage) and Belgium—all-cargo routes, actively promoting 24-hour barrier-free customs clearance; Ningbo Airport introduced the first South American cargo charter flight, and Wenzhou Longwan International Airport (WNZ) recently received approval (December 2019) for its master plan from the Civil Aviation East China Bureau to pursue development at the airport.[43] The WNZ's master plan aims to dramatically grow capacity at the airport and perhaps rank it among the world's top 50 airports by 2050. The master plan seeks to develop WNZ into a modern hub within China's Yangtze River Delta region, with development planned over the next three decades. By 2030, in addition to growth on the passenger side of airport operations, cargo throughput at WNZ is expected to reach 285,000 tonnes. By 2050, the airport is targeting a capacity of 650,000 tonnes.[44] To achieve its growth goals, the WNZ will build four terminals and three runways. In 2019, the Zhejiang Airport Group's revenue was 5.84 billion yuan (US$ 871.64 million), a year-on-year increase of 7.73 per cent.[45] It is an immediate contender to neighbouring Shanghai Airport (Group) Co. Ltd.'s Shanghai Pudong International Airport and Shanghai Hongqiao International Airport.

Besides, at the G20 Hangzhou Summit, provincial enterprises undertook dozens of engineering renovations and constructions to provide full protection for many significant events in the province. Simultaneously, several inter-provincial city-terminals in Shanghai and Jiangsu are to be connected with the province. Zhejiang provincial enterprises do not lose any opportunity to be a part of the nationally acclaimed strategy of Yangtze River Delta Integration.

Besides big provincial enterprises, the province also emphasises on making these entities play a significant role in ensuring stable development of the economy and society. In April 2018, the provincial government announced a scheme that focused on *rural revitalisation* (乡村镇兴 *xiangcun zhenxing*).[46] Over the past year or so, 23 provincial enterprises and their affiliates completed pairings with 85 weak collective economic villages in Quzhou and Lishui.[47]

Moreover, provincial enterprises are also supposed to create jobs and are essential pillars for serving the people's livelihood, providing social employment and thereby add to their tally of achievements. In 2018, the province's SOEs handed over 8.13 billion yuan (US$ 1.21 billion) in state-owned capital gains, which was transferred to the public budget of 3.18 billion yuan (US$ 474.62 million);[48] amongst this, 10 per cent of the state-owned equity of 10 provincial enterprises was transferred to bolster the social security fund, which accounted for more than 9 billion yuan (US$ 1.34 billion) in the state capital and equity.[49]

Known for its innovative and business acumen, the province also emphasises driving innovation development. From the challenges of overcoming core technologies such as ultra-low emissions and new fluorine refrigerants to applying new technologies and new products such as smart highways and high valued industries, Zhejiang provincial enterprises attempted to stay ahead of their neighbours and honed innovation capabilities. In 2018, there were 254 provincial enterprises with the digital economy as their core industry.[50] Total assets and operating incomes were 188.74 billion yuan and 66.80 billion yuan (US$ 9.97 billion), an increase of 19.5 per cent and 23.9 per cent from the previous year (2017), in proportion to the total assets and operating income of the provincial enterprises, accounting for 3.1 per cent and 3.9 per cent, respectively.[51] Additionally, the R&D investment in the core industries of the digital economy increased significantly, with 82 enterprises investing in scientific research, accounting for 32.3 per cent of this industry's provincial enterprises.[52]

Provincial funding is increasingly focused on high-tech industries. The provincial government operated a large number of financial incentives and funding programmes through key funding bodies.[53] The list includes,

- **Zhejiang Provincial S&T Department**: unlike other regions, it is responsible for nearly all the funding programmes in Zhejiang.
- **Zhejiang Provincial Economy and Informatisation Department**: responsible for a minimal number of technology upgrading programmes, e.g., the Zhejiang Provincial Enterprise Technology Centre recognition programme.
- **Municipal-level governments** (e.g., Hangzhou Municipal S&T Bureau, Hangzhou Municipal Bureau of Economy and Informatisation; Ningbo Municipal S&T Bureau, etc.).
- **National Innovation Demonstration Zones**, high-tech zones, and other industrial parks (Ningbo European Industrial Park, etc.).

Besides funding, Zhejiang pays close attention to specialised talent drives and programs so that local talent can be nourished and encouraged to stand out in the national and international competition. Major talent programs like (a) Thousand Talents Recruitment Programme (千人计划 *Qian ren jihua*), are being encouraged by the national authorities throughout China. Zhejiang has its own version of the talent-hunt program with the title of *Zhejiang Provincial 1000 Talents Plan*.[54]

The program is exclusively designed to further the provincial economic interests and open to only those who would contribute to provincial growth. In addition to the Thousand Talents Recruitment Programme, the Zhejiang government also runs (b) *Hangzhou "115"*[55] and *"521"*[56] *Foreign Talent Recruitment Plans* to encourage local enterprises and institutes to introduce high-level foreign experts that could contribute to the development of key priority industries and sectors. In addition to the *"115"* and "*521*" *programs*, the Hangzhou municipal government also extends several (c) patent subsidies to local entities and individuals applying, obtaining, and conducting patent-related activities.[57] This is conceived to promote and accelerate the research activities, which would help the local economy to benefit from cutting-edge patents and promote their commercialisation, particularly in strategic emerging industries. The city of Ningbo is also aggressively using the fund programs being noticed by the provincial administration to be used as a platform to promote S&T projects. In 2018, the Ningbo municipal bureau established a

Map 7.4: Yangtze River

series of (d) *"2025 S&T Megaprojects"*[58], supporting local enterprises, universities and research structures to conduct exploratory research, technology development, and commercialisation activities in areas surrounding the establishment of Ningbo as the first "Made in China 2025" Pilot Model City. The projects which are supported under the scheme cover new energy vehicles, intelligent devices, advanced semiconductor chips and software, advanced materials, high-performance CNC machines (CNC machines are machine tools that cut or move material as programmed on the controller), robotics and high-end equipment, biopharmaceuticals and high-performance medical machinery, new energy, energy-saving and environment-friendly technologies, key fundamental components. Similar to Hangzhou's Patent subsidies, the (e) Ningbo municipal government also offers several patent subsidies[59] to local entities and individuals applying, obtaining, and conducting patent-related activities.

Map 7.5: Yangtze River Delta

Source: Multidisciplinary Digital Publishing Institute (MDPI), Basel

The above-mentioned programs and plans help the province claim the top spot in the national tally of innovation-driven provincial economies. As a result, provincial enterprises consider factors like geography and demography before developing any plans. Guangdong, Jiangsu, Shandong and Zhejiang are the top four provinces in China's national GDP tally (municipalities not included but only provinces), of which Guangdong province is located in the southern coastal area of China and almost exclusively enjoys the Pearl River

Delta region. Similarly, Shandong Province is located in the northern part of the country and is located in the Bohai Bay Rim. Noticeably, in 2018, the permanent residents of Guangdong Province and Shandong Province both exceeded 100 million. Between these two delta regions, Jiangsu province and Zhejiang province are located in China's eastern coastal area. The southern region of Jiangsu province and the northern region of Zhejiang province are both parts of the core area of the Yangtze River Delta. The provincial leaders have been funding new industries focusing on these advantageous positions. Zhejiang has been taking considerable lead by gaining an economic edge over its close competitors like Jiangsu, Shanghai and Fujian. Just for the sake of curious readers, the competition between provinces in delta regions has been part of the recorded history of China. There was a saying in ancient times that "There is heaven and there are Su Hang" (上有天堂下有苏杭 *Shang you tiantang xia you su hang*). "Su" is Suzhou of Jiangsu, and "Hang" is Hangzhou of Zhejiang. The provincial agencies from Zhejiang are aware that they have to deal with the implicit competition with their industry and party peers from the adjacent provinces as everyone expects to excel. Since centuries, Yangtze River Delta has been the focal geographical point for imperial contests and centuries later it still remains one of the most aspired territories for buzzing economic opportunities. This region witnesses contests between mammoth urban clusters, crowded giant industrial hubs and a number of cities that have sprouted in the past couple of decades. The spill-overs, in terms of economic dynamism, in super-regions, are being exploited by industries and the local economy of Zhejiang.

The Zhejiang provincial administration considers the intra-provincial and inter-provincial calculations before proposing schemes across the physical pockets of the province. Compared with southern Zhejiang, northern Zhejiang is located at or close to the Yangtze River Delta's core cities. It has concentrated on a number of scientific research platforms. The concentration of talents has allowed these pockets to incubate many new economy-related enterprises, plus policy support. North Zhejiang has thus emerged as a growing centre of innovation-led investments. In recent years, on the broader note, in a run-up to pursue the national strategy of integrated development in the Yangtze River Delta, cities in Northern Zhejiang, namely, Jiaxing and Huzhou, lined up a large number of innovative resources. Jiaxing has built a number of technology innovation platforms, including Jiaxing Science and Technology City, Jiashan

Science and Technology City, Zhangjiang Yangtze River Delta Science and Technology City Pinghu Park, Xiuzhou High-tech Zone, and Shanghai Talent Pioneer Park. Huzhou has set up the "Huzhou Global Investment Promotion Centre" in Shanghai and has introduced a group of high-end talents and advanced scientific research and technology projects in the Yangtze River Delta.

The provincial government has been active in welcoming and supporting strategic and leading industries. To meet the increased investments demand in establishing emerging industries, the provincial government has been optimising and improving the structure of state-owned assets. The establishment of a group of industrial investment funds such as the Zhejiang State-owned Enterprise Reform and Development Fund (ZSERDF) is a result of those efforts. Regarding efficiency and overcapacity, Zhejiang had to follow in the footsteps of large Central and competing provinces from South China. The provincial administration cut down the excess capacity in steel, shipping, and coal and the destocking of real estate. For example, Hangzhou Iron and Steel Group shut down the Banshan Iron and Steel Base and accelerated its transformation into a national steel enterprise model to reduce capacity.

As per the list of "2019 Zhejiang Top 100 Enterprises",[60] which was jointly issued by the Zhejiang Enterprise Confederation, Zhejiang Entrepreneur Association, and Zhejiang Industrial Economic Federation, there are a total of 16 enterprises in Zhejiang province with operating income exceeding 100 billion yuan (US$ 14.92 billion), of which three enterprises have operating income exceeding 300 billion yuan (US$ 44.77 billion). Alibaba Group Holding Co. Ltd. (376 billion yuan—US$ 56.11 billion), Zhejiang Geely Holding Group Co. Ltd. (328 billion yuan—US$ 48.95 billion) and private players like Wuchan Zhongda Group Co. Ltd., a provincial enterprise (300 billion yuan—US$ 44.77 billion), qualified for the 300 billion yuan club (US$ 44.77 billion).[61] Of the 100 top enterprises in 2019, one-third are provincial enterprises.[62] Judging from the list of top 100 enterprises in Zhejiang (in 2019), the enterprises are spread over 19 industries, namely, metallurgy, chemical raw materials and chemical products, textiles, construction, component manufacturing, etc. Overall, the manufacturing industry still accounts for the largest share.

From the perspective of quality and efficiency, the profitability of high-tech industries is steadily on the rise. In 2018, the total assets and operating income of the high-tech industry (manufacturing) of the provincial enterprises were 107.01 billion yuan (US$ 15.97 billion) and 70.57 billion yuan (US$ 10.53 billion), respectively.[63] The profitability of the enterprise was 71.7 per cent, an increase of 1.5 per cent compared with the previous year (2017), and the profitability of the entire provincial enterprises was 62.1.[64] By standards of innovation investment, which focuses on R&D, technological transformation, and technological innovation investment, in 2018, 315 provincial enterprises invested in research and development, technological change, and technological innovation, with a total investment amounting to 9.31 billion yuan (US$ 1.38 billion), a year-on-year increase of 5.7 per cent, and scientific research investment accounted for 0.5 per cent of operating income.[65]

Among them, Zhejiang Zheneng Technology Research Institute Co. Ltd. invested 74.8 million yuan (US$ 11.56 million) in scientific research in 2018, an increase of 89.1 per cent over the previous year, accounting for 53.1 per cent of its operating income.[66] From the perspective of core competitiveness, more attention is paid to improving trademarks and patents. In its April 2020 circular, the provincial SASAC office directed the enterprises to work on enterprise layout structure, quality and efficiency, industry competitiveness, continuous innovation capability, capital function, and modern enterprise system and proposed more than 40 specific indicators in 17 areas to achieve high goals for state-owned enterprises in Zhejiang province.[67]

Several other provincial enterprises have also overcome domestic competition. They have been giving the provincial economy the much-needed fundamental thrust like Hunan, a Yangtze riverside province from Central China that ranked 14th on the list of China's provincial GDP.[68] The contribution of secondary and tertiary industry in 2019 was 96.4 per cent (44.4 per cent and 52 per cent, respectively).[69] In the '2019 list of top 100 Chinese cities by GDP', five were from Hunan province were in it including Changsha, Yueyang, Changde, Hengyang, and Zhuzhou.[70] Yueyang, Changde, Hengyang, and Zhuzhou were listed at the bottom of the list. Like the Hunan Valin Iron and Steel Group Co. Ltd. and the Hunan Construction Engineering Group, two provincial enterprises from Hunan are performing on domestic and international fronts despite hidden competition.

To better illustrate how Zhejiang struggles to pursue innovation-oriented economic growth, the patent index can be used as an example. The information derived from the innovation index also gives a glimpse at the geographical distribution of innovation-led economic activities in the provinces and the category of industries where Zhejiang beats its competitors. By its active involvement in bolstering innovation and talent, Zhejiang ensures that it remains an influential economy and contributes to the national GDP. Table 7.5 uses the data provided by the Zhejiang Provincial Market Supervision Bureau (Intellectual Property Office)[71] to list enterprises based on the invention patents they hold. An invention patent is used as the primary indicator to rank the top 100 creative enterprises of Zhejiang province. This is undoubtedly in favour of the provincial economy as the listed enterprises hold a total of 21,572 effective invention patents, accounting for 18.6 per cent of all the effective invention patents of enterprises.[72]

This book further expanded the data by looking at the type of enterprises and dividing them between Subsidiaries of the Central SOEs, provincial enterprises and private enterprises. The research zeroed in to check if the private players had any investments or stocks held by the local government. The results disclose that the provincial administration has been dominating the list of top 100 creative enterprises. The provincial government's footprint was visible in 42 enterprises directly owned by the local administration or those private enterprises supported by the provincial subsidies or stocks held by the provincial government.

Table 7.5: List of Top 100 Creative Enterprises in the Zhejiang Province (category and real ownership)

Sr. No.	*Company Name*	*No. of valid invention patents (pieces)*	*City*	*Local area*	*Category*	*Stakeholder/s*
1	New H3C Technology Co. Ltd.	4356	Hangzhou City	Binjiang District	Private	State Council/SASAC - Subsidiary of Tsinghua Holdings Co. Ltd. (largely funded & monitored by State Council & Ministry of Education, PRC)
2	Zhejiang Geely Automobile Research Institute Co. Ltd.	961	Taizhou	Linhai	Private	*Private - Zhejiang Geely* Holding Group
3	Zhejiang Yushi Technology Co. Ltd.	856	Hangzhou City	Binjiang District	Private	*Private* - Hong Kong Securities Clearing Co. Ltd.
4	Hangzhou Hikvision Digital Technology Co. Ltd.	542	Hangzhou City	Binjiang District	Private	Provincial Government stakes involved
5	Ningbo Fangtai Kitchenware Co. Ltd.	459	Ningbo City	Cixi City	Private	Private
6	Zhejiang Dahua Technology Co. Ltd.	458	Hangzhou City	Binjiang District	Private	Provincial Government stakes involved
7	NetEase (Hangzhou) Network Co. Ltd.	457	Hangzhou City	Binjiang District	Private	Private
8	Huzhou Youyan Intellectual Property Service Co. Ltd.	444	Huzhou	Nanxun District	Private	N.A.
9	Zhejiang Geely Holding Group Co. Ltd.	438	Hangzhou City	Binjiang District	Private	Private
10	Hangzhou DPtech Technology Co. Ltd.	393	Hangzhou City	Binjiang District	Private	Provincial Government stakes involved
11	Silicon Power Semiconductor Technology (Hangzhou) Co. Ltd.	383	Hangzhou City	Binjiang District	Private	Provincial Government stakes involved
12	Zhejiang China Tobacco Industry Co. Ltd.	365	Hangzhou City	Uptown	Provincial Enterprises (省级企业 Sheng ji qiye)	Provincial Government stakes involved
13	Chaowei Power Group Co. Ltd.	297	Huzhou	Changxing County	Private	Chaowei Power Group Co. Ltd., HK

Sr. No.	*Company Name*	*No. of valid invention patents (pieces)*	*City*	*Local area*	*Category*	*Stakeholder/s*
14	Zhejiang Geely Automobile Research Institute Co. Ltd. Hangzhou Branch	279	Hangzhou City	Xiaoshan Strict	Private	Private - Zhejiang Land Rover Automobile Co. Ltd.
15	Jack Sewing Machine Co. Ltd.	275	Taizhou	Jiaojiang District	Private	Provincial Government stakes involved
16	Hengdian Group Dongci Co. Ltd.	269	Jinhua City	Dongyang City	Private	Provincial Government stakes involved
17	Hangzhou Silan Microelectronics Co. Ltd.	250	Hangzhou City	Binjiang District	Private	Provincial Government stakes involved
18	Zhejiang Sanhua Intelligent Control Co. Ltd.	224	Shaoxing City	Xinchang County	Private	Provincial Government stakes involved
19	State Grid Zhejiang Electric Power Co. Ltd. Electric Power Research Institute	215	Hangzhou City	Downtown area	SSPs	State Council/SASAC
20	Ningbo Jiangfeng Electronic Materials Co. Ltd.	208	Ningbo City	Yuyao	Private	Provincial Government stakes involved
21	Hangzhou Huawei Digital Technology Co. Ltd.	202	Hangzhou City	Binjiang District	Private	Huawei Technologies Co. Ltd. & Provincial Government stakes involved
22	Haining Economic Development Industrial Park Development and Construction Co. Ltd.	198	Jiaxing City	Haining	Provincial Enterprises (省级企业 Sheng ji qiye)	Provincial Government stakes involved
23	Zhejiang Chint Electric Co. Ltd.	197	Wenzhou city	Yueqing City	Private	Provincial Government stakes involved
24	Zhejiang Sanhua Refrigeration Group Co. Ltd.	195	Shaoxing City	Xinchang County	Private	Provincial Government stakes involved
25	Haining High-tech Zone Technology Innovation Centre Co. Ltd.	189	Jiaxing City	Haining	Provincial Enterprises (省级企业 Sheng ji qiye)	Provincial Government stakes involved
26	Oaks Air Conditioning Co. Ltd.	184	Ningbo City	Yinzhou District	Private	Private
27	Hangzhou Zhongya Machinery Co. Ltd.	182	Hangzhou City	Gongshu District	Private	Private
28	China Mobile Communications Group Zhejiang Co. Ltd.	181	Hangzhou City	Downtown area	SSPs	State Council/SASAC

Sr. No.	*Company Name*	*No. of valid invention patents (pieces)*	*City*	*Local area*	*Category*	*Stakeholder/s*
29	Zhejiang Hisun Pharmaceutical Co. Ltd.	179	Taizhou	Jiaojiang District	Provincial Enterprises (省级企业 Sheng ji qiye)	Provincial Government stakes involved - A subsidiary of Zhejiang International Trade Group Co. Ltd.
30	TCL Communication (Ningbo) Co. Ltd.	172	Ningbo City	Yinzhou District	Private	Private
31	Zhejiang Shaoxing Supor Life Electric Co. Ltd.	166	Shaoxing City	Yuecheng District	Private	Provincial Government stakes involved
32	Zhejiang Sanhua Auto Parts Co. Ltd.	159	Hangzhou City	Jianggan District	Private	Provincial Government stakes involved
33	Ningbo Aux Electric Co. Ltd.	157	Ningbo City	Yinzhou District	Private	Private
34	Med Medical Industrial Equipment Co. Ltd.	154	Taizhou	Yuhuan County	Private	Provincial Government stakes involved
35	State Grid Zhejiang Electric Power Co. Ltd.	150	Hangzhou City	West Lake District	SSPs	State Council/SASAC
36	Jiashan County Weitang Asset Management Co. Ltd.	150	Jiaxing City	Jiashan County	Provincial Enterprises (省级企业 Sheng ji qiye)	Provincial Government stakes involved
37	TCL Mobile Communication Technology (Ningbo) Co. Ltd.	148	Ningbo City	Yinzhou District	Private	Private
38	Zhejiang Shuangyou Logistics Equipment Co. Ltd.	144	Taizhou	Yuhuan County	*Not Available*	*Not Available*
39	HC Semitek (Zhejiang) Co. Ltd.	144	Jinhua City	Yiwu City	Private	Private – A subsidiary of Huacan Optoelectronics Co. Ltd.
40	Zhejiang Huahai Pharmaceutical Co. Ltd.	142	Taizhou	Linhai	Private	Provincial Government stakes involved
41	Jiashan Chuangyue Intellectual Property Service Co. Ltd.	138	Jiaxing City	Jiashan County	Private	Provincial Government stakes involved
42	Haining Huangwan Town Asset Management Co. Ltd.	136	Jiaxing City	Haining	Provincial Enterprises (省级企业 Sheng ji qiye)	Provincial Government stakes involved – Collective Assets Management Committee of Huangwan Town, Haining City
43	Concentrator Technology (Hangzhou) Co. Ltd.	133	Hangzhou City	Binjiang District	Private	Provincial Government stakes involved
44	Ningbo Sunny Optoelectronics Information Co. Ltd.	130	Ningbo City	Yuyao	Private	Private

Sr. No.	*Company Name*	*No. of valid invention patents (pieces)*	*City*	*Local area*	*Category*	*Stakeholder/s*
45	Hangzhou Sanhua Micro Channel Heat Exchanger Co. Ltd.	128	Hangzhou City	Jianggan District	Private	Provincial Government stakes involved
46	Eastern Communications Co. Ltd.	126	Hangzhou City	Binjiang District	Private	Provincial Government stakes involved
47	Zhejiang Changxing Green Battery Technology Co. Ltd.	123	Huzhou	Changxing County	Private	Provincial Government stakes involved
48	State Grid Zhejiang Electric Power Company Huzhou Power Supply Company	122	Huzhou	Wuxing District	SSPs	State Council/SASAC
49	Zhejiang Supcon Technology Co. Ltd.	120	Hangzhou City	Binjiang District	Private	Private
50	Zhejiang Xitang Industrial Co. Ltd.	120	Jiaxing City	Jiashan County	Provincial Enterprises	Provincial Government stakes involved
51	Jushi Group Co. Ltd.	118	Jiaxing City	Tongxiang City	SSPs	State Council/SASAC
52	Zhejiang Xin'an Chemical Group Co. Ltd.	117	Hangzhou City	Jiande City	Private	Provincial Government stakes involved
53	Zhejiang Sunny Optical Co. Ltd.	116	Ningbo City	Yuyao	Private	Private
54	Power China East China Survey, Design and Research Institute Co. Ltd.	116	Hangzhou City	Downtown area	SSP	State Council/SASAC – Operating directly under China Electric Power Engineering Consulting Group Corporation (CPECC)
55	Toka Benma Electromechanical Technology Co. Ltd.	113	Taizhou	Linhai	Private	Provincial Government stakes involved
56	Zhejiang Shuangjin Machinery Group Co. Ltd.	112	Hangzhou City	Yuhang District	Private	Private - Subsidiary of Jack Sewing Machine Co. Ltd.
57	Sailfu Electronics Co. Ltd.	111	Ningbo City	Yinzhou District	Private	N.A
58	Zhejiang Runtu Co. Ltd.	111	Shaoxing City	Shangyu District	Private	Provincial Government stakes involved
59	Huzhou Xinbeilian Network Technology Co. Ltd.	108	Huzhou	Wuxing District	Private	Provincial Government stakes involved
60	The 715th Research Institute of China Shipbuilding Industry Corporation	106	Hangzhou City	West Lake District	SSPs	State Council/SASAC - Subsidiary of China Shipbuilding Industry Corporation
61	Delixi Electric Co. Ltd.	105	Wenzhou city	Yueqing City	Private	Private
62	Huzhou Peiyou Incubator Co. Ltd.	105	Huzhou	Wuxing District	N.A.	N.A.

Sr. No.	Company Name	No. of valid invention patents (pieces)	City	Local area	Category	Stakeholder/s
63	Hangzhou Sanhua Research Institute Co. Ltd.	104	Hangzhou City	Jianggan District	Private	Provincial Government stakes involved
64	Zhejiang Qinyuan Water Treatment Technology Co. Ltd.	103	Ningbo City	Cixi City	Private	Provincial Government stakes involved
65	Huzhou Qiqi Electromechanical Technology Co. Ltd.	100	Huzhou	Wuxing District	Private	Provincial Government stakes involved
66	Great Wall Motor Co. Ltd. Pinghu Branch	100	Jiaxing City	Pinghu	Private	Private
67	Zhejiang Dafeng Industrial Co. Ltd.	99	Ningbo City	Yuyao	Private	Provincial Government stakes involved
68	Ningbo Changyang Technology Co. Ltd.	97	Ningbo City	Jiangbei District	Private	Provincial Government stakes involved
69	Inventronics (Hangzhou) Co. Ltd.	97	Hangzhou City	Binjiang District	Private	Private
70	Ningbo Shupu Electromechanical Co. Ltd.	96	Ningbo City	Yinzhou District	N.A.	N.A.
71	Sinochem Blue Sky Group Co. Ltd.	96	Hangzhou City	Binjiang District	SSP	State Council/SASAC
72	Zhejiang Longsheng Group Co. Ltd.	96	Shaoxing City	Shangyu District	Private	Private
73	Zhejiang Qicai Environmental Technology Co. Ltd.	96	Shaoxing City	Yuecheng District	Private	Private
74	Ningbo Samsung Medical Electric Co. Ltd.	95	Ningbo City	Yinzhou District	Private	Private
75	Sinopec Ningbo Engineering Co. Ltd.	95	Ningbo City	Yinzhou District	SSP	State Council/SASAC
76	Yinjiang Co. Ltd.	95	Hangzhou City	Binjiang District	Private	Private
77	Zhejiang Jiuzhou Pharmaceutical Co. Ltd.	94	Taizhou	Jiaojiang District	Private	Private
78	Haining Yanguan Industrial Investment Co. Ltd.	94	Jiaxing City	Haining	Private	Provincial Government stakes involved
79	Zhejiang Lingpao Technology Co. Ltd.	93	Hangzhou City	Binjiang District	Private	Provincial Government stakes involved
80	Zhejiang Supor Home Appliance Manufacturing Co. Ltd.	92	Hangzhou City	Binjiang District	Private	Provincial Government stakes involved
81	Haining Qianjiang Industrial Investment Development Co. Ltd.	92	Jiaxing City	Haining	Provincial Enterprises (省级企业 Sheng ji qiye)	Provincial Government stakes involved

Sr. No.	Company Name	No. of valid invention patents (pieces)	City	Local area	Category	Stakeholder/s
82	Ningbo Cixing Co. Ltd.	91	Ningbo City	Cixi City	Private	Private
83	Zhejiang Yate Electric Co. Ltd.	90	Jiaxing City	Nanhu District	Private	Private
84	Ningbo Minth Auto Parts Technology R&D Co. Ltd.	90	Ningbo City	Beilun District	Private	Private
85	Zhejiang Tianlan Environmental Technology Co. Ltd.	88	Hangzhou City	Xiaoshan Strict	Private	Private
86	Weihong Power System (Huzhou) Co. Ltd.	88	Huzhou	Wuxing District	Private	Private
87	Zhejiang Weixing Industrial Development Co. Ltd.	87	Taizhou	Linhai	Private	Private
88	He Ye Health Technology Co. Ltd.	87	Huzhou	Anji County	Private	Private
89	Haining Yuanhua Town Industrial Investment Co. Ltd.	86	Jiaxing City	Haining	Provincial Enterprises (省级企业 Sheng ji qiye)	Provincial Government stakes involved
90	Zhejiang Haining Warp Knitting Industrial Park Development Co. Ltd.	86	Jiaxing City	Haining	Private	Private
91	36th Research Institute of China Electronics Technology Group Corporation	83	Jiaxing City	Nanhu District	SSPs	State Council/SASAC
92	Zhejiang Haiyue Automation Machinery Co. Ltd.	83	Huzhou	Changxing County	Private	Private
93	New Thinking Motor Co. Ltd.	82	Jiaxing City	Jiashan County	Private	Private
94	Ningbo Haitian Precision Co. Ltd.	81	Ningbo City	Beilun District	Private	Private
95	Huzhou Modern Textile Machinery Co. Ltd.	81	Huzhou	Wuxing District	Private	Private
96	Geely Automobile Research Institute (Ningbo) Co. Ltd.	81	Ningbo City	Cixi City	Private	Private
97	Aibo Biomedical (Hangzhou) Co. Ltd.	81	Hangzhou City	Jianggan District	Private	Private
98	Zhejiang Real Madrid Technology Co. Ltd.	79	Shaoxing City	Shangyu District	Private	Private
99	Ningbo Fangzheng Automobile Mould Co. Ltd.	79	Ningbo City	Ninghai County	Private	Private
100	Ningbo CRRC New Energy Technology Co. Ltd.	79	Ningbo City	Yinzhou District	SSPs	State Council/SASAC

Conclusion: The Strategic Alliances

While each enterprise under the provincial SASAC tries to perform, there are efforts to reduce these competitive tensions among the provincial SOEs and between themselves. The Provincial SOEs work under the Party's guidelines but avoid any head-on public spats. Work pressures are kept under control to minimise cut-throat competition. The provincial enterprises are also strengthening the local economy and reinforce the foundations of local party leaders. To avoid unnecessary competition and wastage of resources, Central enterprises, SSPs, and provincial enterprises initiated intensive reorganisation, mainly concentrated on competitive industries. The present trend indicates that the current round of reorganisation, mergers and acquisitions leaves no stone unturned and shows detailed plans on the drawing board of provincial and central leadership. The *first* trend is the reorganisation of Central enterprises and local SOEs; the *second* is the reorganisation of the leading businesses, and the *third* is the reorganisation of the industrial chain by syncing the upstream and downstream processes of the industrial chain. The last one has especially picked up pace since the plans to cut overcapacity and streamlining of overproduction have become priority targets.

An industry integration case of Guiyan Platinum and Tin Co. Ltd., a provincial SOE and China Minmetals, a Central SOE, can be referred here to illustrate the emerging dynamics between the provincial and Central SOEs. The Yunnan Provincial Government reached a cooperation framework agreement with China Minmetals as early as in 2017. One of the plans was to develop and utilise non-ferrous metal resources by both the parties. From the perspective of upstream resource integration, the SOE reforms of Guiyan Platinum and Tin Co. Ltd. were seen as critical to boosting China Minmetals' precious metal resources. Simultaneously, the introduction of Central enterprises in Yunnan was strategic for integrating the industrial chain from upstream resources to downstream plans. Guiyan Platinum and the Tin Industry Co. Ltd. in Yunnan are both resource-based provincial enterprises. Guiyan Platinum is a national high-tech enterprise engaged in the research, development, and production of precious metals. It is also the only domestic company applying core technology and innovation in precious metal materials. A listed company integrating production, education, and research, Tin Industry Co. Ltd. is a comprehensive non-ferrous metal company focusing on tin and a leading company in the global industry.

The merger of Central enterprises and SOEs in Yunnan and Liaoning provinces shows how integration has been maintained whereby Central SOEs assign the task to provincial SOEs, and inter-provincial SOEs keep their in-fighting under control. Yunlu, Chihong Zinc and Germanium, and Maanshan Iron & Steel plan to change their regulators from the local SASAC to the State Council's Central SASAC. Central SOEs acquired local SOEs, which has been a frequent trend since the second half of 2018. Since 2019, cooperation between central and local governments has mainly been through equity transfer. Central enterprises and local SOEs hold shares, primarily in competitive industries such as steel, aluminium, tin, and trade and logistics.

The significance of Central-local cooperation (cooperation between Central enterprises and local state-owned enterprises) stays at the level of promoting the reform of local SOEs and encourages local government officials to start businesses and achieve high-quality development. Future Central-local cooperation is one way of equity diversification, and equity mergers are viewed by Chinese leaders as attaining strategic reorganisation. Also, the general investment quota of Central enterprises is relatively large, so it can also drive the downstream industrial chain, which is of great significance to local economic development. Through cooperative action, the medium and long-term funds structure is optimised to provide development opportunities for digesting local debt. The strategic alliance between the administratively divided SOEs can undoubtedly help these entities utilise existing resources rationally and form an industrial chain. The subtle competitive dimensions between Central, SSPs, and provincial enterprises need serious attention by the Party.

NOTES

1. *HLJNews.cn.* 2020. 'Guoqi fuzhai zong'e 94 wan yi yuan fuzhai lu da 65.6% Ruhe qu ganggan?' (国企负债总额 94 万亿元负债率达 65.6% 如何去杠杆?) [Firmly grasp the initiative of economic work], 16 December, http://www.hljnews.cn/article/252/212682.html (accessed on 17 January 2021).
2. Ibid.
3. National People's Congress of the PRC. 1993. 'Civil and Commercial Laws >> Company Law of the People's Republic of China', 29 December, http://www.npc.gov.cn/zgrdw/englishnpc/Law/2007-12/12/content_1383787.htm (accessed on 23 August 2020).
4. Liu Jianming. 2017. 'Smart Grids Open Up New Opportunities', 10 January, https://e.huawei.com/in/publications/global/ict_insights/201711060837/energy/201711091519 (accessed on 7 March 2021).

5. National Energy Administration of the PRC. 2020. 'Guojia nengyuan ju fabu 2019 nian quan shehui yong dian liang' (国家能源局发布2019年全社会用电量) [National Energy Administration releases total electricity consumption of 2019], 20 January, http://www.nea.gov.cn/2020-01/20/c_138720877.htm (accessed on 7 March 2021).
6. *Fortune*. 2020. 'Global 500: China Communications Construction', 8 October, https://fortune.com/global500/2019/china-communications-construction/ (accessed on 20 November 2020).
7. Fitch Ratings. 2020. 'What Investors Want to Know: SGCC' *Special Report*. 9 August, https://www.fitchratings.com/research/corporate-finance/what-investors-want-to-know-sgcc-09-08-2020 (accessed on 8 March 2021).
8. Energy Iceberg. 2019. 'Severe Investment Cuts of the Chinese Grid Companies: Battery Energy Storage the First Casualty', 10 December, https://energyiceberg.com/chinese-grids-cut-investment-hurting-battery-storage/ (accessed on 23 August 2020).
9. State Grid Corporation of China (SGCC). 2017. 'Zuzhi jiegou' (组织结构) [Organizational structure], 25 January. http://www.sgcc.com.cn/html/sgcc_main/col2017012538/column_2017012538_1.shtml (accessed on 17 January 2021).
10. Ibid.
11. Ibid.
12. International Energy Association (IEA). 2020. 'World Energy Investment', May, https://sun-connect-news.org/fileadmin/DATEIEN/Dateien/New/WEI2020.pdf (accessed on 17 January 2021).
13. Ibid.
14. *SMM News*. 2020. "Ultra-high-voltage projects to limitedly drive copper consumption in 2020", 26 March, https://news.metal.com/newscontent/101049371/Ultra-high-voltage-projects-to-limitedly-drive-copper-consumption-in-2020/ (accessed on 26 August 2020).
15. *Power Technology*. 2020. 'China Develops $26bn Ultra High Voltage Electrical Grids to Stimulate Economic Recovery', 22 May, https://www.power-technology.com/comment/china-26bn-uhv-grids/ (accessed on 15 August 2020).
16. Herbert Smith Freehills. 2020.'Zhongguo qiye touzi haiwai jichu sheshiPPP xiangmu: Falu jiaodu de guancha' (中国企业投资海外基础设施 PPP 项目：法律角度的观察) [Chinese companies invest in overseas infrastructure PPP project: a legal perspective], 1 March, https://www.herbertsmithfreehills.com/file/33151/download?token=2roohJ18 (accessed on 20 August 2020).
17. *Bloomberg News*. 2020. 'A 1,000-Mile Long Clean Energy Artery Is Completed in China', 4 June., https://www.bloomberg.com/news/articles/2020-06-04/china-state-grid-completes-3-17-billion-clean-power-uhv-line (accessed on 23 August 2020).
18. *Xinhua*. 2012. 'China Completes Cross-Border Power Transmission Project With Russia', 1 January, http://www.geni.org/globalenergy/library/technical-articles/transmission/xinhua/china-completes-cross-border-power-transmission-project-with-russia/index.shtml (accessed on 15 August 2020).
19. Benjamin Kang Lim and Megha Rajagopalan. 2014. 'China audits State Grid as corruption crackdown seen widening' *Reuters*. 9 May, https://www.reuters.com/article/us-china-power-corruption/china-audits-state-grid-as-corruption-crackdown-seen-widening-idusbrea4802d20140509 (accessed on 15 November 2020).

20. State-owned Assets Supervision and Administration Commission (SASAC). 2020f. 'State Grid in Full Swing on UHV Construction', 22 April, http://en.sasac.gov.cn/2020/04/22/c_4880.htm (accessed on 15 November 2020).
21. *Hangzhou.gov.cn.* 2020. '"Shisiwu" qijian hangzhou jiang mai ru shijie yiliu dianwang hanglie' ("十四五"期间杭州将迈入世界一流电网行列) [During the "14th Five-Year Plan" period, Hangzhou will enter the ranks of world-class power grids], 27 December, http://www.hangzhou.gov.cn/art/2020/12/27/art_812262_59023317.html (accessed on 17 January 2021).
22. Guangdong Provincial Development and Reform Commission (GPDRC). 2019. 'Guangdong sheng fazhan gaige wei guanyu xiada guangdong sheng 2019 nian zhongdian jianshe xiangmu jihua de tongzhi' (广东省发展改革委关于下达广东省2019年重点建设项目计划的通知) [Notice of Guangdong Provincial Development and Reform Commission on Issuing Guangdong Province's 2019 Key Construction Project Plans], 27 March, http://drc.gd.gov.cn/ywtz/content/post_2264242.html (accessed on 17 January 2021).
23. Anhui Development and Reform Commission (ADRC). 2020. '2020 Nian yi jidu sheng fazhan gaige wei yi shenqing gongkai xinxi mulu' (2020年一季度省发展改革委依申请公开信息目录) [Catalogue of Information Disclosure by the Provincial Development and Reform Commission in the first quarter of 2020], 6 May, http://fzggw.ah.gov.cn/public/7011/140946821.html (accessed on 17 January 2021).
24. Author's interview with SGCC employees, September 2019, Beijing.
25. Ibid.
26. Frank Tang. 2019. 'China to give local governments bigger share of tax revenues to continue crucial infrastructure investments' *South China Morning Post.* 11 October, https://www.scmp.com/economy/china-economy/article/3032597/china-give-local-governments-bigger-share-tax-revenues (accessed on 15 November 2020).
27. *Jones Day.* 2008. 'Chinese Local Governments Fight for Their Share of Tax Revenue', March, https://www.jonesday.com/en/insights/2008/03/chinese-local-governments-fight-for-their-share-of-tax-revenue (accessed on 15 November 2020).
28. *Sina Finance.* 2017. 'Guoqi fuzhai zong'e 94 wan yi yuan fuzhai lu da 65.6% Ruhe qu ganggan?' (国企负债总额94万亿元负债率达65.6%如何去杠杆?) [The total debt of state-owned enterprises is 94 trillion yuan with a debt ratio of 65.6%. How to deleverage?], 7 August, http://finance.sina.com.cn/roll/2017-08-07/doc-ifyitamv6769829.shtml (accessed on 17 January 2021).
29. *Sina Finance.* 2020a. '2019 Nian guoyou qiye shouru tongbi zengzhang 6.9% Lirun zeng 4.7%' (2019年国有企业收入同比增长6.9%利润增4.7%) [In 2019, the revenue of state-owned enterprises increased by 6.9% year-on-year, and profits increased by 4.7%], 22 January, http://finance.sina.com.cn/roll/2020-01-24/doc-iihnzhha4438696.shtml (accessed on 17 January 2021).
30. Ibid.
31. Margit Molnar and Jiangyuan Lu. 2019. 'State-owned firms behind China's Corporate Debt', *OECD Working Papers*, No. 1536, 7 February, https://www.oecd.org/officialdocuments/publicdisplaydocumentpdf/?cote=ECO/WKP(2019)5&docLanguage=En (accessed on 23 August 2020).
32. State-owned Assets Supervision and Administration Commission (SASAC). 2020a. '48

Jia yangqi 32 jia difang guoqi shang bang 2020 shijie 500 qiang' (48家央企32家地方国企上榜2020世界500强) [48 state-owned enterprises and 32 local state-owned enterprises on the list of 2020 world top 500], 10 August, http://www.sasac.gov.cn/n2588020/n2877938/n2879597/n2879599/c15338531/content.html (accessed on 12 October 2020).

33. Lin Xiaozhao. 2018. 'Zhejiang Grows to Economy the Size of Netherlands in 40 Years of Opening Up', 1 November, https://www.yicaiglobal.com/news/china-time-zhejiang-grows-to-economy-the-size-of-netherlands-in-40-years-of-opening-up (accessed on 13 October 2020).

34. State-owned Assets Supervision and Administration Commission (SASAC). 2019a. '[Goujian guozi jianguan da geju] zhi san: Jin kou fuwu daju goujian si ge tixi gao zhiliang tuijin zhejiang guozi tongyi jianguan gongzuo' (【构建国资监管大格局】之三：紧扣服务大局构建四个体系高质量推进浙江国资统一监管工作) [Part III of 'The establishment of State-owned Assets Supervision pattern', focusing closely on the general subject of serving, to build four systems to promote the unified supervision of state-owned assets in Zhejiang.], 5 December, http://www.sasac.gov.cn/n4470048/n10286230/n12974073/n12974173/c12970250/content.html (accessed on 15 November 2020).

35. The State Council Information Office of the People's Republic of China (SCIO). 2018. 'Zhejiang juxing guozi guoqi gaige fazhan qingkuang xinwen fabu hui' (浙江举行国资国企改革发展情况新闻发布会) [Zhejiang holds a Press Conference on the reform and development of state-owned assets and state-owned enterprises], 13 December, http://zj.cnr.cn/zjyw/20181213/t20181213_524448854.shtml (accessed on 15 November 2020).

36. *CNR.CN*. 2018. 'Zhejiang sheng guoyou qiye zichan 10.44 Wan yi ju quanguo di er' (浙江省国有企业资产10.44万亿居全国第二) [The assets of state-owned enterprises in Zhejiang Province rank second in the country at 10.44 trillion yuan], 13 December, http://zj.cnr.cn/zjyw/20181213/t20181213_524448854.shtml (accessed on 15 November 2020).

37. Ibid.

38. *Sohu.com*. 2020. 'Zhejiang juxing guozi guoqi gaige fazhan qingkuang xinwen fabu hui' (热烈祝贺物产中大集团在 2020《财富》世界 500 强榜荣登第 210 名) [Congratulations to Wutan Zhongda Group for ranking 210th on the 2020 Fortune Global 500 list], 13 December, http://zj.cnr.cn/zjyw/20181213/t20181213_524448854.shtml (accessed on 15 November 2020).

39. *Zhejiang Daily*. 2019a. 'Zhejiang juxing guozi guoqi gaige fazhan qingkuang xinwen fabu hui' (18年建成22条高速公路，参与建成16条铁路，浙江省交通集团-"一小时交通圈"建设主力军) [Built 22 expressways in 18 years, participated in the construction of 16 railways, Zhejiang Transportation Group - the main force in the construction of "one-hour traffic circle"], 25 December, http://www.meiligaosu.com/h-nd-1175.html?from=groupmessage (accessed on 15 November 2020).

40. *Zhejiang Daily*. 2018b. 'Zhejiang san da jichang jishen "qian wan julebu"' (浙江三大机场跻身"千万俱乐部") [Zhejiang's three major airports rank among the "ten million clubs"], 24 November, http://www.wzs.org.cn/hg/201811/t20181124_294486.shtml (accessed on 15 November 2020).

41. *Zhejiang Daily*. 2018a. 'Wenzhou jichang ying lai jinnian di 1 qian wan ming luke jishen qian wan ji jichang' (温州机场迎来今年第1千万名旅客跻身千万级机场) [Wenzhou Airport

welcomed 10 millionth passenger this year], 24 November, https://baijiahao.baidu.com/s?id=1617973628147446817&wfr=spider&for=pc (accessed on 15 November 2020).

42. *Hangzhou Daily.* 2021. 'Ji guonei shouzuo luse hang zhan lou hou, hangzhou jichang zai jianxin lou zai huo luse jianzhu pingjia biaozhi' (继国内首座绿色航站楼后，杭州机场在建新楼再获绿色建筑评价标识) [Following the first domestic green terminal building, Hangzhou Airport's new building under construction again received the green building evaluation mark], 4 February, https://baijiahao.baidu.com/s?id=1690758686150271142&wfr=spider&for=pc (accessed on 5 February 2021).
43. Wenzhou Airport Group Co. Ltd. 2019. 'Wenzhou jichang xinban zongti guihua huo minhang huadong ju pifu' (温州机场新版总体规划获民航华东局批复) [Wenzhou Airport's new master plan was approved by the East China Bureau of Civil Aviation], 19 November, https://www.wzair.cn/jtdt/jtxw/2019/12/11/259534.html (accessed on 20 November 2020).
44. *Wenzhou Daily.* 2020. 'Wenzhou jueqi "qian wan ji" daxing guoji jichang' (温州崛起"千万级"大型国际机场) [The rise of Wenzhou, a large-scale international airport "ten million"], 12 July, http://www.wenzhou.gov.cn/art/2020/7/12/art_1217832_50326389.html (accessed on 6 December 2020).
45. *CARNOC.com.* 2020. '2019 Nian 2 jia jichang jituan zhuan xiale suoyou jichang de lirun' (2019 年 2家机场集团赚下了所有机场的利润) [In 2019, 2 airport groups made profits from all airports], 15 July, http://news.carnoc.com/list/538/538595.html (accessed on 17 January 2021).
46. The Chinese government has launched a campaign of rural revitalization (乡村镇兴 *xiangcun zhenxing*) which promises to modernize the rural economy and bring wealth to villagers through innovating new pathways of development in the countryside.
47. State-owned Assets Supervision and Administration Commission of Zhejiang Province (SASAC-Zhejiang). 2019. 'Zhejiang guozi guoqi quanli da hao "xiao bao" gongjianzhan zhuli xiangcun zhenxing' (浙江国资国企全力打好"消薄"攻坚战助力乡村振兴) [State-owned and state-owned enterprises in Zhejiang Province do their best to fight the "depletion" battle to help rural revitalization], 4 April, http://www.sasac.gov.cn/n2588025/n2588129/c10888800/content.html (accessed on 6 December 2020).
48. *Zhejiang Daily*. 2019b. 'Zai dan dang zuowei zhong dili qian xing — 70 niandai zhejiang guozi guoqi gaige fazhan huimou' (在担当作为中砥砺前行 — 70年代浙江国资国企改革发展回眸) [Forge ahead in the role - Looking Back on the Reform and Development of Zhejiang State-owned Assets and Enterprises in the 1970s], 27 September, http://zjrb.zjol.com.cn/html/2019-09/27/content_3269446.htm?div=-1 (accessed on 14 December 2020).
49. Ibid.
50. *Eastmoney.com.* 2019. 'Zhejiang sheng shichang jianguan ju 2018 niandu sheng shu qiye nianbao qingkuang fenxi baogao: Sheng shu qiye jingji fazhan "touyan" zuoyong mingxian' (浙江省市场监管局 2018 年度省属企业年报情况分析报告：省属企业经济发展"头雁"作用明显) [Analysis of Zhejiang Provincial Market Supervision Bureau's 2018 Annual Report - Provincial Enterprises: The "head goose" role of Provincial Enterprises in Economic Development], 6 September, http://finance.eastmoney.com/a/201909061230563245.html (accessed on 14 December 2020).
51. Ibid.

52. Ibid.
53. European Union. 2020. 'Improving EU Access to National and Regional Financial Incentives for Innovation in China', December, http://chinainnovationfunding.eu/rd-innovation-funding-china-project/? (accessed on 2 February 2021).
54. Zhejiang Institute of Science and Technology, The University of Hong Kong (ZIRI-HKU). 2019b. 'Zhejiang sheng qian ren jihua' (浙江省千人计划) [Zhejiang Thousand Talents Plan], 6 September, http://www.ziri.hku.hk/en/talent/talent_details/25.html (accessed on 14 December 2020).
55. Hangzhou Municipal Science and Technology Bureau. 2019. 'Guanyu gongbu 2019 niandu hangzhou shi "115" yinru guo (jing) wai zhili jihua xiangmu jihua de tongzhi' (关于公布2019年度杭州市"115"引入国（境）外智力计划项目计划的通知) [Notice on the announcement of the 2019 Hangzhou "115" project plan for the introduction of foreign (overseas) intelligence], 6 December, http://kj.hangzhou.gov.cn/art/2019/12/6/art_1693961_40803586.html (accessed on 14 December 2020).
56. Zhejiang Institute of Science and Technology, The University of Hong Kong (ZIRI-HKU). 2019a. 'Hangzhou shi quanqiu yin cai "521" jihua' (杭州市全球引才"521"计划) [Hangzhou "521" Plan for Global Talent Attraction], 6 September, http://www.ziri.hku.hk/en/talent/talent_details/24.html (accessed on 14 December 2020).
57. *Hangzhou.gov.cn*. 2015. 'Hangzhou shi zhuanli zhuanxiang zijin guanli banfa de tongzhi' (杭州市专利专项资金管理办法的通知) [Notice of the General Office of the Hangzhou Municipal People's Government on Issuing the Measures for the Administration of Hangzhou Patent Special Funds], 19 October, http://www.hangzhou.gov.cn/art/2015/10/19/art_1256295_7049377.html (accessed on 17 December 2020).
58. Ministry of Science and Technology of the People's Republic of China. 2018. 'Ningbo shi "keji chuangxin 2025" zhongda zhuanxiang fu jing tuijie' (宁波市"科技创新 2025"重大专项赴京推介) [Ningbo City's "Technology Innovation 2025" Major Special Project Goes to Beijing for Promotion], 14 June, http://www.most.gov.cn/dfkj/zj/zxdt/201806/t20180613_140106.htm (accessed on 17 December 2020).
59. *Ningbo.gov.cn*. 2019. 'Guanyu xiada ningbo shi 2018 niandu di san pi keji xiangmu buchong jihua de tongzhi' (关于下达宁波市 2018 年度第三批科技项目补充计划的通知) [Notice on the issuance of the third batch of funding plans for Ningbo City in 2018], 8 January, http://www.most.gov.cn/dfkj/zj/zxdt/201806/t20180613_140106.htm (accessed on 17 December 2020).
60. *Xinhua.net*. 2019. '"2019 Zhejiang sheng bai qiang qiye" bang dan fabu 16 jia qi ye ying shou chao qian yi' ("2019 浙江省百强企业" 榜单发布 16 家企业营收超千亿) ["2019 Zhejiang Top 100 Enterprises" lists 16 companies with revenue exceeding 100 billion], 11 September, https://baijiahao.baidu.com/s?id=1644379781031387530&wfr=spider&for=pc (accessed on 17 December 2020).
61. *Sohu.com*. 2018. 'Zhejiang sheng guoyou qiye zichan zong'e 10.44 Wan yi yuan, wei lie quanguo di er!' (浙江省国有企业资产总额 10.44 万亿元，位列全国第二!) [The total assets of state-owned enterprises in Zhejiang Province are 10.44 trillion yuan, ranking second in the country!], 13 December, https://www.sohu.com/a/281891253_821103 (accessed on 17 January 2021).
62. *Xinhua.net*. 2019. '"2019 Zhejiang sheng bai qiang qiye" bang dan fabu 16 jia qi ye ying

shou chao qian yi' ("2019 浙江省百强企业" 榜单发布 16 家企业营收超千亿) ["2019 Zhejiang Top 100 Enterprises" lists 16 companies with revenue exceeding 100 billion], 11 September, https://baijiahao.baidu.com/s?id=1644379781031387530&wfr=spider&for=pc (accessed on 17 December 2020).

63. *Eastmoney.com.* Zhejiang sheng shichang jianguan ju 2018 niandu sheng shu qiye nianbao qingkuang fenxi baogao'.
64. Ibid.
65. Ibid.
66. Ibid.
67. State-owned Assets Supervision and Administration Commission of Zhejiang Province (SASAC-Zhejiang). 2020. 'Zhejiang sheng guozi wei jianli "465" guoqi gao zhiliang fazhan mubiao tixi' (浙江省国资委建立"465"国企高质量发展目标体系) [The State-owned Assets Supervision and Administration Commission of Zhejiang Province established a "465" high-quality development target system for state-owned enterprises], 23 April, http://www.sasac.gov.cn/n2588025/n2588119/c14416599/content.html (accessed on 17 January 2021).
68. *Rednet.cn.* 2019. 'Five Hunan Cities Make the List of Top 100 Chinese Cities by GDP', 16 August, https://english.rednet.cn/content/2019/08/16/5816563.html (accessed on 17 January 2021).
69. *Hunan.gov.cn.* 2020. 'Statistical Communiqué on Hunan's Economic and Social Development in 2019', 24 April, http://www.enghunan.gov.cn/hneng/Business/EconomyCommunique/202004/t20200423_11969012.html (accessed on 17 January 2021).
70. *Rednet.cn.* 'Five Hunan Cities Make the List of Top 100 Chinese Cities by GDP'.
71. *China Quality News Network.* 2020. 'Shou lun zhejiang chuangzao li qiye bai qiang zuoci pai ding zhe 100 jia qi ye yongyou quan sheng 18.6%Youxiao faming zhuanli' (首轮浙江创造力企业百强座次排定这 100 家企业拥有全省 18.6%有效发明专利) [The first round of ranking of the top 100 creative enterprises in Zhejiang. These 100 enterprises have 18.6% of valid invention patents in the province], 22 April, http://www.cqn.com.cn/zj/content/2020-04/22/content_8548584.htm (accessed on 24 August 2020).
72. Ibid.

8

The Story of *Guojin Mintui*

The script on the plight of private enterprises at the hands of the state runs through the timeline of decades. *Guojin Mintui* (国进民退—the state firms advance, the private sector retreats), the Chinese phrase describing a phenomenon where state firms force a retreat of the private sector. The existence of this phenomenon dates back to the days when the People's Republic of China (PRC) was founded in 1949 but this old tendency does have traces in the past seven decades of economic plans and political set-up. Political leaders, under pressure not to overtly pursue privatisation and become victim of its own ideological trap, often tried to rekindle their interest in private sector economy. The private sector economy was used to mimic the grandiose and real-life consumerism but with shallow political pruning. Public-Private Partnership (PPP) is the best case to elaborate this phenomenon more effectively. This chapter would use PPP as a case to substantiate how the state has advanced at the cost of private businesses, often dwarfing the private sector's role in making China a miracle a reality.

The PPP model provides a feasible framework for the delivery of public services. The official term for PPP is used differently to underline the distinction between the Chinese perceptions of such partnerships vis-à-vis global cases of public-private cooperation. As a result, in recent years, the PPP scheme was introduced in China on a narrow scale. The top brass political leaders follow what President Xi and Premier Li Keqiang termed "government and social capital".[1] The term has been in use for the corporation over the customary 'PPP' in their speeches, formal reports, and other theoretical references. The PPPs' success and failure can be analysed carefully by evaluating the party's role and the Chinese state. The partnerships are part of the apparatus where the private enterprises were utilised to toil, and SOEs reaped the harvest. The private enterprises were curated and used by the party to serve its more considerable interest in "welfare" and cultivate its legacy. Hence, private enterprises never overcame the anxieties to deal with the party, state, and existential challenges in modern China. The Chinese state continues to use the PPP model to benefit the state economy more and presents another case where the model of development has been compromised for political reasons.

Amidst Propaganda and Slogans, Private Businesses Lose Hope of Market Liberalism

Since the mid-1990s, the PPP scheme adopted in many advanced and industrialised countries has been increasingly introduced in developing parts of the world. In China's case, a vital discussion on the PPP scheme as a suitable way to innovate the current governance framework has come to light. "Welfare" is one of the core concepts of socialism that generations of Chinese leadership had fondly and vividly followed. The party's philosophy and State's governance model conceptually followed what welfare would mean in *the Chinese way* (with the party's interests and State's intervention uncompromised). Beginning with the revolutionary ideas to Zhou Enlai's balancing acts, the pre-reform was iconic concerning extreme measures adopted by the State to manifest its control over every aspect of the socio-political life of the ordinary Chinese to realise welfare in reality. Early attempts of welfare and 'kick-start modernisation' can be traced back to the *Four Modernisations* (四个现代化 *Si ge Xiandaihua*),[2] announced by Premier Zhou Enlai in the mid-1960s and revived by Deng to launch his economic reform program in 1978. Welfare was combined with the State's ambition to achieve all-round modernisation. Deng further integrated his narratives of a strong and developed China by furthering "three steps" (三步走 *San bu zou*).[3] His "Three Steps" involved (i) doubling the real GDP level by 1990 and thus solve the problem of insufficient clothing and food (温饱问题 *Wenbao Wenti* —"温饱" literally means, "warm and full");

(ii) to build a well-off (小康 *Xiaokang*) society by 2000 by quadrupling the real GDP level and; most importantly (iii) to raise the per capita GDP within 30 to 50 years to the level of an intermediate developed country. The "steps" suggested by Deng provided the best vision and practical model for the successive leadership.

The following generation of leadership devised various supplementary ways to secure future development, which were realistic too. And all steps revolved around the welfare and well-being of Chinese society and state. Follow-through policies were swiftly undertaken by Deng's successor, Jiang Zemin, who re-emphasised "socialism with Chinese characteristics". As Shambaugh observes, Jiang's managerial style coincided perfectly with systemic changes and has been the right leader for the right time.[4] The Hu Jintao period marked organised and focused attempts to side-track political chambers of influence and drive *Scientific Development* (科学发展 *Kexue fazhan*)[5] and a *Harmonious Society* (和谐社会 *Hexie shehui*),[6] adopting a more comprehensive approach for development. Keeping in line with Deng's "Three Steps", the following generations turned the reform process open to include other fields and development dimensions. Attempts to reconcile social interest with economic growth and political solidification were a noticeable change. These generations of leadership and reforms can be highlighted with the notions of social welfare and an equal distribution of income according to the rule of law. But public delivery of services and attempts to widen the spectrum of welfare remains a challenging task. Party and state make sure that public institutions do the indispensable job of political socialisation by harnessing the ideologies and thoughts of elite leaders. Against the backdrop of insufficient and inefficient delivery of public service and the growing challenge to meet the fiscal challenges, a *well-off* and *harmonious society* needed a well-thought out integration of efforts and partnerships.

Public infrastructure in China has long been regarded as a social-welfare issue, and due to the speedy urbanisation and improvement of living standards, conventional sources of financing such as governmental transferring of payments and borrowing from banks could no longer meet the fast-growing demands, and PPP was the result of these pressures. However, the definition of public and private ownership and economy has consistently been kept intertwined with Chinese politics. The public institutions—even in the realm of administration, hold immeasurable control over private businesses. Ever since the establishment of Communist rule in China, the political setup has put a noose around private players to control the economy and fix it with the political 'superstructure.' Since 1949, and after the 1989 student protests, the hidden anxieties towards the private economy flared up. Private businesses were shepherded to deliver what the state intended and as and when it wished. The concepts of State Capitalism and Market Socialism indicate how the Chinese state allowed the entry of non-public entities to provide momentum for growth. Private businesses were shunned after the Communist struggle succeeded in China. The expanding non-public enterprises were seen as detrimental for the ideological set up of the newly-founded Communist rule under Mao Zedong's leadership. A research report by Wai-yip So reiterates this growing threat among the leaders and public sector managers as they failed to maintain pace in the limited market of the Communist state. Bennis writes "even though the Party urged the private sector to improve its efficiency, an ambivalent attitude within the Party was anxious about a subsequent strengthening of capitalists. A threat came from the increasing tendency of joint operations among private".[7] Despite the State's intervention and support to the public sector, private businesses created enough worries for the Communist leadership.

Incidentally, private businesses have always been growing and functioning without swimming against the tide. The facilitation of private businesses was planned to make the public sector competitive. Going forward, in any experiment where non-public enterprises were made stakeholders continued to chase the goals set by the State. Non-public enterprises remained under constant pressure to oblige and perform. Unlike in the developed countries where private enterprises bring disruptive transformations, in China, such disruptions are controlled so that they do not grow more prominent than the state. One classic example could be the introduction of partnerships between public and private institutions. The Chinese state controls every aspect of the economic juggernaut; the role of the private and public sectors is managed to suit the best interests of the State and not the market. Private enterprises could not afford any margin of error by accruing the State's confidence, and it was logical for private enterprises to follow the said or unsaid norms laid down by the party and the State. The PPP model carried structural flaws for an extended period. Since the State was inviting bidding for large urban infrastructures, the SOEs were mostly ending up bagging them. The SOEs were bidding against and manipulating the major PPP projects in China. PPP turned out to be a "Public-Public" partnership, and the role of private enterprises was limited in many ways. Hence, the partnerships in the real sense of PPP remained unfulfilled. Today, many private firms do not have the essential financial wherewithal to take on the SOEs and bid for large-scale projects. On the other hand, the SOEs continue winning a large number of bids. Against this backdrop, the new round of PPP launched in 2014 aims to fix these fundamental problems and expects private players to come forward to construct public utilities.

Private Businesses Slip into Hibernation

Privatisation seems to have influenced government policies in the twentieth century. It has been the centrepiece of political ideologies, movements, and radical political initiatives across nations. During the turbulent years of the early 20th century, private businesses faced steep resistance as the public ownership of production relations was brought under the state's direct rule. Amidst the post-Bolshevik revolutionary waves of ideological influences, the socialist political undercurrents turned into a dominant political force, providing new alternatives to social and economic strife, which initiated a trend to turn private businesses into national properties. Most of the Communist regimes under the influence of the former Soviet Union, and following World War II, pursued aggressive nationalistic policies by nationalising all private businesses.[8] The trend was picked up by the new stream of ideologies in the rest of the world when they secured control over the state. The ongoing political struggle in China since the 1920s picked up some of these socialist habits from Soviet Russia.

During the Civil war and transition to a role model of communist rule under Mao, China showed mixed approaches to private players in China. Cities like Tianjin, Guangzhou, and Shanghai have a sizable merchant population and exert a level of influence over civic policies. Eventually, Mao did increase his focus on public enterprises, but he maintained a balance by not over-taxing and forcing them into the contract system. Mao's "new urban policy" was shaping a transition whereby its real purpose was to increase production to enlarge the volume of supplies, munitions, and money available to the CPC for waging the Civil War.[9] The private sector was given space to earn political support and was made part of the 'New Democracy' that the Communist Party would establish.[10] Post-1949, Mao envisioned a continuing political struggle process favouring both the state sector of the economy over the private sector and the private sector workers over the capitalists.

Since its founding in 1949, China joined the wave of transforming privately-owned domestic and foreign businesses into national enterprises. However, China kept its options open by allowing private companies to function on their own until 1953. Bennis Wai-yip notes that "under the policy framework of 'New Democracy,' put forward by Mao in 1940, the Party promised that all private firms, except for those owned by foreign and bureaucratic capitalists, were to be allowed to carry on their business for a reasonably long period even under Communist rule because the Chinese economy was backward and still needed capitalism to boost its economic development."[11] In 1953, the Party promulgated the transition period by adopting a 'socialist transformation of capitalist industry and commerce,' which underlined the private sector's gradual nationalisation. In a practical sense, the privatisation did not find a way to hold its ground as the premise to do business changed dramatically since the communists took over state control. The People's government was now primarily concerned not about profits but with employment for Chinese workers and not establishing goodwill in foreign capitals, but with increased production.

Moreover, the idea of private ownership or private businesses faced a direct setback given the external crisis which the Chinese state faced. It was not only the ideology that pushed back privatisation but the perceived threat on all fronts made the leaders feel less impressed with privatisation, especially when Chiang Kai Shek controlled the Republic of China (ROC-Taiwan) and successfully implemented ideas and policies to encourage private ownership and entrepreneur activities across the island. William Kirby described this as an event, in which the central planning seemed essential for national defence at a time of crisis, and a valuable means by which to bring Chinese industrial and technological development under the control of the central government, as opposed to foreign, provincial, or private interests.[12] The public-private conflict was apparent within a few years of the Communists coming to power. The then leadership under Mao was inclined to control the merchants and the influence of private businesses from contesting the state's role. Many archival sources covering '*Economic Reorganisation*,' that contain Mao's speeches over a transformation to socialism indicate how the 'private' was about to disappear from China. Chen Yun, the then Vice-Premier and director of the financial and economic committee, played the lead in exploring ways to reduce the role of private enterprises vis-à-vis public enterprises, eventually reducing them to non-existent entities. As per Chen Yun's plans, state production contracts were used to 'fasten' the private industry to the state-capitalist economy.[13] Between 1949 and 1952, the number of private enterprises declined, but the share of the private industry's marketed output also fell sharply.

Table 8.1: The Share of Private Industrial Output for the Market and State Contracts during 1949-1952 (%)

	1949	*1950*	*1951*
Output for the market	88.12	71.17	57.29
Output for state contracts	11.88	28.83	42.71

Source: Wai-yip So, p. 694.

The size of the labour force in urban private businesses was reduced from 8,830,000 to 1,040,000 between 1952 and 1957 and to a mere 150,000 by 1978.[14] These attempts sent the private companies in China into a spiral of hibernation. The Chinese state did not want to see anti-revolutionary forces challenging its economic measures under the Party's direction. While the policies attempted to control the emergence of a free and independent private sector in the economy, there were parallel examples globally, indicating the inconsistencies in promoting the private sector. This is especially valid against the backdrop of failing economic policies, which pushed the Chinese economy into the danger zone of collapsing. While China was hesitant to revive the private sector, many revisionist leaders in China observed what was happening in the East European economies. The attempts to revisit privatisation were taking a definite shape. For example, in its efforts to balance ideology and objective, Poland needed to restructure the economy and let the controls on private business loosen multiple times, between 1956 and 1957, 1965 and 1968, 1977 and 1980 and after 1982.[15] These policy cycles reflected the tension between Communist ideology, which was opposed to any private-sector activity, and the desire of Communist governments to maintain an adequate supply of goods and services.[16] China had to wait until the 1970s when local experiments with non-public businesses started under state control, but those were not termed explicitly private. Slow and having a negligible presence in the 1960s and 70s, the private sector was maintained at a safe distance. The Party did not endorse or even mention it anywhere in their communications. Still, at the same time, the Party knew that it had to keep a check on such experiments.

The private enterprises, which had prospered in the early half of the twentieth century, were forced to enter into systematic hibernation. Here, the word 'hibernation' is used with an undertone that the State lately revived the private sector, which was forced to shut down and die its death in the 1970s. Even when private businesses were legal, they faced many constraints and were aware of the political circumstances. Among the most significant were the difficulties associated with obtaining material inputs. Industrial supplies were hard to get, and the most desirable supplies were tightly controlled by state planning and supply agencies. Any private manufacturing operation, howsoever small and unskilled, relied on the state for its inputs and was therefore always vulnerable to political mood swings.

There were also restrictions on the private sector's labour in many cases, usually in statutory limits on the maximum number of employees in a private firm. Such were the state's and the Party's motives that the private sector was expected to perform when the reforms were announced. But until then, the stricter laws and humiliation at the hands of revolutionary guards discouraged the private enterprises. The private sector knew that the days of doing unrestricted business were over. In his book *The Party: The Secrets World of China's Communist Rulers*, McGregor cites examples of how thousands of Chinese landed in prisons and faced atrocities at the hands of revolutionary guards on the mere suspicion of owning and buying private goods.[17] The end of private businesses and the aftermath left a deep mark on the private sector in China. Hence the reforms and opening up allowed private enterprises to pave their way forward, but doubts were raised over the ravages wrought on the non-public sector. The impact was irreversible and was evident in different forms.

Reverse-thrust: Reviving Private Sector and Early Attempts at Public-Private Partnerships

With the weakening of the old school within the radical communist faction, the contending Chinese leaders were inclined to open up the non-public sector economy again. In the broadest sense, privatisation is the process of structural change that involves non-nationalisation, liberalisation or relaxation of regulations, and utilisation of private sector capabilities in providing service. Of course, the relaxation to the non-public sector was not meant to 'revitalise' the sector but assist it in opening up and providing additional assistance.[18] As a result, China began its privatisation policy by introducing a market economy, that is, by creating a 'non-state sector' consisting of non-state enterprises. The Chinese attempt was more cautious than the Russian and East European privatisation experience, representing the more dominant and more favoured privatisation approach.[19] Hence the party did not intend private personal opinions to challenge its role and centrality. In this regard, Blumental observes, that on the backdrop of the so-called post-hibernation and reforms in 1978, 'privatisation with Chinese characteristics' emphasised not the immediate privatisation of the state sector but rather the retention of the state sector with the concomitant creation of a parallel non-state sector designed to supplement the state sector and to serve as a social 'shock absorber' if the state sector itself is to be eventually 'privatised' or as Chinese officials prefer it, 'corporatised' or 'securitised'.[20]

The opening up and reforms did serve a role in letting non-state actors turn into a decisive factor in decades to come, as was the case in the rest of the world. The last two decades of the 20th century were like turning around a decade-old structure of the global economy. It was not only Margaret Thatcher but also new leaders and political streams in Eastern Europe, Soviet Russia and China that were on the verge of revitalising the private sector. This meant letting the State-controlled sector face competition and count their last days. As a result, the private sector's subsequent entry into the economy created a contest for all players who were protected by the state.

Along with other countries, China also started thinking about transferring the ownership of State firms back from the government to private investors. But does privatisation improve performance? Economic theory suggests that enhanced management accountability resulting from the transfer to capital market funding and competitive product markets should enhance financial performance. The failure of a centralised economy, rigidity in the organisation, inefficiency in management, and low productivity of the SOEs were seen as hindrances to China's modernisation.[21] As a result, China started embracing the non-public sector, and this time, the State wanted the non-state sector to generate employment and growth. The private sector's role in China's economy was redefined as 'complementary to state and collectively owned enterprises,' where their development would benefit production, market supply, and employment.[22] The number of employments in the urban private sector doubled from 150,000 in 1978 to 316,000 in 1979.[23]

The rise of the non-public enterprises surpassed the speed and quality of the products and services of the SOEs turned out to be the game-changer for China. The State-owned and controlled sectors were drastically reduced in terms of their contribution to output and employment. The declining productivity could not offer any political refuge. This transformation through the non-state industry was evident in agriculture, industry and construction, and services. The non-state sector was given the priority over SOEs. Moreover, to stimulate the non-state sector to continue performing, the Chinese state steadily introduced ways to 'manage' the rise of non-state entities. Direct control over the non-state sector was avoided, but indirect rules were put in place. The non-state entities were glorified for their growth momentum, and SOEs were asked to learn some of their non-state peers' practices. The rise of private businesses in China since 1978 is primarily the result of what might be called the 'displacement' of SOEs. But the experience of running private business under communist rule was not ensuring exclusive and outright access to the market and freedom for expansion. The private businesses did grow in large numbers, but most of them were not registered as private but as collective enterprises for political reasons.[24] In 1982, for the first time after the founding of the PRC, the Chinese Constitution was revised to include a provision protecting private property rights. The 'private' sector's growth was used profoundly to show the political commitment of the Chinese state, but private enterprises remained consistently under pressure. The control of the party over other aspects of the rules, regulations, and economy restricts the natural growth of private enterprises. One must note that the private businesses turned into a success without any direct support from the state.

Regarding financing, the role of the private businesses was fuelled by household savings and loans from family and friends rather than funds borrowed from the formal financial system.[25] The fate of private businesses was determined by political logic, and it impacted the growth of the private sector qualitatively. As Lardy points out, "a few key prices remain administered rather than market-determined, distorting the allocation of resources and slowing economic growth".[26] Amid the growing need to catch up with growth, China has to devise a way to carry out large-scale projects so that private players could be employed to serve the state's interests with their expertise. The construction of economic infrastructure such as roads, bridges, public transport, and social infrastructure such as schools, prisons, and hospitals forced the State to look for partnerships with private players.

In an ideal world, PPP should refer to the partnership between the public and the private sectors by providing products and services to ally with 'benefit-sharing, risk-sharing, and full cooperation.' The advantages of PPP were to enable the partnering entities to cooperate to achieve results that are more favourable than expected by acting alone. The story of PPP in China has numerous exciting aspects. The Chinese State primarily uses PPP to save the government's fiscal expenditure and use the private enterprise's investments and agility to fulfil public projects. The State entities often propose these projects, and partnerships are sought to bring them to reality. SOEs have been on the lookout for private partners, and private players are convinced that it is the best way for them to show their natural leadership to promote growth. No wonder that in a Communist state where everything belongs to the state, private players are allowed to rise and serve the state's purpose, and in return, they act as the country's economic *protégé*. Against this backdrop, PPP dynamics in China has mixed results. The SOEs have been innovative to include private players in their dream projects. In other words, PPP resonates with the State's growing control over markets and how State capitalism has come a long way: first, let the private players play an independent role and then develop PPP as a tool to employ private players to help the State deliver public services.

Since the 1980s, private players are part of the China development story. Over the past 40 years, one could not become a wealthy and successful private entrepreneur in China without understanding the requirements and wants of the state. Private players comply with the State's unending guidelines. The PPP has turned into a serious experiment for the present leadership, who would like to take a more risk-defused approach to construct public infrastructure. The earliest case of PPP dates back to the year 1985. The Chinese PPP experiment set off with a Build-Operate-Transfer model (BOT)[27] and was introduced in the mid-1990s into the infrastructure field such as power plants and highways. In 1984, the Shenzhen Shajiao Power Station began its modelling on the PPP idea.

As discussed briefly, the Chinese public utility SOEs were poor performers as far as the urban-related projects were concerned. This included water supply, electricity management, drain water and wastewater management, and other civic utilities. Besides, the local SOEs were non-compliant with environmental standards. Water pollution in China had reached the worst levels in the early 1990s. The Asian Development Bank's (ADB) involvement in funding water management projects resulted from these inefficiencies. Residential and industrial waste discharges, primarily untreated, had contributed to the deterioration of many rivers, lakes, and reservoirs throughout the country. With many of its cities dumping their urban wastes in rivers and lakes, China produced as much organic water pollution as the USA, Japan, and India put together.[28] According to the ADB, negligence towards water management and over-industrialisation put enormous pressure on urban infrastructure. The government-owned facilities managed by the SOEs proved inefficient to deal with this in time. The failure of the SOEs to achieve environmental improvement and ensure financial and economic returns were further problematised when the public sector lending limitations were exposed due to high technology and market risks associated with industrial projects. Some of the SOEs, which were impacted, include the Chaohu Dongya Cement Company (CDCC), Chaohu Wastewater Treatment Engineering Company (CWTEC), Hefei Chemical Fertilizer Plant (HCFP), Hefei Chemical Works (HCW), Hefei Iron and Steel Corporation (HISC), and Hefei Sewerage Treatment Company (HSTC).[29]

In 1993, the ADB partly financed the Hefei Development and Planning Commission (HDPC) and constructed a wastewater treatment plant. In 2002, due to increasing operating costs, HDPC decided to sell the operating rights. The bid was won by Berlinwasser International and East China Engineering and Technology Co. Ltd. The consortium formed a *'special purpose company'*, the Hefei Wangxiaoying Sewage Treatment Co. Ltd. (HWC), to operate the wastewater treatment plant through a concession Transfer-Operate-Transfer (TOT) agreement of 23 years. In 1995, the first Guangxi Laibin Power Station was led by the State Planning Commission to attract foreign investment, and it was considered the first real BOT project in China. Since then, several BOT pilot projects were carried out in succession as per the directions of the State Planning Commission. However, compared with the advanced countries in the PPP field, China's theoretical research and practical application of PPP were yet to mature and improvise.

Between 1995 and 2003, the World Bank and ADB introduced the PPP model in China as an emerging project financing method, which coincided with the Chinese government's urgent need for foreign investment. Before the current wave of the PPP boom, two PPP waves surged in China, beginning with foreign investment in the mid to late 1990s to participate in China's infrastructure construction; the other was in 2002 when the Ministry of Construction promoted municipal public utilities. The reform of the business franchise system[30] generated a massive wave of PPP. The prime reason behind the PPP boom was China's urbanisation and the growing pressure on public institutions to efficiently meet those needs. For an extended period, urbanisation turned into the main driving force of China's economic development. As a result, the Ministry of Construction and local construction administrative departments began to test the waters by introducing a municipal public utilities franchise model. The ADB-funded wastewater treatment project in Hefei was the one to focus on developing an appropriate model to suit local needs.

During the operation of the Wangxiaoying project, all the parties involved in the project, including intermediary consulting agencies, attempted to standardise, specialise and localise Chinese PPP, forming a relatively mature project structure and agreement over issues. It laid a good foundation for Chinese PPP to enter the next stage of development. The effects were seen when Guangxi Laibin B Power Plant, Chengdu Water Supply Plant No. 6, and Changsha Power Plant were commissioned as PPP projects. Besides, in 2002, the Beijing Municipal Government took up the implementation of the Beijing 10th Water Plant BOT project.

In 2004, the Ministry of Construction took the lead in implementing the 'Municipal Public Utilities Franchise Management Measures' (hereafter referred to as "*Order No. 126*"), and officially introduced the concept of 'franchising municipal public utilities' and used it in urban water supply, sewage treatment, and gas supply. This initiated the practice of large-scale projects in other fields as well. Local governments also adopted *'Order No. 126'* as a template and issued several local regulations, government regulations, and policy documents to guide and regulate the development of franchise projects within their respective administrative jurisdictions. At this stage, the departments responsible for planning and development were no longer the only leading agencies in endorsing the application of PPP models. Still, various factors, including stakeholders from construction, transportation, environmental protection, state-owned assets, and other industry authorities, and local governments, looked at the PPP model as an opportunity to take the lead. Because of its remarkable pragmatism, the Chinese call it the stage of 'black cat and white cat' (黑猫白猫 *hei mao bai mao*), a term Deng once used. But in recent times, the name is referred to by those who focus on the objectives which drive the PPP projects based on the wisdom derived from Deng and dismiss the morality debate.

Regardless of their nature or distinctions, as long as these stakeholders, the proverbial 'cats', could catch the 'social capital', that is the wizard 'mouse', the cats were regarded as 'good cats'. Although China's PPP projects no longer favoured foreign capital blindly, its single funding orientation remained unchanged. The former shed the burden between the public and private parties, while the latter's mentality of occupying the market gave the projects traction. Amidst the run for PPP and 'social capital', the PPP model's 'institutional principles'—the efficiency of public products or services, risk control, social and economic benefits, lost centrality in the Chinese case. It led to the development of Chinese-style PPP, which encountered 'loop-snag' in the middle and late stages of this drive with instances of a large number of low-price or irrational bidding, even the withdrawal of state-owned and private capital.

From a realistic perspective, considering the preferences of China's local governments for governance and the unique interest demands of different types of 'social capital,' the occurrence of the above-mentioned tendencies was understandable. It is nothing more than a realistic reflection of the concept of 'black cats and white cats' in the PPP field. It also reveals the trend of objective classification of the PPP model in China to a considerable extent and facilitates putting aside the highest political order and prioritising short-term practical value. Specifically, at the micro-level, Chinese PPP models are still oriented towards raising social funds, pushing public products or services that the government lacks money for and poorly done to an immature market. The long-term development often superseded the project's social and economic benefits because it is often not the focus of the current leadership or managers. The long-term planning, even if external financial and legal advisers are involved, their professional opinions are usually not fully understood and accepted by the project parties. PPP projects also aimed to reduce these tensions between hyper-growth and sustainable growth. Due to negligence, a large number of potential risks gradually accumulated despite spikes in growth in a few areas. In present times, in the case of PPP projects in China, governments or investors have been neglecting to perform or even breach contracts. Given the sensitivity of the matter and the possible economic backlash, information regarding the infringement of contracts is not openly accessible. This study could locate a couple of cases despite restrictions over data accessibility.

The PPP projects have been marred by disputes and undefined administrative, commercial, and legal complexities. One prominent case between Hainan Gas Co. Ltd. (henceforth HG) and a municipal people's government (a municipal government of a city in Hainan – the name is undisclosed) is interesting to refer to here. HG alleged the municipal government of flouting the rules while awarding the PPP project. It was alleged that in the absence of competitive procurement, the municipal government granted the franchise of pipeline gas within the administrative division of a city to a regional branch of a gas company by issuing a series of administrative communications (mail interactions) and signing the agreement on the development of a pipeline gas project. A gas company (HG) and its regional branch objected to the arbitrary decision to allot an administrative licence of a city government as it infringed the franchise rights they enjoyed; as a result, HG filed a lawsuit to cancel the administrative permit granted by a city government to another company. The court rejected the plea on the pretext that the petitioner could not furnish strong evidence supporting its case and directed the government to follow the rules to select the franchise by applying a strict code of conduct in future franchise allotments.

For the Chinese state, the litigations or the breach of contracts were teething periods, and the net result of expanding the PPP program was seen as more important than anything else. The arbitrations never pulled the trigger against the State. The 'black cat and white cat' stage turned out to be an essential process for developing the PPP model in China. The water supply and sewage treatment industry experience was replicated and improved to be used in a more comprehensive, open, and complex project system instead of being limited to an independent operating unit. The main body of project participants and the factors affecting project implementation has also become more diverse.

Two PPP projects of Beijing Metro Line 4 and the National Stadium are classic cases.

According to the goals set out in the 12th Five-Year Plan, China's urbanisation rate increased by 4 per cent from 2011 to 2015. For every one per cent of the increase in urban population, infrastructure investment also increased by at least 10,000 yuan, thus creating enormous pressure on state agencies. Faced with a steep rise in urbanisation requirements, China had to devise a way to innovate the financing and provision of infrastructure through multiple channels, optimise the policy environment, and accelerate PPP application. The Chinese state looks at PPP as an essential measure for China to innovate financial management models and improve financial management efficiency. PPP is a way to make up for the budget gap and efficiently share risks and costs.

The New PPP Drive since 2014

Beginning in 2012, the 18th NPC affirmed the reform measures of 'Allowing Social Capital to Participate in Urban Infrastructure Investment and Operation through Franchising,' and the Ministry of Finance launched a comprehensive deployment of PPP model promotion since the end of 2013. In the Third Plenum of the 18th Chinese Communist Party Central Committee in November 2013, the Chinese government set out the vision of expanding the application of PPPs to infrastructure investment. The most striking decision was the relaunch of franchise legislation. This was regarded by the National Development and Reform Commission (NDRC) as the primary legal system in the PPP field. It was first launched in February 2014, and its draft for comments has undergone eight revisions. The PPP models were further standardised after the 2014 legislations (Table 8.2). In May 2014, the Ministry of Finance established the "Government and Social Capital Cooperation (PPP) Working Leading Group". In addition to the Ministry of Finance's moves, in May 2014, the NDRC launched 80 demonstration projects to encourage 'social capital' to participate in construction and operation,[31] covering traditional infrastructure, information infrastructure, clean energy, oil and gas, and coal. However, in September 2014, the legislative work was unexpectedly suspended. The 'Administrative Measures for Infrastructure and Public Utilities Franchising,' which was first published in April 2015, became legally less effective. The Laws and Regulations Department of the NDRC formulated the 'Infrastructure and Public Utilities Franchising Law (Draft for Comment)' and was sent to industry to seek its opinions on the revisions. In 2016, the legislative work in PPP (government and social capital cooperation, as referred officially) accelerated rapidly in China. The institutionalisation of the PPP model officially gained much-needed traction, especially since the beginning of 2016, General Secretary Xi Jinping, Premier Li Keqiang, and Vice Premier Zhang Gaoli issued instructions on many occasions, requesting all departments and regions to strengthen coordination, improve PPP mechanisms, and promote PPP reform to play its due role and achieve more significant results.[32]

Table 8.2: 2014 Official Documents Promoting the Development of PPPs

Date	*Issuing Institution and Title*	*Reference*
May 18, 2014	National Development and Reform Commission (NDRC), "Notice to encourage private capital to invest in first infrastructure projects".	NDRC, 2014a[33]
September 21, 2014	State Council, "Opinions of the State Council on strengthening the management of local government debt".	State Council, 2014a[34]
September 23, 2014	MOF, "Notice on questions relating to expanding the use of PPPs".	MOF-PRC, 2014a[35]
November 16, 2014	State Council, "Guiding opinions on the innovative investment mechanism and encouraging social investment in key sectors."	State Council, 2014b[36]
November 29, 2014	MOF, "Guide on the operation of public-private partnership projects (interim)"	MOF-PRC, 2014b[37]
December 2, 2014	NDRC, "Guidelines on development of public-private partnership projects".	NDRC, 2014b[38]
July 2, 2015	NDRC, State Council "Infrastructure and public project franchise law".	NDRC, 2015[39]

Source: Hubert Thieriot & Carlos Dominguez, 2015. "Public-Private Partnerships in China in 2014 as a landmark year, with past and future challenges". The International Institute for Sustainable Development (IISD) Discussion Paper.

Overall, the year 2014 was regarded by industry insiders as the first year of developing the next generation of the PPP model in China, while the following years turned into a standardised development stage of Chinese-style PPP. The NDRC took a lead role in organising seminars and meetings on infrastructure and public utility franchising legislation. These brainstorming sessions focused on several specific legislative contents involving franchising relevant fields, applicable conditions and expanding the areas of cooperation in more fields. Table 8.3 identifies how the PPP started taking a detour from its earlier path set by the first generation of PPP trials and the defaults. In the successive years, the State spent time identifying the scope of franchise projects, the institutional stakeholders and partners (Central enterprises), and the project equity transaction. It further paid attention to market exit mechanisms and asset securitisation of project financing, and the intervention of financial institutions. Table 8.3 gives the time-lapse based distinction between the pre and post-2014 approaches towards PPP projects.

Through PPP models, the Chinese State found a new way to drive the economy in specific directions. The government and social capital cooperation model were supposed to link and pursue a long-term cooperative relationship established in infrastructure and public services. According to the usual model, social capital undertakes most of the work of designing, constructing, operating, and maintaining infrastructure and obtains a reasonable return on investment through 'user payment' and necessary 'government payment' whereas the government departments are responsible for infrastructure and public service prices and quality supervision to ensure maximum public interest. In essence, PPPs provide a contractual structure to allow the private investor to undertake projects generally executed by the government using their capital to recouping the investment via delayed payments funded by user charges, government budgets, or third-party revenues.

In current times, China is implementing a new urbanisation development strategy, which is the principal starting point for stabilising growth, promoting reform, and adjusting structure. Based on the post-reform period's experience and the lessons learnt from international experience, the Chinese state had to dive in and work on a new strategy to overcome critical micro-economic transitions. As discussed above, the short-term benefits of the goals were evident from the Chinese economy's fiscal and federal challenges, but it was inevitable that the PPP model would be discarded. The recent wave, starting from the 18th NPC and focusing on PPP investment, aimed the Chinese state to these two sets of goals. To begin with, the short-term strategy was to offload debt from the government account to corporate accounts through PPP arrangements, and in the long-run, the Chinese state wanted to use the PPP models to precipitate the transformation from asset-focused to service-focused

Table 8.3: 2014: New Wave of PPP Augmentation

PPP Policy indicators	*Pre-2014*	*Post-2014*
Financing	• Government guided fund financing • Trust financing • Insurance fund • Others (bank loans and bonds)	On December 21, 2014, NDRC and China Securities Regulatory Commission (CSRC) jointly issued the notice on promoting asset securitisation of government social capital cooperation (PPP) projects in the field of traditional infrastructure, titled "Special Asset Management Plan (asset securitisation)"
The approach by the leaders/state	No specific policy booster	The New Urbanisation Plan (March 2014).[40] Targets in the plan include an urbanisation rate of 60 per cent by 2020, up from 53.7 per cent in 2013 (representing roughly 100 million new urban residents with an estimated cost of CNY 42 trillion by 2020)[41]
Financing and Local governments	Since 1994, local governments have been forbidden to borrow money directly. 2013 - High level of debt among local governments reached CNY 17.9 trillion, about one-third of China's GDP.	2014 - The National Budget Law was amended in August. The law now authorises local governments to raise debt and issue bonds only with State Council approval. Debt can be raised only for non-profit public project investments; for other infrastructure projects with potential cash returns, such as public utilities and transportation, the State Council encourages the use of PPPs or project-specific bonds.
Main sectors (the nature of the agreements between the public & private actors)	Telecom infrastructure, Energy, Transport, Water, and Sewerage.	In 2015, the MOF, NDRC, and the PBoC jointly issued a notice to promote cooperation between government and social capital in the field of public services and proposed to encourage "the use of government and social capital" (PPP) in the areas of energy, transportation, water conservancy, environmental protection, agriculture and forestry, science and technology, affordable housing projects, medical care, health, pension, education, culture, and other public services. The State swung into action to attract social capital participation where franchising was required in specific fields such as energy, transportation, water conservancy, environmental protection, and municipal engineering. PPP mode was applied to new municipal projects and new urbanisation pilot projects.
Monitoring	No centralised or consistent monitoring of PPP projects	

Source: Author's analysis.

public investment. The former, short-term goals were primarily set to achieve through the Transfer-Operate-Transfer (TOT) model. Simultaneously, the latter relied upon PPP models devised by the government to purchase asset-based services from private suppliers, e.g., Private Finance Initiative (PFI).

Since 2014, the government has made it clear, through the 2015 Measures and elsewhere, that the Chinese state expects PPPs to be bankable and contestable between private and state-owned bidders and transfer critical risks over the project life-cycle. This message has been progressively reinforced by successive guidance intended to promote private sector participation in PPP. According to anecdotal reports, projects with no real risk transfer and few (or no) life-cycle obligations have been awarded to local state-owned construction firms, not necessarily in a competitive procedure, while still being labelled as PPP.[42] This is the so-called 'fake PPP' phenomenon, on which the Chinese government has now launched a crackdown. Since 2014, however, new guidance and encouragement from the central government have given PPPs a new drive where they have expanded into every conceivable sector, and there has been an explosion in planning and proposing new projects. However, not all these projects could be accurately described as PPPs, as discussed below.

The noteworthy aspect about PPP is that it has caught the attention of the political masters and that Premier Li Keqiang and Finance Minister Lou Jiwei are actively promoting the PPP wave. In his *2019 Work Report,* Premier Li openly proposed implementing private investment support policies and cooperation between the government and social capital.[43] The experiences have helped the Chinese develop its models to reap maximum benefits from newer PPP patterns (refer to PPP contracts mentioned in Table 8.4). These models include outsourcing, franchising, and privatisation. The history of introducing new 'systemic disruptions' informally is not unique to China. All socio-economic experiments in China have been the result of a chain of experiments where many failed and few survived. The Chinese state co-opted the best examples and replicated them. Once a policy is officially endorsed along party lines in China, it gathers natural attention. Whether it is SEZ, privatisation of agriculture production, or PPP, the Party opened up for reforms at a gradual speed. But to their disappointment, the PPP models have been widely subscribed to by all the entities in China where the private players still find discomfort to invest in public services unless they are pushed to do so or see strong incentive, whether short-term or long-term and in both cases explicit political pressures are being exerted.

PPP and the Rise of State Enterprises

While the State propagates that it attempts to achieve synergy between the private and public enterprises, it promotes cooperation between central enterprises and enterprises of various ownerships to make the best for SOEs. Starting with mixed ownership, the SOEs were facilitated in strengthening pragmatic cooperation with the new generation of private players. For example, Internet companies such as Tencent deeply integrate artificial intelligence, big data, etc., with the real economy and promote the transformation and upgrading of traditional industries. By doing so, the Central enterprises vigorously developed strategies to learn from new sectors. The PPP model sets different milestones for SOEs. The development of PPP was required to solve the need of urbanisation funds. As a result, the leadership looked at the PPP model as the mainstream financing channel for large-scale urbanisation under sound fiscal and monetary policies. This was the most critical aspect of SOEs and their regulators looked at areas where they could partner with private players. SOEs play a much more significant role in China's PPP market than in probably any other area.

For the large Central SOEs, PPP was a minuscule fixture enticing them to show any interest. Still, but for their tiny subsidiaries at the local level, this was crucial to finding niche areas to work with private players. PPPs were seen as an effective channel to promote stable and long-term State-owned Small and Medium-sized Enterprises (SOSMEs). As PPP focuses on 'social capital,' local SOSMEs took advantage to complete the supply of public products such as infrastructure and public services while achieving the sustainable development of the enterprise itself.

Besides, PPPs were capable of improving the market operation capabilities of SOSMEs, and follow the national policies issued by the CSRC and NDRC. The Central SOEs issued a series of policies focusing on strengthening the standardised management of PPP, critical areas of PPP promotion, and encouraging PPP development. Simultaneously, the local SOE guidelines directed PPP development from regulating local PPP project management and strengthening life cycle management to promote PPP development from a more ground-based reality. The implementation and application of PPP policies allowed SOEs, financial institutions, and governments to find a way to see a connection with the ordinary Chinese as well as society. Local SOSMEs grasped it from the perspective of standardised operation, and at the same time, used it to protect their rights and interests in implementing projects.

Under the Central government's financial policy of preventing local government debt risks and reducing society's leverage, the Chinese government's investment and financing system requires establishing a more open, transparent, and diversified government financing supply system. In this context, the SOEs, particularly SOSMEs, needed innovative financing ideas for sustainable development. By restructuring corporate credit, assets, and projects, SOSMEs were expected to cultivate more capital, management, and operation. Market-oriented models, such as social capital to participate in the development of PPP urban projects, comprehensive development covering municipal level engineering, ecological, environmental protection, water conservation, and action, are seen as a step towards improving the capital efficiency of enterprises and optimising the resource allocation of state-owned enterprises as well. This would eventually help ease the operating pressure of traditional SOEs and enhance the profitability of enterprises.

PPP is also a challenge for the SOSMEs to get out of their comfort zone and collaborate with private enterprises. It is also true that private enterprises become more visible by working with the SOSMEs and SOEs. PPP helps SOSMEs to strengthen the training of professional skills for managers. With the operation and development of the PPP model, China's laws and policies for the project are gradually showing signs of departure from bureaucratic holds over approvals and public services management. The PPP model is also crucial to alleviate the government's financial pressure and improve the supply and efficiency of public projects. With the best public and private participation, PPP disallows any margin for errors and is showcased as an efficient model for higher efficiency. This was expected to generate a high rate of professional qualifications. This undoubtedly posed challenges to the operation and management of SOSMEs. The quality and efficiency in the supply of infrastructure and public services were seen as helpful for PPPs to break the local administrative hold over market change, the backward management methods of business. The thumb-rule of going local always monopolised the local and grassroots markets. By way of PPP, the information asymmetry in service pricing and quality was addressed.

On the flip side, the SOEs dominated the PPP (see Table 8.4) because private players fell short of fulfilling the central role of PPP projects. One can refer to the empirical findings to validate how SOEs have been winning bids and causing the private sector to shrink (see Table 8.4). As a case, Table 8.4 shows the SOEs centred classification, indicating that Central SOEs have been dominating PPP projects across sectors. The Table takes a sample timeline and demonstrates the range of PPP projects being approved and conducted by the significant Central SOEs. These eight large Central enterprises include China Construction Group Corporation, China Communications Construction Group Co. Ltd., China Railway Construction Group Co. Ltd., China Railway Engineering Group Co. Ltd., China Metallurgical Corporation, China Power Construction Group Co. Ltd., China Energy Construction Group Co. Ltd., and China National Chemical Engineering Corporation. The data scans projects by sector and province. As sample data, the author looked at the PPP projects being approved and managed by the Central SOEs between January and June 2017, whereby 440 projects were studied to classify them as per the successful bidding entities. Moreover, the Table also indicates that some of the PPP projects bagged by the large Central SOEs do have small private partners.

The government budgets PPP projects as it owns the land and controls significant financing challenges. Bidding and tendering have been increasingly used to find partners to lead the projects and complete them. The bid winners are usually the Central enterprises, SOEs, and other enterprises with state-owned assets, amongst which the SOEs are ahead in winning the project's contract as the bidding thresholds are high and only SOEs can meet them. SOEs could win PPP projects as they possess the required registered capital, enterprise net assets, and essential credit ratings to win the project; indicators set by the governments to fulfil even entry to the bidding process. Small and private firms have low capital and assets to win projects. Based on documents (for evaluating the bidding) of the "PPP Project of the Outer Ring North Road (Anqing City)", it was confirmed that the conditions for enlisting qualified bidders include having a good bank credit, financial status, and corresponding investment, financing, and solvency capabilities. The project listed net assets not less than 7 billion yuan (or equivalent in foreign currency)

Table 8.4: SOEs' Centred Classification of PPP Projects (Sample Timeline—January to June 2017)

Central SOE	*Major bid-winning PPP projects*	*Province*	*Project cost (100 million yuan)*	*Private partner/s (if any)*
China Construction Group Corporation	PPP project of underground comprehensive pipe construction in extension section of Tongan Road and Shengtang Road in Tongcheng City	Anhui	7.67	–
	G4012 Liyang to Ningde Highway, Huangshan to Qiandaohu section, G42S Shanghai to Wuhan Highway Wuwei to Yuexi section, G3W Dezhou to Shangrao Highway Hefei to Zongyang of section 2	Anhui	92.28	–
	Fuyang City Urban Water System Comprehensive Treatment (including black and poisonous water treatment) PPP project (Tender 3)	Anhui	30.66	Lingnan Eco-Cultural Tourism Co. Ltd.
	PPP project of Minjiang Mawei-Taiwan Comprehensive Passenger Terminal Project	Fujian	3.03	–
	Suixi County Fenglang River Basin Ecological Restoration Project (Phase I) (Investment and Financing, Survey, Design, Construction, Operation, and Maintenance Integrated Service Project)	Guangdong	5.8	–
China Communications Construction Group Co. Ltd.	G4012 Liyang to Ningde Highway—Huangshan to Qiandao Lake section; G42S Shanghai to Wuhan Highway—Wuwei to Yuexi section; G3W Dezhou to Shangrao Highway—Hefei to Zongyang section	Anhui	228.93	–
	Maanshan Zhengpu Port Railway PPP Project	Anhui	17.69	–
	The PPP project of the construction of the highway from Lintun to Shitun section of Zhenghe County; Zhenghe Railway Station, and related connecting line road engineering	Fujian	9.17	–
	Maintenance and construction of supporting engineering PPP project of Zhujiayao to Zhongchuan railway line (the newly constructed lines were built by Lanzhou New Area Urban and Rural Construction)	Gansu	18.6	–
	Construction of Qingyang City Sponge City Pilot Model Project	Gansu	12.7	–

Central SOE	*Major bid-winning PPP projects*	*Province*	*Project cost (100 million yuan)*	*Private partner/s (if any)*
China Railway Construction Group Co. Ltd.	PPP project of Five Way Network engineering including Wangershan Road in Jinzhai Modern Industrial Park	Anhui	5.79	–
	PPP project of Lu'an Sports Centre	Anhui	7.3	–
	PPP project of Wuyi New District Tourism Rail Transit—Wuyi Shandong Station to Wuyishan Scenic Area Line Project	Fujian	27.58	–
	PPP project of municipal road engineering (Phase I) of Hanjiang District Housing and Urban-rural Construction Bureau of Putian City	Fujian	8.82	–
	Zhanjiang Diaoshun Sea Bridge PPP Project	Guangdong	21.275	–
China Railway Engineering Group Co. Ltd.	Huanggang City Urban Underground Comprehensive Pipe Gallery PPP Project	Hubei	31.05	Wuhan Jiuyi
	Traffic Facilities Engineering Co. Ltd.			
	PPP project of Aifeike Aviation Science and Technology Museum in Jingmen City	Hubei	5	–
	Infrastructure PPP project of Hankou Riverside International Business District	Hubei	53.6	CITIC Pacific (China) Investment Co. Ltd.
	PPP project of integrated pipe construction in Dali City	Yunnan	25.5	Shanghai Horizon Infrastructure Investment Co. Ltd.
	PPP project of comprehensive environmental management in Xingye County, Yulin City	Guangxi	4.8	–
China Metallurgical Corporation	PPP project in Dongji Town—Heixiazi Island Supporting Function Zone (Fuyuan City)	Heilongjiang	48.8	–
	PPP project of Yuliangzhou Island	Hubei	8.92	Beijing Oriental Garden Environment Co. Ltd.
	Xiema-Caijia Section of Expressway; Xiema Tunnel East-West Trunk Road PPP Project	Chongqing	16.43	–
	PPP project of road and comprehensive pipeline corridor construction project of Chunyu Road and Jinma Road in Kunming	Yunnan	42.1	–
	PPP project for the construction and operation of the "13th Five-Year" tourist trunk road in Xiangxi Prefecture	Hunan	57.96	–

Central SOE	*Major bid-winning PPP projects*	*Province*	*Project cost (100 million yuan)*	*Private partner/s (if any)*
China Power Construction Group Co. Ltd.	PPP project of the construction project of the Eastern Medical and Health Centre of Jimo City (Shandong Provincial Hospital Qingdao Hospital)	Shandong	10.81	–
	Wuhan Xingfu Innovation Ecological Peninsula Infrastructure Project (Phase I) PPP Project	Hubei	9.59	–
	Chengdu Rail Transit Line 18 PPP project	Sichuan	347	–
	Zhaoqing Medical College Upgrade and Relocation Project PPP Project	Guang-dong	16.39	–
	PPP project of comprehensive development and construction of Ruijin Culture and Art Centre	Jiangxi	4.21	–
China Energy Construction Group Co. Ltd.	Dongjiang Dike (Zhongkai Section of Jiangnan Avenue) Road Construction Project PPP Project	Guang-dong	43.1	–
	Jiangmen City promotes a new round of construction of domestic sewage treatment facilities in the East, West, and North of Guangdong PPP project	Guang-dong	5.12	–
	Nanning City Xinjiang to Chongzuo Fusui First Class Highway (Nanning Section) PPP Project	Guangxi	20.83	–
	PPP project of water conservancy, trans-portation, and municipal infrastructure construction in Wu'an City	Hebei	63.27	–
	Linlu Industrial Park—Comprehensive urbanisation construction program (Phase II)	Anhui	9.51	–
China National Chemical Engineering Corporation	PPP project in Zhongshan Street, Fengtai County	Anhui	13.3	–
	Ezhou Aviation Metropolitan Area Community Resettlement Project (EPC+PPP model)	Hubei	80.64	–
	PPP project of Duwei Urban Ecological Wetland Park in Nanjing Chemical Industry Park	Jiangsu	8.8	–
	PPP project for the construction of 22 roads including Dagongxue Road in New District of Xingyuan District, Hanzhong City and the laying of pipeline corridor along the West Second Ring Road	Shaanxi	10.41	–
	Kaifeng City Airport East Road Construction Project—Phase I (Airport North Road-310 National Road) PPP project	Henan	2.87	–

Note: *Sponge city* is a new generation concept of urban storm water management. It means that the city can be like a sponge and has good flexibility in adapting to environmental changes and coping with natural disasters caused by rain. It can also be called a "water elastic city".

Source: Author's analysis based on various reports by provinces and press release.

and the enterprise's registered capital above 500 million yuan as the minimum social capital qualification.[44] In a subsequent development, due to the excessively high capital threshold requirements, the bidding was cancelled for the first time, and therefore the second bidding was conducted after lowering the threshold.

On 12 February, 2015, according to the pre-qualification announcement issued by the urban and rural construction committee of Anqing city, after analysing the reasons for the bid flow, the qualification conditions for social capital funds were revised. The requirements were set at lower levels. The required level for net assets was lowered to 'not less than 500 million yuan (or equivalent in foreign currency)', and the minimum limit for the enterprise's registered capital was set at 305 million yuan.[45] As per the government's original guidelines, the project did not see anyone showing interest in it. After the revised guidelines, the project hoped to attract more bidders and avoid the risk of bidders being dissatisfied. This indicates that the thresholds were too high for the private sector and SOEs as well.[46] To put it into perspective, in China, small enterprises generally have a registered capital of 5 to 40 million yuan and medium-sized enterprises have above 40 million yuan.[47] Those with more than 100 million yuan are considered to be promising small and medium-sized enterprises.[48] In addition to these requirements, PPP projects require fulfilment of stringent quality standards, and private enterprises with experience of a mere 10 to 15 years often lack experience in meeting these certifications. Since several municipal projects have to deal with construction departments, water and electricity projects, the list of qualifications and licences is usually lengthier. The licence requirements of the project itself affect the qualifying rounds.[49] Even if the private enterprises meet the requirements, their technical qualifications fall short in applying for the bidding. This affects the private players' ability to independently contest PPP bids without relying on prospective partner SOE certification and is evident in the case of several small and medium-sized enterprises that lack qualified licences.

In comparison, SOEs have more experience in dealing with the government's expectations and institutional familiarities, which help them influence the contracts. Therefore, compared with small and medium-sized enterprises with incomplete certificates and qualifications, SOEs successfully bid for the project and possess the abilities to implement it without any snag making it natural for the government, i.e., the bidding party, biased towards choosing the SOEs. In the Outer Ring North Road Project in Anqing City, the Beijing Urban Construction Design and Development Group Co. Ltd., an SOE, won the bid.[50] The controlling shareholder of the Beijing Urban Construction Design Development Group Co. Ltd. is the Beijing Urban Construction Group Co. Ltd., and the actual controller is the Beijing Municipal People's Government.

Anqing PPP is just one example in which the SOEs have taken centre stage and running the entire show. Mengnan Shi, who works at the Xiamen Municipal Construction Group, has empirically established that State institutions are ahead in influencing PPP bids. Shi uses data from 2017 and takes into account the 1,062 PPP projects awarded to Central SOEs.[51] The analysis reflects that during 2017, Central SOEs invested about 5.7 trillion yuan in PPP projects accounting for 59 per cent of PPP project total turnover in China.[52] SOEs poured substantial capital into the projects, but the average transaction value of each PPP project in SOEs was 2.07 billion yuan. In contrast, the average transaction value in private enterprises was 760 million yuan. The private players' role does not look like a game-changer, which was the core motive behind launching the PPP model in China. As per the latest *2019 Annual Report of the National PPP Integrated Information Platform Management Database Project*, the role of the private enterprises is 'stable',[53] which one may read cautiously given the growing reservations among private players about the PPP models. In 2018, the All-China Federation of Industry and Commerce, in its report to the Ministry of Commerce, revealed that since the end of 2015, the market share of private capital in the PPP programs continued to decline.[54] The report further enlists[55] specific reasons for this:

1. The current PPP project cooperation model and procurement model restrictions and financial support policies are challenging and are not helpful given the intensified market competition;
2. The current cooperation model and procurement method of PPP projects emphasise the integration of investment, construction, and operation life-cycle service capabilities and investment capabilities making private companies with weak overall creditworthiness lose even before they start to compete for the projects;
3. The current financial support policies for private enterprises to participate in PPP projects have not helped improve the overall financing conditions of private enterprises. They, especially non-

private private enterprises, find it difficult to gain the favour of financial institutions without external credit enhancement. A large amount of financial resources are practically essential. The investment is obtained by central enterprises and local state-owned enterprises easily, and the disadvantages in financing channels and financing costs restrict the ability of private enterprises to continue participating in PPP projects; and

4. Lastly, intensified market competition affects the market share of private enterprises, which is mainly manifested in the large number of local state-owned enterprises participating in PPP projects through cross-level or cross-regional investment. In the past, many private enterprises in China primarily invested in real estate, industrial manufacturing, and tertiary industries. They had relatively little participation in infrastructure, poor experience, and a lack of capabilities. Compared with large state-owned enterprises, the competitiveness of private enterprises was weak.

The report was critical as it underlined several loopholes in the PPP model favouring SOEs. It not only insisted that the PPP was implemented in short-sightedness, in a way but also substantiates that private players are involved in reducing the burden on SOEs but without giving away any significant share.[56] This indicates that the PPP model lacks a long-term development policy expectation, reflects apathy over a fair and just risk distribution system, and is highly secretive. The report recommended improving the information disclosure mechanism in the PPP field. It seems that favours to SOEs are an anticipated factor while drafting PPP laws and guidelines. The report criticises the "hidden discrimination" (隐性歧视 *yin xingqishi*) in implementing projects. This indicates how stubborn SOEs get and how their owners (State Council or local governments) are reluctant to the idea of allowing private players a lead role.

Based on the data,[57] if one analyses the participation rate of private enterprises in PPPs, the picture is not promising. Their participation has been implicitly restricted. On the one hand, when the government wants private players to play an increasing role in PPPs, the number of PPP projects won by private enterprises and the proportion of investment have undergone a double drop. PPP is an essential way of stimulating private investment, and the problem of declining private investment growth has been a matter of anxiety, but the share of provincial and central enterprises has increased over the past five years, i.e., 2015 to 2019. Since the vigorous promotion of the PPP model in 2014, the traditional public service market was gradually opened up to various types of social capital, and the participation of private enterprises has always been the focus of the market. As data in Table 8.5 indicates, in February 2015, the total investment scale of PPP projects won by private enterprises accounted for 35.50 per cent, which slipped to 24.77 per cent in July 2017. By February 2019, it fell further to 23.27 per cent. The decrease in investment is proportionate to the decline in private enterprise success in the PPP project bidding. According to data, private players consistently lost PPP bids since 2015. In 2015, the private sector won a majority of PPP projects registering a share of 55.75 per cent in February 2015. This declined to 47.62 per cent by July 2017, and until February 2019, the share of private players winning PPP bids witnessed a record drop by reaching 42.12 per cent.[58] As most of the earlier analysis points out, restrictions on PPP project cooperation and procurement models, difficulty in implementing financial support policies, and intensified market competition are the main reasons for the gradual decline in private enterprise participation in the PPP field and the rise of state firms.

Table 8.5: Measuring Private Players' Participation in PPP Projects (2015-2019)

	February 2019	*July 2017*	*February 2015*
Proportion of private enterprise investment scale	23.27%	24.77%	35.50%
Proportion of bids won by private enterprises	42.12%	47.62%	55.75%

Source: Author's analysis based on various reports by Ministry of Finance and *First Finance News* (第一财经 *Di Yi Caijing*)

The collated data given here provides further insights into how the SOEs have become a dominant player in winning and implementing PPP projects. Of the 3,000–odd projects, select declarations of provinces and municipalities were used as base data and matched with the Ministry of Finance data. Nearly 103 declared projects by select provinces and endorsed by the Ministry of Finance were used as panel data to develop a detailed PPP project classification. While taking stock of these 103 PPP projects, Table 8.6 classifies them by year, province, majority stakeholder, nature of the stake-holder, investment amount, and contract types. Between 2016 and 2019, these provinces approved

85 BOT projects, and private players could successfully bag only ten projects (see Table 8.6). Some of the projects are as small as US$ 10 million and as big as US$ 2.49 billion. For obvious reasons private players exceptionally win big projects. The big projects were regarding ecological conservation and poverty alleviation, and hence the SOEs were not the apparent takers. In recent times, President Xi has been directing SOEs to adopt PPP models to deal with environmental issues as it has successful models from the West to study. In May 2018, in his speech at the National Ecological Environmental Protection Conference, Xi emphasised that various methods should be adopted to support the government and social capital cooperation projects to improve environmental governance.[59]

Most of the small projects won by private players across various types of PPP projects—Build-Operate-Transfer (BOT), Rehabilitate-Operate-Transfer (ROT), Transfer-Operate-Transfer (TOT), Build-Own-Operate (BOO), Build-Operate-Lease-Transfer (BOLT), Build-Own-Operate-Transfer (BOOT), Commissioned Operation (O&M), Lease-Operate-Transfer (LOT), Engineering Procurement Construction (EPC), and Reconstruction-Lease-Operation-Handover (RLOT)—are specialised categories which the SOEs would not have any interest to invest in, and includes medical, health-care, communication and software (see Table 8.6). The data also reveals that the private players presently run the two BOOT projects in Zhejiang, a province that is incubating ground for China's successful private players, e.g., Alibaba and Geely Group. In other categories, BOT+O&M and BLOT, Guanxi province could not find a suitable match from the SOEs as the project requirement needed a match on the computing and technological front (see Table 8.6).

The collated table is comprehensive and provides a glimpse of PPP project management. Although PPP bidding is tightly controlled and even general information (bidder's name, number of bidders, process, and qualification) is not disclosed, for most China observers, such a table provides an in-depth look into the whole mechanism.

As described in Table 8.6, the project categories are spread across various infrastructure projects; the sub-categories include municipal engineering projects, rail transit, civic-recreational facilities, water treatment plants, healthcare projects, waterways, shipping, housing, etc. Another striking thing which the data reveals is that the private enterprises and the SOEs are local. The respective administrative units preferred Subsidiary SOEs in the provinces (SSP) to award the PPP projects, and if not the SSPs, then the provincial private players were given weightage to bid for the project. This indicates how the provinces manipulated the projects to keep them limited to the local players making it easier for local governments to exercise complete control over project management. The findings reveal that the municipal administrations have limited choices in the case of municipalities and award them to giant State enterprises. The data drawn from Beijing, Chongqing and, Tianjin indicates that the projects have been dominated by the large SOEs and not private players. While the Autonomous Region was given a free hand to award projects to local investors, it widens the local CPC leaders' social and political prospects. The same case is evident in the case of Tibet, but while preparing the data set for this ongoing project, the team could not focus on other provinces other than those mentioned here.

PPP: A Saviour for Local Governments

Urban spaces in China are witnessing a rising number of PPP modelling. Municipalities like Beijing, Guangzhou, Nanjing, Shanghai, Shenzhen, and Tianjin are ahead in inviting newer projects. Along with these cities, the second-tier metropolises such as Chongqing, Hangzhou, Harbin, Kunming, Shenyang, Qingdao, and Xi'an are also taking the lead, inviting bids for projects which are for metropolitan authorities. The scale of expansion of Chinese cities has been unprecedented in the last two decades, creating the need to seek alternative financing methods and carry out projects. However, it is also a fact that most of the urban infrastructure has been turned into a burden on the already shrinking fiscal options open to provinces. A few municipalities under the state's direct control find ways to raise their budget requirements for meeting infrastructure costs, but this is not the same with many other provinces/cities in China. Many cities in China face rising challenges to meet the increasing demands for funds. The PPP model has found greater acceptance in the PRC in recent years as an acceptable funding model. The benefits associated with PPP projects include greater transparency, improved operational efficiency and professionalism, lower costs, and more substantial innovation incentives.[60] But more than the funds, the State needs to look at ways to innovate the

Table 8.6: Profiling of PPP Projects in Select Provinces, Municipalities and the Autonomous Region (2016-2019)

Sr. No.	*PPP Project*	*Province/ Municipality*	*Year*	*Project type*	*Investor/s*	*Major Investor/ Stakeholder's nature*	*Total investment ($ Billion)*	*PPP Contract type*
1	National Highway 109 New Line Expressway (West Sixth Ring Road-City Boundary Section) PPP project	Beijing Municipality	2020	Transportation-Highway	- China Railway Corporation Ltd., - China Railway Second Bureau Group Co. Ltd., - Beijing Municipal Road and Bridge Co. Ltd., - Beijing Construction Engineering Group Co. Ltd., and - Beijing Zhuhai Group Co. Ltd.	SOE	3.20	BOT
2	PPP project of the National Speed Skating Hall of the Beijing 2022 Winter Olympic Games	Beijing Municipality	2018	Sports	- Beijing Capital Development Co. Ltd., - Beijing Urban Construction Group Co. Ltd., - Beijing Residential Group Co. Ltd., - China Sports Group Co. Ltd.	SOE	0.22	BOT
3	Beijing New Airport North Line Expressway (Beijing Section)	Beijing Municipality	2017	Transportation-Highway	- China Railway Construction Corp. Ltd., - China Railway 16th Bureau Group Co. Ltd., and - China Railway Construction Bridge Engineering Bureau Group Co. Ltd.	SOE	1.57	BOT
4	Beijing Big Data Research Platform	Beijing Municipality	2017	Technology	Beijing Beizi Engineering Consulting Co. Ltd.	Private	0.01	BOO
5	Government and Social Capital Cooperation Project of Beijing Global Health Drug R&D Centre	Beijing Municipality	2016	Technology	Tsinghua University Education Foundation and Bill & Melinda Gates Foundation (USA) Beijing Representative Office Consortium	Other	0.14	BOO
6	The Capital Region Ring Expressway (Tongzhou-Daxing Section)	Beijing Municipality	2016	Transportation-Highway	- China Communications Construction Co. Ltd., - China Communications First Highway Engineering Bureau Co. Ltd., and - China Communications Road and Bridge Construction Co. Ltd.	SOE	1.74	BOT

Sr. No.	*PPP Project*	*Province/ Municipality*	*Year*	*Project type*	*Investor/s*	*Major Investor/ Stakeholder's nature*	*Total investment ($ Billion)*	*PPP Contract type*
7	Beijing Xingyan Expressway	Beijing Municipality	2016	Transportation-Highway	- China Railway Construction Corp. Ltd., - China Railway 12th Bureau Group Co. Ltd., and - China Railway 14th Bureau Group Co. Ltd.	SOE	1.87	BOT
8	Beijing Rail Transit's New Airport Line's Social capital projects	Beijing Municipality	2016	Municipal Engineering-Rail Transit	- Beijing Rail Transit Construction Management Co. Ltd., - Beijing Rail Transit Operation Management Co. Ltd., - Beijing Urban Construction Group Co. Ltd., - Beijing Municipal Road and Bridge Co. Ltd., - Beijing Municipal Construction Group Co. Ltd., - China Railway Construction Co. Ltd., - China Railway 14 Bureau Group Co. Ltd., and - China Railway 12th Bureau Group Co. Ltd.	SOE	2.14	BOT
9	Beijing Rail Transit Line 14	Beijing Municipality	2016	Municipal Engineering-Rail Transit	Not available	Not available	6.36	BOT
10	Beijing Rail Transit Line 16	Beijing Municipality	2016	Municipal Engineering-Rail Transit	Beijing Jinggang Metro Co. Ltd.	SOE	7.07	BOT
11	Government and Social capital cooperation project between Beijing New Airport and Dezhou Expressway	Hebei Province	2019	Transportation-Highway	Hebei Transportation Investment Group Corporation	SOE	2.73	BOT
12	Government and social capital co-operation project from the Beijing-Taiwan Expressway to the Beijing-Hong Kong-Macao Expressway on the new line of the Rongwu Expressway	Hebei Province	2019	Transportation-Highway	China Railway Fifth Bureau Group Co. Ltd.	SOE	2.85	Not available

Sr. No.	PPP Project	Province/ Municipality	Year	Project type	Investor/s	Major Investor/ Stakeholder's nature	Total investment ($ Billion)	PPP Contract type
13	The first phase of the construction project of the new campus of Hebei University of Engineering	Hebei Province	2016	Infrastructure	Not available	Not available	0.03	Not available
14	Taihangshan Expressway (Project Package (1) + Project Package (2))	Hebei Province	2016	Transportation-Highway	- China Power Construction Road and Bridge Group Co. Ltd. (Leader of the consortium), - China Power Construction Co. Ltd., - Chengdu Huachuan Highway Construction Group Co. Ltd.	SOE	12.83	BOT
15	Beijing-Xinjiang-Beijing-Tibet Express Link Project	Hebei Province	2016	Transportation-Highway	MCC Jingcheng Engineering Technology Co. Ltd.	Private	0.14	BOT
16	Tianjin-Jincang Expressway Reconstruction	Tianjin Municipality	2019	Transportation-Highway	China Railway 14th Bureau Group Co. Ltd.	SOE	0.10	BOT
17	Tianjin Metro Line 7 (Phase I)	Tianjin Municipality	2019	Municipal Engineering-Rail Transit	China State Construction Corporation	SOE	2.70	BOT
18	Tianjin Metro Line 11 (Phase I)	Tianjin Municipality	2019	Municipal Engineering-Rail Transit	China Communications Construction Co. Ltd.	SOE	2.60	BOT
19	Tianjin Metro Line 4	Tianjin Municipality	2019	Municipal Engineering-Rail Transit	- China Railway Corporation Limited, - China Railway Second Bureau Group Co. Ltd.	SOE	2.52	BOT
20	Tianjin Metro Line 3	Tianjin Municipality	2019	Municipal Engineering-Rail Transit	China Communications Construction Co. Ltd.	SOE	2.53	TOT
21	Tianjin Metro Line 2	Tianjin Municipality	2019	Municipal Engineering-Rail Transit	China Communications Construction Co. Ltd.	SOE	2.01	BOT

Sr. No.	*PPP Project*	*Province/ Municipality*	*Year*	*Project type*	*Investor/s*	*Major Investor/ Stakeholder's nature*	*Total investment ($ Billion)*	*PPP Contract type*
22	Tianjin Metro Line 8 (Phase 1)	Tianjin Municipality	2017	Municipal Engineering-Rail Transit	Not available	Not available	2.52	TOT
23	Tianjin-Shijiazhuang Expressway Project (in the West Section of Tianjin)	Tianjin Municipality	2017	Transportation-Highway	China Communications 1st Public Bureau Group Co. Ltd.	SOE	0.45	BOT
24	Sponge City project construction at Jiefang South Road, Tianjin	Tianjin Municipality	2017	Municipal Engineering-Sponge City	Beijing Bishuiyuan Technology Co. Ltd.	Private	0.36	BOT
25	Road surface reconstruction project in Shanxi Province (in Xinzhou)	Shanxi Province	2019	Transportation-Other	Shanxi Transportation Investment and Financing Group Co. Ltd.	SOE	0.10	BOT
26	Road surface reconstruction project in Shanxi Province (in Luliang area)	Shanxi Province	2019	Transportation-Other	Shanxi Road and Bridge Construction Group Co. Ltd.	SOE	0.11	BOT
27	Road surface reconstruction project in Shanxi Province (in Linfen)	Shanxi Province	2019	Transportation-Other	China Highway Engineering Consulting Group Co. Ltd.	SOE	0.10	BOT
28	Road surface reconstruction project in Shanxi Province (in Taiyuan & Yangquan)	Shanxi Province	2019	Transportation-Other	China Communications First Public Bureau Group Co. Ltd.	SOE	0.07	BOT
29	Road surface reconstruction project in Shanxi Province (in Jinzhong)	Shanxi Province	2019	Transportation-Other	Shanxi Construction Engineering Group Co. Ltd.	SOE	0.14	BOT
30	Road surface reconstruction project in Shanxi Province (in Changzhi)	Shanxi Province	2019	Transportation-Other	China Communications Road & Bridge Construction Co. Ltd.	SOE	0.11	BOT
31	Road surface reconstruction project in Shanxi Province (in Datong and Shuozhou)	Shanxi Province	2019	Transportation-Other	Shanxi Road and Bridge Construction Group Co. Ltd.	SOE	0.13	BOT
32	Road surface reconstruction project in Shanxi Province (in Yuncheng and Jincheng)	Shanxi Province	2019	Transportation-Other	Shanxi Road and Bridge Construction Group Co. Ltd.	SOE	0.14	BOT

Sr. No.	PPP Project	Province/ Municipality	Year	Project type	Investor/s	Major Investor/ Stakeholder's nature	Total investment ($ Billion)	PPP Contract type
33	Shanxi Province Hubei National Expressway—Shuocheng to Shenchi Section (Shanxi Province)	Shanxi Province	2019	Transportation-Highway	Shanxi Expressway Group Co. Ltd.	SOE	0.39	BOT
34	Shanxi Province Hubei National Expressway - Lishi to Xixian Section (Shanxi Province)	Shanxi Province	2019	Transportation-Highway	China Railway Third Bureau Group Co. Ltd.	SOE	1.54	BOT
35	Shanxi Province G3511 Hebao Line Linyi Yellow River Bridge and Leading Project - Project of Yunsan Expressway Sanmenxia Highway-Rail Yellow River Bridge Connection Line	Shanxi Province	2019	Transportation-Highway	China Railway Third Bureau Group Co. Ltd.	SOE	1.09	BOT
36	Shanxi Province Forestry Ecological Poverty Alleviation PPP Project	Shanxi Province	2019	Forestry	Jinzhong Forestry Development Investment Co. Ltd.	Private	2.49	BOT
37	PPP project of Xixian-Jixian section of Hubei National Expressway in Shanxi Province	Shanxi Province	2018	Transportation-Highway	Shanxi Road and Bridge Construction Group Co. Ltd.	SOE	1.76	BOT
38	PPP project of the National Northern Football Training Base	Inner Mongolia Autonomous Region	2018	Sports	MCC Communications Construction Group Co. Ltd.	SOE	0.92	BOT
39	International Mongolian Medicine and Medical Care PPP Project	Inner Mongolia Autonomous Region	2017	Elderly Care-Integrated Medical Care	- Inner Mongolia Aochun Investment Co. Ltd., - Tiankai Ruixiang Health and Elderly Care Centre in Yanqing District, Beijing, - Inner Mongolia Jinji Construction and Installation Engineering Co. Ltd.	Private	0.17	BOT

Sr. No.	*PPP Project*	*Province/ Municipality*	*Year*	*Project type*	*Investor/s*	*Major Investor/ Stakeholder's nature*	*Total investment ($ Billion)*	*PPP Contract type*
40	Sewage treatment plant and supporting construction project in Yangguanhe, Lagu Industrial Park, Shenfu New District, Liaoning Province	Liaoning Province	2019	Municipal Engineering-Sewage Treatment	China Nuclear New Energy Investment Co. Ltd.	SOE	0.03	BOT
41	A project of Comprehensive Service System of Reproductive Medicine Centre of Beihua University Hospital	Jilin Province	2019	Healthcare-Hospital	Jilin Lichuang Medical Co. Ltd.	Private	0.01	BOT
42	A project of Comprehensive Service System of Reproductive Medicine Centre of Yanbian Hospital of Jilin Province	Jilin Province	2018	Healthcare-Hospital	Haikou Broad Medical Investment Management Co. Ltd.	Private	0.01	BOT
43	Jishuang Expressway (Tonghua-Meihekou section) in Jilin Province	Jilin Province	2016	Transportation-Highway	Jilin Expressway Group Co. Ltd.	SOE	1.01	TOT
44	Jiamusi Transit Section of He-Da Expressway, Heilongjiang Province	Heilongjiang Province	2016	Transportation-Highway	- CCCC First Navigation Engineering Bureau Co. Ltd. - Longjian Road and Bridge Co. Ltd. - CCCC Highway Planning and Design Institute Co. Ltd.	SOE	0.30	other
45	Hangzhou-Wenzhou Railway National Mixed Ownership Reform Pilot and PPP Demonstration Project	Zhejiang Province	2018	Transportation-Railway (excluding rail transit)	Parkson United Group Co. Ltd.	Private	5.47	BOOT
46	Hangzhou-Shaoxing-Taiwan High-Speed Railway project	Zhejiang Province	2018	Transportation-Railway (excluding rail transit)	Zhejiang Fosun Commercial Development Co. Ltd.	Private	5.66	BOOT
47	The Reconstruction and Expansion Project of the Hushan (Hurong) National Expressway in Anhui Province - Hefei to Dagudian Section of Anhui Province	Anhui Province	2019	Transportation-Highway	Anhui Transportation Holdings Co. Ltd.	SOE	1.09	ROT

Sr. No.	PPP Project	Province/ Municipality	Year	Project type	Investor/s	Major Investor/ Stakeholder's nature	Total investment ($ Billion)	PPP Contract type
48	Reconstruction and Expansion Project of Wuhu-Litou Section of Wuhu-Hefei National Expressway in Anhui Province	Anhui Province	2019	Transportation-Highway	Anhui Transportation Holdings Co. Ltd.	SOE	0.80	ROT
49	Hefei-Zongyang section of G3W Dezhou-Shangrao Expressway in Anhui Province	Anhui Province	2018	Transportation-Highway	Anhui Transportation Holdings Co. Ltd.	SOE	1.49	BOT
50	G4012 Liyang-Ningde Expressway from Huangshan to Qiandao Lake in Anhui Province	Anhui Province	2018	Transportation-Highway	Anhui Transportation Holdings Co. Ltd.	SOE	0.68	BOT
51	G42S Shanghai-Wuhan Expressway - Wuwei to Yuexi Section (Yuewu East Extension) in Anhui Province	Anhui Province	2018	Transportation-Highway	Anhui Transportation Holdings Co. Ltd.	SOE	2.81	BOT
52	Fujian Children's Hospital (Regional Children's Medical Centre)	Fujian Province	2018	Healthcare-Hospital	Fujian Construction Engineering Group Co. Ltd.	SOE	0.41	BOT
53	Digital Fujian wireless government-private network and demonstration application project based on TD-LTE ubiquitous network technology in Fujian Province	Fujian Province	2018	Technology-Information Network Construction	Fuzhou Yundong Information Technology Co. Ltd.	Private	0.01	BOT
54	Jingxi Branch of Fujian Provincial Government Hospital	Fujian Province	2016	Healthcare-Hospital	- Fujian Branch of Jiangsu Construction Association Engineering Consulting Co. Ltd., - Fujian Branch of Sichuan Schindler Engineering Consulting Supervision Co. Ltd.	Private	0.12	BOT

Sr. No.	PPP Project	Province/ Municipality	Year	Project type	Investor/s	Major Investor/ Stakeholder's nature	Total investment ($ Billion)	PPP Contract type
55	Fujian Emergency Communication Project	Fujian Province	2016	Technology-Information Network Construction	Nanwei Software Co. Ltd.	Private	0.07	BOT
56	Construction of Nanchang Xianghu Elderly Care Centre	Jiangxi Province	2019	Healthcare-Elderly Care	- Hunan Puqin Aging Industry Development Co. Ltd., - Jiangxi Kangyang Industrial Investment Co. Ltd., - Jiangxi Construction Engineering Group Co. Ltd.	Private	0.08	BOT
57	Jiangxi Province Smart Agriculture Project	Jiangxi Province	2016	Agriculture	- Beijing Rural Credit Technology Co. Ltd., - Chongqing Xingnong Equity Investment Fund Management Co. Ltd.	Private	0.03	BOT
58	Jiangxi Elderly Service Centre	Jiangxi Province	2016	Elderly Care-Integrated Medical Care	- Jiangxi Provincial Construction Engineering Group Co. Ltd., and - China Love Senior Apartment Consortium	SOE	0.16	LOT
59	Xiaoqinghe Re-navigation Project	Shandong Province	2018	Transportation-Waterway Shipping	- China Railway Construction Group Co. Ltd., - China Railway Construction Investment Fund Management Co. Ltd., - Shandong Ocean Group Co. Ltd., and - China Railway Construction Port and Shipping Group Co. Ltd.	SOE	1.94	BOT
60	Xiaolangdi North Bank Irrigation District Project in Henan Province	Henan Province	2019	Water Conservancy Construction-Irrigation	- Henan Water Conservancy Investment Group Co. Ltd., - Henan Provincial Water Conservancy First Engineering Bureau	SOE	0.46	BOT
61	River Diversion Project (Henan Section) of Henan Province	Henan Province	2018	Water Conservancy Construction-Irrigation	- Henan Water Conservancy Investment Group Co. Ltd., and - Henan Provincial Water Conservancy First Engineering Bureau	SOE	1.09	BOT

Sr. No.	*PPP Project*	*Provincel Municipality*	*Year*	*Project type*	*Investor/s*	*Major Investor/ Stakeholder's nature*	*Total investment ($ Billion)*	*PPP Contract type*
62	Henan Provincial Youth Talent Apartment (First Phase)	Henan Province	2018	Housing-Affordable Housing	Henan Yuzi Youth Talent Apartment Real Estate Co. Ltd.	SOE	0.69	other
63	New District Hospital Construction Project of the Second Affiliated Hospital of Zhengzhou University, Henan Province	Henan Province	2016	Healthcare-Hospital	- Shaanxi International Trust Co. Ltd., and - Henan Wujian Construction Group Co. Ltd.	SOE	0.24	BOT
64	National Highway G107—Guandu Yellow River Bridge	Henan Province	2016	Transportation-Bridge	China Communications 1st Highway Engineering Bureau Co. Ltd.	SOE	0.56	BOT
65	National Highway G234—Jiaozuo to Xingyang Yellow River Bridge and Connecting Line Project	Henan Province	2016	Transportation-Bridge	Zhengzhou Road and Bridge Construction Investment Group Co. Ltd.	SOE	0.53	BOT
66	Expansion project of the Liling to Loudi section of the Shanghai-Kunming National Expressway in Hunan Province	Hunan Province	2019	Transportation-Highway	Hunan Expressway Group Co. Ltd.	SOE	3.53	BOT
67	The 2nd line of the Meijiang-Huaihua section of the Yuhuai Railway in Hunan Province	Hunan Province	2018	Transportation-Railway (excluding rail transit)	Hunan Railway Investment Development Co. Ltd.	SOE	0.78	BOT
68	Hunan Province Zhangjihuai Railway Project	Hunan Province	2018	Transportation-Railway (excluding rail transit)	Hunan Railway Investment Development Co. Ltd.	SOE	2.82	BOT
69	Mengxi-Huazhong Railway (Hunan section)	Hunan Province	2016	Transportation-Railway (excluding rail transit)	Hunan CDB Railway Construction Private Equity Fund Partnership Enterprise	SOE	0.24	BOT
70	Hangzhou-Kunming Passenger Dedicated Railway (Hunan Section)	Hunan Province	2016	Transportation-Railway (excluding rail transit)	Hunan CDB Railway Construction Private Equity Fund Partnership Enterprise	SOE	1.06	BOT

Sr. No.	PPP Project	Province/ Municipality	Year	Project type	Investor/s	Major Investor/ Stakeholder's nature	Total investment ($ Billion)	PPP Contract type
71	Loudi-Shaoyang Railway Expansion and Reconstruction Project	Hunan Province	2016	Transportation-Railway (excluding rail transit)	Hunan CDB Railway Construction Private Equity Fund Partnership Enterprise	SOE	0.28	BOT
72	Land acquisition and demolition of Qianzhang-Changzhou Railway	Hunan Province	2016	Transportation-Railway (excluding rail transit)	Hunan CDB Railway Construction Private Equity Fund Partnership Enterprise	SOE	0.71	BOT
73	PPP project of land acquisition and demolition of Huaishoheng Railway	Hunan Province	2016	Transportation-Railway (excluding rail transit)	Hunan CDB Railway Construction Private Equity Fund Partnership Enterprise	SOE	1.21	BOT
74	Guangxi E-government Extranet Cloud Computing Centre Project (Phase I) - Computer Room Supporting and IT Equipment Engineering Project	Guangxi Province	2018	Technology-Information Network Construction	Inspur Software Group Co. Ltd.	Private	0.06	BLOT
75	Environmental IoT Project in Guangxi District	Guangxi Province	2016	Ecological/ environmental	- Zhongxing Instrument Co. Ltd., and - Concentration Technology Co. Ltd.	Private	0.04	BOT+ O&M
76	Hainan Railway Mixed Ownership Reform PPP Project	Hainan Province	2018	Transportation-Railway (excluding rail transit)	Not available	Not available	2.56	other
77	Chongqing Rail Transit Line 5A (Fuhua Road-Tiaodengnan) project	Chongqing Municipality	2019	Transportation-Other	- China Communications Construction Co. Ltd., - Beijing Jingcheng Metro Co. Ltd.	SOE	3.11	BOT+ EPC
78	Chongqing Rail Transit Line 4 (Min'an Avenue-Shichuan) (Phase II)	Chongqing Municipality	2018	Transportation-Other	- China Communications Construction Co. Ltd., and - Beijing Jingcheng Metro Co. Ltd.	SOE	2.83	other
79	Hongyan Village Bridge and Tunnel Project in Chongqing	Chongqing Municipality	2018	Transportation-Bridge	- Huarong Tianze Investment Co. Ltd., - China Construction Eighth Engineering Bureau Co. Ltd., and - China Construction 6th Engineering Bureau Co. Ltd.	SOE	0.85	BOT

Sr. No.	PPP Project	Province/ Municipality	Year	Project type	Investor/s	Major Investor/ Stakeholder's nature	Total investment ($ Billion)	PPP Contract type
80	West Section of the 2nd Horizontal Line of Chongqing Expressway	Chongqing Municipality	2017	Transportation-Bridge	- China Construction Fifth Engineering Co. Ltd., and - China Tunnel Construction Co. Ltd.	SOE	0.79	BOT
81	West Section of Xiema Tunnel	Chongqing Municipality	2017	Municipal Engineering-Municipal Road	Not available	Not available	0.23	BOT
82	Suburban Railway—Moxinpo to Hechuan Line	Chongqing Municipality	2016	Transportation-Railway (excluding rail transit)	Not available	Not available	1.09	BOT
83	Chongqing Guojiatuo Bridge and South Extension Project	Chongqing Municipality	2016	Municipal Engineering-Municipal Road	China State Construction Corporation	SOE	0.84	BOT
84	Chongqing Zengjiayan Jialing River Bridge Project	Chongqing Municipality	2016	Transportation-Bridge	- China Merchants Chongqing Transportation Research and Design Co. Ltd., and - China Railway Tunnel Group Co. Ltd., and - China Communications Second Navigation Engineering Bureau Co. Ltd.	SOE	0.47	BOT
85	Chongqing suburban railway (rail transit extension line) Connecting to Jiangjin line Package B	Chongqing Municipality	2016	Transportation-Railway (excluding rail transit)	Not available	Not available	0.46	BOO
86	Baijusi Yangtze River Bridge	Chongqing Municipality	2016	Transportation-Bridge	CCCC 2nd Navigation Engineering Bureau Co. Ltd.	SOE	0.48	BOT
87	Tongzi-Xinpu Expressway Project in Guizhou Province	Guizhou Province	2019	Transportation-Highway	- China Railway Corporation Limited, - China Railway Construction Kunlun Investment Group Co. Ltd., - China Railway First Bureau Group Co. Ltd., - China Railway Second Bureau Group Co. Ltd.	SOE	1.77	BOT

Sr. No.	*PPP Project*	*Province/ Municipality*	*Year*	*Project type*	*Investor/s*	*Major Investor/ Stakeholder's nature*	*Total investment ($ Billion)*	*PPP Contract type*
88	Weng'an to Kaiyang section of Jiangkou-Duge Expressway in Guizhou Province	Guizhou Province	2018	Transportation-Highway	- China Railway Corporation Limited, and - China Railway 6th Bureau Group Co. Ltd.	SOE	1.03	BOT
89	A project of the network upgrade and construction of the electromechanical system of the highway in Guizhou Province	Guizhou Province	2017	Transportation-Other	Guizhou QiantongZhilian Technology Industry Development Co. Ltd.	SOE	0.14	RLOT
90	Qianxi-Dafang Expressway—Dongguan-Qingfeng Section	Guizhou Province	2016	Transportation-Highway	- Guizhou Provincial Highway Engineering Group Co. Ltd., - Guizhou Bridge Construction Group Co. Ltd.	SOE	0.59	BOT
91	G8012 Maitreya-Chuxiong Expressway in Yunnan Province—Yuxi-Chuxiong Section	Yunnan Province	2019	Transportation-Highway	China Railway Corporation Limited	SOE	4.56	BOT
92	G56 Chuxiong (Guangtong)-Dali Expressway Expansion Project of Yunnan Province Government and Social Capital Cooperation Project	Yunnan Province	2017	Transportation-Highway	Yunnan Transportation Investment Construction Group Co. Ltd.	SOE	6.13	BOT
93	Shangri-La-Lijiang National Highway in Yunnan Province	Yunnan Province	2016	Transportation-Highway	Yunnan Construction Engineering Group Co. Ltd.	SOE	2.78	BOT
94	General hospital of Xinkunhua Hospital, Yunnan 1st People's Hospital (First phase)	Yunnan Province	2016	Healthcare-Hospital	Not available	Not available	0.34	BOT
95	Meixian-Taibai Highway in Shaanxi Province	Shaanxi Province	2019	Transportation-Highway	Not available	Not available	1.76	BOT
96	Xunyi to Fengxiang and Hancheng to Huanglong Expressway Project in Shaanxi Province	Shaanxi Province	2018	Transportation-Highway	China Railway Corporation Limited	SOE	3.20	BOT

Sr. No.	PPP Project	Province/ Municipality	Year	Project type	Investor/s	Major Investor/ Stakeholder's nature	Total investment ($ Billion)	PPP Contract type
97	Shaanxi Province Extension to Huanglong, Ningshan to Shiquan Expressway Project	Shaanxi Province	2017	Transportation-Highway	- China Gezhouba Group Co. Ltd., and - Baihe No. 6 Investment Partnership	SOE	3.55	BOT
98	Heyang-Tongchuan and Wuqi-Huachi Expressway in Shaanxi Province	Shaanxi Province	2017	Transportation-Highway	China Railway Construction Corporation	SOE	2.84	BOT
99	G85 Yinchuan-Kunming National Expressway Pengyang (Gan-Ning boundary) to Pingliang to Daqiao Village (Gan-Shan boundary) project	Gansu Province	2019	Transportation-Highway	- Gansu Highway Transportation Construction Group Co. Ltd., - Gansu Road and Bridge Construction Group Co. Ltd., - Gansu Shunda Road and Bridge Construction Co. Ltd.	SOE	1.73	BOT
100	Reconstruction project of the Qingshuiyi to Kushui section of the G312 highway from Shanghai to Horgos in Gansu Province	Gansu Province	2018	Transportation-First Class Highway	- Gansu Provincial Communications Construction Group Co. Ltd., and - China State Construction Engineering Corporation, etc.	SOE	2.96	BOT
101	Highway G309—Jinya to Hekou (Zhangjiatai) section, Gansu Province	Gansu Province	2017	Transportation-Highway	- Gansu Communications Construction Group Co. Ltd., and - Gansu Road and Bridge Construction Group Co. Ltd.	SOE	3.06	BOT
102	Liuge Guogao (G3011) Dunhuang-Dangjin Mountain Pass Highway Construction Project, Gansu Province	Gansu Province	2016	Transportation-Highway	- Gansu Communications Construction Group Co. Ltd., and - Gansu Wantai Construction Engineering Co. Ltd.	SOE	1.71	BOT
103	Longnan City G316 Highway. Changle-Tongren Highway Liangdang County Yangdian (Ganshan-Shaan border) to Huixian highway	Gansu Province	2016	Transportation-Highway	- Gansu Road and Bridge Third Highway Engineering Co. Ltd., and - Gansu Fifth Ring Road Engineering Co. Ltd.	SOE	1.06	BOT

Contract Type: BOT—Build-Operate-Transfer; ROT—Rehabilitate-Operate-Transfer; TOT—Transfer-Operate-Transfer; BOO—Build-Own-Operation; BLOT—Build-Lease-Operate-Transfer; BOOT—Build-Own-Operate-Transfer; O&M—Commissioned Operation; LOT—Lease-Operate-Transfer; EPC—Engineering Procurement Construction; RLOT—Reconstruct-Lease-Operate-Transfer.

Source: Ministry of Finance, Data from Provincial/Municipal and administrative Information bureaus and case-based investigation by the author

current governance structure by not only looking at the PPPs scheme's launch but also how to apply it to address China's ever-increasing number of civic challenges such as clean water, clean air and clean energy.

Based on Table 8.3, it is established that provincial governments have been using PPP as a model to out-survive budgetary forces. In recent years, municipalities promulgated policies to encourage non-public economies to invest in public utilities including the Central to the local governments. Some places have tried to adopt the PPP model in public utilities such as highways, water supplies, and electric power, such as the Hubei Xiangjing Expressway, Hong Kong Subway, Changsha Power Plant, Beijing No. 10 Water Plant, Beijing Subway Line 4, etc., and gained experience to experiment further.

Besides, PPP was seen as supplementary to the *treasury reforms,* which involved strengthening budget management and clarification of the central bank's decentralisation of the treasury. Moreover, *local debt reforms* covered issues like improving the budget management of local debt and strengthening China's fiscal role in multilateral development institutions. PPP turned out to be the saviour especially for local governments. They carried liabilities to support local enterprises and bear the burden to finance public projects. Local debt in China reached a dead end, and local governments, under pressure from GDP, were tempted to look at land finances. Local governments borrowed money and did not consider their future fiscal revenue and were accustomed to borrowing the new to repay the old and maintain stability. Local governments saw an opportunity to leverage from the promotion of PPP and clean up local debts and promote the budget system's reform.

The PPP is a new economic algorithm on the rise in China, and SOEs have been reaping benefits from all sides. While the Central SOEs look at the private enterprises to take a lead role in shouldering responsibilities, the provincial economies see these as opportunities to circumvent financing issues. Local economies have been facing severe criticism for threatening the country's financial stability by a reckless build-up of local-government debt. PPP is seen as the model to alleviate local government from financial and hard resources required to support growth and compete for the larger pie in GDP.

The PPP model is envisioned to bring local debt under control which has been burgeoning and causing tensions in China's entire financial policymaking. While the local government debt and financing platform models are being reformed, the government is always looking for alternatives. According to data from the National Audit Office, as of the end of June 2013, local government debt was 17.9 trillion yuan (US$ 2.75 trillion), of which bank loans were 10.1 trillion yuan (US$ 1.55 trillion). It can be said that the loan model of urban investment companies is now the primary mode of local government financing and a primary reason why it is difficult to monitor it (compared to issuing government bonds). According to Moody's data, the national average of provincial government debt to the province's GDP ratio is 31.4 per cent, and Guizhou, at the highest, is close to 80 per cent. The repayment ability of financing platforms depends heavily on land transfer fees, which has created a situation where local governments and financing platforms bet on the national economy, especially the land economy's upturn. Even if real estate has not faced a sharp fall at present, financing platforms have begun to borrow afresh and repay old debts in large chunks. One can also doubt how effective these measures would be because if the macro-economy and the real estate collapse in the future, there will be a systemic risk of local debt.

The future approach is to strictly control the use of government debt for projects, administer loans, and additionally use government bond issuance or PPP. Local governments increasingly use the PPP model to repay existing debts that the government is obligated to settle. Moreover, by excluding debt incurred through the PPP model and converting it into corporate debt, local governments manage to control the government debt. But the non-performing, debt-ridden projects were given special concessions to be included in the general debt. In the name of 'Public welfare' (公益性 *Gongyi xing*), local government borrowing was allowed mainly for public welfare undertakings but prohibited to borrow for current expenditure. Besides, the future development of public welfare undertakings with certain benefits was permitted to secure financing by special bonds issued by local governments or in the PPP mode.

Local governments in China lacked the spirit of partnerships for many years. The economy attempted to create its aura, priorities, and ways to compete and co-exist with rival provinces and the centre. Under the premise of government dominance and public funds investment, it is understandable that the government remained hegemonic. While implementing the PPP models of public-private tug-of-opportunities, local governments must know how to deal with private investors and how they can be improved. It can also be said that the anti-corruption task force created a better environment for PPP to take root in China. The growing number of Chinese leaders and economists from the mainland hope that the real PPP model will be implemented and accelerated in China in a few more decades to come. Given the fact that the urban investment company's absolute reliance on loans is unchanged, it will be too early to reach such a conclusion as to how PPP will bring about a landmark transformation unless the dependence on the need for a loan can be changed in the future, and the BT model of fake PPPs are dealt with resolve. Local governments need to evaluate how much debt they can bear and improve budgetary supervision. Private capital must benefit from PPP in the future, and private rights in PPP need to be introduced one after another.

Major Drawbacks of China's PPP Model

However, the recent history of PPPs in China shows that challenges remain to be overcome before a new PPP phase can bear fruition. Some of the significant impediments were discussed earlier and have been underlined clearly. In addition to the political legacies and historical reasons for failing the PPP models, few other factors are more systemic and could be posing a threat of turning the PPP business into a mega-failure.

China has to deal with its BT model seriously. BT is a variant of BOT but created a range of imperfections in the overall PPP scheme. It happens to give government construction and repurchase two significant fiscal buffers. After the construction (B), investors do not want to fall into the quagmire of long-term operation (O), but want to take money away as soon as possible; at the same time, the government, under pressure from various infrastructure construction, wants to repurchase as soon as possible to control the infrastructure fully but is unable to repurchase in full at once. In practice, the BT model is the second-largest financing model after government platform loans, far more extensive than local government bond financing. The BT model is essentially a short-term and limited participation of 'social capital.' It is a disguised model in which local governments use their advantageous position to request contractors to utilise their funds. It has always concealed the essence of the real PPP model. As early as 2012, the "Notice on Stopping Local Governments' Illegal Financing Activities" (Circular 463 on Stopping Local Governments' Illegal Financing Activities) has long restricted the BT model.[61]

Broadly, PPP refers to the cooperative relationship established between the government and the private sector, a partnership, to provide public goods or services. It is often characterised by franchise authorisation and mainly includes BOT, BOO, PFI, and other models. In the case of Chinese experiments, PPP is a way for enterprises to obtain government franchise rights and provide infrastructure and public utility construction and services that are traditionally the responsibility of the government. This is proving to be a way to be in the good books of the State. The State also uses the context of private players to consolidate its legacy by utilising complementary gestures. One must even notice that securing authorisation through a franchise system, commonly adopted by the PPP model, may lead to monopoly. The franchise system widely used in the PPP model enables the winning investment operator to obtain a certain degree of monopoly, and guarantees the returns. This uncompetitive environment will, in some cases, weaken the private sector's motivation to reduce costs and improve service quality.

Another critical issue with the PPP model is the subjective and often non-standard format of the game. Among central leadership, local authorities, and private entities, the project was conceptualised not to let private enterprises rise above SOEs. The provinces do not allow domicile to private players from outside. The operation of PPP projects is not standardised. First, the operating procedures are not transparent enough, and many projects lack bidding regularities and are often accused of not being allotted entry to stand a chance even after competitive bidding; secondly, the operating personnel lacks professional acumen, the public servants in charge of PPP projects often change, and the relevant experience is not enough when selecting consulting agencies. Thirdly, business conditions are not yet settled and have not turned mature. In the end, this all costs the project since it may not be completed on time and stands blacklisted as a defaulter.

China is expected to implement the PPP on competitive models and scale, but in reality, competition between PPP projects is non-existent and is a mere formality. The purpose of the government's promotion of PPP is to change the mechanism and improve efficiency. In the case of insufficient or no competition for entry, the local government's price for PPP projects exceeds the traditional system, resulting in a breach of contract by social investors after the change of local government. It also shadows the PPP making others believe that it runs low on the scale of efficiency.

The government, local or central, have been arbitrarily controlling the functioning of PPP projects. It is common for local governments to sign contracts in haste and default at will. On the one hand, government default undermines the confidence of investors in the government; on the other, when social investors reduce services, they need to be compensated sooner or later. The local government can play its role at its will. The government's PPP mode carries these inherited characteristics, making the public-private partnership's real motive ineffective.

This chapter has discussed another major drawback in the earlier sections, and the problems with regard to missing financial instruments is a significant blow to the PPP model. Most foreign PPP projects use project financing, that is, the project itself is qualified to seek credit support and obtain financing from financial institutions, without the need for shareholders to provide guarantees, and the debt does not enter the shareholders' balance sheet. China's PPP projects are primarily financed under the premise of shareholder guarantees. Project financing is only a matter of a few banks and a few investors. When the company's debt ratio is high, it restricts the development of PPP. This contradiction is even more prominent when the leverage ratio of China's local governments and SOEs is generally high.

The lack of intermediary organisations or consultants has failed to play its due role in the Chinese case. Having consultants certainly cannot be an excellent reason to standardise the PPP projects and their functions. Still, where the Chinese have fondly accepted the advice of prominent corporate consultants in other sectors of the economy, the PPPs' lack in seeking intervention seems to have added to the Chinese inexperience of operationalising the projects. It is common for developed countries to hire consultants for PPP projects, and the most crucial point when hiring consultants use their experience. The practice of hiring intermediaries for PPP projects in China has not been widespread and Chinese reluctance in hiring and appointing consultants in areas of critical significance indicates the apathy of Chinese leadership.

Conclusion

After nearly two years of policy adjustments, PPP has begun to gradually develop from a stage of rational return to that of standardisation. Many PPP projects have been put under supervision for financing purposes, as many 'pseudo' PPP projects are in disguise. The standards to launch PPP have certainly been elevated. There have been noticeable changes; for example, the proportion of projects that meet the essential characteristics of PPP projects and the norms about environmental protection and people-friendly projects have increased significantly. As the counter-cyclical adjustment of macroeconomic policies continues to grow, in terms of stabilising investment, authorities are also exploring the best combination of PPP and special debt, trying to leverage more social investment and exert a more substantial pulling effect on the stable growth of the national economy.

However, it can be seen that the two waves of generalised PPP are primarily conducted in the BOT or BT modes. The initial applications of Public-Private models were mainly concentrated in the field of hard economic infrastructure, including roads, highways, railways, bridges, tunnels, airports, communications, power, and then gradually extended to the field of social infrastructure, including hospitals, schools, government office buildings, residential buildings, water supply, sewage treatment, prisons, urban reconstruction, etc. Now, the application of PPP covers all infrastructure, including 'soft economic infrastructure' (research and development, technology transfer, vocational training, prisoner reform) and 'soft social infrastructure' (community services, social welfare, security, environmental planning). As mentioned above in the PPP application field, the roadmap has particular significance for China to promote PPP comprehensively. Still, in the process, non-state players were deprived of gaining traction to develop their game plan and create additional legroom. Like any other economic experiment in the past, the State wields complete control over the PPPs' evolving dynamics.

As the Chinese economy slowly opened up, private businesses sprang into action. Still, their role never evolved bigger than that of the state or state enterprises. Research shows that the attempt to transplant PPP policies to China has led to the emergence of two significant transitions: the rise of PPP from 1993 onwards and its subsequent fall from about 2007 and throughout the process, the SOEs maintained full control over the two generations of PPP (post-78 reforms—running through the 1990s—and post-2014 booster reforms). The first-generation experience of PPP reforms concentrated mainly on heavy infrastructure and private players had to fight to make some space for themselves. As a relatively newcomer, China is still developing a clear vision for the role of private participation in infrastructure. It is unbelievable that while Chinese authorities are keen to extend the PPP model into new areas of the economy, private players find it equally uncomfortable to let their experience being brushed aside when it comes to the matrix of political interest and business incentives. In the long run, if the aforementioned supporting problems cannot be resolved, the PPP model currently promoted by China may become a temporary measure to solve the local debt crisis and abducting private capital for fire-fighting measures.

NOTES

1. *Social Capital* can refer to state-owned as well as private enterprise.
2. David Mason. 1984. 'China's Four Modernizations: Blueprint for Development or Prelude to Turmoil?', *Asian Affairs*, Vol. 11, No. 3, 47-70.
3. *China.org.cn.* 2018. 'Three Step Development Strategy (Reform and Opening Up)', 29 October, http://www.china.org.cn/english/china_key_words/2018-10/29/content_68860874.htm (accessed on 24 August 2020).
4. David Shambaugh. 2016. 'The Dynamics of Elite Politics during Jiang Era', *Brookings Institution.* https://www.brookings.edu/wp-content/uploads/2016/06/2001chinajournal.pdf (accessed on 26 July 2020).
5. Wu Guoguang. 2011. 'China in 2010: Dilemmas of "Scientific Development', *Asian Survey*, Vol. 51, No. 1, February, 18-32.
6. John P. Geis and Blaine Holt. 2009. '"Harmonious Society": Rise of the New China', *Strategic Studies Quarterly*, Vol. 3, No. 4, 75-94.
7. Bennis Wai-yip So. 2002. 'The Policy-Making and Political Economy of the Abolition of Private Ownership in the Early 1950s: Findings from New Material', *The China Quarterly*, Vol. 171, September, 682-703.
8. Klaus Uhlenbruck and Julio O. De Castro. 2000. 'Foreign Acquisitions in Central and Eastern Europe: Outcomes of Privatization in Transitional Economies', *The Academy of Management Journal*, Vol. 43, No. 3, June, 381-402.
9. Kenneth Lieberthal. 1971. 'Mao versus Liu? Policy towards Industry and Commerce 1946-49', *The China Quarterly*, Vol. 47, July/September, 494-520.
10. The New Democracy was to be an alliance of four classes: the national bourgeoisie, the petit bourgeoisie, the proletariat and the peasantry. This categorisation left only the bureaucratic capitalists, landlords and "remnant feudal elements" (mostly secret society members, gangsters and other criminals) beyond the pale of the new society.
11. So. 'The Policy-Making and Political Economy of the Abolition of Private Ownership in the Early 1950s'.
12. William C. Kirby. 1990. 'Continuity and Change in Modern China: Economic Planning on the Mainland and on Taiwan, 1943-1958', *The Australian Journal of Chinese Affairs,* No. 24, July, 121-141.
13. So. 'The Policy-Making and Political Economy of the Abolition of Private Ownership in the Early 1950s'.

14. Sun Sheng Han and Clifton W. Pannell. 1999. 'The Geography of Privatization in China, 1978-1996', *Economic Geography*, Vol. 75, No. 3, July, 275-76.
15. Anders Aslund. 1985. *Private Enterprise in Eastern Europe.* New York: St. Martin. Quoted in Simon Johnson. 1992. 'Private Business in Eastern Europe', in Olivier Blanchard, Kenneth Froot and Jeffrey Sachs (eds.), *Transition in Eastern Europe, Volume 2.* (Chicago: University of Chicago Press), 245-92.
16. Simon Johnson. 1992. 'Private Business in Eastern Europe', in Olivier Blanchard, Kenneth Froot and Lan Cao (eds.), *Transition in Eastern Europe,* Volume 2 (Chicago: University of Chicago Press), 245-92.
17. Richard McGregor. 2010. *The Party: The Secret World of China's Communist Rulers* (New York: Harper Collins), 194.
18. Sun and Pannell. 'The Geography of Privatization in China, 1978-1996', 272.
19. David Blumental. 1998. '"Reform" or "Opening"? Reform of China's State-Owned Enterprises and WTO Accession: The Dilemma of Applying Gatt to Marketizing Economies', *UCLA Pacific Law Basin Journal,* Vol. 16, No. 2, Spring, 198-262. Quoted in Lan Cao. 2001. 'Chinese Privatization: Between Plan and Market'. *Law and Contemporary Problems,* Vol. 63, No. 4, 13-62.
20. Blumental. '"Reform" or "Opening"? Reform of China's State-Owned Enterprises and WTO Accession', 14.
21. Sun and Pannell. 'The Geography of Privatization in China, 1978-1996', 272.
22. Sun and Pannell. 'The Geography of Privatization in China, 1978-1996', 277.
23. Ibid.
24. Nicholas R. Lardy. 2014. *Markets over Mao: The Rise of Private Business in China* (Washington D.C.: *Peterson Institute Press*).
25. Ibid.
26. Ibid.
27. It is the conventional PPP model in which the private partner is responsible to design, build, operate (during the contracted period) and transfer back the facility to the public sector.
28. Asian Development Bank. 2011. 'Engaging Private Sector Companies for Wastewater Management in Asia' *ADB Project Results and Case Studies.* 31 August, https://www.adb.org/results/country-water-action-engaging-private-sector-companies-wastewater-management-asia (accessed on 20 August 2020).
29. Asian Development Bank. 2005. 'Anhui Environmental Improvement Project for Municipal Wastewater Treatment/Industrial Pollution Abatement' *ADB Performance Evaluation Report.* Decemberhttp://www.oecd.org/derec/adb/36065250.pdf (accessed on 20 August 2020).
30. Ministry of Construction of the People's Republic of China. 2004. 'Zhonghua renmin gongheguo jianshe bu ling di 126 hao' (中华人民共和国建设部令第126号) [Order No. 126 of the Ministry of Construction of the People's Republic of China], 1 May, http://www.jjgas.com.cn/statute/18.html (accessed on 21 January 2021).
31. Xin Bao. 2020. 'Intelligent Heating Business Model based on PPP Mode', *IOP Conference Series,* IOP Publishing, https://iopscience.iop.org/article/10.1088/1757-899X/768/5/052005/pdf (accessed on 17 August 2020).
32. Shi Yaobin. 2016. 'Caizheng bu fu buzhang: Zai quanguo caizheng xitong PPP gongzuo tuijin hui ji shifan xiangmu dudao hui shang de jianghua' (财政部副部长：在全国财政系统

PPP工作推进会暨示范项目督导会上的讲话) [Deputy Minister of Finance: Speech at the PPP Work Promotion Meeting and Demonstration Project Supervision Meeting of the National Financial System], (Ministry of Finance, PRC), 15 December, http://www.gov.cn/xinwen/2016-12/15/content_5148452.htm#1) (accessed on 16 August 2020).

33. National Development and Reform Commission (NDRC). 2014b. 'Guanyu fabu shou pi jichu sheshi deng lingyu guli shehui touzi xiangmu di tongzhi (fa gai jichu [2014]981 hao' (关于发布首批基础设施等领域鼓励社会投资项目的通知(发改基础[2014]981号) [Notice to encourage private capital to invest in first infrastructure projects], 21 May, http://www.sdpc.gov.cn/zcfb/zcfbtz/201405/t20140521_612322.html) (accessed on 26 July 2020).
34. The State Council of the People's Republic of China. 2014b. 'Guowuyuan guanyu jiaqiang difang zhengfu xing zhaiwu guanli de yijian' (国务院关于加强地方政府性债务管理的意见) [Opinions of the State Council on strengthening the administration of local government debt], 21 September, http://www.gov.cn/zhengce/%20content/2014-10/02/content_9111.htm (accessed on 26 July 2020).
35. Ministry of Finance of the People's Republic of China. 2014b. 'Guanyu tuiguang yunyong zhengfu he shehui ziben hezuo moshi youguan wenti de tongzhi' (关于推广运用政府和社会资本合作模式有关问题的通知) [Notice on questions relating to expanding the use of PPPs], 23 September, http://jrs. mof.gov.cn/zhengwuxinxi/zhengcefabu/201409/t20140924_1143760. html (accessed on 20 August 2020).
36. The State Council of the People's Republic of China. 2014a. 'Guowuyuan guanyu chuangxin zhongdian lingyu tou rongzi jizhi guli shehui touzi de zhidao yijian' (国务院关于创新重点领域投 融资机制鼓励社会投资的指导意见) [Guiding opinions on the innovative investment mechanism and encouraging social investment in key sectors], 26 November, http://www.gov.cn/zhengce/content/2014-11/26/content_9260.htm (accessed on 20 August 2020).
37. Ministry of Finance of the People's Republic of China. 2014a. 'Guanyu yinfa zhengfu he shehui ziben hezuo moshi caozuo zhinan (shixing) de tongzhi' (关于印发政府和社会资本合作模式操作指南(试行)的通知) [Guide on operation of public–private partnership projects (interim)], 29 November, http://jrs.mof.gov.cn/zhengwuxinxi/zhengcefabu/201412/t20141204_1162965.html (accessed on 26 August 2020).
38. National Development and Reform Commission (NDRC). 2014a. 'Guojia fazhan gaige wei yinfa kaizhan zhengfu he shehui ziben hezuo de zhidao yijian' (国家发展改革委印发开展政 府和社会资本合作的指导意见) [Guidelines on development of public–private partnership projects], 4 December, http://www.sdpc.gov.cn/zcfb/zcfbtz/201412/t20141204_651012.html (accessed on 16 July 2020).
39. National Development and Reform Commission (NDRC). 2015. 'Guojia fazhan gaige wei guanyu qieshi zuo hao "jichu sheshi he gongyong shiye texu jingying guanli banfa" guanche shishi gongzuo de tongzhi' (国家发展改革委关于切实做好"基础设施和公用事业特许经营管理办法" 贯彻实施工作的通知) [Guidelines on the Implementation of the 'Administrative Measures for Infrastructure and Public Utilities Franchising'], 7 July, https://www.ndrc.gov.cn/xwdt/ztzl/pppzl/zcfg/201507/t20150707_1033191.html (accessed on 16 July 2020).
40. The State Council of the People's Republic of China. 2014c. 'Guojia xinxing chengzhen hua guihua (2014-2020 nian) zhonghua renmin gongheguo zhongyang renmin zhengfu menhu

wangzhan' (国家新型城镇化规划 (2014-2020 年) 中华人民共和国中央人民政府门户网站) [National New Urbanization Plan 2014-2020], 16 March, http://www.gov.cn/zhengce/2014-03/16/content_2640075.htm (accessed on 15 July 2020).

41. *Xinhua*. 2014. "财政部推 PPP 模式助地方融资城镇化资金缺口42万亿", (Caizheng bu tui PPP moshi zhu difang rongzi chengzhen hua zijin quekou 42 wan yi), [The Ministry of Finance is encouraging a PPP model to help local governments, providing the CNY 42 trillion required for urbanization], 2 April. Retrieved from http://news.xinhuanet.com/house/bj/2014-04-02/c_1110055180.htm (accessed on 12 August 2020).
42. Lavanchy Rene. 2018. 'PPP in China', *IJ Global Project Finance & Infrastructure Journal*, July, 1-12. https://ijglobal.com/articles/134411/ppp-in-china-report (accessed on 10 December 2020).
43. The State Council of the People's Republic of China. 2019. 'Full Text: Report on the work of the Government (13th National People's Congress of CPC)', 16 March, http://english.www.gov.cn/premier/speeches/2019/03/16/content_281476565265580.htm (accessed on 26 July 2020).
44. China Tendering & Bidding Association. 2016. 'PPP xiangmu zhaobiao shehui ziben zige shencha de falu yingyong fenxi' (PPP 项目招标社会资本资格审查的法律应用) [Analysis on the Legal Application of Social Capital Qualification Examination for PPP Project Bidding], 24 March, http://www.ctba.org.cn/list_show.jsp?record_id=241727) (accessed on 15 August 2020).
45. *China Economic Weekly* (中国经济周刊). 2016. 'Zhongguo PPP shifan xiangmu xunli] anqing shi wai huanbei lu gongcheng xiangmu: PPP xiangmu shi yi zhong touzi xingwei, bushi jiandan "zhao huo er gan"' (中国PPP示范项目巡礼]安庆市外环北路工程项目：PPP项目是一种投资行为，不是简单"找活儿干") [China PPP Demonstration Project Tour] Anqing Outer Ring North Road Project: PPP project is an investment behaviour, not simply "an act of work"], 15 August, http://finance.sina.com.cn/roll/2016-08-15/doc-ifxuxnak0328418.shtml?cre=finance pagepc&mod=f&loc=4&r=9&doct=0&rfunc=100 (accessed on 9 September 2020).
46. Sun Jie. 'Guoyou qiye canyu PPP de jiyu yu tiaozhan' (国有企业参与 PPP 的机遇与挑战) [Opportunities and challenges for state-owned enterprises to participate in PPP], *State-owned Enterprise Management*, No. Z6, December, 28-29.
47. *Guojingmao SME* (国精贸中小企业).2003. 'Interim Provisions on the Standards for Small and Medium-sized Enterprises', National Economic and Trade Commission, the National Development Planning Commission, Ministry of Finance and National Bureau of Statistics. 19 February. http://www.lawinfochina.com/display.aspx?lib=law&id=2636&CGid= (accessed on 15 July 2020).
48. Shenzhen Huiyongxin Technology (深圳市慧用心科技有限公司). 2020. 'Huaqiang bei zhongxiao gongsi zhuce-zhongxiao qiye de zhuce ziben shi duoshao' (华强北中小公司注册-中小企业的注册资本是多少) [Huaqiangbei Small and Medium-sized Company Registration—What is the registered capital of small and medium-sized enterprises], 22 September, http://www.rousin.com/view-95556.html (accessed on 14 March 2021).
49. Sun Jie. 'Guoyou qiye canyu PPP de jiyu yu tiaozhan'.
50. Anqing City Public Administration Bureau (安庆市公管局). 2015. 'Anqing shi wai huanbei lu gongcheng PPP xiangmu zhongbiao gongshi' (安庆市外环北路工程 PPP 项目中标公示) [Anqing City's Outer Ring North Road Project PPP Project Winning Public

Announcement], 24 April, http://aqxxgk.anqing.gov.cn/show.php?id=361283 (accessed on 9 September 2020).

51. Mengnan Shi. 2018. 'Analysis on the Obstacles of Private Capital Participating in the Construction of Municipal PPP in China: A Case Study of PPP Project of Underground Utility Tunnel in a New Airport Area of a City', *Advances in Economics, Business and Management Research*, Vol. 71, 94-98.
52. Ibid.
53. *Songyuan.yccsrj.cn.* 2015. 'Songyuan 2019 nian quanguo PPP zonghe xinxi guanli ku nianbao chulu: Xin ru ku xiangmu 1434 ge' (松原2019年全国PPP综合信息管理库年报出炉: 新入库项 目1434个) [Songyuan's 2019 National PPP Comprehensive Information Management Database - Annual Report - 1434 Newly Projects Included], 18 March, https://songyuan.yccsrj.cn/industry/514.html (accessed on 9 September 2020).
54. Ministry of Finance of the People's Republic of China. 2018. 'Jianyi wanshan zhengce guli minjian ziben canyu PPP' (建议完善政策鼓励民间资本参与PPP) [It is recommended to improve policies to encourage private capital to participate in PPP], 13 March, http://www.ccgp.gov.cn/ppp/llyj/201803/t20180313_9656828.htm (accessed on 9 September 2020).
55. Ibid.
56. Ibid.
57. *First Finance.* 2017. 'Min zi PPP canyu du shuang jiang, guowuyuan juexin rang huibao geng heli' (民资 PPP 参与度双降，国务院决心让回报更合理) [The participation rate of private PPP has dropped, and the State Council is determined to make the return more reasonable], 19 September, https://m.21jingji.com/article/20170919/herald/dfa45bf8690143dcdde77763f4 efb107.html (accessed on 9 January 2021).
58. *Beijing Mingshu Data Technology Co. Ltd.* (北京明树数据科技有限公司). 2019. 'Beijing ming shu shuju ke zhi youxian gongsi' (明树数据-2019年全国 PPP 项目市场动态报告) [Mingshu Data-2019 National PPP Project Market Dynamics Report], 3 April, https://max.book118.com/html/2019/0402/6025151044002021.shtm(accessed on 9 January 2021).
59. *China Net Finance.* 2018. 'Jishi jiuzheng PPP fazhan zhong de mohu renshi' (及时纠正 PPP 发展中的模糊认识) [Timely Correction of Ambiguous Understanding in PPP Development], 9 August, https://finance.ifeng.com/c/7fE0QH83DSL (accessed on 6 March 2021).
60. Asian Development Bank. 2010. 'Sustainable Urban Development in the People's Republic of China—Urban Public Transport—A Case Study of Public–Private Partnerships (PPPs) in Beijing'. *ADB Urban Innovations and Best Practices.* November, https://www.adb.org/sites/default/files/publication/27867/urbandev-prc-nov2010-transport-beijing.pdf (accessed on 20 August 2020).
61. Urban Management Information Network. 2020. 'Local Governments may assume certain debt relief obligations', 20 September, http://www.yljs79.com/hyxw/2020/0920/8844.html (accessed on 28 October 2020).

9

Belt and Road Initiative and SOEs

For a long time, Chinese SOEs primarily operated to meet the needs of the domestic market and slowly and steadily developed a robust introverted characteristic. Compared to foreign and private enterprises, Chinese SOEs have had less exposure to international operations and were limited to foreign partners and investors in the mainland. The big SOEs did venture to expand their portfolios, but their existence was limited to resources and not the market. About 25-30 years before the BRI was launched, Chinese SOEs were trying their hands-on learning from their early association and gained first-hand knowledge about operations and management. These years were crucial for enterprises to provide much-needed respite to domestic needs for minerals and other essential commodities and later enter into global finance. Although the "going out" (走出去 *Zou chuqu*)[1] and internationalisation strategies[2] were suggestive, the SOEs needed to diversify their basket. The diversification meant upstream production vulnerabilities and downstream sales and services. Building on these intricacies, the Chinese state devised yet another but novel mainframe of its statecraft—named the Belt and Road Initiative (BRI) and launched in 2013 with fanfare.[3] The "internationalisation" or "going out" were the directions and independent strategies that were partly a natural course of trade-related adjustments. In contrast to these policies, BRI emerged as the politico-economic statecraft of China, which the Chinese leaders endorsed as an unparallel initiative in Chinese history.

The BRI was launched when Chinese growth plummeted dramatically, whereby global growth showed no signs of recovery, and Chinese industries did not know how to circumvent it. While slow growth gives rise to 'nationalism-stoked-protectionist' policies, China's global ambition is a by-product of its nationalistic policies. The difference is that while some economies would protect themselves from external shocks, the Chinese are doing it by making the external shocks subsumed by localised but assured growth projections as it protects its economic interest, which serves to fulfil its centenary goals. The BRI is not a free aid-and-recovery program for the world but a recovery program for China. In other words, as a few strategists view,[4] the BRI as China's *Marshall Plan*[5] for itself as the Chinese and their trading partners need it. Each country would decide when it should agree or disagree with China, but largely the BRI has its costs.

Looking at the BRI's political canvassing and going by McKinsey research,[6] SOEs do have a conducive environment to scale up globally, which nowhere indicates the excellence and capabilities of Chinese SOEs but rather the conducive market conditions that offer opportunities. According to the McKinsey research (Figure 9.1), in the past 12 years, the presence of Chinese enterprises has grown exponentially as global exposure to China has widened.[7] While the world economy looks at the profitability in working with the Chinese, the Chinese are busy grabbing everything they could. From T-shirts to T-bonds (treasury bonds), the global economy was excited about working with China. While major Western economies developed selective measures to allow the Chinese to engage with their economies, many countries still wanted to *feel* the upswing with China offering its irresistible offers.

On the other hand, China has been increasingly becoming a closed economy where it does not want the global players to squeeze the local industries' performance. Chinese leaders would least think of banning *Apple* products, but the markets are already flooded with foreign products. The CPC has been discreetly 'indicating' to its members to desist from using Western-made electronic consumables, and accordingly, one would see officials and party members buying *Huawei* and *Oppo* over *Apple* products. It is believed

Figure 9.1: China and the World Exposure Indices Over Time[1] Index

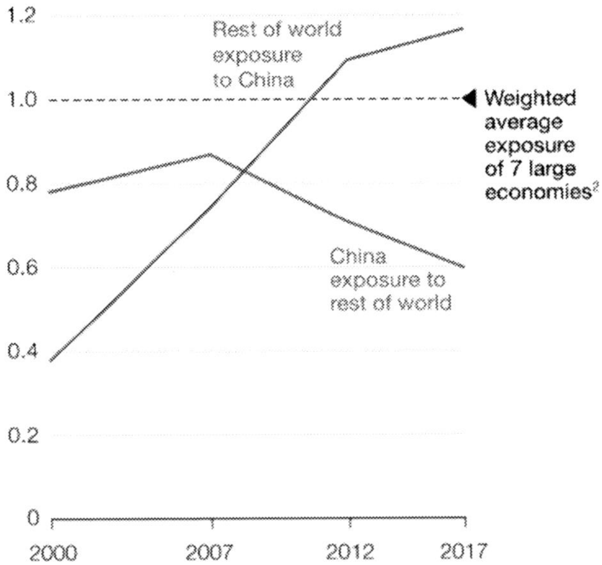

[1]Includes trade, technology and capital exposure metrics.
[2]China, France, Germany, India, Japan, United Kingdom, and United States.
Source: IHS Global Insight; International Monetary Fund; Organisation for Economic Co-operation and Development; World Input-Output Database; McKinsey Global Institute analysis.
McKinsey & Company

that party members own iPhones but refrain from displaying them in public. Moreover, the Chinese have been building parallel domestic brands to create a formidable challenge for the biggest western competitors, such as Starbucks, an American brand, and the world's biggest coffee shops. Party officials prefer *Lantian* (a Chinese luxury hotel chain) and similar high-end Chinese hotels and restaurants. The Chinese implicitly have a taste for Western brands and services. Although there are competing theories with regard to foreign products losing their symbolic value in the Chinese market,[8] it does not emerge as a rationale driving Chinese consumerism. While modernity, lifestyle and prestige related to the usage of foreign brands are challenging the global marketers (in the form of adaptation and positioning strategies in the PRC), one cannot negate that the political-cultural influence predominantly shaped some of these dynamics. McKinsey's report does not elaborate on all these aspects in great detail but points out that the Chinese have reduced their exposure to global players, leaving fewer or zero level playing options. This indicates how China has been peddling its interests unilaterally, and in all this, SOEs provide them with the best platform to fulfil their intentions.

Here is another illustration to prove the point, as mentioned earlier. One can see how amidst the USA-China trade war, the global banking legend—HSBC (Hongkong and Shanghai Banking Corporation)—had to pay heed to Chinese concerns rather than stand by its commitment to global standards of corporate values. The USA was critical of HSBC's ethical stand in the wake of intensifying trade conflicts between the two countries.[9] The HSBC is headquartered in London but focuses on Hong Kong and Mainland China to expand its business prospects where China has been replacing the dollar. It uses the dollar to fund global trade and has been falling into a political feud. The CPC has been using HSBC's vulnerability, which draws 90 per cent of its business from Asia[10] to execute its decisions in the region.

A Rise in the International Ranks of SOEs

In the 19th National Congress of the Communist Party of China,[11] the leaders put forward the new goal of cultivating world-class enterprises with global competitiveness to reform and develop SOEs in the modern era. Global economic competitiveness is generally manifested in the international market-oriented operation and competitiveness of large enterprises. As of 2018, there were more than 11,028 projects owned and run by Central enterprises overseas, with total assets exceeding 7.6 trillion yuan (US$ 1.13 trillion), and 185 countries and regions where they invested and were engaged in business. The registered annual operating income of these SOEs amounted to 5.4 trillion yuan (US$ 805.97 billion), with a profit of 131.89 billion yuan (US$ 19.68).[12]

The role of Chinese SOEs always remained at the centre of China's political economy. As elaborated earlier, the SOEs had undergone reforms and restructuring when private players outperformed in innovation, quality, and market share, raising questions over the role of SOEs in the coming decades of reforms and opening up. But SOEs have been brought back into the mainstream to cushion political ideology related to development, growth, and connectivity. While China talks more about global governance, connectivity, and building institutions of global common interests, SOEs were expected to deliver a strategic result and that too with precision. Being an arm of the State, SOEs do not limit their involvement to global economic affairs alone but also help the Chinese State to append its enhancing soft power role globally. Today, when it comes to geo-economics, SOEs influence some strategic areas, including banking, finance, media, and public policy.

The SOEs play a crucial role in any given nation-state's international narrative. In China's case, SOEs are often called the 'eldest son' (长子 *Zhang zi*)[13] of the Chinese economy as they seem to carry a particular plan reflected in the realm of economic affairs. This could be in competition or cooperation or other related matters to gain comparative advantage over neighbours and competitors. The State enterprises from China carry political communication both ways because, as national carriers, SOEs have a strong political interest, as is evident. Still, it is equally valid that they play a central role in China's economic statecraft globally and have carried forward its geo-economic agenda.

The international competition among large countries is not new in a globalised scheme of things. Still, China has been overtly supporting and using its advantageous position of the SOEs to influence international trade competition. At this juncture of globalisation and geo-economics, large Chinese corporations comprising large local enterprises and international multinational companies play a crucial role in advocating the state plan. In the last 20 years, the number of Chinese enterprises functioning globally has risen sharply, breaking the European and American enterprises' long-term myth and monopoly. Among them, SOEs in banking and financial verticals play the lead role.

On the one hand, the exposure of SOEs to global competitiveness has improved; on the other, this has also created severe non-competitive investments by prominent Chinese enterprises raising regulatory issues. Enhancing the competitiveness of SOEs and promoting and deepening corrective measures is an inevitable requirement for China's economic and social transformation and a significant driving force for China's sustained development. The SOEs' role has been seen as a method to achieve an invincible position in a fierce international competition. Most of China's trading partners have been accusing and holding SOEs responsible for breaching corporate values. At the height of the USA-China trade war, the USA added 24 Chinese SOEs to its "sanctions list".[14]

Traditionally, much of the outward engagements of Chinese SOEs lie in conventional areas comprising chemicals, construction companies, shipbuilding, mining, utilities, and traditional energy. SOEs have been at the forefront to underline their role in internationalising the Chinese economic agenda. Hence, most of the foreign acquisitions were dominated by SOEs making foreign acquisitions. However, as China grew, so did its appetite for foreign acquisitions. The trend has recently shifted to private Chinese companies investing in real estate, fashion, entertainment houses, etc.

In recent years, political underpinnings have influenced the economic orientations of state enterprises. It seems, and has been observed too, that the geopolitical agenda has been camouflaged by the mirage of connectivity, overseas investment, and 'shared destiny.' State enterprises play a critical role in this strategy, and in their attempts to exploit maximum political incentives, the SOEs went overboard and launched over-ambitious projects. With the launch of the BRI, the tendencies for overseas investments among the SOEs increased multi-fold. China's overseas deal-making has been the subject of much attention by the Chinese government, especially in recent times. It began as a hunt for raw materials[15] (especially energy) required to support its domestic industrial production, but the present trend does not attribute the logic of dependency or economic co-operation. After 40 years, China's SOEs have made some reform and development achievements, and today, among the latest *Fortune 500* companies, 119 Chinese companies were shortlisted, out of which 82 are SOEs.[16]

Fortune magazine's "World Top 500" list has been an authoritative and reliable source of the world's largest enterprises. It publishes a list of 500 companies with the highest total global operating revenue each year with fundamental indicators such as profits, total assets, and the number of employees and bases its ranking on the company's total operating income. In 1989, the Bank of China (BOC) became the first company from mainland China to enter the world's top *Fortune 500* list,[17] after which many Chinese companies continued to enter the elite club. By 2012, seventy mainland companies entered the list of world's top 500. Among the world's top *Fortune 500* enterprises from China, state-owned and state-owned holding companies account for a significant share. Of 70 companies, 42 were Central enterprises that the SASAC supervised. The new entrants from China displaced other global companies from richer economies. In the first decade of the 21st century, Japan's percentage in the list shrunk from 88 to 68,[18] and for the USA, the number shrunk from 197 to 132.[19]

For the past 15 consecutive years, Chinese SOEs have increased their global list of the wealthy and influential, and although the list includes both the private and the SOEs, three of the top five companies in the list are SOEs from China with the State Grid ranking second, followed by the State-owned energy giants, Sinopec Group and China National Petroleum Corp. (CNPC).[20] Thirteen Chinese companies made it to the list for the first time, including China Merchants Group (CMG), Xiamen Xiangyu Group (XXG), Ansteel Group, China Taiping Insurance Group (CTIG), and Haier Group. In the coming years, the number of Chinese enterprises may see an upward trend; as Scott Cendrowski wrote, the number of Chinese companies appearing on the *Fortune 500* list should continue growing in the coming years because it is a government priority to raise the global rankings of Chinese enterprises.[21]

BRI, Economic Statecraft and SOEs

The 'Belt and Road' (BRI) Initiative is the strategic framework of China's global expansions through a complex mesh of projects and partnerships. Its two features include the 'Silk Road Economic Belt' (SREB)[22] and the '21st Century Maritime Silk Road' (MSR)[23] proposed by Xi Jinping in 2013. After the BRI was put into action, it has brought a profound impact on the Chinese SOEs. A 4 billion strong population along the route is involved in providing broad market opportunities for the SOEs. Premier Li specifically pointed out that SOEs should seize the opportunities brought about by the BRI. The Chinese SOEs have been asked to adapt to local conditions and improve brand services. After the BRI was advocated, the orientation of the SOEs for participating in the BRI construction and investment increased significantly. According to a research report by Deloitte,[24] 70 per cent of the SOEs surveyed indicated that the future direction of internationalisation would lean towards the BRI; 78 per cent of SOEs planning to participate in the BRI said they would increase the scale of overseas investment in the future. Affected by this, the focus of SOE overseas mergers and acquisitions began to shift from developed economies in Europe and the USA to the BRI-subscribed countries. The Asian region adjacent to China has undoubtedly become the first choice for enterprises to expand their existence beyond Chinese borders.

The continuous engagement of the SOEs with the international market has more meaning attached to it than what seems to be and is not only limited to the diversification strategy but also an important geopolitical step. In the past 40 years, China's SOEs experienced exponential growth in quantity and quality and a stellar performance on the world stage. In 2018, as per the *Fortune 500* list, 120 Chinese enterprises and 126 US-listed companies marked their entry in the list.[25] According to the data, among the 120 Chinese enterprises, 48 were Central enterprises supervised by the SASAC, 11 treasury-funded enterprises (banks and financial enterprises), and 24 local SOEs. The total number of SOEs stood at 83.[26] In 2019, the Chinese nearly levelled the USA number of *Fortune 500* companies. Over 119 companies from mainland China and Hong Kong made it to the list, while that of the USA declined from 126 to 121.[27] This is not all. As it is happening each year, the SOEs have been consistently rising to the need of the hour and industry expectations. The *Fortune 500* figures indicate that SOE contribution has also increased, representing 80.2 per cent of Chinese companies on the list, up from 76.3 per cent last year.[28] Given the trade war, the Chinese state is certainly glad that the state enterprises are not losing their pole positions.

SOEs' BRI Specific Strategies

While Chinese love invoking their country's rich and glorious past with talk about porcelain, silk, and trade across the Eurasian belt to Europe, modern-day conversations have shifted. They are inclined more towards soft diplomacy wired in initiatives of 'shared prosperity.' The SOEs and state financial institutions are being pushed to invest overseas in areas beyond infrastructure and construction. A discussion on BRI is incomplete without mentioning the role of the SOEs, and on the other hand, the agenda is unfinished for SOEs if the BRI does not reflect in their routine reports. The giant SOEs with close links to the CPC lobby around for bagging projects by focusing on the BRI. Although the intensity of such lobbying has decreased after the initial prodigious surge, it certainly indicates how the SOEs are pursuing nuanced strategies to benefit from the BRI and help the Chinese state build economic influence in the long run.

Relying on Technical Strength and Improving Competitiveness

Enterprises are continuously required to enhance global competitiveness to achieve long-term development, and against the backdrop of the BRI, Chinese enterprises have constantly been advancing in the international market. The BRI provides new opportunities for SOEs. But one can also notice that Chinese SOEs face challenges that include deficiency of high-end talents, insufficient innovation capabilities, and backend management when conducting foreign trade. The BRI put extraordinary pressure on Chinese enterprises to strengthen strategies such as attracting talent, attaching importance to cooperation in science and innovation, and strengthening corporate management to help develop the international competitiveness of Chinese enterprises.

The BRI sets out susceptible targets forcing SOEs to rely on technological strength to open up the international market and develop international competencies. Since China's opening up in 1978, SOEs have accumulated technical experience, which helps Chinese enterprises to optimise their technological advantages and develop business in their expertise areas and as per the destination economy.

Creating High-quality Services

At present, China is transitioning from *Made in China* to *Service in China.* The potential to promote Chinese standards and services can be found in the Digital BRI, because of which SOEs were bound to take the lead.[29] Based on *'Service in China,'* most SOEs are involved in a series of cross-border mergers and acquisitions. Improving service levels and creating high-quality services challenged SOEs to gain a good reputation in the international market and enhance competitiveness in the global market to a certain extent. Chinese SOEs are strategising to use the BRI to expand their 'services' business. Opportunities to work in joint ventures (JVs) in the fields of smart electricity grids and intelligent transport logistics, common standards for telecommunications, infrastructure for the 'internet of things' are a few examples of how Chinese SOEs would be planning their rise.

Effective Overseas Partnerships

To ensure that SOEs achieve sound development by participating in BRI construction, in 2015, the State Council proposed creating a conducive environment for regional investment to guide SOEs to participate in the international market in clusters and form complementary advantages and cooperation models. Overseas mergers and acquisitions were seen as an essential means for enterprises to internationalise rapidly under the BRI banner. Since the BRI was launched, SOEs were aware that only strong alliances can achieve the strategic goal of 'going out' of SOEs swiftly. With the rapid growth of China's economy and the accelerated pace of enterprises 'going global', Chinese enterprises increased their overseas investment. The analysis indicates that the overall share of SOEs is diminishing with the advent of the private sector. SOEs still hold a dominant position in China's outward foreign direct investment (OFDI) stock. By the end of 2005, the OFDI stock share held by Chinese SOEs under the Central government administration stood at around 84 per cent of its entire outstanding OFDI stock.[30] In 2009, SOEs accounted for nearly 70 per cent of China's foreign investment stock, with 30 per cent for private enterprises'.[31] By the end of 2019, Chinese Central SOEs still held more than half of China's OFDI stock.[32] Most of the SOEs belonged to the energy and heavy chemical industries. For profitable growth in these sectors, SOEs in the energy, power, and industrial sectors have always focused on overseas mergers and acquisitions.

Provide Systemic Guarantees

Generally, the international markets are like far-away waters to sail through that involves more risks than challenges for the Chinese SOEs. Under the banner of the BRI, the international expansions of SOEs face more significant operational risks. Therefore, risk prevention and control, managing and supervising global operations became a new experience. Unlike the domestic market, the international scenario comprised political and economic risks and competition with the already existing dominant players. SOEs had to take the risk to perform without compromising the standardised operations. The levels of compliances and local restrictions multiplied, and the Chinese SOEs had to pay closer attention to these new environments. As SOEs have taken the risk of investing in BRI countries, the scope of Chinese SOEs grew, and so did the risks.

Against this backdrop, the systemic guarantees were seen as critical, and SOEs have been counting on regulators and leaders (read *the State)* to provide guarantees in crises. Interestingly, one of the SOEs, China Export & Credit Insurance Corporation (中国出口信用保险公司 *Zhongguo chukou xinyong baoxian gongsi*), which is also known as *Sinosure* (中国信保 *Zhongguo xinbao*), provides the SOEs respite from rising risk levels calculated against the enterprise's instinct to take risks and support the national policies. If the risks are taken by developing BRI compatible 'going out' 'internationalisation,' such risks have political benefits. *Sinosure* itself identifies rising risk in getting involved with geopolitically and economically stormy geographies. The general debt risk involving bankruptcy and liquidation, risks related to asset depreciation, exchange rate restrictions, foreign exchange, government default risk caused by changes in policy rules, and geopolitical risks are the set of risks, which the SOEs operating under the banners of the BRI seek protection from. *Sinosure* has been pressed into service to provide the much-needed protective umbrella for SOE overseas operations.[33] The data by *Sinosure* indicates that since 2017, the company has insured the SOEs, which primarily operate out of politically and commercially riskier BRI countries. Globally, in 2018, *Sinosure's* insured value totalled over US$ 612 billion.[34] The insurance and indemnities ensure that the SOEs do not avoid their role in extending the BRI against any excuses. In 2017, the total loan amount underwritten by *Sinosure* reached US$ 176.94 billion.[35] Given the nature of state protection, SOEs sail through unchartered global waters without any doubt, where the rest of their competitors hesitate to engage in. This gives Chinese enterprises immense benefits. It does not mean competition, but on the contrary, the hosts allow Chinese enterprises free access and freebies to stay on and expand. These SOEs further make headway towards pursuing well-calibrated geopolitical ambitions.

Relying on Team Talent

With the advent of the knowledge economy era, the role of talent in economic development has increased manifold. In the process of internationalised economic development, skills occupy a dominant position. Therefore, SOEs needed to accelerate the growth and training of internationalised talent, actively introduce talent, and protect the talent team. At the international level, SOEs attempt to train the company's employees and solve talent shortage were tuned according to BRI designs.

The SOEs seeking to outcompete foreign players in their market and create space is an uphill task without working on the soft infrastructure, i.e., human resources. As Chinese-funded enterprises continue to go global, many Chinese are sent to work in foreign nations. Traditionally, SOEs have been facing difficulties in recruiting expatriates due to high attrition rates and cultural conflicts. Moreover, the foreign talent in SOEs insists on low-key talent acquisition and includes assembly lines and those required for labour-intensive profiles, high skilled jobs, and talent gaps that were either left vacant or filled by the Chinese. Acquiring and broadening the talent base is an inevitable choice. SOEs have lately understood the critical importance of talent and cutting-edge technology. Starting with banks and the energy sector, a few Chinese SOEs have introduced high-level overseas skills and adopted a broader vision.

Conventionally, talent development remained less dynamic and underestimated for the international expansion and growth trajectories of SOEs. The BRI schemes accelerated the revolution in strategic human resource management (SHRM), as the relationship between Human Resource Management and organisational performance impacted enterprises. The SOEs, beginning from the 1980s, started introducing high-performance work systems and human resource management practices domestically. But as China and its enterprises set to internationalise their operations to cover BRI ambitions, the relationship between high-performance work systems and organisational performance was seen equally crucial while operating outside China. In the post-BRI launch, SOEs attempted to adopt and adapt the high-performance work system model to fit their current cultural (Chinese work styles) and economic context. SOEs adopted strategies such as "reverse migration" to attract talent under the "1000 talent" plan. The key "1000 talent" program was introduced in 2008 by Politburo member Li Yuanchao.[36] It did help the Chinese enterprises to some extent but not entirely.

It is observed that the talent strategies of the SOEs are being implemented in a piecemeal manner and include team-based learning, on-the-job learning, and global exposure.[37] The Chinese Ministry of Commerce has been indicating to SOEs to strengthen the cultivation of local and international talents under the national schemes of "Thousand Talents Plan" and "Thousand Talents Plan for Youth" (千人计划 *Qian ren jihua*; 青年千人计划 *Qingnian qian ren jihua*).[38]

In the previous chapter on sub-national contests between types of enterprises, readers have noticed that SOEs' talent has been fed by the SOE subsidiaries at the provincial levels (SSPs).

Establish Brand Goals

Chinese products have been facing severe problems concerning their brands.[39] When a company enters a foreign market, the brand becomes more important. With the BRI in place, Chinese State agencies make sure they get enough cushion to let the Chinese SOEs expand their brand equity. In the initial stages of internationalisation, the Chinese could not make a dent in the international brands. The brand has become a centre-piece of China's BRI as China is looking to export services and value-added products. In the past two decades, the Chinese have been discreetly building their capacity by relying on R&D to gain an advantage in products and then driving the brand through products. Although the initial speed of taking this path was slow, the Chinese state believes the efforts would pay off in good numbers. Price is no more a prerequisite. The Chinese attempt to venture into new markets. Their companies no more keep the prices intentionally low compared to their competitors, but China still enjoys low-cost marketplaces compared to their high-end Western brands. Chinese enterprises sabotage the reliance of Western brand on countries like China as a great way of reducing core production expenses. The low-price tactics are no more a USP that the Chinese enterprises would like to use. The enterprises from China claim to have patented technologies and time-tested R&D brains involved in producing world-class products. And in the process, if they can benefit from the low cost of production that adds to their edge over their rivals; that is what the Huawei advertisement even denotes. Cases of acquisitions to enter the international market are temporary, and enterprises will eventually have to launch quality products through R&D and then use these products to drive the brand.

Chinese SOEs have been conscious of making the Chinese brands stand out. A brand is a concentrated expression of national economic strength for Chinese SOEs, the torch bearers of Chinese identity globally. An opportunity to build brands requires SOEs to put stress on technological and product innovation. Therefore, against the backdrop of the BRI, SOEs attempt to strengthen the brand building and increase their brand influence, which globally remains a vital issue. With the long-term goal of building a "Chinese brand", SOE efforts to build factories and R&D institutions overseas, driving Chinese equipment, technology, standards, and services to go abroad with technological innovation, and enhancing corporate credit influence have been made on a war footing. For example, in Africa, through grand schemes under the BRI, the SOE brands such as Chinese Railway, Sinotrans, CITIC Guohua, CITIC Guoanzhi, China Petroleum, and Petrochemical are emphasising Chinese brands and promoting the development and growth of the SOEs internationally.

SOEs' Span of Work under BRI

Until the first BRI forum was held in Beijing in May 2017, the Central enterprises played a formidable role in supporting the BRI agenda. As per SASAC data, until May 2017, Central enterprises actively responded and participated in 1,676 projects.[40] In response to the State's grand plans, 47 Central enterprises invested and participated in projects spread across all the continents.[41] By the beginning of 2019, more than 80 Central enterprises participated in various BRI schemes and implemented 3,116 projects along the route, primarily focused on infrastructure construction and energy security.[42] In January 2020, the number made a little more progress when China's 81 Central enterprises undertook over 3,400 projects covering BRI demarcated landscape.[43]

The internationalisation strategy of the SOEs spanned across several sectors. In terms of building infrastructure, Central enterprises have distinct advantages. For example, Central Enterprises initiated many railway and high-speed rail projects such as the Mombasa-Nairobi Railway and many highways and transportation facilities such as the Karakoram Highway. Further, the Chinese SOEs laid cross-sea communication optical cables, terrestrial communication optical cables, and communication networks and facilities. Sometimes referred to as the construction of interconnection infrastructure along the BRI, Central enterprises undertook more than 60 per cent of the projects, and the contracted investment exceeded 80 per cent.[44] A detailed list of SOE projects has been put together in Table 9.1.

Regarding projects related to energy, the Central enterprises completed more than 60 energy projects and oil and gas cooperation projects in more

Table 9.1: SOEs' Span of Work under BRI

Sr. No.	*Name of the SOE*	*Country of Investment*	*Sector and Services*	*Year/month*
1	China Jiangxi International Economic and Technical Cooperation Co, Ltd. and JinkoSolar Holdings Co. Ltd. form a consortium	Kenya	China-Africa Photovoltaic Cooperation, Garissa 50 MW Solar Power Station	24/08/20
2	China Railway Bridge Bureau	Ghana	The renovation project of Ghana's coastal road project starts	24/08/20
3	Long Jian Road & Bridge Co. Ltd. and China Investment Corporation (CIC)	Russia	Construction of the 2,200-metre bridge between Nizhneleninskoye in Russia and Tongjiang city in China. While CIC is one of the funding agencies, LJRB constructed the bridge on the Chinese side	13/08/20
4	China Harbour Investment and Construction under China Communications Group	Sri Lanka	Port City of Colombo	03/08/20
5	China Export-Import Bank	Bangladesh	Export-Import Bank and Bangladesh Ministry of Finance signed a loan agreement for power grid expansion and upgrade project	19/06/20
6	China Shandong High-Speed Group	Serbia	Construction of Serbian Expressway Contracted by Chinese Enterprises Started	18/06/20
7	China Railway Shanghai Engineering Bureau	Malaysia	Chinese enterprises undertook to complete the second phase of the southern line tunnel of Kuala Lumpur MRT	16/06/20
8	Shandong Port Qingdao Port	Italy	The construction of the second phase of civil works of the Chinese-invested Vado project in Italy completed	15/06/20
9	Harbin Electric Group	Ecuador	Handover of civil engineering contracted by Chinese enterprise to build Menas Hydropower Station in Ecuador	05/06/20
10	China Railway Eighteenth Bureau Group	Dubai, UAE	The construction of the world's highest hotel project by a Chinese company starts	04/06/20
11	Harbin Electric Group	Dubai, UAE	The first Chinese built clean coal-fired power station in the Middle East was connected to the grid for power generation	19/05/20
12	China Huaneng Group	Cambodia	China Huaneng Cambodia Sanhe II Hydropower Station	17/05/20

Sr. No.	*Name of the SOE*	*Country of Investment*	*Sector and Services*	*Year/month*
13	China Communications Construction Co. Ltd.	Kenya	Chinese enterprise undertook the construction of berths 1-3 at Lamu Port	05/05/20
14	Energy China Gezhouba Group	Argentina	Chinese enterprise undertakes construction of Argentina's Conra Hydropower Station	05/05/20
15	China Railway Tunnel Bureau	Uzbekistan	Chinese enterprises undertook the construction of the Uzbekistan coal mine modernisation project to complete phase tasks; status - on schedule	05/05/20
16	China Power Construction Group Co. Ltd.	Indonesia	Tunnel No. 3 of Indonesia's Jakarta-Bandung High-speed Rail Project was completed	27/04/20
17	China Power Construction Group	Laos	Laos La Mengshan Tunnel Level Guide No. 3 Cross Pass	05/04/20
18	Sichuan Railway Industry Investment Group Co. Ltd.	Norway	The second bridge built by Sichuan Road Bridge in Norway opens to traffic	04/04/20
19	China Railway Construction International Group Co. Ltd.	Qatar	Unloading of the main steel structure of the Qatar World Cup main stadium under construction by China; status - completed	10/04/20
20	State Grid Corporation of China	Brazil	The second phase of the Meilishan Hydropower UHV DC transmission project (referred to as the Meilishan Phase II project) put into operation, with a cumulative transmission of 7.2 billion kWh	08/04/20
21	China Railway 20th Bureau	Mozambique	Agricultural cooperation project	28/03/20
22	China Energy Construction Group (Anhui Electric Power Construction First Engineering Co. Ltd.)	Turkey	Installation of the No. 2 boiler of Hunutlu Thermal Power Project begins the construction	25/03/20
23	Sinopec	Russia	West Siberian Petrochemical Project finishes trial runs; Progress made in Sino-Russian Petrochemical Cooperation	01/04/20
24	National Energy Group	France	The joint venture wind power project signed between National Energy Group and EDF-the 502 MW Jiangsu Dongtai offshore wind power project, China's first Sino-foreign joint venture offshore wind power project, was officially launched	13/03/20

Sr. No.	Name of the SOE	Country of Investment	Sector and Services	Year/month
25	China Power Construction Nuclear Power Company and Shandong Power Construction Company	Saudi Arabia	The world's largest combined-cycle power plant was successfully connected to the grid in Saudi Arabia	02/03/20
26	China Railway Corporation Limited	Peru	The Lima Green Coast Project in Peru was completed	29/02/20
27	Chinese Enterprise Shanghai Construction Engineering Group	Cambodia	Chinese enterprises undertook to build Cambodian Highway 58 and open to traffic	27/02/20
28	COSCO Shipping Piraeus Port Co. Ltd.	Greece	The expansion project of the cruise terminal of Piraeus Port in Greece started	27/02/20
29	China Railway Eighteenth Bureau Group	Saudi Arabia	Saudi Arabia's Jizan Aramco Emergency Response Centre project was completed	26/02/20
30	China Railway Tunnel Bureau	Israel	Chinese enterprises completed the Tel Aviv light rail red line tunnel	25/02/20
31	China Railway Construction Corporation	Sri Lanka	Sri Lanka's southern expressway extension line opens to traffic on 23 February 2020	24/02/20
32	China Tianchen Company	Georgia	The completion and commissioning of the Georgian key power station project undertaken by a Chinese company	18/01/20
33	China Nonferrous Metals Group	Congo (DRC)	Chinese enterprises invested in the construction of Congo (DRC) Dizwa mining and LCS project were completed and put into production	18/01/20
34	China State Power Investment Corporation	Malta	The Montenegro wind power project invested by a Chinese company and Malta is officially completed	20/11/19
35	China State Construction Engineering Corporation (CSCEC)	Pakistan	Peshawar to Karachi Motorway (PKM) project, the largest transportation infrastructure project in the China-Pakistan Economic Corridor, was completed	06/11/19
36	Hengyi Industrial (Brunei) Co. Ltd.	Brunei	China's most prominent investment project in Brunei was put into operation (Hengyi Petrochemical Damorra Island Comprehensive Refining and Chemical Project)	04/11/19

Sr. No.	*Name of the SOE*	*Country of Investment*	*Sector and Services*	*Year/month*
37	China Railway 21st Bureau	Mongolia	The construction of the municipal road in Zamyn-Uud, Mongolia, was completed	18/10/19
38	China Railway Construction 20th Bureau Group Co. Ltd.	Angola	The Chinese company completed the construction of Kuito Airport in central Angola	20/10/19
39	China State Power Investment Corporation	Turkey	The Hunutlu Power Plant, China's largest direct investment project in Turkey, officially started construction on the 22nd in Adana's southern province	24/09/19
40	Power Construction Nuclear Power Company	Brazil	Priority implementation project of China-Pakistan Economic Corridor-Sahiwal Coal-fired Power Station	13/08/19
41	China Road and Bridge Engineering Co. Ltd.	Kenya	The Kenya Nairobi Expressway project started	17/10/19
42	China National Chemical Engineering Group	Russia	China and Russia will jointly build the world's largest ethylene integration project	12/10/19
43	China National Engineering Corporation	Bangladesh	Chinese company completed the construction of the Padma Water Plant in Bangladesh	12/10/19
44	State Grid Corporation of China	Brazil	Substantial breakthrough in the second phase of the ±800 kV UHV DC transmission project in Brazil	09/10/19
45	China Gezhouba Group Co. Ltd.	Pakistan	Chinese companies have achieved initial results in the construction of Sugikinari Hydropower Station in Pakistan	30/09/19
46	China Railway	Indonesia	Indonesia's Jakarta-Bandung high-speed rail project's first continuous beam closure	25/09/19
47	China National Electric Import & Export Corporation	Belarus	A Chinese company completes its first railway electrification project in Belarus	12/09/19
48	China Power Construction	Togo	A Chinese company undertook the Togo Radio and Television Facilities Renovation Project was officially handed over	12/09/19
49	China Intercontinental Petroleum Corporation	Albania	The Banks Oilfield in Albania to be transformed into the largest onshore oil field in Europe	15/09/19

Sr. No.	*Name of the SOE*	*Country of Investment*	*Sector and Services*	*Year/month*
50	China Petroleum Pipeline Bureau Engineering Co. Ltd.	Sri Lanka	The construction of the drainage tunnel project in the capital of Sri Lanka by a Chinese company starts	06/09/19
51	China Dongfang Electric Group Co. Ltd.	Bosnia and Herzegovina	Chinese enterprise enters into a contract to build thermal power plants in Bosnia and Herzegovina	21/08/19
52	China Gezhouba Group Co. Ltd.	Papua New Guinea	Chinese enterprises sign Papua New Guinea Edwu Hydropower Project Contract	20/08/19
53	China Harbour Company	Cote d'Ivoire	Construction of the C™te d'Ivoire Industrial Park by a Chinese company starts with a contract value of approximately US$ 97 million	06/08/19
54	China Earth Corporation and China Railway 15th Bureau	Tanzania	Chinese-funded enterprises to undertake the construction of Lake Victoria Bridge in Tanzania	06/08/19
55	China Zhongman Petroleum and Natural Gas Group Co. Ltd.	Egypt	Chinese enterprises undertake Egyptian water well drilling project	21/07/19
56	China Communications Construction Co. Ltd., China Road and Bridge Engineering Co. Ltd.	Montenegro	The Montenegro North-South Expressway connects the southern port of Bar with the main transportation corridors of Central and Eastern Europe	12/06/19
57	State Grid Corporation of China	Laos	The construction of the 500/230 kV ring network project in Vientiane, Laos, starts	22/04/19
58	China Railway International	East Timor	Chinese enterprises undertook to build East Timor's first expressway	18/04/19
59	Energy China Gezhouba Group	Pakistan	China and Pakistan signed a general contract for the construction of the Mohmand Hydropower Project	09/04/19
60	China Power Construction Group International Engineering Co. Ltd.	Guinea	Chinese company to build Guinea's Kukutamba hydropower station to supply power to four countries in the Senegal River Basin	14/03/19
61	Shanghai Construction Engineering Group Co. Ltd.	Cambodia	The construction of the third ring road project in Phnom Penh, Cambodia, started by a Chinese enterprise	15/01/19

Sr. No.	*Name of the SOE*	*Country of Investment*	*Sector and Services*	*Year/month*
62	China Civil Engineering Group Co. Ltd.	Bangladesh	Chinese company to undertake the construction of 173 km double-track railway project in Bangladesh	19/12/18
63	China Civil Engineering Group Co. Ltd.	Tanzania	Chinese company won the bid for the second phase of Tanzania's BRT project	11/12/18
64	Hebei Iron and Steel Group	Philippines	Chinese companies signed an 8 million tons steel project in the Philippines with a total investment of approximately US$4.4 billion	19/12/18
65	China National Petroleum Corporation	Russia	The third production line of the Yamal LNG project officially put into operation	12/12/18
66	COSCO Shipping Group	Abu Dhabi	COSCO Shipping Abu Dhabi Terminal was formally opened	11/12/18
67	Sichuan Railway Investment Group	Norway	Harrow Grand Bridge, under contract by a Chinese company, opens	10/12/18
68	China Communications Construction Co. Ltd. and China Harbour Engineering Co. Ltd.	Panama	Chinese companies to build the fourth bridge of The Panama Canal, benefiting more than 1.7 million residents	13/11/18
69	China Machinery Engineering Corporation	Ukraine	Chinese companies to build large solar power plants in central Ukraine	08/04/18
70	Dongfang Electric and Shanghai Electric	Egypt	Two Chinese companies jointly won the bid for the Egyptian thermal power EPC project	29/06/18
71	China Railway Construction Corporation	Saudi Arabia	China Railway Construction won a light rail operation contract in Mecca, Saudi Arabia	21/06/18
72	China Railway Corporation Limited	Bangladesh	Bangladesh Padma Bridge Connection Project Signs Loan Agreement; status–delayed, the budget has increased by 12 per cent	24/05/18
73	China Road and Bridge Corporation	Croatia	Chinese companies sign contracts to build Croatian sea-crossing bridge project	24/04/18
74	Beijing Urban Construction Group	Maldives	Chinese company undertook to build Maldives airport project started	02/02/18
75	China Harbour Engineering Co. Ltd.	Sri Lanka	Chinese enterprises to invest in the construction of the first comprehensive building complex in the Port City of Colombo	26/01/18

Sr. No.	Name of the SOE	Country of Investment	Sector and Services	Year/month
76	China Harbour Engineering Co. Ltd.	Ghana	Chinese enterprises undertake the expansion project of Tema Port in Ghana to train local talent	21/01/18
77	China Construction Group	The Republic of Congo	Chinese enterprises undertook to build National Highway No. 1 to open up the economic artery of Congo (Brazzaville)	08/01/18
78	China State Construction Corporation	Egypt	Chinese enterprises undertook to develop the new capital central business district of Egypt	12/10/17
79	State Grid Corporation	Brazil	Chinese companies participate in the start of Brazil's UHV transmission project	29/09/17
80	China Road and Bridge	Madagascar	A Chinese company signs a loan agreement for the Madagascar Airport Expressway Project. Design and construction adopt Chinese standards	15/09/17
81	China Energy Construction Co. Ltd.	Malaysia	Chinese companies sign a general contract for Balik Hydropower Station in Malaysia	12/09/17
82	China Energy Construction Co. Ltd.	Egypt	China-Egypt sign railway project	16/08/17
83	China Power Construction Group	Bangladesh	Chinese company won the bid for Bangladesh Heavy oil power station project	12/09/17
84	China Hydropower Construction Group International Engineering Co. Ltd.	Russia	Chinese companies to build a bridge across the Lena River in the Irkutsk Region	12/09/17
85	China Power Construction Group	Poland	A Chinese company undertakes the most massive bid for the Polish flood control project	29/08/17
86	China Communications Construction Co. Ltd.	Malaysia	Construction of the Malaysian East Coast Railway project undertaken by a Chinese company starts	10/08/17
87	CRRC Zhuzhou Electric Locomotive Co. Ltd.	Malaysia	China's fully automated driverless light rail vehicles to be built in Malaysia	04/08/17

Sr. No.	*Name of the SOE*	*Country of Investment*	*Sector and Services*	*Year/month*
88	China Gezhouba Group Company Limited	Russia	Russia's largest natural gas processing project started, and to become the source of the Sino-Russian East Route natural gas pipeline project	04/08/17
89	China Southern Power Grid Co. Ltd., China Power International Co. Ltd.	Vietnam	Chinese companies to build garden-style power plants in Vietnam	14/07/17
90	China Shenzhen Regional Economic Cooperation Promotion Association	Azerbaijan	China and Azerbaijan will jointly build China-Arab Free Trade Industrial Park	30/06/17
91	Africa Star Railway Operation Company (Afristar)	Kenya	Africa Star Railway Operation Company (Afristar) is contracted to run and maintain the 592-km Standard Gauge Railway (SGR) for ten years, after which management will revert to the Kenyans.	31/05/17
92	China Railway Tunnel Group	Uzbekistan	"One Belt One Road" Central Asia's first long tunnel	27/04/17
93	China Atomic Energy Industry Co. Ltd.	Iran	Chinese and Iranian companies sign the first commercial contract for the reconstruction of the Arak heavy water reactor	25/04/17
94	China Atomic Energy Industry Co. Ltd.	Oman	China-Oman Industrial Park launched	21/04/17
95	China Atomic Energy Industry Co. Ltd.	Netherlands	Eurasian Economic and Trade Cooperation Industrial Park	13/04/17
96	China Water Resources and Hydropower Construction Co. Ltd.	Niamey	Chinese enterprises undertook to build Niger heavy oil power station officially completed	04/04/17
97*	Shanghai Tunnel Engineering Co. Ltd.	India	Chinese companies help India's rail modernisation	04/04/17
98	Shanghai Tunnel Engineering Co. Ltd.	Pakistan	Sino-German joint venture assists the construction of the China-Pakistan Economic Corridor and builds Pakistan's largest cement plant	30/03/17
99	China Communications Services Co. Ltd.	Africa	Chinese enterprises connect with the development plan of African countries, and it is expected to lay tens of thousands of kilometres of optical cables	29/03/17
100	CNMC	Kazakhstan	Aktogai copper mine processing plant completed ahead of schedule; Chinese enterprises help Kazakhstan's industrial upgrading	28/03/17

Sr. No.	Name of the SOE	Country of Investment	Sector and Services	Year/month
101	China Red Lion Group	Nepal	China's investment in the construction of Nepal's largest cement plant	23/03/17
102	China Construction Third Bureau	Pakistan	Construction of China-Pakistan Economic Corridor Expressway	
103	China Construction Third Bureau	Pakistan	Peshawar-Karachi Expressway, Pakistan (Sukur-Multan section)	2015
104	China Construction Third Bureau	Malaysia	Malaysia-China Kuantan Industrial Park	14/02/17
105	China Communications Construction Co. Ltd. (CCCC)	Italy	Chinese company designs a port for the historical and cultural city of Venice	13/02/17
106	China Communications Construction Co. Ltd. (CCCC)	Hungary	Hungary China-Europe Business Logistics Park	04/02/17
107	China Communications Construction Co. Ltd. (CCCC)	Russia	Russia Longyue Forestry Economic and Trade Cooperation Zone	04/02/17
108	China Communications Construction Co. Ltd. (CCCC)	Egypt	Egypt Suez Economic and Trade Cooperation Zone	03/02/17
109	China Communications Construction Co. Ltd. (CCCC)	Laos	Saisetta Comprehensive Development Zone, Vientiane, Laos	03/02/17
110	China Communications Construction Co. Ltd. (CCCC)	Zambia	Zambia-China Economic and Trade Cooperation Zone	03/02/17
111	China Communications Construction Co. Ltd. (CCCC)	Pakistan	Pakistan Haier-Ruba Economic Zone	03/02/17
112	China Communications Construction Co. Ltd. (CCCC)	Vietnam	Longjiang Industrial Park, Vietnam	03/02/17
113	China Communications Construction Co. Ltd. (CCCC)	Uzbekistan	Uzbekistan ÒPengshengÓ Industrial Park	03/02/17
114	China Communications Construction Co. Ltd. (CCCC)	Hungary	Baoside Economic and Trade Cooperation Zone	03/02/17
115	China Communications Construction Co. Ltd. (CCCC)	Thailand	Thailand-China Rayong Industrial Park	03/02/17
116	China Communications Construction Co. Ltd. (CCCC)	Indonesia	China-Indonesia Economic and Trade Cooperation Zone	03/02/17
117	China Communications Construction Co. Ltd. (CCCC)	Cambodia	Sihanoukville Special Economic Zone, Cambodia	03/02/17
118	Sinopec	Saudi Arabia	Yanbu Refinery Project officially started production	20/01/16
119	Hong Kong Zhongke International Oil and Gas Investment Group Co. Ltd.	Kazakhstan	Sukh Oil and Gas, Kazakhstan	11/11/16
120	China Communications Construction Co. Ltd. (CCCC)	Bangladesh	Padma Bridge and River Dredging Project	2012-2016
121	China Communications Construction Co. Ltd. (CCCC)	Bangladesh	Seven Bridges of China-Bangladesh-China Friendship	2012-2016

Sr. No.	*Name of the SOE*	*Country of Investment*	*Sector and Services*	*Year/month*
122	China Communications Construction Co. Ltd. (CCCC)	Laos	China Laos Railway	2012-2016
123	China Communications Construction Co. Ltd. (CCCC)	Myanmar	China-Myanmar Railway	2012-2016
124	China Merchants Group	Belarus	Belarus China-Belarus Industrial Park	29/09/16
125	China Merchants Group	Horgos border	Horgos International Border Cooperation Centre	01/04/12
126	China Merchants Group	Malaysia	Malaysia Malaysia-China Kuantan Industrial Park	01/04/12
127	China National Petroleum Corporation	Myanmar	China-Myanmar Natural Gas Pipeline Project	01/12/09
128	China Petroleum	Russia	PetroChina and Gazprom signed the ÒChina-Russia Eastern Route Gas Supply ContractÓ.	01/05/14

*India is a non-signatory to any BRI schemes, but the name is included as the primary link describes the project under BRI.

Note: The table is arranged chronologically.

The list includes Chinese SOEs, which are either funding, constructing, or operating the projects. The list implies giving readers a general impression of the number of countries, regions, and sectors they are globally involved in. This is not an exhaustive list and represents select cases considering the paucity of sources and time.

Source: Author's compilation. From SASAC, NDRC, Press Release by State Council, Data extracted from a foreign news bulletin.

than 20 countries, which focused on energy and local resource development[45] and energy construction. Central enterprises undertook the construction of China-Russia, China-Kazakhstan, China-Myanmar crude oil pipelines, China-Russia, Central Asia, China-Myanmar gas pipelines, etc., to solve the problem of resource and energy output. Besides, over the years, Central SOEs have also undertaken many projects related to thermal power plants, hydropower plants, nuclear power plants, and power grids.

Apart from infrastructure and energy projects, the Chinese SOEs are engaged in expanding production capacity cooperation and industrial park cooperation (Table 9.1). The Central enterprises made special efforts to strengthen production capacity cooperation with BRI countries and intensified industrial park construction. The Central SOEs have keenly pursued several industrial and manufacturing projects. For example, the China-Belarus Industrial Park (CBIP), led by a Central enterprise, made time-bound progress.[46] As of the end of 2018, Chinese enterprises had established 933 enterprises in 46 countries in the overseas economic and trade cooperation zones with a total investment of US$ 20.96 billion, paid US$ 2.28 billion in taxes and fees to the host country and claims to have created 147,000 jobs.[47] Simultaneously, relying on resource and energy development as the primary support, Chinese SOEs have accelerated the development of related industries, forming an industrial synergy effect of gathering power and mutual assistance among sectors. For example, the Zambia-China Economic and Trade Cooperation Zone (ZCETCZ) and Nigeria's Lekki Free Trade Zone (LFTZ) focus on developing oil processing. In the process of 'going global', Chinese SOEs have led other domestic enterprises too to go global.[48]

Since implementing the BRI project, Chinese SOE investment has focused on manufacturing, information transmission, computer services and software, mining, and transportation. As per the annual report titled "China International Project Contracting", jointly issued by the Chinese Ministry of Commerce and China International Contractors Association, 63 countries along the BRI have completed a turnover of US$ 89.33 billion in foreign contracted projects, built 75 overseas economic and trade cooperation zones, and invested more than US$ 27 billion.[49] Not only have the Central enterprises completed all these investments, they have also been looking to expand their outreach in equipment, technology, management, and other areas.[50]

Risks and Challenges

While the SOEs are speeding up to go global, there are also many shortcomings and problems.

To start with the basics, one has to ask whether the Chinese SOEs are better equipped to handle international operations. Looking at the scale of operation, an enterprise's ability to operate internationally is reflected in its ability to occupy and lead the global market and generate profits from it. So far, SOEs have been facing problems in the domestic market. Weak international competitiveness and low profitability in the global market became severe when SOEs started looking for international markets. From the perspective of net import and export value, from 2008 to 2018, Chinese SOEs net export value remained negative. In 2018, the net export value reached US$ 290.1 billion, which was twice that of 2008.[51] Besides, a few SOEs have low overseas operations, poor returns, and have even committed investment mistakes. The large-scale asset management of SOEs contrasts with the profitability of overseas international markets, reflecting the problem. Strengthening the global competitiveness of SOEs, especially Central enterprises, and optimising state-owned capital has become the top priority for promoting further market-oriented reforms and enhancing core competitiveness.

Given that Chinese SOEs face challenges, the state has shored up scrutiny of overseas spending by private and state-owned firms amidst growing concerns about rising debt levels and potential systemic financial risk.[52] The stakes are rising after all the outbound investments by centrally controlled state firms. The issues of SOEs profitability and competitiveness raise questions regarding the failure of Chinese SOEs to operate their businesses globally, which has been more evident especially given the rising global costs of operations and against the hostile market conditions. After the financial crisis in 2007, the performance of the SOEs declined, but specifically, if one looks at the post-BRI time frame, the global needs to operate internationally have been riskier. SASAC made a detailed comparison of the operating performance of Central enterprises with world-class companies in the same industry. It concluded that the current management of SOEs is competent to face global competition.[53] Against the rising operating cost, size of assets, and non-profitable acquisitions, as well as stricter market conditions, Moody's reported that the leverage ratio of most Chinese SOEs is set to decline continuously.[54] This is one of the several financial measurements that look at how much capital comes in the form of debt (loans) or assesses a company's ability to meet its financial obligations. The recently released report titled "China Overseas Investment Country Risk Rating (2020)"[55] by the Institute of World Economics and Politics (IWEP) of the Chinese Academy of Social Sciences (CASS) shows that the risk of overseas investment by Chinese companies continues to rise.

The Chinese SOEs have been hardly deviating from the BRI layouts. While, on the one hand, internationalisation helped them to explore markets, on the other, tools like merger and acquisition (M&A) have been adopted by the SOEs management, resulting in serious problems. According to a research report released by the Boston Consulting Group (BCG) in 2014,[56] the completion rate of overseas M&A transactions by Chinese companies is only 67 per cent, which is far lower than that of companies in developed countries such as Europe, America and Japan. The M&A strategies adopted are unclear and lack due diligence, which is the main reason for business failure and operational transactions. Some SOEs did not fully demonstrate the selection of target companies, corporate valuation, and the operation of M&A projects before overseas mergers and acquisitions, resulting in losses of state-owned assets. Even if the procedures are completed, SOEs often fail to achieve their expected goals for which poor integration planning and execution after M&A are responsible.

The result of empirical research by scholars generally shows that the performance level of overseas M&A of SOEs is significantly lower than that of private enterprises.[57] An important reason for this is that some SOEs have misunderstood participation in BRI construction and regard it as a political task, which leads to blindly following the trend where the strategic goals remain unclear. For example, many SOEs regard the expansion of scale as an essential goal of overseas M&A. Enterprises believe that by expanding the scale, economies of scale and efficiency, improving production can be achieved. However, based on the microeconomic theory, with the expansion of production scale, production costs will initially notice a rapid decline. The decline rate slows eventually achieving the minimum efficient scale (Figure 9.2), that is, to achieve the smallest production scale with the lowest long-term average cost.

Figure 9.2: The Minimum Efficiency Scale of Enterprise Production

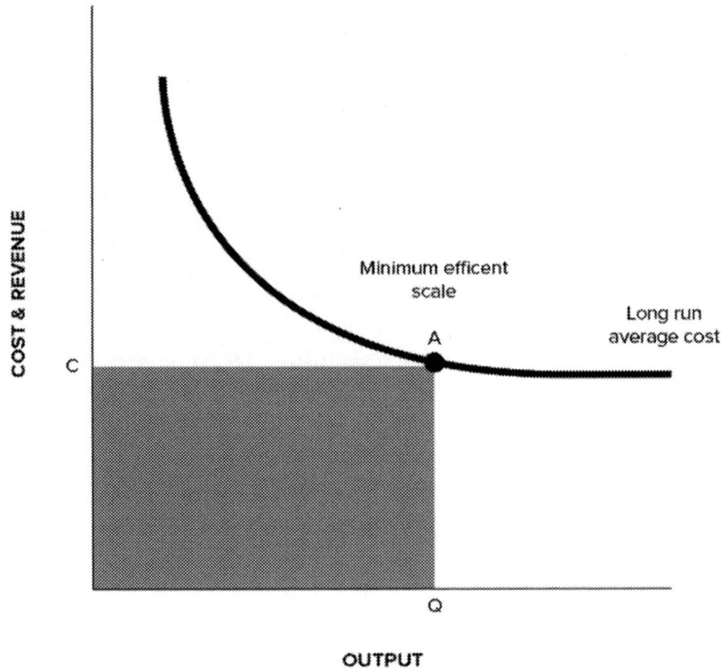

Source: Author's analysis based on *the theory of "minimum efficient scale".*

And technically, at this stage, expanding the scale through M&A may not increase production efficiency. On the contrary, after the merger, the economy of scale is likely to be affected due to the sharp increase in management costs. Based on this case, the vast majority of SOEs have reached or exceeded the minimum efficiency scale[58] (Figure 9.2), and there is no room left to expand and achieve higher returns. As a result, M&A may not serve the core purpose and should be differentiated from the market acquisition or the influencer factor. The Chinese enterprise, which sees M&A as the best way to infiltrate the international market, fails to keep up with monetary returns. It has been over three decades now that some of the Chinese SOEs have been operating globally. They fell short in innovating cooperation models, strengthening risk management and control and formulating scientific strategic plans. On the finances front, the SOEs have been unable to expand their financing channels further to increase the success rate of overseas mergers and acquisitions and achieve corporate transformation and upgrading through overseas M&A.

In addition to operationability, flawed schemes of overseas M&As, the SOE capital management and control capabilities have been a severe disciplinary matter for the Chinese State and leadership. For a Chinese State, which believes in public ownership and state control over assets and wealth, the splurge by SOEs is taken seriously by the regulators. With the same logic, the State-owned capital belongs to the ordinary Chinese, and overseas state-owned capital is the long-term accumulation and hard-won precious wealth of all the Chinese people. Against this backdrop, the Third Plenary Session of the 18th Central Committee of the CPC proposed strengthening state-owned capital with capital management.[59] SOEs have been scrutinised for their role against preserving and appreciating state-owned capital as the top priority of state-owned capital management and strengthening the power of overseas state-owned capital. Given that there is an apparent gap between Chinese SOEs and Western multinational giants regarding corporate governance structure and capital management and control capabilities, SOEs still meet roadblocks due to management failures. Hence, the construction of capital management and control capabilities is a significant issue for SOEs to perform globally.

In addition to the above problems, institutional pre-emption has been a long-standing problem for Chinese SOEs. They increasingly lack the institutional maturity to support BRI investment plans. Multinational operations of enterprises require sound decision-making mechanisms and market-oriented flexible operating choices, and international operating systems and tools to better and efficiently integrate multiple international and domestic resources and use the same towards developing international and domestic markets. The strategy of business internationalisation requires internationalised talents and incentive and restraint mechanisms for internationalised operations. These are some of the shortcomings of the internationalised operations of China's SOEs. Besides, compared with the more localised operations of Chinese companies, Chinese SOEs are mostly selective in using local labour and materials and rarely hire and train local employees. Some companies operate and live in the host country isolated from the residents, forming a relatively closed small circle. These long-term corporate operations failures to integrate with local society are inevitably affecting the corporate image and long-term operating capabilities of Chinese SOEs working remotely. As a result, Chinese SOEs proved to be unprepared to manage risks. Compared with international multinational companies, Chinese SOEs participating in international competition have inadequate risk management capabilities. Against the backdrop of rising numbers of non-compliance, Chinese SOEs are accustomed to exploiting loopholes in policies and regulations, making decisions in violation of rules, and over-authorising to engage in high-risk business activities instead of having had to develop a strong awareness for operating compliance.

Finally, the lack of planning and coordination for overseas development of enterprises has made the internationalisation of SOEs noticeable but, unfortunately, non-sustainable in the long run. Looking at the lack of strategic planning and coordination in overseas expansion, one can doubt how long the Chinese enterprises will be on the global horizon and leave a permanent mark on international economic affairs. There have been disorderly and even vicious competition in overseas markets, and the phenomenon of mutual mistrust, and even fierce competition between different companies managed by the same investor in the same market. While these situations seriously damage investor interests, they also hurt the international image of Chinese enterprises going global.

The performance of SOEs is affected by a multitude of factors. Planning and coordination are not the concern of the enterprises, and this involves political and institutional stakeholders in China. The government's multi-functional departments manage the implementation of internationalised operations in Chinese SOEs. The approval items involve the National Development and Reform Commission (NDRC), the Ministry of Finance, the Ministry of Commerce, the State Administration of Foreign Exchange, etc. The institutional distances within China affect the role of the SOEs. Moreover, as Leutert[60] concludes, the performance of SOEs is weighed against its political rather than market logic. Moreover, mere shuffling of executives cannot eliminate their multiple and often conflicting incentives, which remains the truth across various regulatory bodies and ministries.

Apart from the above limitations, SOEs have been facing an increasing number of litigations globally. They are one of the primary means of sovereign investment. In recent years, Chinese SOEs have seen significant growth in scale, quantity, and impact. With the increase in SOE overseas investments, the settlement of overseas investment disputes has become an inevitable problem, and dispute resolution between investors and host countries has become increasingly important. SOE investments are primarily made by the state agencies, and as a result, attracted investigation. Most of the time, the larger subsidiaries of the SOEs have been bidding in several countries without disclosing their connections with the parent SOE or any distant ties with the Chinese State. The relationship between the SOE and State meant that the chances of bidding low and winning contracts are higher and, on the other hand, the bidding is for a Chinese State-owned project. As a result, in the wake of bidding, Chinese enterprises and the state support have been brought up at numerous levels. Litigation over the status of bidding Chinese enterprises in international courts and arbitration is underway. Globally it is assumed that the Chinese enterprises end up winning the bids as the State does play an invisible hand in influencing them.

A legal debate on defining a 'public institution' and how it can be called the subsidy provider has been causing problems in the USA-China relations and the role of the Chinese SOEs widely. The Chinese enterprises are increasingly undergoing investigations on their origin, details on project feasibilities, and whether or not the Chinese have procured projects through fair competition. If the projects are the results of the state-to-state agreements, they certainly enjoy sovereign backing and protection from both the investor and host states. Still, in some cases, the subsidiary companies of the SOEs have been bidding and winning projects independently and without referring to their relations with the Chinese state. Some of the Chinese companies, with their parent SOEs, have been winning bids in developing countries.[61] The worries over the non-discrimination between the state-owned and private company investments shed significant light on the influence on international market access by state giants against those that are confidential in having limited leverage as a non-state entity.

The Case—China Communications Construction Company Limited (CCCC) (中国交通建设集团有限公司 *Zhongguo jiaotong jianshe jituan youxian gongsi*) and BRI

The Chinese SOEs have been in a hurry to take a leading role in BRI schemes. The SOEs hardly found any resistance in their overseas plans as state banks backed them due to the predominance of trade in bilateral relations. But when it comes to projects funded by liberal democracies and project processes pinned to due diligence, the Chinese SOEs maintain a low profile. A few cases where these companies have participated did result in a confluence of crisis. Even well before the BRI was announced, Chinese SOEs have been squarely refusing to comply with global standards and were exposed to inconsistencies. Most of the time, SOEs have been questioned over these practices more than the risks associated with expanding business outside of China.

It will be instructive to take the case of the China Communications Construction Company Limited (CCCC). It was initiated and founded by the China Communications Construction Group (CCCG) and was incorporated on 8 October 2006. Among the 97 Central enterprises[62] governed by SASAC, CCCC ranked 15th for its revenue and profit in the entire list of China's top 500 list of enterprises[63] and fifth amongst the top 100 Chinese construction enterprises.[64] In the BRI scheme of things, the CCCG is engaged in the design and construction of transportation infrastructure, dredging, and heavy machinery manufacturing business. The company signed contracts and agreements with 58 countries along the route for nearly US$ 40 billion.[65] The investment and construction of the China-Pakistan Economic Corridor series projects, Colombo Port City, East Africa Railway, China-Malaysia Friendship Bridge, and other projects have become milestones under the BRI and currently ranks 93rd[66] in the world's top 500 and 22nd in the Chinese SOE list in *Fortune 500*.[67] The Hong Kong-Zhuhai-Macao Bridge, the Kenya Railway, and the Port City of Sri Lanka built by the group have received widespread attention.

Despite its shining progress and rising fortunes on the domestic front, CCCC was one of the enterprises blacklisted by the World Bank Group and other joint funding agencies for eight years.[68] The World Bank Sanctions Committee, after a joint investigation, found the company involved in fraud, corruption, and bid manipulation in the procurement or contract execution process. The company and its affiliated companies were prohibited from participating in any World Bank project and other cooperative banks for several years. All the associated parties that were part of the World Bank Group, the African Development Bank, the Asian Development Bank, the European Bank for Reconstruction and Development, and the Inter-American Development Bank were part of the joint implementation of sanctions and resolution agreements, forced the CCCC to close its projects. According to the arrangements, those companies and their affiliated subsidiaries were subject to collective sanctions by the above-mentioned joint banks and prohibited from participating in bidding for any projects invested by these banks for a specified time. Despite the ban, the CCCC went ahead and lied about the prohibitions and won several other overseas contracts. This again underlines the strength or weaknesses of the corporate governance of the Chinese SOEs. Sometimes, the lucrative arrangements made by the CCCC in offering to host countries also help it disguise its mischievous acts. Host countries even fail to verify some of the credibility of the Chinese SOEs and fall victim to the risks, and dangers. For example, the Malaysian government was unaware of these bans and conferred one of Malaysia's most significant contracts for a single company. A 55 billion ringgit contract (US$ 12.3 billion) for the East Coast Rail Link, was awarded to the CCCC without a competitive tender.[69]

Like the CCCC, the SOEs have been the best examples to indicate how they remained a much-sought medium for China's internationalisation and statecraft despite being a serial violator at home. By fulfilling all the duties regarding the BRI, the group earned particular respect among the top leaders to be spared for a serious disciplinary violation. The CCCC group of companies has been indulging in acts of severe non-compliance within China as well. The Shanghai Zhenhua Group has been exposed for its negligence towards environmental protection and waste management.[70] Moreover, in its recent report, the Chongqing Municipal Commission of Housing and Urban-Rural Development criticised the CCCC. The SASAC Party Committee even inspected the other three companies for illegal activities in April 2020.[71] The group was discreetly advised to carry out the rectification process. But these revelations failed to deter the group from refraining from corruption, poaching, and other activities when it comes to international projects, especially BRI-related ones.

The CCCC has been subject to widespread criticism. The record shows that its projects accelerated soon after the BRI was announced. The group has a complex history; while it expanded its work and went on to win political favours by exploring opportunities that kept the party happy; it also continued to create disciplinary issues for the leadership. Here, we may take the CCCC as an example of the Chinese state's plan to expand. With a highly complex network of subsidiaries, CCCC continues to play the charm offensive. The same group pleased the State leaders by taking up the responsibility to perform and continue dredging in the South China Sea. The disclosed information at the Shenzhen Stock Exchange reveals that the company has expertise in capital dredging and reclamation dredging, container crane, heavy marine machinery, large steel structure, road machinery manufacturing, and international project contracting. It created suspicion over its activities and invited stern internal criticism on its listing in the Entity list.[72] Another subsidiary of the CCCC, the China Harbour Engineering Company (CHEC), has been performing well for the Chinese State as it continued bagging mega projects. The list includes Cebu International and Bulk Terminal Project in the Philippines, Colombo New Port city, and Hambantota Port project in Sri Lanka, the Deepwater Port in Kyaukpyu, Myanmar, and the East Coast Rail Link, a flagship BRI project in Malaysia. The projects in Africa, however, have a different story to tell.

Conclusion

In addition to inherent challenges, Chinese influence over global affairs has been dramatically enhanced by the SOEs. In the process, Chinese SOEs identified and selected partners to ensure that the political and legal factors remain within their control. International projects invested in by SOEs are easily affected by regime change in the destination country, resulting in frequent suspension of investment projects and frustration. As a result, Chinese firms increasingly look for opportunities where power wielding authorities help.

In the 40 years since the opening up of the economy, SOEs have been actively expanding their international operations while promoting their corporate reforms. The rise of the SOEs has been significant in many respects, from reverse engineering learning to personnel training; from establishing Sino-foreign joint ventures in China to facilitating and amplifying foreign direct investment, transnational mergers and acquisitions, integration of foreign resources, technology, and market resources; and transforming a group of enterprises from the production unit under the planned economic system to a strategic organisation in the international market. In the present context, Chinese enterprises face a new pattern of opening up to the outside world. With the BRI in place and concrete bilateral setups (because the BRI is an amplification of bilateral commercial arrangements), the SOEs know their targets. The Chinese State has been paying increasingly close attention to SOEs' challenges and balancing their role by letting private players balance the act.

In the end, one should not be misled by the rising status of Chinese SOEs in *Fortune 500* list because more than 80 per cent of their revenue is still earned at home. The Chinese State has full control over SOE international operations and risks. If the government had not had any control over the SOEs, by this time, they would have lost the game to their competitors. Despite plenty of challenges, SOEs remain the Chinese state's best bet.

NOTES

1. Hongying Wang. 2016. 'A deeper look at China's 'Going Out' Policy' *Centre for International Governance Innovation.* 8 March, https://www.cigionline.org/publications/deeper-look-chinas-going-out-policy (accessed on 24 July 2020).
2. Eunsuk Hong and Laixiang Sun. 2006. 'Dynamics of Internationalization and Outward Investment: Chinese Corporations' Strategies.', *The China Quarterly*, No. 187, September, 610-34.
3. Asif Amin. 2018. 'Belt and Road Initiative Five Years Later' *China Daily.* 10 August, http://www.chinadaily.com.cn/a/201808/10/WS5b6d46f5a310add14f38525f.html (accessed on 26 August 2020).
4. Michael Clarke. 2017. 'The Belt and Road Initiative: China's New Grand Strategy?' *Asia Policy*, No. 24, 71-79.
5. A comprehensive plan to rebuild war-ravaged Europe, prepared by the then US Secretary of State George C. Marshall. The US Congress passed the Economic Cooperation Act in March 1948 and approved funding that would eventually rise to over US$ 12 billion for the rebuilding of Western Europe.
6. Jacques Bughin, James Manyika and Jonathan Woetzel. 2009. 'China and the World: Inside the dynamics of a changing relationship' *Mckinsey Global Institute.* July, https://www.mckinsey.com/-/media/mckinsey/featured%20insights/china/china%20and%20the%20world%20inside%20the%20dynamics%20of%20a%20 changing%20relationship/mgi-china-and-the-world-full-report-june-2019-vf.ashx (accessed on 26 July 2020).
7. Ibid.
8. Zhou Lianxi, and Michael K. Hui. 2003. 'Symbolic Value of Foreign Products in the People's Republic of China'. *Journal of International Marketing*, Vol. 11, No. 2, 37, 39.
9. *Financial Times.* 2020. 'Mike Pompeo renews attack on HSBC as banks walk lines between US and China', 26 August, https://www.ft.com/content/c2e3407f-9d0f-484b-825f-111239c7362b (accessed on 26 November 2020).
10. Ibid.
11. *Gov.cn.* 2017. '19th National Congress of the Communist Party of China', 18-24 October, http://english.www.gov.cn/19thcpccongress/ (accessed on 28 July 2020).
12. *China Central Television (CCTV).* 2019. 'Guowuyuan guozi wei: Dao 2018 niandi yangqi jingwai zichan zong'e 7.6 Wan yi yuan' (国务院国资委：到 2018 年底央企境外资产总额 7.6 万亿元) [State-owned Assets Supervision and Administration Commission of the State Council: By the end of 2018, the total overseas assets of central enterprises is 7.6 trillion yuan], 17 October, http://news.cctv.com/2019/10/17/ARTIZBCpnvYxtj06dE7qZVEe191017.shtml (accessed on 28 July 2020).

13. *People's Daily.* 2018a. 'Guoyou qiye zuoyong buke tidai' (国有企业作用不可替代) [The role of state-owned enterprises is irreplaceable], 29 November, http://www.gov.cn/xinwen/2018-11/29/content_5344296.htm (accessed on 12 August 2020).
14 . Siladitya Ray. 2020. 'US adds 24 Chinese Companies, associated individuals to sanctions list' *Forbes,* 26 August, https://www.forbes.com/sites/siladityaray/2020/08/26/us-adds-24-chinese-companies-associated-individuals-to-sanctions-list/?sh=e84d9673fe2e (accessed on 30 August 2020).
15. David Zweig and Bi Jianhai. 2005. 'China's Global Hunt for Energy', *Foreign Affairs,* September/October, https://www.foreignaffairs.com/articles/asia/2005-09-01/chinas-global-hunt-energy (accessed on 12 August 2020).
16. Scott Kennedy. 2020. 'The biggest but not the strongest: China's place in the Fortune Global 500' *CSIS Blogs.* 18 August, https://www.csis.org/blogs/trustee-china-hand/biggest-not-strongest-chinas-place-fortune-global-500 (accessed on 20 August 2020).
17. Bank of China. 2008. 'Bank of China Listed in Fortune Global 500 for 16 Consecutive Years Since 1989', 7 July, https://www.boc.cn/en/aboutboc/ab2_1/2003/200807/t20080707_1601883.html (accessed on 12 August 2020).
18. J. Stewart Black and Allen J. Morrison. 'The Globe: A Cautionary Tale for Emerging Market Giants', *Harvard Business Review,* September, https://hbr.org/2010/09/the-globe-a-cautionary-tale-for-emerging-market-giants (accessed on 12 August 2020).
19. *CNN Money.* 2012. 'Global 500: Annual Ranking of the World's Largest Corporations', 23 July, https://money.cnn.com/magazines/fortune/global500/2012/countries/US.html?iid=top3 (accessed on 12 August 2020).
20. Fan Feifei. 2018. 'More Chinese firms make Fortune Global 500' *China Daily.* 21 July, http://www.chinadaily.com.cn/a/201807/21/WS5b52735ea310796df4df7ce2.html (accessed on 20 November 2020).
21. Scott Cendrowski. 2015. 'China's Global 500 Companies are bigger than ever – and mostly State-owned Enterprises' *Fortune.* 22 July, https://fortune.com/2015/07/22/china-global-500-government-owned/ (accessed on 18 July 2020).
22. Yan Hang and Wen Zongduo. 2019. 'Belt and Road reached out to the World', *China Daily.* 30 September, https://global.chinadaily.com.cn/a/201909/30/WS5d9160e4a310cf3e 3556e4a0_2.html (accessed on 18 August 2020).
23. Emesto Gallo and Giovanni Biava. 2017. 'A Maritime Silk Road to peaceful seas' *China Daily.* 16 May, https://www.chinadaily.com.cn/opinion/2017-05/16/content_29359861.htm (accessed on 15 August 2020).
24. Norman Sze and Flora Wu. 2015. 'One Belt One Road: The Internationalization of China's SOE's' *Deloitte Perspective.*https://www2.deloitte.com/content/dam/Deloitte/cn/Documents/about-deloitte/dttp/deloitte-cn-dttp-vol5-chapter2-en.pdf (accessed on 18 August 2020).
25. Zhang Jie. 2018. 'Global 500: Chinese companies race ahead' *China Daily.* 20 July, https://www.chinadaily.com.cn/a/201807/20/WS5b518b77a310796df4df7b77.html (accessed on 18 August 2020).
26. *Daily Economic News.* 2018. 'Gaige kaifang 40 nian guoqi chengji liang yan: Wei guojia zan xia 183.5 Wanyi "jiadi" daidong quan shehui fazhan jinbu' (改革开放40年国企成绩亮眼：为国 家攒下183.5万亿"家底" 带动全社会发展进步) [State-owned enterprises have achieved outstanding results in the 40 years of reform and opening up: they have saved 183.5 trillion "family assets" for the country to drive the

development and progress of the whole society], 30 November, https://m.nbd.com.cn/articles/2018-11-30/1277470.html (accessed on 24 July 2020).

27. Geoff Colvin. 2019. 'It's China's World', *Fortune*. 22 July, https://fortune.com/longform/fortune-global-500-china-companies/ (accessed on 16 August 2020).
28. Zheng Yangpeng. 2019. 'In a first, China has more companies on Fortune Global 500 list than the US' *South China Morning Post*. 22 July, https://www.scmp.com/business/companies/article/3019632/first-china-has-more-companies-fortune-global-500-list-us (accessed on 12 August 2020).
29. OECD. 2018. 'China's Belt and Road Initiative in the Global Trade, Investment and Finance Landscape' *OECD Business and Finance Outlook 2018*. https://www.oecd.org/finance/Chinas-Belt-and-Road-Initiative-in-the-global-trade-investment-and-finance-landscape.pdf (accessed on 12 August 2020).
30. OECD. 2008. 'China's Outward Direct Investment', *OECD Investment Policy Reviews: China 2008*, November, https://www.oecd.org/investment/investmentfordevelopment/41792683.pdf (accessed on 12 August 2020).
31. Douglas Ritchie. 2013. 'Chinese Outward Foreign Direct Investment', 4 December, http://www.chinagoabroad.com/en/commentary/chinese-outward-foreign-direct-investment (accessed on 21 October 2020).
32. Meg Rithmire. 2019. 'Going Out or Opting Out? Capital, Political Vulnerability, and the State in China's Outward Investment', *Harvard Business School Working Paper*, No. 20-009, June, 1-40, https://www.hbs.edu/ris/Publication%20Files/20-009_664c9264-f0ee-4e43-acbd-d5da9f08caf1.pdf (accessed on 21 October 2020).
33. *Sina Finance*. 2016b. 'Zhongguo xinbao wei zhong qi jinjun "yidai yilu" cheng qi qian yi meiyuan "baohusan"' (中国信保为中企进军"一带一路"撑起千亿美元"保护伞) [SINOSURE supports Chinese companies to enter the "Belt and Road" "protective umbrella" of 100 billion US dollars], 9 September, https://finance.sina.com.cn/roll/2016-09-09/doc-ifxvukuq4092206.shtml (accessed on 12 August 2020).
34. Cheng Leng, Samuel Shen and Engen Tham, 2019. 'As trade war deepens, a state-owned insurer in China helps soften the blow', *Reuters*, September, https://www.reuters.com/article/us-usa-trade-china-insurers-idUSKCN1VX0L3 (accessed on 12 August 2020).
35. *China Securities Network*. 2018. 'Zhongguo xinbao wei "yidai yilu" jianshe tigong xin dongneng' (中国信保为"一带一路"建设提供新动能) [Sinosure provides new momentum for the "Belt and Road" construction], 7 June, http://www.cs.com.cn/sylm/jsbd/201806/t20180607_5820117.html (accessed on 15 August 2020).
36. David Zweig and Huiyao Wang. 2013. 'Can China Bring Back the Best? The Communist Party Organizes China's Search for Talent', *The China Quarterly*, Vol. 215, September, 590.
37. Chih-shian Liou. 2009. 'Bureaucratic Politics and Overseas Investment by Chinese State-Owned Oil Companies: Illusory Champions', *Asian Survey*, Vol. 49, No. 4, 671.
38. Ministry of Commerce of the People's Republic of China. 2018. 'Zhongguo guoqi "zou chuqu" de guoji hua rencai zhanlue' (中国国企"走出去"的国际化人才战略) [The internationalized talent strategy of Chinese state-owned enterprises "going out"], 29 March, http://fec.mofcom.gov.cn/article/ywzn/xgzx/guonei/201803/20180302725618.shtml (accessed on 11 August 2020).
39. Lance Eliot Brouthers and Kefeng Xu. 2002. 'Product Stereotypes, Strategy and Performance Satisfaction: The Case of Chinese Exporters', *Journal of International Business Studies*, Vol. 33, No. 4, 658.

40. *Yicai.com. (Shanghai First Financial Media Co. Ltd.).* 2017. 'Guozi wei: 47 Jia yangqi canyu yidai yilu jianshe yi jian 1676 ge xiangmu' (国资委：47 家央企参与一带一路建设已建 1676 个项目) [State-owned Assets Supervision and Administration Commission: 47 state-owned enterprises have participated in the construction of the Belt and Road Initiative, 1676 projects have been built], 8 May, https://www.yicai.com/news/5280261.html (accessed on 17 January 2021).
41. Ibid.
42. *Economic Information Daily.* 2019. 'Yangqi gong jian "yidai yilu" zou shen zou shi' (央企共建"一带一路"走深走实) [Central enterprises' joint construction of the "Belt and Road" is deepening and realizing], 18 January, http://dz.jjckb.cn/www/pages/webpage2009/html/2019-01/18/content_50060.htm (accessed on 17 January 2021).
43. *Sina Finance.* 2020b. 'Zhongguo 81 jia yangqi zai "yidai yilu" yanxian chengdan chao 3400 ge xiangmu' (中国81家央企在"一带一路"沿线承担超3400个项目) [China's 81 central enterprises have undertaken over 3,400 projects along the "Belt and Road"], 15 January, https://baijiahao.baidu.com/s?id=1655797097367459931&wfr=spider&for=pc (accessed on 17 January 2021).
44. Ibid.
45. *Financialnews.com.cn.* 2020. '81 Jia yangqi zai "yidai yilu" yanxian chengdan chao 3400 ge xiangmu' (81 家央企在"一带一路"沿线承担超 3400 个项目) [China's 81 central enterprises have undertaken over 3,400 projects along the "Belt and Road"], 15 January, https://www.financialnews.com.cn/cj/hyfx/202001/t20200115_175279.html (accessed on 17 January 2021).
46. *CGTN News.* 2015. 'Ask China: China's largest overseas business park is open to the world', 12 May, https://news.cgtn.com/news/3d6b444d33597a4d/share_p.html (accessed on 28 July 2020).
47. *Xinhua.* 2019b. '2018 Nian woguo duiwai touzi 1298.3 Yi meiyuan baochi pingwen jiankang fazhan' (2018年我国对外投资1298.3亿美元保持平稳健康发展) [my country's foreign investment of US$ 129.83 billion in 2018 maintained steady and healthy development], 16 January, http://www.xinhuanet.com/2019-01/16/c_1123999786.htm (accessed on 24 October 2020).
48. *People's Daily.* 2019. 'Zhongguo qiye "zou chuqu" ge cengmian xu zuo hao juese dingwei' (中国企业"走出去"各层面需做好角色定位) [Chinese companies' "going out" need to be well positioned at all levels], 28 April, http://world.people.com.cn/n1/2019/0428/c1002-31053828.html (accessed on 30 August 2020).
49. Ministry of Commerce of the People's Republic of China. 2020. 'Annual Report on China International Project Contracting 2018-19', 9 May, http://images.mofcom.gov.cn/fec/202005/20200509174729295.pdf (accessed on 20 August 2020).
50. Zhang Xiaozhe. 2020. 'Guozi wei shenru tuijin guoyou zhongdian qiye dui biao shijie yiliu guanli tisheng xingdong' (国资委深入推进国有重点企业对标世界一流管理提升行动) [The State-owned Assets Supervision and Administration Commission of the State-owned Assets Supervision and Administration Commission further promotes the benchmarking of world-class management improvement actions for key state-owned enterprises], June, http://www.gdasc.cn/news_3376.shtml (accessed on 24 August 2020).
51. *Siyiou Foreign Trade Express.* 2019. '2008-2018 Nian shi nian zhongguo waimao jin chukou quanjing tu' (2008-2018 年十年中国外贸进出口全景图) [A panoramic view of China's foreign trade imports and exports from 2008 to 2018], 29 January, https://www.syoseo.com/post/529.html (accessed on 24 August 2020).

52. *Reuters*. 2017. 'China issues rules to curb state firm's overseas investment risks', 2 August, https://www.reuters.com/article/china-investment/china-issues-national-security-rules-on-foreign-investment-idUSKBN28T0FS (accessed on 24 August 2020).
53. State-owned Assets Supervision and Administration Commission (SASAC). 2012. 'Guozi wei: Yangqi yu shijie yiliu qiye reng cunzai jiao da chaju' (国资委：央企与世界一流企业仍存在较大差距) [SASAC: There is still a big gap between state-owned enterprises and world-class enterprises], 25 March, http://www.china.com.cn/news/shanghui/2012-03/25/content_24978872.htm (accessed on 24 August 2020).
54. Moody's Investor Research. 2018. 'Moody's: Rated China SOE's to lower leverage gradually through 2018', 8 January, https://www.moodys.com/research/Moodys-Rated-China-SOEs-to-lower-leverage-gradually-through-2018—PR_377781 (accessed on 24 August 2020).
55. *21st Century Business Herald Economy*. 2020. 'Zhongguo haiwai touzi guojia fengxian pingji baogao (2020) fabu "yidai yilu" diqu touzi fengxian jiao di' (中国海外投资国家风险评级报告（2020）发布"一带一路"地区投资风险较低) [China Overseas Investment Country Risk Rating Report (2020) released the "Belt and Road" region has low investment risk], 1 July, https://www.investgo.cn/article/yw/zctz/202007/494163.html (accessed on 5 December 2020).
56. Steven Yuan, Veronique Yang, Yves-Pierre Willers, David Lee and Ying Luo. 2015. 'Gearing up for the new era of China's outbound M&A' *BCG Publications*. 24 September, https://www.bcg.com/publications/2015/mergers-acquisitions-globalization-gearing-up-for-new-era-chinas-outbound-m-a (accessed on 24 August 2020).
57. Xu Wenjing. 2018. 'Jiyu chuangxin nengli shijiao de minying qiye haiwai binggou jixiao pingjia yanjiu' (基于创新能力视角的民营企业海外并购绩效评价研究) [Research on Performance Evaluation of Private Enterprises' Overseas M&A Based on the Perspective of Innovation Ability], Yanshan University Masters' Thesis, May 2018, https://kns.cnki.net/KCMS/detail/detail.aspx?dbcode=CMFD&filename=1018877596.nh (accessed on 23 July 2020).
58. The minimum efficient scale (MES) is the lowest point on a cost curve at which a company can produce its product at a competitive price. At the MES point, the company can achieve the economies of scale necessary for it to compete effectively in its industry.
59. *People's Daily Online*. 2017. 'Zhonggong zhongyang guanyu jianli guowuyuan xiang quanguo renda changwei hui baogao guoyou zichan guanli qingkuang zhidu de yijian' (中共中央关于建立国务院向全国人大常委会报告国有资产管理情况制度的意见) [Opinions of the Central Committee of the Communist Party of China on Establishing a System for the State Council to Report State-owned Assets Management to the Standing Committee of the National People's Congress], 17 January, http://npc.people.com.cn/big5/n1/2018/0117/c14576-29770394.html (accessed on 16 August 2020).
60. Wendy Leutert. 2016. 'Challenges ahead in China's Reform of State-owned Enterprises', *Asia Policy*, No. 21, January, 83-99, https://www.brookings.edu/wp-content/uploads/2016/07/Wendy-Leutert-Challenges-ahead-in-Chinas-reform-of-stateowned-enterprises.pdf (accessed on 12 August 2020).
61. Herbert Smith Freehills. 2019. 'Zhongguo qiye touzi haiwai jichu sheshiPPP xiangmu: Falu jiaodu de guancha' (中国企业投资海外基础设施PPP项目：法律角度的观察) [Chinese companies invest in overseas infrastructure PPP project: a legal perspective], 1 March, https://www.herbertsmithfreehills.com/file/33151/download?token=2roohJ18 (accessed on 20 August 2020).

Also read *People's Daily Overseas Edition*. 2018. 'Guoyou qiye zuoyong buke tidai' (国有企业作用不可替代) [The role of state-owned enterprises is irreplaceable], 29 November, http://www.gov.cn/xinwen/2018-11/29/content_5344296.htm (accessed on 23 August 2020).

62. The State-owned Assets Supervision and Administration Commission of the State Council (SASAC) released the latest directory of Central State-owned enterprises (SOEs) on June 29.
63. *Chinese Fortune Network* (财富中文网出品). 2020. 'Zhongguo jiaotong jianshe gufen youxian gongsi' (中国交通建设股份有限公司) [China Communications Construction Co. Ltd.], 1 August, http://www.caifuzhongwen.com/fortune500/gongsi/china500/2020/11.htm (accessed on 12 October 2020).
64. *China Construction Enterprise Management Association*. (中国建筑企业管理协会). 2020. '2020 Nian zhongguo jianzhu qiye zonghe shi li 100 qiang bang" long chong fabu' (2020 年中国建筑企业综合实力100强榜隆重发布) [The "Top 100 Chinese Construction Enterprises in Comprehensive Strength in 2020" is released], 31 August, https://www.sohu.com/a/415732171_120646104 (accessed on 6 March 2021).
65. Ibid.
66. Slipped from 91st from the 2018 list.
67. *Fortune*. 2020. 'Global 500: China Communications Construction', 8 October, https://fortune.com/global500/2019/china-communications-construction/ (accessed on 20 November 2020).
68. World Bank. 2011b. 'World Bank Applies 2009 Debarment to China Communications Construction Company Limited for Fraud in Philippines Roads Project', *World Bank Press Release*, 29 July, https://www.worldbank.org/en/news/press-release/2011/07/29/world-bank-applies-2009-debarment-to-china-communications-construction-company-limited-for-fraud-in-philippines-roads-project (accessed on 23 August 2020).
69. Mlex Market Insight. 2017. 'China Communications Construction debarment row brews as concerns grow over Malaysia's award of $12.3bn rail project', 5 January, https://mlexmarketinsight.com/insights-center/editors-picks/area-of-expertise/anti-bribery-and-corruption/china-communications-construction-debarment-row-brews-as-concerns-grow-over-malaysias-award-of-$12.3bn-rail-project (accessed on 12 October 2020).
70. *BJNews*. 2019. 'Zhong jiao jituan zi gongsi 17 nian lao wenti reng wei zhenggai' (中交集团子公司 17 年老问题仍未整改) [The 17-year-old problem of the subsidiary of China Communications Group has not been rectified], 12 August, http://www.bjnews.com.cn/news/2019/08/12/614192.html (accessed on 23 August 2020).
71. State-owned Assets Supervision and Administration Commission (SASAC). 2020b. 'Zhonggong zhongguo jiaotong jianshe jituan youxian gongsi weiyuanhui guanyu xunshi zhenggai jinzhan qingkuang de tongbao' (中共中国交通建设集团有限公司委员会关于巡视整改进展情况的通报) [Announcement of the Committee of the Communist Party of China and China Communications Construction Group Co. Ltd. on the inspection and improvement of the exhibition], 2 April, http://www.sasac.gov.cn/n2588020/n2588072/n2591770/n2591772/c14213702/content.html (accessed on 24 August 2020).
72. Companies listed in the Entity List prevents them from doing business with U.S. companies.

Epilogue

The *March* and *Fate* of State Capitalism and Economic Statecraft

In 2021, China claimed to have accomplished one of the centenary goals, i.e., eradicating extreme rural deprivation. Moreover, it is also celebrating its victory against the COVID-19 pandemic and lays out its 14th Five-Year Plan (14th FYP) (2021-25). The economy is set to record remarkable growth figures, largely due to the spiked government spending, net export boom and rise in investment through public capital outlays (contrary to collapse in private investment). This promises China to manage a GDP growth target of above 6 per cent for 2021.

There are some important corollaries to take away from this scenario. The Chinese state capitalism proudly walks away from mere welfarism and liberal values; it is constantly compared to an alternative idea; meritocracy. China does not want to stop short at creating an economic and political setup with Chinese characteristics alone, but it is developing a comprehensive system as an alternative to the Western system. The state has successfully made such a transition where liberal Western-style ideas and functions have been firmly ruled out. In Xi's China, a 2000-year old history of China's complex imperial bureaucratic system proves more useful when efforts to institutionalise the ideal meritocracy are constantly imbibed as an appropriate standard for evaluating progress—political and economic. As a result, with multiple course corrections, Chinese state capitalism understates the "crisis" and emphasises how liberal and compatible their practice stands vis-à-vis most democratic values and practices in Western-style state systems. China has established that whether or not liberal democracies in the West accept China as a suitable partner or an outlier, China's model is not at a dead end. Moreover, it was the liberal democracies that crossed the fence to forge economic ties with China in the past four decades or so.

In the platitudes creatively crafted through his speeches at Davos (World Economic Forum—January 2017 and January 2021), New York (UN headquarters—September 2015 and September 2020), Biarritz (Group of 7 summit meeting—August 2019), and Saint Petersburg (St. Petersburg International Economic Forum—June 2019), Xi presents a newer and more reformist China than what Deng Xiaoping had visualised, and more nationalist than what Mao Zedong had spelt out. The scheme of state capitalism and economic statecraft even look unprecedented for liberal schools across global disciplines.

Nobody can contest that in today's China, working with the government requires more than just merit and practice. The series of controls administered by Xi and his team in order to navigate the Chinese state through hazards while keeping reforms on course was visible during rallies of political receptions and meetings in March 2021.

The plans, as indicated through the 'two sessions' (两会 *Lianghui*)[1] held in early March 2021, carefully spread over the next fifteen years, aimed at launching the next generation of development blueprint of socialist modernisation. The year 2021 signifies the centenary of the Communist Party of China (CPC), and as a result, this year's *lianghui* was more than a routinely scripted exercise. Among several aspects, the top areas discussed during the two sessions included law-based governance, social security, rural revitalisation, anti-corruption, environment, financial risk prevention, education system, housing, digital lifestyle and social governance. All these plans and strategies signify the pursuance of 'the great rejuvenation of the Chinese nation'. While the CPC would continue to monitor and control the broader game plan, China expects to achieve the status of a "mid-tier developed country" by 2035. In order to accomplish the wide band of expectations from society, the economy, and the political setup, China has to balance control and release the pressure over certain sectors.

As indicated in the beginning of this note, China has been re-framing state capitalism, where it does want to control the way the market influences resources at home and thereby not withdrawing control entirely. State-led capitalism is directed to pursue long-range objectives through the year 2035. This is in tandem with China's roadmap towards the country's second centenary goal of building a fully modern socialist country, ushering China into a new stage of development.

China would increasingly concentrate on deep structural issues such as unleashing domestic demand and raising innovation capacity without succumbing to international pressures, global economic and political fluctuations. Alongside, it would attempt not to let its global, economic and political impact wear off. Over the past decade, China's openness towards foreign brands in the domestic market is witnessing a sharp downfall. It strategises to maintain its global market share intact, i.e., to defend its share of export markets.

Chinese state capitalism *marches* ahead by balancing between a socialist modernisation drive and the pursuance of a 'great power' status. The state deploys long-trusted state enterprises and other agencies to deliver the job meticulously. Given the geopolitical uncertainties, state enterprises walk on a tightrope to infuse growth on the domestic front and insulate the national economy from external shocks. History has proved that every time China stumbled upon serious structural readjustments domestically, global crises or non-performance, the SOEs gathered attention from the leadership. The *march* is arduous as the state's challenges have multiplied, and China is unlikely to loosen up.

The role of private enterprises also needs to be seen from the narratives of *statisation* or the advent of state capitalism. When the economy was opened in 1978, SOEs were the flag-bearers of reforms and had to undergo a stress test and later had to accept 'existence' over 'perishing' through liquidations of assets, large-scale layoffs, and restructuring. Private enterprises, along with SOEs, provided the Chinese state with the much-needed thrust to survive economic pressures. Private banks and private tech players were just adding critical mass and edge to the entire state-driven capitalism. The private firms left the public banks with panic in the coffers. UnionPay, a Chinese financial services corporation and the world's most extensive card network, lost its shine when Alipay was given a freeway to rule e-trade and commerce. In the 2010s, officials gave tech firms such as Alibaba and Tencent just enough space to grow into giants, and in Tencent's case, to create a messaging app, WeChat, which later became an instrument of party control. Alipay was ahead of UnionPay to sign-up for global payment gateways. Alipay and WeChat Pay together constitute over 90 per cent of the payment systems market[2], and state-owned banks are taking this with a pinch of direct rivalry. Digital payments monopolised by private players have routed state-backed China UnionPay, which controls the large majority (90 per cent) of the card-based transactions market.[3] Likewise, private businesses provided every sector of the Chinese economy with much-needed life support alternatives. If private players were not allowed to walk through the narrow political and regulatory alleys, we would not have witnessed the e-commerce boom in China, and the eventual unleashing of consumerism and rise in private spending. In a state-dominated network of businesses, private players rose and gave state capitalism the much-needed facelift. Against such a backdrop, state capitalism in China consists of intricate issues of legacy and political crisis. It is singular in its manifestation (state-driven market and market forces subjected to political scrutiny) and has a linear approach (the state drives growth and not the other way round) towards the complementary relations between politics and economic growth.

In the past few years, the Chinese state noticed that it could no longer function at the mercy of a global network of production bases, supply lines and a web of industrial value-added chains. China attempts to take a long leap into the future and overcome the hurdles by guarding its core economic interests against global rivals. Insulation from hostile foreign forces and overcoming a shortfall in stranglehold technologies (卡脖子技术 *Qia bo zi jishu*) are the most critical bottlenecks for state capitalism. How China defies the sceptics depends upon the control the Party exercises over its economy. If one connects the futuristic plans of the Chinese state to rejuvenate its nation into a 'great nation' and not just a 'superpower', state capitalism has a considerable task left unfinished. Investments in robotics and electric vehicles, pursuing frontier technologies such as quantum computing, semiconductors, and artificial intelligence, dominate in the Chinese state.

Additionally, one cannot discount the infrastructure China continues to invest in to maintain its position as the leading global production hub with the most updated technological marvels at work. Chinese SOEs in transport and communication are expanding China's high-speed rail network. These efforts are planned to turn the Chinese economy agile and resistant to any global economic shocks emitted from political or other risks. The big targets are set, and the Chinese state is ready to deploy all possible force to make its way through. Advancement will ultimately enable the state enterprises and the state-owned economy to play a greater role in China's high-quality development in the future.

Keeping these milestones in sight, SOEs are obviously the natural choice for the Chinese leadership to count upon. But the SOEs keep running into trouble and fail to deliver what the mega plans stipulate. For example, the much-celebrated Ultra-High-Voltage electricity transmission (UHV electricity transmission) network lines are not performing to their optimum. According to China News Agency, many UHV lines are running just a bit more than 60 per cent of their design capacity due to technological limits and conflicts of interest between power generators, grid companies, and the local government.[4] The apathy over non-return of investments in these projects is growing high. To cite another example, the XCMG Group, the country's biggest construction machinery business (world's fourth largest), was rocked by defaults, raising concerns about the wider financial system and the efficacy of performance. Amidst financial crisis and competition, the SOEs are tasked to fulfil steep targets at a breakneck pace. The XCMG blamed "[unreasonable] performance targets" and also alleged "mismanagement by local governments" for defaults.[5] In the wake of the rising influence of central SOEs over sub-national economies, the subnational forces have displayed a heads-on attempt to wield more financial power vis-à-vis the central SOEs in recent years, and the XCMG is the most recent case (November 2020).

Given the duty of SOEs to build superlative projects, this obsession, unless controlled, may lead to a number of problems, especially pertaining to financial sustainability. In this regard, SOEs still have a lot of work to do. This includes the development of its industry sectors and the strategic reorganisation of the state-owned economy, optimisation of layout, structural adjustment, and asset management system reforms focusing on capital management. To record the rising role of SOEs, the 14th FYP plans to pitch the R&D of SOEs at higher levels and envisions that they take up R&D to ensure that the annual growth rate of central state-owned industrial enterprise R&D expenditure significantly exceeds the national average. The plan also mentions improving the preferential tax policies that encourage small and medium-sized technological enterprise innovation.[6]

All analysis and primary empirics indicate that the CPC expects SOEs to remain trustworthy choices for spatial growth. This also requires the Chinese state to be equally liberal to both SOEs and private players. Li Keqiang, in his 2021 Government Work Report, [7]underlines the importance of the private players, but actually, that does not seem to fit into the Chinese state capitalism of any era. On the contrary, the 'overcorrection' administered over the private sector may stifle innovative areas of industry as well as services and, ultimately, economic growth. While SOEs are unwilling to take risks, private players are advised to leap forward and collaborate with state firms in unchartered waters.[8] This dichotomy was once again established when Chinese leaders objected to the Ant Group's US$ 37 billion initial public offering that was scheduled in November 2020. This would have been the world's largest public offering, outshining and miniaturing any equivalent on the mainland. It was none other than President Xi who himself decided to pull the plug. *National rejuvenation* conceptualised by the present leadership does represent the tenets of the old school, which are more Marxist and socialist in nature. The Chinese state relies upon state enterprises in asserting total Party control over the actions, incentives and even the thoughts of entrepreneurs.

Political security (read 'firm and stable political leadership') and development (read 'spin-off of moderate society and well-being') are now seen as inextricably linked, but security trumps all other considerations. In the coming years, risk aversion, albeit economic in its primary form, would continue to focus on identifying and pre-empting political challenges rather than waiting to deal with them once they arise. Undoubtedly, plummeting growth rates across global economies and rising political polarisation and hostility over matters of global interests have been used to illustrate China's 'rightful' position and rise to power. To reinforce his plans to solidify state capitalism and China's weight in global affairs, Xi delivers another masterstroke by exposing 'contractions' in global affairs, in Mao style.

NOTES

1. The *lianghui* (two meetings) refers to two annual plenary meetings - the meeting of the National People's Congress (NPC) and the Chinese People's Political and Consultative Conference (CPPCC). Both meetings are highly scripted affairs meant to display the government's achievements of the past year and introduce plans for the future.
2. CGAP (Consultative Group to Assist the Poor). 2019. 'China: A Digital Payments Revolution' CGAP Research Publications. 1 September, https://www.cgap.org/research/publication/china-digital-payments-revolution (accessed on 15 March 2021).
3. J. P. Morgan. 2019. E-commerce payments trends: China' *2019 J.P. Morgan Global Payment Trends—China e-commerce insights*. 30 August, https://www.jpmorgan.com/merchant-services/insights/reports/china (accessed on 15 March 2021).
4. Bill Bishop. 2021. 'Two Sessions and the "国之大者" the big national priority' *Sinocism*. 11 March, https://sinocism.com/p/two-sessions-and-the-the-big-national (accessed on 26 February 2021).
5. Sun Yu. 2020. 'China state group says official meddling contributed to default wave' *Financial Times*. 20 November, https://www.ft.com/content/157310ef-d404-479e-9566-3503b77d49e9 (accessed on 26 February 2021).
6. *Gov.cn*. 2020. 'Zhonggong zhongyang guanyu zhiding guomin jingji he shehui fazhan di shisi ge wu nian guihua he er ling sanwu nian yuanjing mubiao di jianyi' (中共中央关于制定国民经济和社会发展第十四个五年规划和二〇三五年远景目标的建议) [Proposals of the Central Committee of the Communist Party of China on Formulating the Fourteenth Five-Year Plan for National Economic and Social Development and the Long-term Goals for 2035], 3 November, http://www.gov.cn/zhengce/2020-11/03/content_5556991.htm (accessed on 12 January 2021).
7. *Gov.cn*. 2021. 'Zhengfu gongzuo baogao' (政府工作报告) [Government Working Report], 12 March, http://www.gov.cn/premier/2021-03/12/content_5592671.htm (accessed on 10 March 2021).
8. The Sponge City projects were forced on private players to sign up for and participate in PPP projects along with state firms.

Bibliography

163.com. 2020. 'Zhongguo zui "juewujinyou" de yangqi! Zhangguan 14 wan gongli tielu, ceng zi dai "gongjianfa"' (中国最"绝无仅有"的央企！掌管 14 万公里铁路，曾自带"公检法") [China's most "unique" central enterprise! In charge of 140,000 kilometers of railways, once brought its own "Public Security Law"], 14 September, https://baijiahao.baidu.com/s?id=16775 28086760256102&wfr= spider&for=pc (accessed on 8 December 2020).

21st Century Business Herald Economy. 2020. 'Zhongguo haiwai touzi guojia fengxian pingji baogao (2020)" fabu "yidai yilu" diqu touzi fengxian jiao di' (《中国海外投资国家风险评级报告（2020）》发布 "一带一路"地区投资风险较低) [China Overseas Investment Country Risk Rating Report (2020)" released the "Belt and Road" region has low investment risk], 1 July, https://www.investgo.cn/article/yw/zctz/202007/494163.html (accessed on 5 December 2020).

Amin, Asif. 2018. 'Belt and Road Initiative Five Years Later' *China Daily*. 10 August, http://www.chinadaily.com.cn/a/201808/10/WS5b6d46f5a310add14f38525f.html (accessed on 26 August 2020).

Anaç, Ilayda. 2020. 'Turkey: Cross-Default Clauses in Loan Agreements' *Mondaq*. 13 March, https://www.mondaq.com/turkey/financial-services/ 903472/cross-default-clauses-in-loan-agreements (accessed on 14 March 2021).

Andor, Laszlo and Martin Summers. 1998. *Market Failure: A Guide to Eastern Europe's "Economic Miracle"*. London: Pluto Press.

Anhui Development and Reform Commission (ADRC). 2020. '2020 Nian yi jidu sheng fazhan gaige wei yi shenqing gongkai xinxi mulu' (2020 年一季度省发展改革委依申请公开信息目录) [Catalogue of Information Disclosure by the Provincial Development and Reform Commission in the first quarter of 2020], 6 May, http://fzggw.ah.gov.cn/public/7011/140946821. html (accessed on 17 January 2021).

Anqing City Public Administration Bureau (安庆市公管局). 2015. 'Anqing shi wai huanbei lu gongcheng PPP xiangmu zhongbiao gongshi' (安庆市外环北路工程

PPP 项目中标公示) [Anqing City's Outer Ring North Road Project PPP Project Winning Public Announcement], 24 April, http://aqxxgk. anqing.gov.cn/ show.php?id=361283 (accessed on 9 September 2020).

Asian Development Bank. 2011. 'Engaging Private Sector Companies for Wastewater Management in Asia' *ADB Project Results and Case Studies.* 31 August, https:// www.adb.org/results/country-water-action-engaging-private-sector-companies-wastewater-management-asia (accessed on 20 August 2020).

Asian Development Bank. 2010. 'Sustainable Urban Development in the People's Republic of China - Urban Public Transport—A Case Study of Public–Private Partnerships (PPPs) in Beijing' *ADB Urban Innovations and Best Practices.* November, https://www.adb.org/sites/default/files/publica-tion/27867/urbandev-prc-nov2010-transport-beijing.pdf (accessed on 20 August 2020).

Asian Development Bank. 2005. 'Anhui Environmental Improvement Project for Municipal Wastewater Treatment/Industrial Pollution Abatement' *ADB Performance Evaluation Report.* December http://www.oecd.org/ derec/adb/ 36065250.pdf (accessed on 20 August 2020).

Aslund, Anders. 1985. *Private Enterprise in Eastern Europe.* New York: St. Martin. Quoted in Simon Johnson. 1992. 'Private Business in Eastern Europe', in Olivier Blanchard, Kenneth Froot and Jeffrey Sachs (eds), *Transition in Eastern Europe, Volume 2.* Chicago: University of Chicago Press, 245-292.

Ban yue tan (Bi-Monthly Talks). 1985. No. 4, February 25. Quoted in Harry Harding. 1987. *China's Second Revolution: Reform after Mao.* Washington D.C.: Brookings, 167.

Bank of China. 2008. 'Bank of China Listed in Fortune Global 500 for 16 Consecutive Years Since 1989', 7 July, https://www.boc.cn/en/aboutboc/ ab2_1/2003/200807/ t20080707_1601883.html (accessed on 12 August 2020).

Becker, Jasper. 2000. *The Chinese.* Oxford: Oxford University Press.

Becker, Jasper. 1999. 'Slump in countryside deepens as bubble bursts for rural enterprises' *South China Morning Post.* 27 August. Quoted in Becker, Jasper. 2000. *The Chinese.* New York: Free Press, 79-80.

Beijing Mingshu Data Technology Co., Ltd. (北京明树数据科技有限公司). 2019. 'Beijing ming shu shuju ke zhi youxian gongsi' (明树数据-2019 年全国 PPP 项目市场动态报告) [Mingshu Data-2019 National PPP Project Market Dynamics Report], 3 April, https://max.book118.com/html/2019/0402/ 6025151044002021.shtm (accessed on 9 January 2021).

Bishop, Bill. 2021. 'Two Sessions and the "国之大者" the big national priority' *Sinocism.* 11 March, https://sinocism.com/p/two-sessions-and-the-the-big-national (accessed on 26 February 2021).

BJNews. 2019. 'Zhong jiao jituan zi gongsi 17 nian lao wenti reng wei zhenggai' (中交集团子公司 17 年老问题仍未整改) [The 17-year-old problem of the subsidiary of China Communications Group has not been rectified], 12 August, http:// www.bjnews.com.cn/news/2019/08/12/614192.html (accessed on 23 August 2020).

Black, J. Stewart and Allen J. Morrison. 2010. 'The Globe: A Cautionary Tale for Emerging Market Giants', *Harvard Business Review,* September, https://hbr.org/2010/09/the-globe-a-cautionary-tale-for-emerging-market-giants (accessed on 12 August 2020).

Bloomberg News. 2020. 'A 1,000-Mile Long Clean Energy Artery Is Completed in China', 4 June, https://www.bloomberg.com/news/articles/2020-06-04/china-state-grid-completes-3-17-billion-clean-power-uhv-line (accessed on 23 August 2020).

Blumental, David. 1998. '"Reform" or "Opening"? Reform of China's State-Owned Enterprises and WTO Accession: The Dilemma of Applying GATT to Marketizing Economies', *UCLA Pacific Law Basin Journal,* Vol. 16, No. 2, Spring, 198-262. Quoted in Lan Cao. 2001. 'Chinese Privatization: Between Plan and Market'. *Law and Contemporary Problems,* Vol. 63, No. 4, 13-62.

Boulter, John. 2018. 'China's Supply-side Structural Reform' *Reserve Bank of Australia Bulletin.* December, https://www.rba.gov.au/publications/ bulletin/2018/dec/chinas-supply-side-structural-reform.html (accessed on 24 August 2020).

Brand Finance Global Forum. 2019. 'Global 500: The annual report on the world's most valuable and strongest brands', *Brand Finance*, February, https://www2.deloitte.com/content/dam/Deloitte/cn/Documents/about-deloitte/deloitte-cn-global-500-2019-en-190215.pdf (accessed on 17 July 2020).

Broadman, Harry G. 2001. 'The Business(es) of the Chinese State', *The World Economy*, Vol. 24, No. 7, July, 849-875.

Brouthers, Lance Eliot, and Kefeng Xu. 2002. 'Product Stereotypes, Strategy and Performance Satisfaction: The Case of Chinese Exporters', *Journal of International Business Studies*, Vol. 33, No. 4, 657-77.

Brus, Wlodzimierz. 1979. 'The East European Reforms: What Happened to Them?', *Soviet Studies*, April, Vol. 31, No. 2, 257-267.

Bughin, Jacques, James Manyika and Jonathan Woetzel. 2009. 'China and the World: Inside the dynamics of a changing relationship' *Mckinsey Global Institute.* July, https://www.mckinsey.com/~/media/mckinsey/featured%20 insights/china/china%20and%20the%20world%20inside%20the%20 dynamics%20of%20a%20changing%20relationship/mgi-china-and-the-world-full-report-june-2019-vf.ashx (accessed on 26 July 2020).

Byrd, William A. 1992. *Chinese Industrial Firms under Reform.* Washington D.C: Oxford University Press.

CARNOC.com. 2020. '2019 Nian 2 jia jichang jituan zhuan xiale suoyou jichang de lirun' (2019年2家机场集团赚下了所有机场的利润) [In 2019, 2 airport groups made profits from all airports], 15 July, http://news.carnoc. com/list/538/538595.html (accessed on 17 January 2021).

Cendrowski, Scott. 2015. 'China's Global 500 Companies are bigger than ever – and mostly State-owned Enterprises' *Fortune.* 22 July, https://fortune. com/2015/07/22/china-global-500-government-owned/ (accessed on 18 July 2020).

Central Committee of the Communist Party of China. 2016. '13th Five-Year Plan for Economic and Social Development of The People's Republic of China (2016-20)', Central Compilation and Translation Bureau, 17 March, https://en.ndrc.gov.cn/newsrelease_8232/201612/P020191101481868235378.pdf (accessed on 24 August 2020).

Central Committee of the Communist Party of China. 1984. 'Decision of the Central Committee of the Communist Party of China on Reform of the Economic Structure (adopted by the Twelfth Central Committee of the CPC at its Third Plenum)'. Quoted in David Wen-Wei Chang. 1988. *China Under Deng Xiaoping: Political and Economic Reform.* Basingstoke: The Macmillan Press.

Central Huijin Investment Ltd. 2008. 'Company Profile', http://www. huijininv.cn/huijineng/About_Us/index.shtml (accessed on 17 July 2020).

CGTN News. 2020. '19th CPC Central Committee to hold 5th Plenary Session', 28 September, https://news.cgtn.com/news/2020-09-28/19th-CPC-Central-Committee-to-hold-5th-plenary-session-Oct-26-to-29-U9HMnelwwE/index.html (accessed on 1 October 2020).

CGTN News. 2015. 'Ask China: China's largest overseas business park is open to the world', 12 May, https://news.cgtn.com/news/3d6b444d33597a4d/ share_p.html (accessed on 28 July 2020).

Chai, Joseph C. H. 1997. *China: Transition to a Market Economy.* New York: Oxford University Press.

Chang, C. Y. 1980. 'Overseas Chinese in China's Policy', *The China Quarterly,* Vol. 82, June, 281-303.

Chang, David Wen-Wei. 1988. *China Under Deng Xiaoping: Political and Economic Reform.* Basingstoke: The Macmillan Press.

Chen Jia and Zhong Nan. 2019. 'Debt burden of State-owned enterprises decreases in 2018' *China Daily.* 24 October, https://www.chinadaily. com.cn/a/201910/24/WS5db10417a310cf3e355723dd.html (accessed on 18 July 2020).

Chen Xuewan and Lu Yutong. 2020. 'State Grid's profit collapses on Covid-19 fallout' *Caixin.* 5 August, https://www.caixinglobal.com/2020-08-05/ exclusive-state-grids-profit-collapses-on-covid-19-fallout-101589230.html (accessed on 26 August 2020).

Cheng Yu. 2020. 'Private firms step up innovation investment' *China Daily.* 15 September, https://www.chinadaily.com.cn/a/202009/15/WS5f601a3ba3101ccd0bee0606.html (accessed on 23 September 2020).

Chien - Min Chao and Bruce J. Dickson (eds). 2001. *Remaking the Chinese State: Strategies, Society, and Security.* London: Routledge.

Chih-shian Liou. 2009. 'Bureaucratic Politics and Overseas Investment by Chinese State-Owned Oil Companies: Illusory Champions', *Asian Survey*, Vol. 49, No. 4, 670-90.

China.org. 2002. 'Full Text of Jiang Zemin's Report at the 16th Party Congress', 17 November, http://www.china.org.cn/english/2002/Nov/ 49107.htm (accessed on 12 October 2019).

China.org.cn. 2018. 'Three Step Development Strategy (Reform and Opening Up)', 29 October, http://www.china.org.cn/english/china_key_words/ 2018-10/29/content_68860874.htm (accessed on 24 August 2020).

China Banking News. 2017. 'Mixed-ownership Reforms of 19 State-owned Enterprises Expected to Draw 300bn Yuan', 4 December, http://www. chinabankingnews.com/2017/12/04/mixed-ownership-reforms-19-state-owned-enterprises-expected-draw-300bn-yuan/ (accessed n 15 September 2020).

China Central Television (CCTV). 2019. 'Guowuyuan guozi wei: Dao 2018 niandi yangqi jingwai zichan zong'e 7.6 Wan yi yuan' (国务院国资委：到 2018 年底央企境外资产总额 7.6 万亿元) [State-owned Assets Supervision and Administration Commission of the State Council: By the end of 2018, the total overseas assets of central enterprises are 7.6 trillion yuan], 17 October, http://news.cctv.com/2019/10/17/ARTIZBCpnvYxtj06dE7q ZVEe191017.shtml (accessed on 28 July 2020).

China Construction Enterprise Management Association. (中国建筑企业管理协会). 2020. '2020 Nian zhongguo jianzhu qiye zonghe shi li 100 qiang bang" long chong fabu' (2020 年中国建筑企业综合实力100 强榜 隆重发布) [The "Top 100 Chinese Construction Enterprises in Comprehensive Strength in 2020" is released], 31 August, https://www.sohu.com/a/415732171_ 120646104 (accessed on 6 March 2021).

China Daily. 2020. 'Chinese brands grab half of domestic auto market share', 17 August, https://www.chinadaily.com.cn/a/202008/17/WS5f39f97aa310834817260c21.html (accessed on 20 Aug 2020).

China Daily. 2017a. 'Full Text of Xi Jinping's Report at 19th CPC National Congress', 18 October, https://www.chinadaily.com.cn/china/19thcpc nationalcongress/2017-11/04/content_34115212.htm (accessed on 20 August 2020).

China Daily. 2017b. 'New Normal in Economic Development', 5 October, https://www.chinadaily.com.cn/china/19thcpcnationalcongress/2017-10/ 05/content_32869258.htm (accessed on 2 August 2020).

China Daily. 2014. 'China names Six SOEs for pilot reforms', 15 July, http://www.chinadaily.com.cn/business/2014-07/15/content_17787248. htm (accessed on 23 September 2020).

China Daily. 2010. 'Sanjia wenhua "yangqi" chengli wei shou pi zhuanzhi de zhongyang wenhua qiye' (三家文化"央企"成立 为首批转制的中央文化企业) [Three Cultural Central Enterprise were established as the first batch of central cultural enterprises to be transformed], 11 August, http://www. chinadaily.com.cn/dfpd/whtzgg/2010-08/11/content_11137762.htm (accessed on 22 July 2020).

China Economic Weekly (中国经济周刊). 2016. 'Zhongguo PPP shifan xiangmu xunli] anqing shi wai huanbei lu gongcheng xiangmu:PPP xiangmu shi yi zhong touzi xingwei, bushi jiandan "zhao huo er gan"' (中国 PPP 示范项目巡礼]安庆市外环北路工程项目：PPP 项目是一种投资行为，不是简单"找活儿干") [China PPP Demonstration Project Tour] Anqing Outer Ring North Road Project: PPP project is an investment behaviour, not simply "an act of work"], 15 August, http://finance.sina.com.cn/roll/2016-08-15/doc-ifxuxnak0328418.shtml?cre=financepagepc &mod=f&loc=4&r=9&doct=0&rfunc=100 (accessed on 9 September 2020).

China Enterprise News. 2016. 'Zhongguo jiancai jituan youxian gongsi xuanbu chengli' (中国建材集团有限公司宣布成立) [China National Building Materials Group Co., Ltd. announced its establishment], 30 August, https://money.163.com/16/0830/00/BVM54OA9002580S6.html (accessed on 8 December 2020).

China National Machinery Industry Corporation (SINOMACH). 2013. 'Zhongguo er chong yu guo ji jituan shishi lianhe chongzu' (中国二重与国机集团实施联合重组) [China Erzhong and SINOMACH to carry out the reorganizsation], 25 July, http://www.sinomach.com.cn/xwzx/zgsdt/2013 zgsdt/201412/t20141218_41384.html (accessed on 11 March 2021).

China Net. 2020. '2020 Nian zhongguo fangdichan ye zonghe shili 100 qiang bang" long chong fabu' (2020年中国房地产业综合实力 100 强榜》隆重发布) [The latest "2020 China Real Estate Industry Top 100 Comprehensive Strength List" is released], 11 September, http://china.qianlong.com/ 2020/0911/4712160.shtml (accessed on 6 March 2021).

China Net Finance. 2018. 'Jishi jiuzheng PPP fazhan zhong de mohu renshi' (及时纠正 PPP 发展中的模糊认识) [Timely Correction of Ambiguous Understanding in PPP Development], 9 August, https://finance. ifeng.com/c/7fE0QH83DSL (accessed on 6 March 2021).

China Quality News Network. 2020. 'Shou lun zhejiang chuangzao li qiye bai qiang zuoci pai ding zhe 100 jia qi ye yongyou quan sheng 18.6%Youxiao faming zhuanli' (首轮浙江创造力企业百强座次排定 这 100 家企业拥有全省 18.6%有效发明专利) [The first round of ranking of the top 100 creative enterprises in Zhejiang. These 100 enterprises have 18.6% of valid invention patents in the province], 22 April, http://www.cqn.com.cn/zj/content/2020-04/22/content_8548584.htm (accessed on 24 August 2020).

China Securities Network. 2018. 'Zhongguo xinbao wei "yidai yilu" jianshe tigong xin dongneng' (中国信保为"一带一路"建设提供新动能) [Sinosure provides new momentum for the "Belt and Road" construction], 7 June, http://www.cs.com.cn/sylm/jsbd/201806/t20180607_5820117.html (accessed on 15 August 2020).

China Social Science Research Network. 2018. '"Zhongguo guojia zichan fuzhai biao 2018" zaijing fabu' ("中国国家资产负债表 2018" 在京发布) ["China National Balance Sheet 2018" released in Beijing], 27 December, http://ex.cssn.cn/ts/bwdj/201812/t20181227_4801366.shtml (accessed on 24 August 2020).

China Tendering & Bidding Association. 2016. 'PPP xiangmu zhaobiao shehui ziben zige shencha de falu yingyong fenxi' (PPP 项目招标社会资本资格审查的法律应用) [Analysis on the Legal Application of Social Capital Qualification Examination for PPP Project Bidding], 24 March, http://www.ctba.org.cn/list_show.jsp?record_id=241727) (accessed on 15 August 2020).

Chinese Fortune Network (财富中文网出品). 2020. 'Zhongguo jiaotong jianshe gufen youxian gongsi' (中国交通建设股份有限公司) [China Communications Construction Co., Ltd.], 1 August, http://www.caifuzhongwen.com/fortune500/gongsi/china500/2020/11.htm (accessed on 12 October 2020).

Clarke, Michael. 2017. 'The Belt and Road Initiative: China's New Grand Strategy?', *Asia Policy*, No. 24, 71-79.

cnafc.com. 2019. 'Dazao "yi zong, yi fen, si de" jiagou, zhuli jituan shixian "san ge pao ying" ——relie zhuhe zhongyuan hai cai beijing fen gongsi zhengshi kaiye' (打造"一总、一分、四地" 架构，助力集团实现"三个跑赢" ——热烈祝贺中远海财北 京分公司正式开业) [Create a structure of "one headquarters, one branch, and four locations" to help the group realize the "three outperforms" —— Congratulations on the official opening of COSCO SHIPPING Beijing Branch], 4 June, http://www.cnafc.org/cnafc/front/detail.action?id=0FF8C1EDDCF84C6E8F69B8B0A101341C (accessed on 12 August 2020).

Cousin, Violaine. 2007. *Banking in China.* London: Palgrave Macmillan.

CNN Money. 2012. 'Global 500: Annual Ranking of the World's Largest Corporations', 23 July, https://money.cnn.com/magazines/fortune/global500/2012/countries/US.html?iid=top3 (accessed on 12 August 2020).

CNR.CN. 2018. 'Zhejiang sheng guoyou qiye zichan 10.44 Wan yi ju quanguo di er' (浙江省国有企业资产 10.44 万亿 居全国第二) [The assets of state-owned enterprises in Zhejiang Province rank second in the country at 10.44 trillion yuan], 13 December, http://zj.cnr.cn/zjyw/20181213/t20181213_524448854.shtml (accessed on 15 November 2020).

CNR News. 2019. '2018 Nian yangqi shixian lirun zong'e 1.7 Wan yi yuan chuang lishi zui hao shuiping' (2018 年央企实现利润总额 1.7 万亿元 创历史最好水平) [In 2018, the total profit of central enterprises reached 1.7 trillion yuan, the best level in history], 17 January, http://news.cnr.cn/native/gd/20190117/t20190117_524485815.shtml (accessed on 16 July 2020).

Colvin, Geoff. 2019. 'It's China's World' *Fortune.* 22 July, https://fortune.com/longform/fortune-global-500-china-companies/ (accessed on 16 August 2020).

Daily Economic News. 2018. 'Gaige kaifang 40 nian guoqi chengji liang yan: Wei guojia zan xia 183.5 Wanyi "jiadi" daidong quan shehui fazhan jinbu' (改革开放40年国企成绩亮眼：为国家攒下 183.5 万亿"家底" 带动全社会发展进步) [State-owned enterprises have achieved outstanding results in the 40 years of reform and opening up: they have saved 183.5 trillion "family assets" for the country to drive the development and progress of the whole society], 30 November, https://m.nbd.com.cn/articles/2018-11-30/1277470.html (accessed on 24 July 2020).

Deng Xiaoping. 1984. 'Make a success of Special Economic Zones and Open more cities to the outside world', in *Selected works of Deng Xiaoping Vol. II*, 24 February, www.english.peoplesdaily.com.cn (accessed on 2 July 2020).

Deng Xiaoping. 1982. 'Opening Speech at the Twelfth National Congress of the Communist Party of China', in *Selected Works of Deng Xiaoping Vol. III*, 1 September, www.english.peoplesdaily.com.cn. (accessed on 24 July 2020).

Deng Xiaoping. 1979a. 'We Can Develop a Market Economy under Socialism', *Selected Works of Deng Xiaoping Vol. II*, 26 November, www.english.peoplesdaily.com.cn (accessed on 24 July 2020).

Deng Xiaoping. 1979b. 'Some Comments on Economic Work', in *Selected Works of Deng Xiaoping Vol. II*, 4 October, www.english.peoplesdaily.com.cn (accessed on 24 July 2020).

Deng Xiaoping. 1979c. 'Uphold the Four Cardinal Principles', in *Selected Works of Deng Xiaoping Vol. II*, 30 March, www.english.peoplesdaily.com.cn (accessed on 8 July 2020).

D'Entreves, Maurizio Passerin and Seyla Benhabib. 1996. *Habermas and the Unfinished Project of Modernity*. Cambridge: Polity Press.

Dernberger, Robert, F. 1984. 'China's New Economic Development: Problems and Prospects', in Ginsberg, Norton and Bernard Lalor (eds), *China: The 80s Era.* Boulder: Westview Press.

Dittmer, Lowell. 1994. *China Under Reform*. New York: Routledge.

Dong Zhang and Owen Freestone. 2013. 'China's Unfinished State-owned Enterprise Reforms', *Economic Roundup,* The Treasury, Australian Government, No. 2, December, 79-102.

Dorn, James. 2000. 'State-owned Enterprises continue to hinder Chinese growth' *Japan Times.* 21 September, https://www.cato.org/commentary/state-owned-enterprises-continue-hinder-chinese-growth (accessed on 24 July 2020).

Eastmoney.com. 2019. 'Zhejiang sheng shichang jianguan ju 2018 niandu sheng shu qiye nianbao qingkuang fenxi baogao: Sheng shu qiye jingji fazhan "touyan" zuoyong mingxian' (浙江省市场监管局 2018 年度省属企业年报情况分析报告：省属企业经济发展"头雁"作 用明显) [Analysis of Zhejiang Provincial Market Supervision Bureau's 2018 Annual Report - Provincial Enterprises: The "head goose" role of Provincial Enterprises in Economic Development], 6 September, http://finance.eastmoney.com/a/201909061230563245.html (accessed on 14 December 2020).

Eckholm, Erik. 1998. 'New China Leader Promises Reform for Every Sector' *New York Times.* 20 March, https://www.nytimes.com/1998/03/20/world/new-china-leader-promises-reforms-for-every-sector.html (accessed on 24 July 2020).

Economic Information Daily. 2019. 'Yangqi gong jian "yidai yilu" zou shen zou shi' (央企共建"一带一路"走深走实) [Central enterprises' joint construction of the "Belt and Road" is deepening and realizing], 18 January, http://dz.jjckb.cn/www/pages/webpage2009/html/2019-01/18/content_50060.htm (accessed on 17 January 2021).

Economic Research Center of Academic School of Chinese Communist Party. 1996. *Research of Reforming the Small SOEs*. Beijing: Economic Science Press.

Economy, Elizabeth C. 1999. 'Reforming China', *Survival,* Vol. 41, No. 3, Autumn, 21-42.

Embassy of the PRC in the USA. 2000. 'China, EU sign bilateral agreement on China's WTO entry', 19 May, http://www.china-embassy.org/eng/zt/wto/t36884.htm (accessed on 26 July 2020).

Energy Iceberg. 2019. 'Severe Investment Cuts of the Chinese Grid Companies: Battery Energy Storage the First Casualty', 10 December, https://energyiceberg.com/chinese-grids-cut-investment-hurting-battery-storage/ (accessed on 23 August 2020).

English.gov.cn. 2018. 'Pilot reform of State-owned capital investing, operating companies', 30 July, http://english.www.gov.cn/policies/latest_releases/2018/07/30/content_281476242418612.htm (accessed on 15 September 2020).

EQ International. 2020. 'China Develops $26bn Ultra High Voltage Electrical Grids to Stimulate Economic Recovery', June 2, https://www.eqmagpro.com/china-develops-26bn-ultra-high-voltage-electrical-grids-to-stimulate-economic-recovery/ (accessed on 15 November 2020).

European Union. 2020. 'Improving EU Access to National and Regional Financial Incentives for Innovation in China', December, http://chinainnovation funding.eu/rd-innovation-funding-china-project/? (accessed on 2 February 2021).

Fan Feifei. 2018. 'More Chinese firms make Fortune Global 500' *China Daily*. 21 July, http://www.chinadaily.com.cn/a/201807/21/WS5b52735ea310796df4df7ce2.html (accessed on 20 November 2020).

Fang Liufang. 1995. 'China's Corporatization Experiment', *Duke Journal of Comparative and International Law*, Vol.5, 149-269.

Fei Xiaotong. 1988. *Chinese Village Close-Up*. Beijing: New World Press. Quoted in David Wen-Wei Chang. 1988. *China Under Deng Xiaoping: Political and Economic Reform.* Basingstoke: The Macmillan Press.

Fenghuang Wang Caijing. 2014. 'Guoziwei 'si xiang gaige' shidian neirong' (国资委'四项改革'试点内容) [SASAC 'four reform' pilot content]. 15 July, http://finance.ifeng.com/a/20140715/12725003_0.shtml (accessed on 23 September 2020).

Fewsmith, Joseph. 1999. 'China and the WTO: The Politics behind the Agreement', *The National Bureau of Asian Research*, November, https://www.iatp.org/sites/default/files/China_and_the_WTO_The_Politics_Behind_the_Agre.htm) (accessed on 26 July 2020).

Fewsmith, Joseph. 1994. *Dilemmas of Reform in China: Political Conflict and Economic Debate.* New York: M. E. Sharpe.

Field, Robert Michael. 1983. 'Slow Growth of Labour Productivity in Chinese Industry, 1952-81', *The China Quarterly*, Vol. 96, December, 641-64.

Financialnews.com.cn. 2020. '81 Jia yangqi zai "yidai yilu" yanxian chengdan chao 3400 ge xiangmu' (81家央企在"一带一路"沿线承担超 3400 个项目) [China's 81 central enterprises have undertaken over 3,400 projects along the "Belt and Road"], 15 January, https://www.financialnews.com.cn/cj/hyfx/202001/t20200115_175279.html (accessed on 17 January 2021).

Financial Times. 2020. 'Mike Pompeo renews attack on HSBC as banks walk lines between US and China', 26 August, https://www.ft.com/content/c2e3407f-9d0f-484b-825f-111239c7362b (accessed on 26 November 2020).

First Finance. 2017. 'Min zi PPP canyu du shuang jiang, guowuyuan juexin rang huibao geng heli' (民资 PPP 参与度双降, 国务院决心让回报更合理) [The participation rate of private PPP has dropped, and the State Council is determined to make the return more reasonable], 19 September, https://m.21jingji.com/article/20170919/herald/dfa45bf8690143 dcdde77763f4efb107.html (accessed on 9 January 2021).

Fischer, Stanley. 1994. 'Russia and the Soviet Union: Then and Now', in Olivier Blanchard, Kenneth Froot and Jeffrey Sachs (eds), *Transition in Eastern Europe, Volume 1.* Chicago: University of Chicago Press, 221-58.

FitchRatings. 2020. 'What Investors Want to Know: SGCC' *Special Report.* 9 August, https://www.fitchratings.com/research/corporate-finance/what-investors-want-to-know-sgcc-09-08-2020 (accessed on 8 March 2021).

Fortune. 2020. 'Global 500: China Communications Construction', 8 October, https://fortune.com/global500/2019/china-communications-construction/ (accessed on 20 November 2020).

Freehills, Herbert Smith. 2020. '"New Infrastructures": China's Massive Stimulus Measures after COVID-19 Outbreak - Part 7: Ultra-High Voltage' *Lexology.* 26 August, https://www.lexology.com/library/detail.aspx?g=555cad5d-0ee7-473c-a389-0c78a18f929a (accessed on 30 August 2020).

Freehills, Herbert Smith. 2019. 'Zhongguo qiye touzi haiwai jichu sheshi PPP xiangmu: Falu jiaodu de guancha' (中国企业投资海外基础设施 PPP 项目：法律角度的观察) [Chinese companies invest in overseas infrastructure PPP project: a legal perspective], 1 March, https://www.herbertsmithfreehills.com/file/33151/download?token=2roohJ18 (accessed on 20 August 2020).

Fung, Ben, Jason George, Stefan Hohl and Guonan Ma. 2011. 'Public asset management companies in East Asia Case studies 1', *Financial Stability Institute (FSI) Papers*, Bank for International Settlements, https://www.bis.org/fsi/publications.htm?m=1%7C17%7C161 (accessed on 21 August 2019).

Gabriel, Satya J. 1998. 'Restructuring State-owned Enterprises in China', https://www.mtholyoke.edu/courses/sgabriel/soe.htm (accessed on 22 July 2020).

Galkin, Philipp, Dongmei Chen and Junyuang Ke. 2020. 'China's Energy Investment Through the Lens of the Belt and Road Initiative' *King Abdullah Petroleum Studies and Research Center Papers.* 12 January, https://www.kapsarc.org/research/publications/chinas-energy-investment-through-the-lens-of-the-belt-and-road-initiative/ (accessed on 12 August 2020).

Gallo, Emesto and Giovanni Biava. 2017. 'A Maritime Silk Road to peaceful seas' *China Daily.* 16 May, https://www.chinadaily.com.cn/opinion/2017-05/16/content_29359861.htm (accessed on 15 August 2020).

Garfinkel, Harold. 1967. *Studies in Ethnomethodology.* Englewoods Cliffs, NJ: Prentice Hall.

Garnaut, Ross, Ligang Song and Cai Fang (eds). 2018. *China's 40 Years of Reform and Development: 1978–2018.* Acton ACT, Australia: ANU Press.

Geis, John P. and Blaine Holt. 2009. '"Harmonious Society": Rise of the New China', *Strategic Studies Quarterly*, Vol. 3, No. 4, 75-94.

Gerstel, Dylan. 2018. 'It's a (Debt) Trap! Managing China-IMF Cooperation Across the Belt and Road', *New Perspectives in Foreign Policy,* Centre for Strategic and International Studies, No. 16, https://www.csis.org/npfp/its-debt-trap-managing-china-imf-cooperation-across-belt-and-road (accessed on 26 August 2020).

Gill, Chriss. 2020. 'China's bureaucrats tussle over control of the treasury' *Asia Financial Times.* 3 September, https://www.asiatimesfinancial.com/china-s-bureaucrats-tussle-over-control-of-the-treasury (accessed on 9 September 2020).

Global Times. 2019. 'Party Leadership helps improve corporate governance', 26 May, https://www.globaltimes.cn/content/1151631.shtml (accessed on 4 August 2020).

Gov.cn. 2021. 'Zhengfu gongzuo baogao' (政府工作报告) [Government Working Report], 12 March, http://www.gov.cn/premier/2021-03/12/content_5592671.htm (accessed on 10 March 2021).

Gov.cn. 2020. 'Zhonggong zhongyang guanyu zhiding guomin jingji he shehui fazhan di shisi ge wu nian guihua he er ling sanwu nian yuanjing mubiao di jianyi' (中共中央关于制定国民经济和社会发展第十四个五年规划和二〇三五年远景目标的建议) [Proposals of the Central Committee of the Communist Party of China on Formulating the Fourteenth Five-Year Plan for National Economic and Social Development and the Long-term Goals for 2035], 3 November, http://www.gov.cn/zhengce/2020-11/03/content_5556991.htm (accessed on 12 January 2021).

Gov.cn. 2017. '19th National Congress of the Communist Party of China', 18-24 October, http://english.www.gov.cn/19thcpccongress/ (accessed on 28 July 2020).

Gov.cn. 2006. 'Shiwu qijian guoyou qiye gufenzhi gaige qude zhongda jinzhan' (十五期间国有企业股份制改革取得重大进展) [Significant progress has been made in state-owned enterprise shareholding reform during the Tenth Five-Year Plan], 24 October, http://www.gov.cn:8080/jrzg/2006-01/06/content_149150.htm (accessed on 12 October 2019).

Gov.cn. 2003. 'Guowuyuan guoyou zichan jiandu guanli weiyuanhui zhuyao zhize nei she jigou he renyuan bianzhi guiding' (国务院国有资产监督管理委员会主要职责内设机构和人员编制规定") [State-owned Assets Supervision and Administration Commission of the State Council, Main Responsibilities, Internal Institutions and Staffing Regulations], 15 April, http://www.gov.cn/zhengce/content/2005-08/12/content_8164.htm (accessed on 12 October 2019).

Gowan, Peter. 1995. 'Neo-Liberal Theory and Practice for Eastern Europe', *New Left Review*, No. 213, September/October, 1-60.

Guangdong Provincial Development and Reform Commission (GPDRC). 2019. 'Guangdong sheng fazhan gaige wei guanyu xiada guangdong sheng 2019 nian zhongdian jianshe xiangmu jihua de tongzhi' (广东省发展改革委关于下达广东省 2019 年重点建设项目计划的通知) [Notice of Guangdong Provincial Development and Reform Commission on Issuing Guangdong Province's 2019

Key Construction Project Plans], 27 March, http://drc.gd.gov.cn/ywtz/content/post_2264242.html (accessed on 17 January 2021).

Guluzade, Amir. 2019. 'The role of China's State-owned companies explained' *World Economic Forum.* 7 May, https://www.weforum.org/agenda/2019/05/why-chinas-state-owned-companies-still-have-a-key-role-to-play/ (accessed on 20 July 2020).

Guojingmao SME (国精贸中小企业). 2003. 'Interim Provisions on the Standards for Small and Medium-sized Enterprises', National Economic and Trade Commission, the National Development Planning Commission, Ministry of Finance and National Bureau of Statistics. 19 February, http://www.lawinfochina.com/display.aspx?lib=law&id=2636&CGid= (accessed on 15 July 2020).

Hangzhou.gov.cn. 2020. '"Shisiwu" qijian hangzhou jiang mai ru shijie yiliu dianwang hanglie' ("十四五"期间 杭州将迈入世界一流电网行列) [During the "14th Five-Year Plan" period, Hangzhou will enter the ranks of world-class power grids], 27 December, http://www.hangzhou.gov.cn/art/2020/12/27/art_812262_59023317.html (accessed on 17 January 2021).

Hangzhou.gov.cn. 2015. 'Hangzhou shi zhuanli zhuanxiang zijin guanli banfa de tongzhi' (杭州市专利专项资金管理办法的通知) [Notice of the General Office of the Hangzhou Municipal People's Government on Issuing the Measures for the Administration of Hangzhou Patent Special Funds], 19 October, http://www.hangzhou.gov.cn/art/2015/10/19/art_1256295_7049377.html (accessed on 17 December 2020).

Hangzhou Daily. 2021. 'Ji guonei shouzuo luse hang zhan lou hou, hangzhou jichang zai jianxin lou zai huo luse jianzhu pingjia biaozhi' (继国内首座绿色航站楼后, 杭州机场在建新楼再获绿色建筑评价标识) [Following the first domestic green terminal building, Hangzhou Airport's new building under construction again received the green building evaluation mark], 4 February, https://baijiahao.baidu.com/s?id=1690758686150271142&wfr=spider&for=pc (accessed on 5 February 2021).

Hangzhou Municipal Science and Technology Bureau. 2019. 'Guanyu gongbu 2019 niandu hangzhou shi "115" yinru guo (jing) wai zhili jihua xiangmu jihua de tongzhi' (关于公布 2019 年度杭州市"115"引入国（境）外智力计划项目计划的通知) [Notice on the announcement of the 2019 Hangzhou "115" project plan for the introduction of foreign (overseas) intelligence], 6 December, http://kj.hangzhou.gov.cn/art/2019/12/6/art_1693961_40803586.html (accessed on 14 December 2020) (accessed on 14 December 2020).

Harding, Harry. 1987. *China's Second Revolution: Reform after Mao.* Washington D.C.: Brookings Institution Press.

Hexun.com. 2019. 'Yinhang fa de lishi yu weilai' (银行法的历史与未来) [The history and future of banking law], 4 November, https://bank.hexun.com/2019-11-04/199126104.html?from=rss (accessed on 6 August 2020).

HLJNews.cn. 2020. 'Guoqi fuzhai zong'e 94 wan yi yuan fuzhai lu da 65.6% Ruhe qu ganggan?' (国企负债总额 94 万亿元负债率达 65.6% 如何去杠杆?) [Firmly grasp the initiative of economic work], 16 December, http://www.hljnews.cn/article/252/212682.html (accessed on 17 January 2021).

Hong, Eunsuk and Laixiang Sun. 2006. 'Dynamics of Internationalization and Outward Investment: Chinese Corporations' Strategies', *The China Quarterly*, No. 187, September, 610-34.

Hongying Wang. 2016. 'A deeper look at China's 'Going Out' Policy', *Centre for International Governance Innovation.* 8 March, https://www.cigionline.org/publications/deeper-look-chinas-going-out-policy (accessed on 24 July 2020).

Hou Qingyang. 2010. 'New steel firm melting pot of consolidation', *China Daily.* 25 February, http://www.chinadaily.com.cn/bizchina//2010-02/25/content_9501486.htm (accessed on 27 August 2020).

Hsu, Immanuel C.Y. 1983. *The Rise of Modern China.* New York: Oxford University Press.

Huang Yiping. 1999. 'State-owned enterprise reform' in Ross Garnaut, and Ligang Song (eds), *China: Twenty Years of Reform.* Canberra: Asia Pacific Press. 95-116.

Hu Bangding. 1990. *Zhongguo wujia nianjian 1990 (China Price Yearbook 1989).* Beijing: China Price Publishing House. Quoted in Joseph C. H. Chai. 1997. *China: Transition to a Market Economy.* New York: Oxford University Press, 53.

Hu Bangding. 1989. *Zhongguo wujia nianjian 1989 (China Price Yearbook 1989).* Beijing: China Price Publishing House. Quoted in Joseph C. H. Chai. 1997. *China: Transition to a Market Economy.* New York: Oxford University Press, 53.

Hubbard, Paul. 2014. 'SOEs are the Champions' *A Natural History of Chinese State-owned Enterprises.* 8 September, https://chinasoe.wordpress.com/tag/sasac/ (accessed on 14 July 2020).

Hui Zhang. 2015. *China's SOE Reforms in the 2000 and 2010s,* Unpublished Post-Graduate Thesis, University of British Columbia.

Hunan.gov.cn. 2020. 'Statistical Communiqué on Hunan's Economic and Social Development in 2019', 24 April, http://www.enghunan.gov.cn/hneng/Business/EconomyCommunique/202004/t20200423_11969012.html (accessed on 17 January 2021).

Innovation Centre Denmark. 2013. 'Smart Grid in China: A R&D Perspective', July, http://assets.fiercemarkets.net/public/sites/energy/reports/chinasgreport.pdf (accessed on 23 August 2020).

Inotai, Andras. 1996. 'Europe: Challenges and Risks at the Turn of the Century — An Economic Approach from Central Europe', *Perspectives,* No. 6-7, 119-28.

International Energy Association (IEA). 2020. 'World Energy Investment', May, https://sun-connect-news.org/fileadmin/DATEIEN/Dateien/New/WEI2020.pdf (accessed on 17 January 2021).

Jefferson, Gary H. and Thomas G. Rawski. 1994. 'Enterprise Reform in Chinese Industry', *Journal of Economic Perspectives,* Vol. 8, No. 2, 47-70.

Ji Wei. 1999. *The Great Tendency of the Chinese SOEs,* Unpublished Master's Thesis, TungHai University.

Johnson, Simon. 1994. 'Private Business in Eastern Europe', in Olivier Blanchard,

Kenneth Froot, Lan Cao (eds), *Transition in Eastern Europe, Volume 2*. Chicago: University of Chicago Press, 245-292.

JonesDay. 2008. 'Chinese Local Governments Fight for Their Share of Tax Revenue', March, https://www.jonesday.com/en/insights/2008/03/chinese-local-governments-fight-for-their-share-of-tax-revenue (accessed on 15 November 2020).

Kam Wing Chan, J. Vernon Henderson and Kai Yuan Tsui. 2008. 'Spatial Dimensions of Chinese Economic Development' in Loren Brandt and Thomas Rawski (eds), *China's Great Economic Transformation*. Cambridge: Cambridge University Press, 776-828.

Kegley (Jr.), Charles W. and Eugene R. Wittcopf. 1993. *World Politics: Trend and Transformation*. New York: St. Martin's Press.

Kennedy, Scott. 2020. 'The biggest but not the strongest: China's place in the Fortune Global 500' *CSIS Blogs*. 18 August, https://www.csis.org/blogs/trustee-china-hand/biggest-not-strongest-chinas-place-fortune-global-500 (accessed on 20 August 2020).

Kirby, William C. 1990. 'Continuity and Change in Modern China: Economic Planning on the Mainland and on Taiwan, 1943-1958', *The Australian Journal of Chinese Affairs*, No. 24, July, 121-141.

Kizilyalli, Husnu. 1998. *Economics of Transition: A New Methodology for Transforming a Socialist Economy to a Market-led Economy*. New York: Routledge.

Knight, John and Sai Ding. 2010. 'Why does China invest so much?', *Asian Economic Papers*, MIT Press, Vol. 9, No. 3, Fall, 87-117.

Koo, Anthony Y. C. 1990. 'The Contract Responsibility System: Transition from a Planned to a Market Economy', *Economic Development and Cultural Change*, Vol. 38, No. 4, July, 797-820.

Kornai., Janos. 1986. 'The Hungarian Reform Process: Visions, Hopes and Reality', *Journal of Economic Literature*, Vol. 24, December, 1687-1737.

Kovacs, Janos Matyas and Martori Tardos (eds). 1992. *Reform and Transformation in Eastern Europe: Soviet type Economies on the Threshold of Change*. New York: Routledge.

Kumiko Okazaki. 2007. 'Banking System Reform in China', *RAND Occasional Papers*, No. 194, 1-73.

Lam, W. Raphael, Markus Rodlauer and Alfred Schipke. 2017. 'State-Owned Enterprise Reform', in W. Raphael Lam, Markus Rodlauer and Alfred Schipke, (eds), *Modernizing China: Investing in Soft Infrastructure. USA: International Monetary Fund*, https://www.elibrary.imf.org/view/IMF071/23209-9781513539942/23209978151353 9942/ch11.xml?language=en&redirect= true#Rch11tab3 (accessed on 21 August 2019).

Lardy, Nicholas R. 2014. *Markets over Mao: The Rise of Private Business in China*. Washington D.C.: Peterson Institute Press.

Lardy, Nicholas R. 1998. *China's Unfinished Economic Revolution.* Washington D.C.: Brookings Institution.

Lawrence, Susan V. 1999. 'Reality-Check: At least Premier Zhu isn't hiding China's problems', *Far Eastern Economic Review,* Vol. 62, No. 11, March, 26.

Leutert, Wendy. 2016. 'Challenges ahead in China's Reform of State-owned Enterprises', *Asia Policy,* No.21, January, 83-99, https://www.brookings.edu/wp-content/uploads/2016/07/Wendy-Leutert-Challenges-ahead-in-Chinas-reform-of-stateowned-enterprises.pdf (accessed on 12 August 2020).

Li Peng. 1991. 'The Current Economic Situation and the Issues of further Improving State-owned Large and Medium-sized Enterprises (CCP Committee Work Meeting, 23rd September)', reproduced by *China Report,* Vol. 27, No. 4, April-June 2000, 329-348.

Li Rongrong. 2008. 'Wu nianlai guoyou qiye gaige fazhan qude zhongda jinzhan' (五年来国有企业改革发展取得重大进展) [Significant progress has been made in the reform and development of state-owned enterprises in the past five years], 29 March, http://paper.ce.cn/jjrb/html/2008-03/29/content_8361.htm (accessed on 2 August 2020).

Lieberthal, Kenneth. 1993. 'The Great Leap Forward and the Split in the Yan'an Leadership, 1958-65,' in Roderick Macfarquhar (ed.), *The Politics of China 1949-1989.* Cambridge: Cambridge University Press, 87-147.

Lieberthal, Kenneth. 1971. 'Mao versus Liu? Policy towards Industry and Commerce 1946-49', *The China Quarterly,* Vol. 47, July/September, 494-520.

Ligang Song. 2018. 'State-Owned Enterprise Reform in China: Past, Present and Prospects', in Ross Garnaut, Ligang Song and Cai Fang (eds), *China's 40 Years of Reform and Development: 1978–2018.* Acton ACT, Australia: ANU Press, 345-73.

Lim, Benjamin Kang and Megha Rajagopalan. 2014. 'China audits State Grid as corruption crackdown seen widening' *Reuters.* 9 May, https://www.reuters.com/article/us-china-power-corruption/china-audits-state-grid-as-corruption-crackdown-seen-widening-idusbrea4802d20140509 (accessed on 15 November 2020).

Lin, Karen, Xiaoyan Lu, Junsheng Zhang and Ying Zheng. 2020. 'State-owned Enterprises in China: A Review of 40 Years of Research and Practice', *China Journal of Accounting Research,* Vol. 13, 31-55.

Lin Xiaozhao. 2018. 'Zhejiang Grows to Economy the Size of Netherlands in 40 Years of Opening Up', 1 November, https://www.yicaiglobal.com/news/china-time-zhejiang-grows-to-economy-the-size-of-netherlands-in-40-years-of-opening-up (accessed on 13 October 2020).

Liu Guoguang and Wang Ruisun. 1984. 'Restructuring of the Economy', in Yu Guangyuan (ed.), *China's Socialist Modernization.* Beijing: Foreign Languages Press, 71-146.

Liu Guoguang (ed.). 1981. *Theoretical Issues in National Economic System Reform.*

Beijing: Chinese Academy of Social Sciences Press. Quoted in Joseph C. H. Chai. 1997. *China: Transition to a Market Economy*. New York: Oxford University Press.

Liu Jianming. 2017. 'Smart Grids Open Up New Opportunities', 10 January, https://e.huawei.com/in/publications/global/ict_insights/201711060837/energy/201711091519 (accessed on 7 March 2021).

Lo, Dic and Hugo Radice. 1998. 'Institutional Change and Economic Development in East-Central Europe and China: Contrasts in the light of the 'East-Asian Model'', in Jeffery Henderson (ed.), *Industrial Transformation in Eastern Europe in the Light of the East Asian Experience*. London: Macmillan Press Ltd.

Lu Fuming and Yang Ye. 2010. 'Shandong Iron and Steel Group to acquire Rizhao Iron and Steel Company', 3 November, http://www.eeo.com.cn/ens/homepage/briefs/2010/11/05/184970.shtml (accessed on 26 July 2020).

Mason, David. 1984. 'China's Four Modernizations: Blueprint for Development or Prelude to Turmoil?', *Asian Affairs*, Vol .11, No. 3, 47-70.

Ma Hung. 1983. *New Strategy for China's Economy*. Beijing: New World Press. Quoted in David Wen-Wei Chang. 1988. *China Under Deng Xiaoping: Political and Economic Reform*. Basingstoke: The Macmillan Press. 86.

Ma Jun. 2000. *The Chinese Economy in the 1990s*. London: Palgrave Macmillan.

Mackerras, Collin, Pradeep Taneja and Graham Young. 1994. '*China since 1978: Reform, Modernization, and Socialism with Chinese Characteristics*. New York: St. Martin's Press.

Mao Zedong. 1967. *Selected Works of Mao Tse-Tung: Vol. I*. Peking: Foreign Languages Press.

Marshall, Gordon (ed.). 1998. *Oxford Dictionary of Sociology*. New York: Oxford University Press.

McCormick, Barrett L. and Jonathan Unger (eds). 1996. *China Under Socialism: In the Footsteps of Eastern Europe or East Asia*. New York: Routledge.

McGregor, Richard. 2010. *The Party: The Secret World of China's Communist Rulers*. New York: Harper Collins.

Mengnan Shi. 2018. 'Analysis on the Obstacles of Private Capital Participating in the Construction of Municipal PPP in China: A Case Study of PPP Project of Underground Utility Tunnel in a New Airport Area of a City', *Advances in Economics, Business and Management Research*, Vol. 71, 94-98.

Mengan Xie and Yuanmin Luo. 1990. *China's Economic Development During Last 40 Years*. Beijing: Chinese Academy of Social Sciences Press. Quoted in Joseph C.H. Chai. 1997. *China: Transition to a Market Economy*. New York: Oxford University Press.

Miller, Robert F. 1992. 'Economic Reform in Former Communist Systems: The Problems of Privatization', paper presented at the *36th Australian Agricultural and Resource Economics Society (AARES) Conference*, https://ageconsearch.umn.edu/record/146546 (accessed on 8 July 2020).

Ministry of Commerce of the People's Republic of China. 2020. 'Annual Report on China International Project Contracting 2018-19', 9 May, http://

images.mofcom.gov.cn/fec/202005/20200509174729295.pdf (accessed on 20 August 2020).

Ministry of Commerce of the People's Republic of China. 2018. 'Zhongguo guoqi "zou chuqu" de guoji hua rencai zhanlue' (中国国企"走出去"的国际化人才战略) [The internationalized talent strategy of Chinese state-owned enterprises "going out"], 29 March, http://fec.mofcom.gov.cn/article/ywzn/xgzx/guonei/201803/20180302725618.shtml (accessed on 11 August 2020).

Ministry of Commerce of the People's Republic of China. 1999. 'The Decision of the Central Committee of the Communist Party of China on major issues concerning The Reform and Development of State-Owned Enterprises (Adopted at the Fourth Plenum of the 15th CPC Central Committee on September 22, 1999)', 22 September, http://english.mofcom.gov.cn/aarticle/lawsdata/chineselaw/200211/20021100053897.html (accessed on 21 October 2018).

Ministry of Commerce of the People's Republic of China. 1993. 'Company Law of the People's Republic of China', 29 December, http://english.mofcom. gov.cn/article/lawsdata/chineselaw/200211/20021100053539.shtml (accessed on 26 July 2020).

Ministry of Construction of the People's Republic of China. 2004. 'Zhonghua renmin gongheguo jianshe bu ling di 126 hao' (中华人民共和国建设部令第 126 号) [Order No. 126 of the Ministry of Construction of the People's Republic of China], 1 May, http://www.jjgas.com.cn/statute/18.html (accessed on 21 January 2021).

Ministry of Finance of the People's Republic of China. 2018. 'Jianyi wanshan zhengce guli minjian ziben canyu PPP' (建议完善政策鼓励民间资本参与PPP) [It is recommended to improve policies to encourage private capital to participate in PPP], 13 March, http://www.ccgp.gov.cn/ppp/llyj/201803/t20180313_9656828.htm (accessed on 9 September 2020).

Ministry of Finance of the People's Republic of China. 2014a. 'Guanyu yinfa zhengfu he shehui ziben hezuo moshi caozuo zhinan (shixing) de tongzhi' (关于印发政府和社会资本合作模式操 作指南(试行)的通知) [Guide on operation of public–private partnership projects (interim)], 29 November, http://jrs.mof.gov.cn/zhengwuxinxi/zhengcefabu/201412/t20141204_1162965.html (accessed on 26 August 2020).

Ministry of Finance of the People's Republic of China. 2014b. 'Guanyu tuiguang yunyong zhengfu he shehui ziben hezuo moshi youguan wenti de tongzhi' (关于推广运用政府和社会资本合作模式 有关问题的通知) [Notice on questions relating to expanding the use of PPPs], 23 September, http://jrs. mof.gov.cn/zhengwuxinxi/zhengcefabu/201409/t20140924_1143760.html (accessed on 20 August 2020).

Ministry of Science and Technology of the People's Republic of China. 2018. 'Ningbo shi "keji chuangxin 2025" zhongda zhuanxiang fu jing tuijie' (宁波市"科技创新2025"重大专项赴京推介) [Ningbo City's "Technology Innovation 2025" Major Special Project Goes to Beijing for Promotion], 14 June, http://www.most.gov.cn/dfkj/zj/zxdt/201806/t20180613_140106.htm (accessed on 17 December 2020).

Mlex Market Insight. 2017. 'China Communications Construction debarment row brews as concerns grow over Malaysia's award of $12.3bn rail project', 5 January, https://mlexmarketinsight.com/insights-center/editors-picks/area-of-expertise/anti-bribery-and-corruption/china-communications-construction-debarment-row-brews-as-concerns-grow-over-malaysias-award-of-$12.3bn-rail-project (accessed on 12 October 2020).

Molnar, Margit and Jiangyuan Lu. 2019. 'State-owned firms behind China's Corporate Debt', *OECD Working Papers*, No.1536, 7 February, https://www.oecd.org/officialdocuments/publicdisplaydocumentpdf/?cote=ECO/WKP(2019)5&docLanguage=En (accessed on 23 August 2020).

Moody's Investor Research. 2018. 'Moody's: Rated China SOE's to lower leverage gradually through 2018', 8 January, https://www.moodys.com/research/Moodys-Rated-China-SOEs-to-lower-leverage-gradually-through-2018—PR_377781 (accessed on 24 August 2020).

Morgan, J.P. 2019. 'E-commerce payments trends: China' *2019 J.P. Morgan Global Payment Trends-China e-commerce insights*. 30 August, https://www.jpmorgan.com/merchant-services/insights/reports/china (accessed on 15 March 2021).

Nathan, Andrew J. 1997. *China's Transition*. New York: Columbia University Press.

National Development and Reform Commission (NDRC). 2015. 'Guojia fazhan gaige wei guanyu qieshi zuo hao "jichu sheshi he gongyong shiye texu jingying guanli banfa" guanche shishi gongzuo de tongzhi' (国家发展改革委关于切实做好"基础设施和公用 事业特许经营管理办法"贯彻实施工作的通知) [Guidelines on the Implementation of the "Administrative Measures for Infrastructure and Public Utilities Franchising], 7 July, https://www.ndrc.gov.cn/xwdt/ztzl/pppzl/zcfg/201507/t20150707_1033191.html (accessed on 16 July 2020).

National Development and Reform Commission (NDRC). 2014a. 'Guojia fazhan gaige wei yinfa kaizhan zhengfu he shehui ziben hezuo de zhidao yijian' (国家发展改革委印发开展政府和社会资本 合作的指导意见) [Guidelines on development of public–private partnership projects], 4 December, http://www.sdpc.gov.cn/zcfb/zcfbtz/201412/t20141204_651012.html (accessed on 16 July 2020).

National Development and Reform Commission (NDRC). 2014b. 'Guanyu fabu shou pi jichu sheshi deng lingyu guli shehui touzi xiangmu di tongzhi (fa gai jichu [2014]981 hao' (关于发布首批基础设施等领域鼓励社会投资项目的通知 (发改基础[2014]981 号) [Notice to encourage private capital to invest in first infrastructure projects], 21 May, http://www.sdpc.gov.cn/zcfb/zcfbtz/201405/t20140521_612322.html) (accessed on 26 July 2020).

National Energy Administration of the PRC. 2020. 'Guojia nengyuan ju fabu 2019 nian quan shehui yong dian liang' (国家能源局发布 2019 年全社会用电量) [National Energy Administration releases total electricity consumption of 2019], 20 January, http://www.nea.gov.cn/2020-01/20/c_138720877.htm (accessed on 7 March 2021).

National People's Congress of the PRC. 1993. 'Civil and Commercial Laws >>

Company Law of the People's Republic of China', 29 December, http://www.npc.gov.cn/zgrdw/englishnpc/Law/2007-12/12/content_1383787.htm (accessed on 23 August 2020).

National People's Congress of the PRC. 2004. 'Constitution of the People's Republic of China', 14 March, http://www.npc.gov.cn/zgrdw/englishnpc/Constitution/2007-11/15/content_1372963.htm (accessed on 8 August 2020).

National People's Congress of the PRC. 2012. 'Jiu cheng guoqi wancheng gongsi zhi gufenzhi gaige' (九成国企完成公司制股份制改革) [90% of state-owned enterprises have completed the reform of the company system and shareholding system], 25 October, http://www.npc.gov.cn/zgrdw/huiyi/cwh/1129/2012-10/25/content_1740654.htm (accessed on 12 October 2019).

Ningbo.gov.cn. 2019. 'Guanyu xiada ningbo shi 2018 niandu di san pi keji xiangmu buchong jihua de tongzhi' (关于下达宁波市 2018 年度第三批科技项目补充计划的通知) [Notice on the issuance of the third batch of funding plans for Ningbo City in 2018], 8 January, http://www.most.gov.cn/dfkj/zj/zxdt/201806/t20180613_140106.htm (accessed on 17 December 2020).

OECD. 2018. 'China's Belt and Road Initiative in the Global Trade, Investment and Finance Landscape' *OECD Business and Finance Outlook 2018*. https://www.oecd.org/finance/Chinas-Belt-and-Road-Initiative-in-the-global-trade-investment-and-finance-landscape.pdf (accessed on 12 August 2020).

OECD. 2015. *G20/OECD Principles of Corporate Governance.* Paris: *OECD Publishing.*

OECD. 2011. *Corporate Governance of Listed Companies in China: Self-Assessment by the China Securities Regulatory Commission.* Ukraine: OECD Publishing.

OECD. 2009. 'State-Owned Enterprises in China: Reviewing the Evidence', *OECD Working Group on Privatisation and Corporate Governance of State-Owned Assets,* 26 January, https://www.oecd.org/corporate/ca/corporategovernanceofstate-ownedenterprises/42095493.pdf (accessed on 12 October 2019).

OECD. 2008. 'China's Outward Direct Investment', *OECD Investment Policy Reviews: China 2008*, November, https://www.oecd.org/investment/investmentfordevelopment/41792683.pdf (accessed on 12 August 2020).

Ogden, Suzanne. 1995. *China's Unresolved Issues: Politics, Development and Culture.* Englewood Cliffs, N.J.: Prentice Hall.

Overholt, William H. 1993. *China: The Next Superpower.* London: Weidenfeld & Nicolson LPB.

Peijun Duan and Tony Saich. 2014. 'Reforming China's Monopolies', *Ash Center Occasional Papers.* No. RWP14-023, May, 1-59.

People's Daily. 2019. 'Zhongguo qiye "zou chuqu" ge cengmian xu zuo hao juese dingwei' (中国企业"走出去"各层面需做好角色定位) [Chinese companies' "going out" need to be well positioned at all levels], 28 April, http://world.people.com.cn/n1/2019/0428/c1002-31053828.html (accessed on 30 August 2020).

People's Daily. 2018a. 'Guoyou qiye zuoyong buke tidai' (国有企业作用不可替代) [The role of state-owned enterprises is irreplaceable], 29 November, http://www.gov.cn/xinwen/2018-11/29/content_5344296.htm (accessed on 12 August 2020).

People's Daily. 2018b. 'Zhongguo xinbao zhuli yangqi kaita "yidai yilu" yanxian shichang' (中国信保助力央企开拓"一带一路"沿线市场) [SINOSURE helps central enterprises develop markets along the "Belt and Road"], 19 July, https://www.sohu.com/a/242052506_114731 (accessed on 8 September 2020).

Peoples' Daily. 2018c. 'Yi dapi yangqi xiangmu ronghuo 2017 niandu guojia kexue jishu jiangli' (一大批央企项目荣获 2017 年度国家科学技术奖励) [A large number of central enterprise projects won the 2017 National Science and Technology Awards], 10 January, http://ccnews.people.com.cn/n1/2018/0110/c141677-29756353.html (accessed on 06 August 2020).

People's Daily. 2014. 'China Huafu Trade Development Group Corporation was merged into COFCO corporation', 26 November, http://politics.people.com.cn/BIG5/n/2014/1126/c70731-26100059.html (accessed on 14 July 2020).

People's Daily.com. 2020. 'Wei guoyou qiye qiang "gen" zhu "hun"' (为国有企业强"根"铸"魂") [To build the "soul" for the strong "root" of state-owned enterprises], 6 January, http://paper.people.com.cn/rmrb/html/2020-01/06/nw.D110000renmrb_20200106_2-04.htm (accessed on 26 July 2020).

People's Daily Online. 2017. 'Zhonggong zhongyang guanyu jianli guowuyuan xiang quanguo renda changwei hui baogao guoyou zichan guanli qingkuang zhidu de yijian' (中共中央关于建立国务院向全国人大常委会报告国有资产管理情况制度的意见) [Opinions of the Central Committee of the Communist Party of China on Establishing a System for the State Council to Report State-owned Assets Management to the Standing Committee of the National People's Congress], 17 January, http://npc.people.com.cn/big5/n1/2018/0117/c14576-29770394.html (accessed on 16 August 2020).

People's Daily Overseas Edition. 2018. 'Guoyou qiye zuoyong buke tidai' (国有企业作用不可替代) [The role of state-owned enterprises is irreplaceable], 29 November, http://www.gov.cn/xinwen/2018-11/29/content_5344296.htm (accessed on 23 August 2020).

Piketty, Thomas, Li Yang and Gabriel Zucman. 2019. 'Income inequality is growing fast in China and making it look more like the US', *LSE Business Review,* 1 April, https://blogs.lse.ac.uk/usappblog/2019/04/06/income-inequality-is-growing-fast-in-china-and-making-it-look-more-like-the-us/ (accessed on 26 July 2020).

Power Technology. 2020. 'China Develops $26bn Ultra High Voltage Electrical Grids to Stimulate Economic Recovery', 22 May, https://www.power-technology.com/comment/china-26bn-uhv-grids/ (accessed on 15 August 2020).

Przeworski, Adam. 1991. *Democracy and the Market: Political and Economic Reforms in Eastern Europe and Latin America*. Cambridge: Cambridge University Press.

Pulsenews.co.kr. 2018. 'Most of the allegations of preferential treatment such as luge and hotel in Tongyeong have been closed', 4 June, https://pulsenews.co.kr/view.php?year=2018&no=354111 (accessed on 11 August 2020).

Qimiao Fan and Peter Nolan (eds). 1994. *China Economic Reforms: The Costs and Benefits of Incrementalism.* New York: Palgrave.

Rappai, M. V. 1999. 'The PLA (People's Liberation Army) sheds its business interests', *The Hindu* .10 February.

Rawski, Thomas G. 1975. 'China's Industrial System', in U.S. Congress, Joint Economic Committee (ed.), *China: A Re-assessment of the Economy.* Washington D.C.: US Government Printing Office. Reproduced in Joseph C.H. Chai (ed). 2000. *The Economic Development of Modern China Vol. II: Socialist Modernization, 1949-1978.* Cheltenham: Edward Elgar, 112-135.

Ray, Siladitya. 2020. 'US adds 24 Chinese Companies, associated individuals to sanctions list' *Forbes*, 26 August, https://www.forbes.com/sites/siladityaray/2020/08/26/us-adds-24-chinese-companies-associated-individuals-to-sanctions-list/?sh=e84d9673fe2e (accessed on 30 August 2020).

Rednet.cn. 2019. 'Five Hunan Cities Make the List of Top 100 Chinese Cities by GDP', 16 August, https://english.rednet.cn/content/2019/08/16/5816563.html (accessed on 17 January 2021).

Rene, Lavanchy. 2018. 'PPP in China', *IJGlobal Project Finance & Infrastructure Journal,* July, 1-12. https://ijglobal.com/articles/134411/ppp-in-china-report (accessed on 10 December 2020).

Reuters. 2017. 'China issues rules to curb state firm's overseas investment risks', 2 August, https://www.reuters.com/article/china-investment/china-issues-national-security-rules-on-foreign-investment-idUSKBN28T0FS (accessed on 24 August 2020).

Ritchie, Douglas. 2013. 'Chinese Outward Foreign Direct Investment', 4 December, http://www.chinagoabroad.com/en/commentary/chinese-outward-foreign-direct-investment (accessed on 21 October 2020).

Rithmire, Meg. 2019. 'Going Out or Opting Out? Capital, Political Vulnerability, and the State in China's Outward Investment', *Harvard Business School Working Paper,* No. 20-009, June, 1-40 https://www.hbs.edu/ris/Publication%20Files/20-009_664c9264-f0ee-4e43-acbd-d5da9f08caf1.pdf (accessed on 21 October 2020).

Romich, Manfred F. 1994. 'Decentralization and the Danwei System: Economic Reform and Its Impact on Social Development in Chinese Cities', *China Report,* Vol. 30, No. 4, October-December, 447-56.

Rosen, Daniel H., Wendy Leutert, and Shan Guo. 2018. 'Missing Link: Corporate Governance in China's State Sector. Rhodium Group' *Rhodium Group.* 5 November, https://rhg.com/research/missing-link-corporate-governance-in-chinas-state-sector/ (accessed on 15 September 2020).

Sachs, Jeffrey (eds). 1994. *Transition in Eastern Europe, Volume 2: Restructuring.* Chicago: University of Chicago Press.

Sachs, Jeffery. 1994. 'Understanding Shock Therapy', *Social Market Foundation Occasional Paper Series,* No. 7, 1-44.

Schram, Stuart R. 1988. 'China after the 13th Congress', *The China Quarterly*, Vol. 114, June, 177-97.

Shambaugh, David. 2016. The Dynamics of Elite Politics during Jiang Era' *Brookings Institution*. https://www.brookings.edu/wp-content/uploads/2016/06/2001chinajournal.pdf (accessed on 26 July 2020).

Sheng Huaren. 2001. 'Striving to Realize the Three-Year Target of State-owned Enterprises Reform and separation of losses', in Laurence J. Bhahm (ed.), *China's Century: The Awakening of the Next Economic Powerhouse*. Singapore: Wiley, 175-183.

Shenzhen Huiyongxin Technology (深圳市慧用心科技有限公司). 2020. 'Huaqiang bei zhongxiao gongsi zhuce-zhongxiao qiye de zhuce ziben shi duoshao' (华强北中小公司注册-中小企业的注册资本是多少) [Huaqiangbei Small and Medium-sized Company Registration-What is the registered capital of small and medium-sized enterprises], 22 September, http://www.rousin.com/view-95556.html (accessed on 14 March 2021).

Shi Yaobin. 2016. 'Caizheng bu fu buzhang: Zai quanguo caizheng xitong PPP gongzuo tuijin hui ji shifan xiangmu dudao hui shang de jianghua' (财政部副部长：在全国财政系统 PPP 工作推进会暨示范项目督导会上的讲话) [Deputy Minister of Finance: Speech at the PPP Work Promotion Meeting and Demonstration Project Supervision Meeting of the National Financial System], (Ministry of Finance, PRC), 15 December, http://www.gov.cn/xinwen/2016-12/15/content_5148452.htm#1) (accessed on 16 August 2020).

Shih, Victor. 2004. 'Dealing with Non-Performing Loans: Political Constraints and Financial Policies in China', *The China Quarterly*, Vol. 180, December, 922-944.

Sina. 2019. 'Xiaoyaqing: Yangqi gongsi zhi gaige quanmian wancheng' (肖亚庆：央企公司制改革全面完成) [Xiao Yaqing: The reform of the state-owned enterprise system is fully completed], 27 March, http://news.sina.com.cn/o/2019-03-27/doc-ihtxyzsm0948191.shtml (accessed on 07 August 2020).

Sina. 2003. 'Shiliu jie san zhong quanhui jingshen jiedu: Guoqi gaige bu ru shizhi neirong' (十六届三中全会精神解读：国企改革步入实质内容) [Interpretation of the spirit of the Third Plenary Session of the 16th Central Committee: State-owned enterprise reform has entered crucial stage]. 24 October, http://news.sina.com.cn/c/2003-10-24/0610978283s.shtml (accessed on 12 October 2019).

Sina Finance. 2020a. '2019 Nian guoyou qiye shouru tongbi zengzhang 6.9% Lirun zeng 4.7%' (2019 年国有企业收入同比增长 6.9% 利润增 4.7%) [In 2019, the revenue of state-owned enterprises increased by 6.9% year-on-year, and profits increased by 4.7%], 22 January, http://finance.sina.com.cn/roll/2020-01-24/doc-iihnzhha4438696.shtml (accessed on 17 January 2021).

Sina Finance. 2020b. 'Zhongguo 81 jia yangqi zai "yidai yilu" yanxian chengdan chao 3400 ge xiangmu' (中国 81 家央企在"一带一路"沿线承担超 3400 个项目) [China's 81 central enterprises have undertaken over 3,400 projects along the

"Belt and Road"], 15 January, https://baijiahao.baidu.com/s?id=1655797097367459931&wfr=spider&for=pc (accessed on 17 January 2021).

Sina Finance. 2019. 'Guojia youqi guan wang gongsi zhengshi chengli xin ju wu ba dansheng' (国家油气管网公司正式成立 新巨无霸诞生) [The National Oil and Gas Pipeline Company was formally established, the new giant was born], 9 December, http://finance.sina.com.cn/wm/2019-12-09/doc-iihnzahi6271079.shtml (accessed on 14 July 2020).

Sina Finance. 2017. 'Guoqi fuzhai zong'e 94 wan yi yuan fuzhai lu da 65.6% Ruhe qu ganggan?' (国企负债总额 94 万亿元负债率达 65.6% 如何去杠杆?) [The total debt of state-owned enterprises is 94 trillion yuan with a debt ratio of 65.6%. How to deleverage?], 7 August, http://finance.sina.com.cn/roll/2017-08-07/doc-ifyitamv6769829. shtml (accessed on 17 January 2021).

Sina Finance. 2016a. 'Zhongguo chubei liang guanli zong gongsi yu zhongguo chubei mian guanli zong gongsi shishi chongzu' (中国储备粮管理总公司与中国储备棉管理总公司实施重组) [China Grain Reserve Management Corporation and China Cotton Reserve Management Corporation reorganized], 23 November, http://finance.sina.com.cn/roll/2016-11-23/doc-ifxyasmv1622811.shtml.

Sina Finance. 2016b. 'Zhongguo xinbao wei zhong qi jinjun "yidai yilu" cheng qi qian yi meiyuan "baohusan"' (中国信保为中企进军"一带一路"撑起千亿美元"保护伞") [SINOSURE supports Chinese companies to enter the "Belt and Road" "protective umbrella" of 100 billion US dollars], 9 September, https://finance.sina.com.cn/roll/2016-09-09/doc-ifxvukuq4092206.shtml (accessed on 12 August 2020).

Singh, Surjit. 1998. 'Economic Reforms and State Enterprises in China', *China Report*, Vol. 34, No. 2, 199-212.

Siyiou Foreign Trade Express. 2019. '2008-2018 Nian shi nian zhongguo waimao jin chukou quanjing tu' (2008-2018 年十年中国外贸进出口全景图) [A panoramic view of China's foreign trade imports and exports from 2008 to 2018], 29 January, https://www.syoseo.com/post/529.html (accessed on 24 August 2020).

Sohu.com. 2020. 'Zhejiang juxing guozi guoqi gaige fazhan qingkuang xinwen fabu hui' (热烈祝贺物产中大集团在 2020《财富》世界 500 强榜荣登第 210 名) [Congratulations to Wutan Zhongda Group for ranking 210th on the 2020 Fortune Global 500 list], 13 December, http://zj.cnr.cn/zjyw/20181213/t20181213_524448854.shtml (accessed on 15 November 2020).

Sohu.com. 2019. 'Guonei yinhang xinyong daikuan, zhizao ye daikuan, zhong changqi daikuan bili shi duoshao? Zhiliang you ruhe?' (国内银行信用贷款、制造业贷款、中长期贷款比例是多少？质量又如何?) [What is the ratio of domestic bank credit loans, manufacturing loans, and medium and long-term loans? How about the quality?], 2 July, https://www.sohu.com/a/324257480_100003691 (accessed on 20 August 2020).

Sohu.com. 2018. 'Zhejiang sheng guoyou qiye zichan zong'e 10.44 Wan yi yuan, wei lie quanguo di er!' (浙江省国有企业资产总额 10.44 万亿元，位列全国第二!) [The total assets of state-owned enterprises in Zhejiang Province are 10.44 trillion yuan, ranking second in the country!], 13 December, https://www.sohu.com/a/281891253_821103 (accessed on 17 January 2021).

Sohu.com. 2016. 'Dongfang Electric and Harbin Electric switch coaches during the trough period, power equipment giants may encounter huge losses', 13 June, https://www.sohu.com/a/82811936_109478 (accessed on 18 July 2020).

Songyuan.yccsrj.cn. 2015. 'Songyuan 2019 nian quanguo PPP zonghe xinxi guanli ku nianbao chulu: Xin ru ku xiangmu 1434 ge' [(松原 2019 年全国 PPP 综合信息管理库年报出炉：新入库项目 1434 个) [Songyuan's 2019 National PPP Comprehensive Information Management Database - Annual Report - 1434 Newly Projects Included], 18 March, https://songyuan.yccsrj.cn/industry/514.html (accessed on 9 September 2020).

Smith, Matt. 2000. 'Clinton signs China trade bill' *CNN*. 10 October, https://edition.cnn.com/2000/ALLPOLITICS/stories/10/10/clinton.pntr/ (accessed on 02 August 2000).

Smith, Richard. 1993. 'The Chinese Road to Capitalism', *New Left Review*, No. 199, May/June, 55-99.

SMM News. 2020. "Ultra-high-voltage projects to limitedly drive copper consumption in 2020", 26 March, https://news.metal.com/newscontent/101049371/Ultra-high-voltage-projects-to-limitedly-drive-copper-consumption-in-2020/ (accessed on 26 August 2020).

So, Bennis Wai-yip. 2002. 'The Policy-Making and Political Economy of the Abolition of Private Ownership in the Early 1950s: Findings from New Material', *The China Quarterly*, Vol. 171, September, 682-703.

State-owned Assets Supervision and Administration Commission (SASAC). 2020a. '48 Jia yangqi 32 jia difang guoqi shang bang 2020 shijie 500 qiang' (48 家央企 32 家地方国企上榜 2020 世界 500 强) [48 state-owned enterprises and 32 local state-owned enterprises on the list of 2020 world top 500], 10 August, http://www.sasac.gov.cn/n2588020/n2877938/n2879597/n2879599/c15338531/content.html (accessed on 12 October 2020).

State-owned Assets Supervision and Administration Commission (SASAC). 2020b. 'Zhonggong zhongguo jiaotong jianshe jituan youxian gongsi weiyuanhui guanyu xunshi zhenggai jinzhan qingkuang de tongbao' (中共中国交通建设集团有限公司委员会关于巡视整改进展情况的通报) [Announcement of the Committee of the Communist Party of China and China Communications Construction Group Co., Ltd. on the inspection and improvement of the exhibition], 2 April, http://www.sasac.gov.cn/n2588020/n2588072/n2591770/n2591772/c14213702/content.html (accessed on 24 August 2020).

State-owned Assets Supervision and Administration Commission (SASAC). 2020c. '2019 Nian zhongyang qiye jingji yun hang qingkuang' (2019 年中央企业经济运行情况) [Economic performance of central enterprises in 2019], 16 January, http://www.sasac.gov.cn/n2588035/n2588330/n2588360/c13551779/content.html (accessed on 20 July 2020).

State-owned Assets Supervision and Administration Commission (SASAC). 2020d.

'Guanyu jiang zhongguo jianyan renzheng (jituan) youxian gongsi lie ru guowuyuan guoyou zichan jiandu guanli weiyuanhui lu hang chuzi ren zhize qiye mingdan de gonggao' (关于将中国检验认证（集团）有限公司 列入国务院国有资产监督管理委员会 履行出资人职责企业名单的公告) [About China Certification & Inspection (Group) Co., Ltd. Listed in the State-owned Assets Supervision and Administration Commission of the State Council Announcement on the list of companies performing the duties of investors], 5 June, http://www.sasac.gov.cn/n2588035/n2641579/n2641660/c14787870/content.html (accessed on 22 July 2020).

State-owned Assets Supervision and Administration Commission (SASAC). 2020e. 'Guanyu shanghai nuojiya bei'er gufen youxian gongsi bu zai lie ru guowuyuan guoyou zichan jiandu guanli weiyuanhui lu hang chuzi ren zhize qiye mingdan de gonggao' (关于上海诺基亚贝尔股份有限公司 不再列入国务院国有资产监督管理委员会 履行出资 人职责企业名单的公告) [About Shanghai Nokia Bell Co., Ltd. No longer listed in the State-owned Assets Supervision and Administration Commission of the State Council Announcement on the list of companies performing the duties of investors], 3 June, http://www.sasac.gov.cn/n2588035/n2641579/n2641660/c14770605/content.html (accessed on 22 July 2020).

State-owned Assets Supervision and Administration Commission (SASAC). 2020f. 'State Grid in Full Swing on UHV Construction', 22 April, http://en.sasac.gov.cn/2020/04/22/c_4880.htm (accessed on 15 November 2020).

State-owned Assets Supervision and Administration Commission (SASAC). 2019a. '[Goujian guozi jianguan da geju] zhi san: Jin kou fuwu daju goujian si ge tixi gao zhiliang tuijin zhejiang guozi tongyi jianguan gongzuo' ([构建国资监管大格局]之三：紧扣服务大局 构建四个体系高质量推进浙江国 资统一监管工作) [Part III of 'The establishment of State-owned Assets Supervision pattern', focusing closely on the general subject of serving, to build four systems to promote the unified supervision of state-owned assets in Zhejiang.], 5 December, http://www.sasac.gov.cn/n4470048/n10286230/n12974073/n12974173/c12970250/content.html (accessed on 15 November 2020).

State-owned Assets Supervision and Administration Commission (SASAC). 2019b. 'Zhongguo chuanbo gongye jituan youxian gongsi yu zhongguo chuanbo zhonggong jituan youxian gongsi shishi lianhe chongzu' (中国船舶工业集团有限公司与中国船舶重工集团有限公司实施联合重组) [China State Shipbuilding Corporation and China Shipbuilding Industry Corporation implement joint reorganization], 25 October, http://www.sasac.gov.cn/n2588035/n2641579/n2641660/c12397252/content.html (accessed on 24 August 2020).

State-owned Assets Supervision and Administration Commission (SASAC). 2019c. 'Zhongguo baoli jituan youxian gongsi yu zhongguo zhong si jituan youxian gongsi shishi chongzu' (中国保利集团有限公司与中国中丝集团有限公司实施重组) [China Poly Group Co., Ltd. and China Silk Group Co., Ltd. reorganized], 8 July, http://www.sasac.gov.cn/n2588035/n2641579/n2641660/c11679355/content.html (accessed on 24 August 2020).

State-owned Assets Supervision and Administration Commission (SASAC). 2019d. 'Guowuyuan guoyou zichan jiandu guanli weiyuanhui gonggao)' (国务院国有资产监督管理委员会公告) [Announcement of the State-owned Assets Supervision and Administration Commission of the State Council], 4 April, http://www.sasac.gov.cn/n2588035/n2641579/n2641660/c10885879/content.html (accessed on 24 August 2020).

State-owned Assets Supervision and Administration Commission (SASAC). 2018a. 'Wuhan youdian kexue yan jiu yuan youxian gongsi yu dianxin kexue jishu yan jiu yuan youxian gongsi shishi lianhe chongzu' (武汉邮电科学研究院有限公司与电信科学技术研究院有限公司实施联合重组) [Wuhan Post and Telecommunications Research Institute Co., Ltd. and Telecommunication Science and Technology Research Institute Co., Ltd. implement joint reorganization], 27 June, http://www.sasac.gov.cn/n2588025/n2588119/c9175370/content.html (accessed on 14 August 2020).

State-owned Assets Supervision and Administration Commission (SASAC). 2018b. 'Zhongguo he gongye jituan youxian gongsi yu zhongguo he gongye jianshe jituan youxian gongsi shishi chongzu' (中国核工业集团有限公司与中国核工业建设集团有限公司实施重组) [China National Nuclear Corporation and China Nuclear Industry Construction Group Co., Ltd. reorganized], 31 January, http://www.sasac.gov.cn/n2588035/n2641579/n2641660/c8551590/content.html (accessed on 14 August 2020).

State-owned Assets Supervision and Administration Commission (SASAC). 2017a. 'Zhongguo guodian jituan gongsi yu shenhua jituan youxian zeren gongsi shishi lianhe chongzu' (中国国电集团公司与神华集团有限责任公司实施联合重组) [China Guodian Corporation and Shenhua Group Co., Ltd. implement joint reorganization], 28 August, http://www.sasac.gov.cn/n2588035/c7795367/content.html (accessed on 14 August 2020).

State-owned Assets Supervision and Administration Commission (SASAC). 2017b. 'Zhongguo baoli jituan gongsi yu zhongguo qing gong jituan gongsi, zhongguo gongyi (jituan) gongsi shishi chongzu' (中国保利集团公司与中国轻工集团公司、中国工艺（集团）公司实施重组) [China Poly Group Corporation, China Light Industry Corporation and China National Arts & Crafts (Group) Corporation reorganized], 21 August, http://www.sasac.gov.cn/n2588025/n2588119/c7768396/content.html (accessed on 14 August 2020).

State-owned Assets Supervision and Administration Commission (SASAC). 2016. 'Guozi wei guanyu zujian zhongguo hangkong fadongji jituan youxian gongsi de gonggao' (国资委关于组建中国航空发动机 集团有限公司的公告) [State-owned Assets Supervision and Administration Commission on the establishment of China's aviation engine Group Co., Ltd. announcement], 13 July, http://www.sasac.gov.cn/n2588035/n2641579/n2641660/c3753618/content.html (accessed on 12 July 2020).

State-owned Assets Supervision and Administration Commission (SASAC). 2015a.

'Nanguang (jituan) youxian gongsi he zhuhai zhen rong gongsi shishi chongzu' (南光（集团）有限公司和珠海振戎公司实施重组) [Nanguang (Group) Co., Ltd. and Zhuhai Zhenrong Company reorganized], 1 December, http://www.gov.cn/xinwen/2015-12/01/content_5018604.htm (accessed on 14 August 2020).

State-owned Assets Supervision and Administration Commission (SASAC). 2015b. 'Zhongguo dianli touzi jituan gongsi he guojia hedian jishu youxian gongsi shishi lianhe chongzu' (国电力投资集团公司和国家核电技术有限公司实施联合重组) [China Power Investment Corporation and State Nuclear Power Technology Co., Ltd. implement joint reorganization], 1 June, http://www.sasac.gov.cn/n2588035/n2641579/n2641660/c3753547/content.html (accessed on 24 July 2020).

State-owned Assets Supervision and Administration Commission (SASAC). 2014. 'Guowuyuan guozi wei juban "si xiang gaige shidian xinwen fabu huì' (国务院国资委举办"四项改革"试点新闻发布会) [State-owned Assets Supervision and Administration Commission of the State Council held a press conference on the "four reforms" pilot]. 15 July, http://www.sasac.gov.cn/n2588025/n2588119/c2668690/content.html (accessed on 23 September 2020).

State-owned Assets Supervision and Administration Commission (SASAC). 2012. 'Guozi wei: Yangqi yu shijie yiliu qiye reng cunzai jiao da chaju' (国资委：央企与世界一流企业仍存在较大差距) [SASAC: There is still a big gap between state-owned enterprises and world-class enterprises], 25 March, http://www.china.com.cn/news/shanghui/2012-03/25/content_24978872.htm (accessed on 24 August 2020).

State-owned Assets Supervision and Administration Commission of Zhejiang Province (SASAC-Zhejiang). 2020. 'Zhejiang sheng guozi wei jianli "465" guoqi gao zhiliang fazhan mubiao tixi' (浙江省国资委建立"465"国企高质量发展目标体系) [The State-owned Assets Supervision and Administration Commission of Zhejiang Province established a "465" high-quality development target system for state-owned enterprises], 23 April, http://www.sasac.gov.cn/n2588025/n2588119/c14416599/content.html (accessed on 17 January 2021).

State-owned Assets Supervision and Administration Commission of Zhejiang Province (SASAC-Zhejiang). 2019. 'Zhejiang guozi guoqi quanli da hao "xiao bao" gongjianzhan zhuli xiangcun zhenxing' (浙江国资国企全力打好"消薄"攻坚战助力乡村振兴) [State-owned and state-owned enterprises in Zhejiang Province do their best to fight the "depletion" battle to help rural revitalization], 4 April, http://www.sasac.gov.cn/n2588025/n2588129/c10888800/content.html (accessed on 6 December 2020).

State Economic and Trade Commission (SETC). 'Creating a Modern Enterprise Mechanisms that suits the Market'. Quoted in You Ji. 1998. *China's Enterprise Reform: Changing State/Society Relations After Mao (Routledge Studies on China in Transition)*. London: Routledge, 163.

State Grid Corporation of China (SGCC). 2017. 'Zuzhi jiegou' (############)

[Organizational structure], 25 January, http://www.sgcc.com.cn/html/sgcc_main/col2017012538/column_2017012538_1.shtml (accessed on 17 January 2021).

Statista. 2020. 'Revenue of State Grid Corporation in China from 2010 to 2019', March, https://www.statista.com/statistics/302451/china-state-grid-corporation-revenue/ (accessed on 26 July 2020).

Stefanova, Katina. 2017. 'China's Rising Wealth Gap and Implications to Markets and the World' *Forbes.* 19 December, https://www.forbes.com/sites/katinastefanova/2017/12/19/chinas-rising-wealth-gap-and-implications-to-markets-and-the-world/#628bbf642311 (accessed on 30 July 2020).

Strategic Comments (Indian Institute for Strategic Studies). 1999. 'The End of China's Era of Growth' *The Hindu.* 9 March.

Sun Jie. 2017. 'Guoyou qiye canyu PPP de jiyu yu tiaozhan' (国有企业参与 PPP 的机遇与挑战) [Opportunities and challenges for state-owned enterprises to participate in PPP], *State-owned Enterprise Management,* No. Z6, December, 28-29.

Sun Sheng Han and Clifton W. Pannell. 1999. 'The Geography of Privatization in China, 1978-1996', *Economic Geography,* Vol. 75, No. 3, July, 272-296.

Sun Yu. 2020. 'China state group says official meddling contributed to default wave' *Financial Times.* 20 November, https://www.ft.com/content/157310ef-d404-479e-9566-3503b77d49e9 (accessed on 26 February 2021).

Sung Yun-wing and Thomas M. H. Chan. 1987. 'China's Economic Reforms: The Debates in China', *The Australian Journal of Chinese Affairs,* No. 17, January, 29-51.

Sze, Norman and Flora Wu. 2015. 'One Belt One Road: The Internationalization of China's SOE's' *Deloitte Perspective.* https://www2.deloitte.com/content/dam/Deloitte/cn/Documents/about-deloitte/dttp/deloitte-cn-dttp-vol5-chapter2-en.pdf (accessed on 18 August 2020).

Tang, Frank. 2019. 'China to give local governments bigger share of tax revenues to continue crucial infrastructure investments' *South China Morning Post.* 11 October, https://www.scmp.com/economy/china-economy/article/3032597/china-give-local-governments-bigger-share-tax-revenues (accessed on 15 November 2020).

Tang Qingliang and Amy Lau 2000. 'Accounting Reforms in China: A Transition from a State Plan and Controloriented System to Capital Marketoriented System', *Managerial Finance,* Vol. 26, No. 5, May, 80-98.

The Economist. 2019a. 'Some Chinese firms turned out to have lied about their state pedigree', 14 November, https://www.economist.com/finance-and-economics/2019/11/14/some-chinese-firms-turn-out-to-have-lied-about-their-state-pedigree (accessed on 26 July 2020).

The Economist. 2019b. 'Pandas can fly: The struggle to reform China's economy', 27 February, https://www.economist.com/leaders/2019/02/21/the-struggle-to-reform-chinas-economy (accessed on 1 January 2021).

The Economist. 2018. 'Why only 2% of Chinese pay any income tax', 1 December, https://www.economist.com/china/2018/12/01/why-only-2-of-chinese-pay-any-income-tax (accessed on 24 August 2020).

The Economist. 2016. 'China's state firms borrow cheaply'. 23 November, https://www.economist.com/graphic-detail/2016/11/23/chinas-state-firms-borrow-cheaply (accessed on 23 September 2020).

The Economist. 2011. 'China's economy and the WTO - All Change'. 10 December, https://www.economist.com/asia/2011/12/10/all-change (accessed on 28 January 2021).

The State Council of the People's Republic of China. 2019. 'Full Text: Report on the work of the Government (13th National People's Congress of CPC)', 16 March, http://english.www.gov.cn/premier/speeches/2019/03/16/content_281476565265580.htm (accessed on 26 July 2020).

The State Council of the People's Republic of China. 2014a. 'Guowuyuan guanyu chuangxin zhongdian lingyu tou rongzi jizhi guli shehui touzi de zhidao yijian' (国务院关于创新重点领域投融资机制鼓励社会投资的指导意见) [Guiding opinions on the innovative investment mechanism and encouraging social investment in key sectors], 26 November, http://www.gov.cn/zhengce/content/2014-11/26/content_9260.htm (accessed on 20 August 2020).

The State Council of the People's Republic of China. 2014b. 'Guowuyuan guanyu jiaqiang difang zhengfu xing zhaiwu guanli de yijian' (国务院关于加强地方政府性债务管理的意见) [Opinions of the State Council on strengthening the administration of local government debt], 21 September, http://www.gov.cn/zhengce/%20content/2014-10/02/content_9111.htm (accessed on 26 July 2020).

The State Council of the People's Republic of China. 2014c. 'Guojia xinxing chengzhen hua guihua (2014-2020 nian) zhonghua renmin gongheguo zhongyang renmin zhengfu menhu wangzhan' (国家新型城镇化规划 (2014-2020 年)中华人民共和国中央人民政 府门户网站) [National New Urbanization Plan 2014-2020], 16 March, http://www.gov.cn/zhengce/2014-03/16/content_2640075.htm (accessed on 15 July 2020).

The State Council Information Office of the People's Republic of China (SCIO). 2018. 'Zhejiang juxing guozi guoqi gaige fazhan qingkuang xinwen fabu hui' (浙江举行国资国企改革发展情况新闻发布会) [Zhejiang holds a Press Conference on the reform and development of state-owned assets and state-owned enterprises], 13 December, http://zj.cnr.cn/zjyw/20181213/t20181213_524448854.shtml (accessed on 15 November 2020).

The US-China Business Council. 2013. 'Third Plenum outcomes settle Top-line Reform Themes, but debate on specifics to continue', https://www.uschina.org/third-plenum-outcomes-settle-top-line-reform-themes-debate-specifics-expected-continue (accessed on 24 July 2020).

The Wall Street Journal. 2019. 'China intends to continue debt-reduction efforts', 25 February, https://www.wsj.com/articles/china-intends-to-continue-debt-reduction-efforts-11551126582 (accessed on 26 July 2020).

Thomson Reuters Practical Law. 2021. 'Practical Law - Glossary', https://

uk.practicallaw.thomsonreuters.com/1-382-3377?transitionType=Default&contextData=(sc.Default)&firstPage=true (accessed on 14 March 2021).

Uhlenbruck, Klaus and Julio O. De Castro. 2000. 'Foreign Acquisitions in Central and Eastern Europe: Outcomes of Privatization in Transitional Economies', *The Academy of Management Journal*, Vol. 43, No. 3, June, 381-402.

United Nations. 2012. *Inclusive Wealth Report 2012: Measuring Progress toward Sustainability*. Cambridge: Cambridge University Press, https://digitallibrary.un.org/record/784798?ln=en (accessed on 23 July 2020).

Urban Management Information Network. 2020. 'Local Governments may assume certain debt relief obligations', 20 September, http://www.yljs79.com/hyxw/2020/0920/8844.html (accessed on 28 October 2020).

Van Ness, Peter (ed.). 1989. *Market in Socialist Societies: Comparing China and Hungary*. Boulder: Lynne Rienner.

Vernon, Raymond. 1979. 'The Fragile Foundations of East-West Trade', *Foreign Affairs*, Vol. 57, No. 5, Summer, 1035-051.

Walter, Carl and Fraser Howie. 2012. *Red Capitalism: The Fragile Financial Foundation of China's Extraordinary Rise*. Singapore: John Wiley and Sons.

Weisskopf, Michael. 1984. 'China caught in cycle of reform and retreat' *The Washington Post*. 26 April, https://www.washingtonpost.com/archive/politics/1984/04/26/china-caught-in-cycle-of-reform-and-retreat/18e492ec-d5d7-4991-aa2e-1149450909c1/ (accessed on 26 July 2020).

Wei-Wei Zhang. 1996. *Ideology and Economic Reform under Deng Xiaoping 1978-199*, London: Kegan Paul International. Quoted in Michael Weisskopf. 1984. 'China caught in cycle of reform and retreat' *The Washington Post*. 26 April, https://www.washingtonpost.com/archive/politics/1984/04/26/china-caught-in-cycle-of-reform-and-retreat/18e492ec-d5d7-4991-aa2e-1149450909c1/ (accessed on 26 July 2020).

Wenzhou Airport Group Co. Ltd. 2019. 'Wenzhou jichang xinban zongti guihua huo minhang huadong ju pifu' (温州机场新版总体规划获民航华东局批复) [Wenzhou Airport's new master plan was approved by the East China Bureau of Civil Aviation], 19 November, https://www.wzair.cn/jtdt/jtxw/2019/12/11/259534.html (accessed on 20 November 2020).

Wenzhou Daily. 2020. 'Wenzhou jueqi "qian wan ji" daxing guoji jichang' (温州崛起"千万级"大型国际机场) [The rise of Wenzhou, a large-scale international airport "ten million"], 12 July, http://www.wenzhou.gov.cn/art/2020/7/12/art_1217832_50326389.html (accessed on 6 December 2020).

WID.world. 2017. *World Inequality Report 2018*, https://wir2018.wid.world (accessed on 30 July 2020).

World Bank. 2011a. *The Changing Wealth of Nations: Measuring Sustainable Development in the New Millennium (Environment and Development)*. Washington D.C.: World Bank.

World Bank. 2011b. 'World Bank Applies 2009 Debarment to China Communications

Construction Company Limited for Fraud in Philippines Roads Project', *World Bank Press Release*, 29 July, https://www.worldbank.org/en/news/press-release/2011/07/29/world-bank-applies-2009-debarment-to-china-communications-construction-company-limited-for-fraud-in-philippines-roads-project (accessed on 23 August 2020).

World Bank. 1997a. 'Understanding the Present', in Vikarm Nehru, Aart Kraay and Xiaoqing Yu (eds), *China 2002: Development Challenges in the New Century.* Washington D.C.: The World Bank, 1-5.

World Bank. 1997b. *China 2020: Sharing Rising Incomes.* Washington D.C.: World Bank. Quoted in Aart Krray. 2000. 'Household Savings in China', *The World Bank Economic Review,* Vol. 14, No. 3, September, 545-570.

World Bank. 1997c. *China 2020: Development Challenges in the New Century.* Washington D.C.: World Bank.

World Bank. 1985. *China: Long Term Development Issues and Options.* Baltimore: World Bank Publication.

Wu Guoguang. 2011. 'China in 2010: Dilemmas of "Scientific Development', *Asian Survey*, Vol. 51, No. 1, February, 18-32.

Wu Zengxian. 1997. 'How Successful Has State-Owned Enterprise Reform Been in China?', *Europe-Asia Studies*, Vol. 49, No. 7, 1237-1262.

Xiaobin Lin, Jianhui Liao, Haiyun Song and Xiaodong Li. 2019. 'Analysis of State-owned Capital Investment and Operating Companies Experimental Units', *2019 3rd International Conference on Informatization in Education, Management and Business Conference Proceedings* (unpublished), 28-29 January, https://www.clausiuspress.com/conferences/AETP/IEMB%202019/IEMB51.pdf (accessed on 15 September 2020).

Xinhua. 2020a. 'Xi Focus: Xi stresses breaking new ground amid changes through reforms', 1 July, http://www.xinhuanet.com/english/2020-07/01/c_139178782.htm (accessed 24 July 2020).

Xinhua. 2020b. 'Kai zu mali bao fang kong fugong fu chan wen jingji——zhongyang qiye quanli yi fu kangji yiqing' (开足马力保防控 复工复产稳经济——中央企业全力以赴抗击疫情) [Strive to ensure prevention and control, resume work and resume production to stabilize the economy-central enterprises go all out to fight the epidemic], 18 February, http://www.xinhuanet.com/politics/2020-02/18/c_1125593316.htm (accessed on 22 July 2020).

Xinhua. 2020c. 'China improves S&T award system to spur innovation', 9 January, http://www.xinhuanet.com/english/2020-01/09/c_138691824.htm (accessed on 2 August 2020).

Xinhua. 2019a. '"Liang chuan" zhengshi heti zhongguo chuanbo jituan youxian gongsi jiepai chengli' ("两船"正式合体 中国船舶集团有限公司揭牌成立) ["Two ships" officially merged China State Shipbuilding Corporation Limited was inaugurated and established], 26 November, http://www.xinhuanet.com//fortune/2019-11/26/c_1125277030.htm (accessed on 12 August 2020).

Xinhua. 2019. '"2019 Zhejiang sheng bai qiang qiye" bang dan fabu 16 jia qi ye ying shou chao qian yi' ("2019 浙江省百强企业" 榜单发布 16 家企业营收超千亿) ["2019 Zhejiang Top 100 Enterprises" lists 16 companies with revenue exceeding 100 billion], 11 September, https://baijiahao.baidu.com/s?id=1644379781031387530&wfr=spider&for=pc (accessed on 17 December 2020).

Xinhua. 2019b. '2018 Nian woguo duiwai touzi 1298.3 Yi meiyuan baochi pingwen jiankang fazhan' (2018 年我国对外投资 1298.3 亿美元 保持平稳健康发展) [my country's foreign investment of US$129.83 billion in 2018 maintained steady and healthy development], 16 January, http://www.xinhuanet.com/2019-01/16/c_1123999786.htm (accessed on 24 October 2020).

Xinhua. 2017. 'Economic Watch: Supply-side structural reform gears up for high-quality development', 30 December, http://www.xinhuanet.com/english/2017-12/30/c_136861755.htm (accessed on 27 July 2020).

Xinhua. 2012. 'China Completes Cross-Border Power Transmission Project With Russia', 1 January, http://www.geni.org/globalenergy/library/technical-articles/transmission/xinhua/china-completes-cross-border-power-transmission-project-with-russia/index.shtml (accessed on 15 August 2020).

Xinhua Finance Agency. 2016. 'SOEs reform to deepen as ten pilots reforms unveiled'. 26 February, http://en.xfafinance.com/html/In_depth/2016/199753.shtml (accessed on 15 September 2020).

Xinhua News Agency. 2019. 'Zhongguo youzheng jituan youxian gongsi jiepai chengli' (中国邮政集团有限公司揭牌成立) [China Post Group Co., Ltd. was inaugurated and established], 28 December, https://baijiahao.baidu.com/s?id=1654156682908150058&wfr=spider&for=pc (accessed on 13 June 2020).

Xinhua News Agency. 2016. 'Baogang yu wugang lianhe chongzu huo pi' (宝钢与武钢联合重组获批) [The joint reorganization of Baosteel and WISCO was approved], 22 September, http://www.gov.cn/xinwen/2016-09/22/content_5110905.htm (accessed on 13 June 2020).

Xin Bao. 2020. 'Intelligent Heating Business Model based on PPP Mode', *IOP Conference Series*, IOP Publishing, https://iopscience.iop.org/article/10.1088/1757-899X/768/5/052005/pdf (accessed on 17 August 2020).

Xu Wenjing. 2018. 'Jiyu chuangxin nengli shijiao de minying qiye haiwai binggou jixiao pingjia yanjiu' (基于创新能力视角的民营企业海外并购绩效评价研究) [Research on Performance Evaluation of Private Enterprises' Overseas M&A Based on the Perspective of Innovation Ability], Yanshan University Masters' Thesis, May 2018, https://kns.cnki.net/KCMS/detail/detail.aspx?dbcode=CMFD&filename=1018877596.nh (accessed on 23 July 2020).

Xu Yi-Chong. 1996. 'Deepening and Widening the Economic Reform in China: From Enterprise Reform to Macroeconomic Stability', *The Journal of Developing Areas*, Vol. 30, No. 3, 361-84.

Xue Muqiao. 2010. *Chinese Economists on Economic Reform - Collected Works of Xue Muqiao*. New York: Routledge.

Yan Hang and Wen Zongduo. 2019. 'Belt and Road reached out to the World' *China*

Daily. 30 September, https://global.chinadaily.com.cn/a/201909/30/WS5d9160e4a310cf3e3556e4a0_2.html (accessed on 18 August 2020).

Yicai.com. (Shanghai First Financial Media Co., Ltd.). 2017. 'Guozi wei: 47 Jia yangqi canyu yidai yilu jianshe yi jian 1676 ge xiangmu' (国资委：47 家央企参与一带一路建设 已建 1676 个项目) [State-owned Assets Supervision and Administration Commission: 47 state-owned enterprises have participated in the construction of the Belt and Road Initiative, 1676 projects have been built], 8 May, https://www.yicai.com/news/5280261.html (accessed on 17 January 2021).

You Ji. 1998. *China's Enterprise Reform: Changing State/Society Relations after Mao (Routledge Studies on China in Transition)*. London: Routledge.

Yuan, Steven, Veronique Yang, Yves-Pierre Willers, David Lee and Ying Luo. 2015. 'Gearing up for the new era of China's outbound M&A' *BCG Publications*. 24 September, https://www.bcg.com/publications/2015/mergers-acquisitions-globalization-gearing-up-for-new-era-chinas-outbound-m-a (accessed on 24 August 2020).

Zhang Jie. 2018. 'Global 500: Chinese companies race ahead' *China Daily*. 20 July, https://www.chinadaily.com.cn/a/201807/20/WS5b518b77a310796df4df7b77.html (accessed on 18 August 2020).

Zhang Shasha 2018. 'State-Owned Capital Guideline' *Beijing Review*. No. 51. 20 December, http://www.bjreview.com/Special_Reports/2018/2018_in_Retrospect/Top_10_Business_News_Stories/201812/t20181227_800152646.html (accessed on 15 September 2019).

Zhang Xiaozhe. 2020. 'Guozi wei shenru tuijin guoyou zhongdian qiye dui biao shijie yiliu guanli tisheng xingdong' (国资委深入推进国有重点企业对标世界一流管理提升行动) [The State-owned Assets Supervision and Administration Commission of the State-owned Assets Supervision and Administration Commission further promotes the benchmarking of world-class management improvement actions for key state-owned enterprises], June, http://www.gdasc.cn/news_3376.shtml (accessed on 24 August 2020).

Zhejiang Daily. 2019a. 'Zhejiang juxing guozi guoqi gaige fazhan qingkuang xinwen fabu hui' (18 年建成 22 条高速公路，参与建成 16 条铁路，浙江省交通集团-建设主力军) [Built 22 expressways in 18 years, participated in the construction of 16 railways, Zhejiang Transportation Group - the main force in the construction of "one-hour traffic circle"], 25 December, http://www.meiligaosu.com/h-nd-1175.html?from=groupmessage (accessed on 15 November 2020).

Zhejiang Daily. 2019b. 'Zai dan dang zuowei zhong dili qian xing — 70 niandai zhejiang guozi guoqi gaige fazhan huimou' (在担当作为中砥砺前行 — 70 年代浙江国资国企改革发展回眸) [Forge ahead in the role - Looking Back on the Reform and Development of Zhejiang State-owned Assets and Enterprises in the 1970s], 27 September, http://zjrb.zjol.com.cn/html/2019-09/27/content_3269446.htm?div=-1 (accessed on 14 December 2020).

Zhejiang Daily. 2018a. 'Wenzhou jichang ying lai jinnian di 1 qian wan ming luke jishen qian wan ji jichang' (温州机场迎来今年第 1 千万名旅客 跻身千万级机场)

[Wenzhou Airport welcomed 10 millionth passenger this year], 24 November, https://baijiahao.baidu.com/s?id=1617973628147446817&wfr=spider&for=pc (accessed on 15 November 2020).

Zhejiang Daily. 2018b. 'Zhejiang san da jichang jishen "qian wan julebu"' (浙江三大机场跻身"千万俱乐部") [Zhejiang's three major airports rank among the "ten million clubs"], 24 November, http://www.wzs.org.cn/hg/201811/t20181124_294486.shtml (accessed on 15 November 2020).

Zhejiang Institute of Science and Technology, The University of Hong Kong (ZIRI-HKU). 2019a. 'Hangzhou shi quanqiu yin cai "521" jihua' (杭州市全球引才"521"计划) [Hangzhou "521" Plan for Global Talent Attraction], 6 September, http://www.ziri.hku.hk/en/talent/talent_details/24.html (accessed on 14 December 2020).

Zhejiang Institute of Science and Technology, The University of Hong Kong (ZIRI-HKU). 2019b. 'Zhejiang sheng qian ren jihua' (浙江省千人计划) [Zhejiang Thousand Talents Plan], 6 September, http://www.ziri.hku.hk/en/talent/talent_details/25.html (accessed on 14 December 2020).

Zheng Xinli. 2014. 'Renmin ribao: Jinyibu shenhua guoyou qiye gaige' (人民日报：进一步深化国有企业改革) [People's Daily: Further deepen the reform of state-owned enterprises], *People's Daily*, 25 December, http://opinion.people.com.cn/n/2014/1225/c1003-26275490.html (accessed on 19 August 2020).

Zheng Yangpeng. 2019. 'In a first, China has more companies on Fortune Global 500 list than the US' *South China Morning Post.* 22 July, https://www.scmp.com/business/companies/article/3019632/first-china-has-more-companies-fortune-global-500-list-us (accessed on 12 August 2020).

Zhou Lianxi, and Michael K. Hui. 2003. 'Symbolic Value of Foreign Products in the People's Republic of China'. *Journal of International Marketing*, Vol. 11, No. 2, 36-58.

Zhu Chuanrui. 2018. 'The Impact of Foreign Strategic Investors' Shareholding Changes on China's Commercial Banks under the Impact of International Liquidity Crisis—Targeting at Bank of China and its Foreign Strategic Investors in Financial Crisis', paper presented at the *2018 International Conference on Economics, Politics and Business Management (ICEPBM 2018),* 23-25 March, https://webofproceedings.org/proceedings_series/ECOM/ICEPBM% 202018/ICEPBM029.pdf (accessed on 13 August 2020).

Zhu Rongji. 2013. *Zhu Rongji on the Record: The Road to Reform 1991-1997.* Washington D.C.: Brookings Institution Press.

Zweig, David and Bi Jianhai. 2005. 'China's Global Hunt for Energy', *Foreign Affairs,* September/October, https://www.foreignaffairs.com/articles/asia/2005-09-01/chinas-global-hunt-energy (accessed on 12 August 2020).

Zweig, David and Huiyao Wang. 2013. 'Can China Bring Back the Best? The Communist Party Organizes China's Search for Talent', *The China Quarterly,* Vol. 215, September, 590-615.

Index

*